Free within Ourselves

FREE WITHIN OURSELVES

OURSELVES

The Development of African American
Children's Literature

RUDINE SIMS BISHOP

GREENWOOD PRESS
Westport, Connecticut • London

The Library of Congress has catalogued the paperback edition as follows:

Bishop, Rudine Sims.
    Free within ourselves : the development of African American children's literature / Rudine Sims Bishop.
        p. cm.
    Includes bibliographical references and index.
    ISBN-13: 978–0–325–07135–0 (alk. paper)
  1. American literature—African American authors—History and criticism. 2. Children's literature, American—History and criticism. 3. African Americans in literature. 4. African American children in literature. 5. African American children—Books and reading. 6. African Americans—Intellectual life. I. Title.
    PS153.N5B526 2007
    810.9'928208996073—dc22   2007000612

British Library Cataloguing in Publication Data is available.

A paperback edition of *Free within Ourselves: The Development of African American Children's Literature* is available from Heinemann, a division of Reed Elsevier, Inc. (978–0–325–07135–0)

Library of Congress Catalog Card Number: 2007000612
ISBN-13: 978–0–313–34093–2
ISBN-10: 0–313–34093–5

First published in 2007

Greenwood Press, 88 Post Road West, Westport, CT 06881
An imprint of Greenwood Publishing Group, Inc.
www.greenwood.com

Printed in the United States of America

The paper used in this book complies with the
Permanent Paper Standard issued by the National
Information Standards Organization (Z39.48–1984).

10 9 8 7 6 5 4 3 2 1

Copyright Acknowledgments

The author and the publisher gratefully acknowledge permission for use of the following material:

The author and publisher wish to thank the Crisis Publishing Co., Inc. the publisher of the magazine of the National Association for the Advancement of Colored People, for the use of this material first published in the January 1928 issue of *Crisis*.

"Straighten Up and Fly Right" words and music by Nat King Cole and Irving Mills 1944 (Renewed) EMI Mills Music, Inc. All rights controlled by EMI Mills Music, Inc. and Alfred Publishing Co., Inc. All rights reserved. Used by permission of Alfred Publishing.

Honoring the memory of
Virginia Hamilton and Tom Feelings—
and for my Gem, my Jim—always

Contents

Acknowledgments   ix

Introduction   xi

1. Before 1900: Sowing the Seeds of African American Children's Literature   1

2. For the Children of the Sun: African American Children's Literature Begins to Bloom   21

3. Breaking New Ground: Arna Bontemps and Some of His Contemporaries   45

4. "Give Them Back Their Own Souls": Change and the Need for Change   67

5. African American Poetry for Children: Soft Black Songs   95

6. African American Picture Books Take Shape: Authenticating the Worlds of Black Children   115

7. African American Picture Books Expand: Celebrating the Past, Reflecting the Present   133

8. African American Illustrators of Children's Books: Nine Pacesetters   153

9. Newer African American Illustrators: Expanding Possibilities, Maintaining Traditions   177

10. African American Children's Fiction: Illuminating the Life of the People   195

11. African American Contemporary Realistic Fiction: Focus on Teens and Preteens   221

12. African American Historical Fiction: Telling a People's Story   249

viii   Contents

Some Concluding Thoughts   273

References   275

Index   283

Acknowledgments

This book owes a debt to many fellow workers in the vineyard of African American children's books. Over the years I have interviewed, corresponded with, or conversed with many of the authors and artists whose work is at the center of this book. They have given generously of their time and willingly shared their insights and perspectives on their work and on children's books, and I am deeply appreciative. The list is long; I hope you all know who you are. I am also grateful for the work of younger academics whose scholarship has informed my own. Violet Harris's in-depth study of *The Brownies' Book* was an invaluable resource, as was her scholarship on other historical developments in African American children's literature. Dianne Johnson's critical examination of *The Brownies' Book* and the children's books of Arna Bontemps, Langston Hughes, and Lucille Clifton in *Telling Tales* was not only insightful and informative, but also an important advance in the recognition of African American children's literature as an appropriate topic for serious literary criticism. I also want to acknowledge the help of two librarians whose generosity contributed to this work. When Diane Newsum came across eight original and well-used issues of *The Brownies' Book*, she passed that treasure on to me, and I cannot thank her enough. Elinor Des Verney Sinnette, founding member of the Council on Interracial Books for Children, generously shared her firsthand knowledge of the council's history.

Although nonfiction is not a focus of this work, I wish also to acknowledge here the work of one of the most prolific creators of African American nonfiction and biography for children, James Haskins, who died in 2005 after writing more than 100 children's and young adult books about African American history and culture and biographies of numerous African American achievers. The body of his work constitutes a substantial portion of African American nonfiction for children and youth. He leaves a rich legacy.

This book has been a long time in the writing. I am grateful to Lois Bridges, the editor who accepted the book originally and patiently waited for it to be completed, all the while expressing her faith that it would happen. My current editor, George Butler, has given thoughtful and insightful feedback, which has helped to make the manuscript better than it was when he first "inherited" it after Lois accepted a different position. Thank you, George, for helping me to see it through.

Finally, my deepest gratitude and appreciation to my one-man support team, the love of my life, my husband, James J. Bishop.

Introduction

We build our temples for tomorrow, strong as we know how, and we stand on top of the mountain, free within ourselves.

Langston Hughes (1926)

This book traces the development of African American children's literature from its early roots to the present. By African American children's literature, I mean books written by African Americans, focused on African American people and their life experiences, and primarily intended for children up to age fourteen. It was not until the late 1960s and the early 1970s that contemporary African American children's literature began to come into its own, but its roots stretch back much earlier, and its evolution can be traced through the history of a people who have had to overcome formidable obstacles on their journey across the American hopescape. African American children's literature bears witness to that journey as a means to offer children and youth wisdom and insights that can serve as part of a foundation on which they can build their own futures. In a sense, African American writers are building, in the words of Langston Hughes, temples for tomorrow.

Twentieth century African American children's literature owes a debt to Hughes and his fellow Harlem Renaissance artists, who helped to open the way for a children's literature that derives from African American sociocultural environments and experiences. In a famous 1926 essay, Hughes, taking on the role of spokesman, declared that he and his fellow "younger Negro artists" intended to create art based on material out of their own racial/cultural background. Rejecting the idea that Black artists should imitate White art, Hughes asserted that the life experiences and cultural expressions of Black people are rich enough to sustain a cultural art, and that he and his fellow artists intended to produce such an art, regardless of the reactions of either White people or Black people. "We stand on top of the mountain," he declared, "free within ourselves."

For African American writers and artists who create children's books, embracing that freedom has resulted in a body of literature that holds within it a good deal of diversity as well as a number of important commonalities that serve to make it a distinctive body of work. Obviously some variation can be attributed to the differing interests and talents of individual creators. African American children's books also often reflect or are influenced by the life experiences of their creators, and African

American life and culture are far from monolithic. Nevertheless, the creators of African American children's literature all share the experience of being members of a society in which race matters a great deal more than it should.

In focusing on the writings of African Americans, therefore, I am embracing the idea that, regardless of how they label themselves as artists or what aspects of Black life they choose to depict or highlight, they share what Ralph Ellison called "that 'concord of sensibilities' through which the group has come to constitute a sub-division of the larger American culture" (1972, 131). Ellison goes on to provide a lengthy enumeration of experiences that shape or define what it means to be, in the terminology of his day, "a Negro." Author Virginia Hamilton (1981) expresses a similar idea more concisely:

> The life of the people is and always has been different in a significant respect from the life of the majority. It has been made eccentric by slavery, escape, fear of capture; by discrimination, and constant despair. But it has held tight within it happiness, and subtle humor, a fierce pride in leadership and progress, love of life and family, and a longing for peace and freedom. Nevertheless, there is an uneasy, ideological difference with the American majority basic to black thought. (57)

My assumption is that this shared concord of sensibilities, this eccentricity, this uneasy ideological difference, shapes the lenses through which Black authors and illustrators of children's books view their work and their world, and helps to coalesce their work into a canon of African American children's literature.

Contemporary African American children's literature, meaning that which has been published since 1965, has roots in African American and American social and literary history. This book connects that literature to its historical and social contexts by describing relevant historical developments and milestones, as well as the work of pioneering individuals who advanced the development of the literature in the late nineteenth and early twentieth centuries. It also identifies key contemporary writers and artists and describes the major thematic and stylistic characteristics of their work across time and within and across the genres of poetry, picture books, and both contemporary and historical realistic fiction.

Because of the historical circumstances from which it has emanated, much of African American children's literature has been purposeful, intended to serve functions that have not been expected of the larger body of American children's literature. A number of Black authors and artists have articulated the goals and objectives they wish to achieve with their children's books, and the philosophical ideas and ideological stances that underlie those books or motivate them to write for children. These statements, many of which are quoted in this book, provide another lens through which to view their work and, because many of the statements are similar, they also help to explain in part the thematic cohesiveness of much African American children's literature.

In spite of major increases in the numbers of children's books about Black people since 1965, African American children's literature continues to exist as a very small subset of the estimated 5000 new children's books published each year in the United States. Within the context of American children's literature, Black writers have never had a monopoly on producing children's books about African American life and culture. This was certainly the case in the nineteenth century and early in the twentieth century, but it was also true in the 1970s, when African American writers first began to be published in increasing numbers, and even through the last two decades of the twentieth century and beyond, the era of multiculturalism in children's books.

Some statistics kept by the Cooperative Children's Books Center (see Table 1) are illustrative. In the eight years from 1994 to 2001, a total of 1,402 new children's books about people of African descent were published. Of those 1,402 books, a total of 730, or just over half (52 percent), were created by Black authors and artists. The highest proportion of books about people of African descent produced by Black writers and artists was 65 percent, achieved only once, in 2000, with 96 of 147 books. In recent years it has usually ranged between 40 percent and 60 percent.

Furthermore, when viewed in the context of the estimated total number of new children's trade books published annually, the percentage of children's books about African Americans by any author is small, averaging about 3.5 percent between 1994 and 2001. The percentage of such books *by and about* African Americans remains dismally low. With the annual total output of new books ranging from about 2,500 in 1985 to about 5,500 in 2001, the percentage of books by African Americans ranges from a low of 0.6 percent in 1986, when only 18 such books were published, to a high of 2.2 percent, or 100 books, in 1995.

Given such disproportionate representation, some mention of Black-centered books by non-Blacks is difficult to avoid in a discussion of African American children's literature. For example, a few White-authored books, such as Ezra Jack Keats's *The Snowy Day*, had an important impact in the field and a consequent

Table 1
CCBC Statistics: Children's Books by and about Black People Published in the United States 1985 to 2001 Statistics Gathered by the Cooperative Children's Book Center, University of Wisconsin* Percentages Calculated by R.S.B.

Year	Est. Total Books Published	Books About Blacks*	% About Blacks*	Books About Blacks BY Blacks	% About Blacks BY Blacks	% of Total BY Blacks
1985	2500			18		0.7
1986	3000			18		0.6
1987	3000			30		1.0
1988	3000			39		1.3
1989	4000			48		1.2
1990	5000			51		1.0
1991	4000			70		1.75
1992	4500			94		2.0
1993	4500			74		1.6
1994	4500	166	3.6	82	49	1.8
1995	4500	167	3.7	100	59.8	2.2
1996	4500	172	3.8	92	53	2.0
1997	4500–5000	216	4.0–4.8	88	40	1.7–1.9
1998	5000	183	3.6	92	50	1.8
1999	5000	150	3.0	81	54	1.6
2000	5000–5500	147	2.6–2.9	96	65	1.7–1.9
2001	5000–5500	201	3.6–4.0	99	49	1.8–1.9

*The CCBC published statistics only on books by Black authors and artists from 1985 to 1993.
Source: http://www.soemadison.wisc.edu/ccbc/books/pcstats.htm.

effect on African American children's literature. Furthermore, in tracing the history of African American children's literature, it is important to understand how historically some of the racist, stereotypical books about Blacks, created by benighted White writers and artists, made it imperative to create an African American literature to contradict and counteract such imagery. Discussions of such books help to reveal the contexts out of which African American children's literature emerged at various times.

One of the most hopeful developments in children's literature in the past couple of decades has been the advent of the multicultural education movement, an educational reform movement that is intended to promote equity and equality in schooling for all students. Part of multicultural curricular reform is the integration of the literatures of underrepresented groups, including African American children's literature, into the classroom, with a view to promoting appreciation and respect for diversity, giving rise to critical inquiry, and ultimately developing a commitment to the democratic ideals of equity and social justice. In that context, African American children's literature can be affirming for children who have historically not found affirmation in classroom materials. It can also connect with other children of color whose life experiences in this society are tainted by the poison of racism and often marked by struggle. Reading such literature has the potential to help all students understand who we are today as a society and how we might become a better society tomorrow.

The question of the role of children's literature in classrooms is one that is crucial in an atmosphere of high-stakes testing, re-segregation of schools, and inequitable educational resources, such as school libraries. Such factors can result in too little time and attention given to the classroom reading of literature, which does not lend itself easily to one-right-answer tests and which requires the availability of a fair number of books. Unlike textbooks, however, literature educates the heart as well as the head. It offers pleasure and enjoyment, as well as insights into what it means to be a decent human being in a society, benefits that will last far longer than the facts that can be tested easily on standardized tests. For children in both ethnically homogeneous and ethnically diverse classrooms, literature can offer self-affirmation and a sense of connection to others like and unlike themselves. Teachers also can enrich their teaching by coming to know a wide variety of literature. It is my hope that this work will speak to educators, librarians, and scholars of children's literature, and that it will also reach a wider audience, including parents and other adults who select and buy books for children.

African American children's literature reflects the social and cultural history of Black people in America. Like African Americans, the literature has undergone a fascinating and sometimes tumultuous journey. This book charts that journey and promotes an understanding of the development of African American children's literature, its rich and sometimes troublesome contexts, and its role in preserving and passing on the values we most want to share with our children.

A WORD ABOUT TERMS

The focus of this volume is literature for *children*. Defining the term *children* in relation to literature is not as simple as it would seem since there appear to be overlapping conceptions of when literary childhood ends and literary adolescence begins. The Association for Library Services to Children (ALSC), a division of the American Library Association (ALA), defines children's literature as that suitable for young people from preschool to eighth grade. Complicating that definition is the designation, by ALA's young adult division, of young adult literature as that for young people between the ages of twelve and eighteen, thus overlapping children's literature and making the middle school/junior high school (ages twelve through fourteen) rather uncertain territory.

Such designations must necessarily function only as flexible guidelines, in any case, since individual books cannot be reliably matched to any fixed grade or age level. Generally, I am defining my territory as literature for children in kindergarten through eighth grade, although because my discussions usually lead with identifying writers or artists and their work, some attention to young adult literature has been inevitable.

I have lived through being colored, Negro, Black, Afro-American, and now African American. All those terms appear in this book. In general, I have used older terms like *colored* or *Negro* only in their historical contexts or in quotations. The use of the term *Afro-American* has been limited to quotations or titles. I have often used *Black* (spelled with an upper case B) and *African American* interchangeably to refer to people of African descent in the United States. All Black people are not American, however; when referring to people of African descent from outside the United States Black is a more appropriate term than African American.

AN OVERVIEW

The first three chapters trace the development of African American children's literature prior to the 1960s. The first chapter discusses the foundations of African American children's literature in an antebellum oral culture, in African Americans' quest for literacy and liberation, and in nineteenth century religious and secular writing addressed to children.

The second chapter discusses W.E.B. Du Bois's *The Brownies' Book* magazine, the first substantial twentieth century effort by African Americans to create a literature addressed to Black children. It also explores part of the legacy of the magazine as embodied in the early work of Langston Hughes and Effie Lee Newsome, both of whom wrote for *The Brownies' Book* and subsequently continued to write for children. It briefly discusses the contributions of another pioneer in creating literature for Black children, Carter G. Woodson.

Chapter 3 examines the period between 1932 and 1967, dominated by the work of Arna Bontemps, whose writing for children in a number of genres was groundbreaking. It also discusses the expansion of African American children's literature in new directions, including the beginnings of African American picture books, the first explorations of black/white racial conflicts in African American children's literature, and the appearance of a number of collections of original poetry.

Chapter 4 describes some parallel and opposing early developments in children's literature about Blacks and argues that an African American children's literature developed in part from the necessity to counteract the pervasive and long-lasting negative imagery that robbed children of the truth about themselves and each other. It also describes the sociopolitical developments that created a context conducive to the growth of an authentic African American children's literature.

Until the late 1960s, African American children's literature developed in a fairly linear fashion, often because of the leadership of one or a few individuals. Once African American children's literature began to come into its own, it increased fairly rapidly in quantity, simultaneously across several genres. Organizing by genre offered an opportunity to explore developments in some detail and to examine the work of important writers and artists whose work was prominent in those genres. Each chapter identifies major writers and landmark books and discusses the main topics, thematic emphases, and some textual features of African American books in the genre. I have also attempted to place the literature in its sociocultural or political context by exploring what writers and artists themselves have to say about their work. In some cases the discussions focus on representative writers or artists and representative books.

Chapter 5 examines developments in poetry from the 1960s to the present, including the work of major African American children's poets and the themes, topics, imagery, and emotions they explore in their work.

Chapters 6 and 7 examine developments in picture books, focusing on the texts created by African American writers. Chapter 6 focuses on the period from 1969 through 1989. Chapter 7 looks at happenings in the 1990s and beyond. Through a critical examination of important texts, these chapters discuss the main topics and themes that characterize the genre, as well as writers' perspectives on their work and its goals and objectives.

Chapters 8 and 9 focus on the work of African American illustrators. Chapter 8 looks at the work of nine "pacesetters" who began illustrating children's books in the 1960s and 1970s and are the premier African American illustrators. It also discusses their perspectives on their work. Chapter 9 describes the work of other important artists who began publishing children's books in the 1980s or later. Both chapters describe the main features of the artists' work and the ways in which they have redefined the image of African American children's books.

Chapters 10 and 11 are concerned with contemporary realistic fiction. Chapter 10 looks at landmark developments in the genre in the 1960s and 1970s. Chapter 11 describes the emergence of a newer group of writers and their focus on fiction for upper elementary and middle school youth. It also discusses the appearance of a group of award-winning authors who mainly write for young adults.

Chapter 12 looks at African American historical fiction, its main themes, and the work of the major authors who produce it.

A final section offers some concluding thoughts, including some speculations about the future of African American children's literature.

A NOTE ABOUT THE DOCUMENTATION OF SOURCES

For the convenience of readers with a special interest in locating children's books in various genres, I have provided documentation of the books for children and young adults that were the primary sources for each chapter in a bibliography at the end of that chapter.

In the two chapters that discuss African American illustrators, Chapters 8 and 9, I have arranged the bibliography alphabetically by the last name of the illustrator. All other documentation is provided including the author, title, date of publication, publisher location, and publisher.

All other sources are documented in a list of references at the end of the book.

CHAPTER 1

Before 1900: Sowing the Seeds of African American Children's Literature

The seeds of an African American children's literature were sown in the soil of Black people's struggles for liberation, literacy, and survival. For those seeds to develop into a body of written literature for children, there first had to be, among other things, a critical mass of child readers, a collective recognition of children as a reading audience distinct from adults, and a significant number of writers willing to address their work to that child readership. Since many of these seeds fell upon the rocks of slavery and among the thorns of racism, these conditions would not be met on any large scale among African Americans until well after emancipation. Nevertheless, the record of African Americans' historical strivings for literacy and education confirms that some of the seeds fell on good ground and began to blossom and bear fruit. At least three aspects of antebellum and late nineteenth century Black life are fundamental to the development of African American children's literature and to some of its distinctive qualities: the vital oral culture; the persistent pursuit of literacy; and late nineteenth century writings addressed to Black children, mainly by women and published primarily in newspapers and periodicals.

ORAL CULTURE: ENTERTAINMENT, KNOWLEDGE, SURVIVAL

Aspiring to control and dominate every aspect of slaves' lives, and fearing possible conspiracies, slaveholders in the United States forbid enslaved Africans to speak their native languages and banned African cultural practices such as religious ceremonies and the use of drums. Literacy learning was, of course, either severely restricted or expressly forbidden lest slaves become infected with yearnings for freedom or equality.

Under those harsh circumstances, enslaved Africans turned to oral forms to build community, to entertain themselves, and to inform and instruct each other and their children. Out of African cultural memories that could not be eradicated, creative impulses that could not be suppressed, and the oppressive social environment that could not be easily transformed, enslaved Africans created an African American oral culture. Many of the songs, stories, and other oral forms they produced have become a part of the African American and American cultural and literary heritage, but at the time of their creation they also helped in forming and passing on a shared worldview and a set of values and attitudes that were essential to African Americans' survival in an environment hostile to their best interests.

This oral culture thrived in segregated enclaves such as slave quarter communities, which operated as informal schools in which both adults and children acquired cultural knowledge that would enable them to resist the slaveholders' efforts to control and dominate their lives. In a well-known study of education in the slave quarter community, Thomas L. Webber (1978) identified both the kind of knowledge the people in the quarters acquired and the means by which they transmitted this knowledge to each other and to their children. Based on his examination of documents, slave folklore, and written or dictated narratives produced by people who had actually lived in slave quarter communities, he specified nine "cultural themes" that challenged the knowledge the slaveholders endeavored to impart and helped to shape the worldview of the quarter slaves.

There is a striking similarity between four of Webber's cultural themes—family, communality, the importance of the spirit world, and the high regard for acquiring literacy—and some of the important thematic threads that are woven through contemporary African American children's literature. Family was particularly significant both as a cultural value and as a vehicle through which the slave quarter community educated itself and maintained itself as a distinctive cultural group. Family values—parental roles, the concept of the extended family, the importance of elders and their roles in the family, and strong sibling relationships—were highly significant in the quarter community. The persistence of these cultural themes, values, and family practices as themes and subthemes in twentieth-century African American children's literature attests to their enduring significance.

Two of the most important and best-known aspects of oral culture, which were also important vehicles for transmitting values and attitudes, were songs and stories. Numerous collections of African American folktales and folklore reveal the wide range of stories, rhymes, jokes, and proverbs, as well as a large repertoire of secular and sacred songs created by African Americans. Regarding children's literature, the best-known and most enduring stories are the animal tales featuring Brer Rabbit and his friends, enemies, and acquaintances. A small animal with very little strength, Brer Rabbit seems an unlikely choice for a hero, but he was a trickster who used his wits to triumph over larger, stronger animals, a characteristic that had great appeal to people held in bondage, and, predictably, enduring appeal to children as well, who sometimes feel weak and powerless in a world of large adults.

Animal tales, however, were just one type of story children in the quarters would have heard. Mothers used ghost stories and tales about a boogeyman, such as "Raw-Head and Bloody Bones" (Weber 1978, 165), as cautionary tales for disobedient children. At evening time, children participated in the family activities, which might include listening to adults sing or tell stories either as they found some little time for quiet relaxation or while they completed household chores. Grandparents who could remember their lives in Africa told stories that would have provided information about the family's African roots and about Africa. Adults who had been in the same location for many years became the transmitters of local history (Webber 1978, 165, 174). Thus, long before a written African American children's literature appeared, African Americans were employing story as a vehicle for socializing children, for providing information, and for helping them survive in a hostile environment.

The songs composed and sung by the people in the slave quarter community served much the same functions. The best-known songs are the spirituals, one of

African Americans' original contributions to American and world music. Much has been written about the way many of the spirituals, such as "Steal Away," functioned as coded messages about meetings and escapes. Spirituals also transmitted some of the cultural values of the quarters, such as the importance of freedom and a strong sense of family. Frequent references were made, for instance, to meeting family members in heaven. The spirituals also imparted specific knowledge; they would have informed children, for example, about certain Biblical heroes such as Daniel ("Didn't My Lord Deliver Daniel?"), Moses ("Let My People Go"), and Joshua ("Joshua Fit the Battle of Jericho").

Some secular songs expressed the slave quarter community's dissatisfaction and its antagonism toward whites, making children aware of the injustice in their situation. One frequently cited example is reported by Frederick Douglass (1892/1962, 146) in his autobiography:

We raise de wheat,
Dey gib us de corn;
We bake de bread,
Dey gib us de crust;
We sif' de meal,
Dey gib us de huss;
We peel de meat,
Dey gib us de skin;
And dat's de way
Dey take us in;
We skim de pot,
Dey gib us de liquor,
And say dat's good enough for nigger.

Such songs and stories functioned as acts of resistance to the domination that slaveholders thought they held over the lives of those they enslaved.

Songs and rhymes were also a part of the children's culture in the quarters. Because acknowledgment of children as an audience distinct from adults is one prerequisite for the development of a children's literature, it is important to note that Black children growing up as plantation slaves did experience something of a childhood before they were forced into hard labor. Although there were certainly exceptions, slave children usually were not required to work in the fields before the age of ten or twelve, although many were assigned other chores before that time. They were generally cared for in a group setting, and for many children younger than eight their main task was to help to take care of the younger children (Genovese 1976). An ex-slave, Rosa Maddox (2002, 76–77), for example, told an interviewer, "I had all the time to play until I was 'bout nine years old. We made rag dolls and played dolls. . . . We used to play church. We would play singin' and prayin' and dyin'. Come to me sometimes little play-game songs." In their play, they also contributed to an oral culture by creating and passing on songs and rhymes that accompanied their ring games and hiding games. Riddles such as the following, cited in Webber (1978, 182), were also popular: "Slick as a mole, black as coal, Got a great tail like a thunderhole" (Answer: Skillet).

The oral expressions of enslaved Black people, which were often improvised on the spot, and the artistic forms they took were testament to the strength of the creative impulses that flourished, even in the oppressive conditions under which enslaved people were forced to live. African American literature, including African

American children's literature, reflects its oral culture roots in numerous and varied ways. A repertoire of stories and songs that have survived from the oral tradition are being retold for children and made available in book form as part of the canon of African American children's literature. Writers of fiction and poetry often weave into their works folk motifs and characters from African American folklore. A number of authors have created literary folktales that emulate the style, forms, and topics of stories from the oral tradition. Poets and writers of fiction incorporate musical forms such as the blues or oral performances such as sermons into their creations. A number of linguistic or stylistic features of these oral forms are reflected and replicated, as for instance in blues poems, in African Americans' written literature, including children's literature.

African American children's literature, then, has roots in African Americans' determination to maintain a sense of themselves as fully human in the face of their legal status as property and to maintain some control over their own lives. Where literacy was forbidden and denied to African Americans, story and song flourished and served to entertain, to discipline, to provide information, to subvert slaveholders' intentions, and to transmit to children the values and attitudes that the community deemed necessary for its survival. It would take some time, however, for a written African American children's literature to develop since the acquisition of literacy among a critical mass of African Americans required years of struggle.

THE PURSUIT OF LITERACY

An obvious precondition for an African American children's literature was a critical mass of adult writers and child readers. Regrettably, however, in the eyes of slaveholders, reading and writing were incompatible with slavery, and although there were thousands of free Blacks prior to 1860, the great majority of antebellum Blacks were enslaved. The 1860 census counted 487,970 "free colored," but about eight times as many (3,953,760) slaves (U.S. Census Bureau 1860). Slaveholders denied the humanity of those they enslaved, but at the same time feared their human compulsion to be free. Consequently, they tended to severely restrict access to literacy and education.

For most people held in slavery, therefore, literacy learning took place when and where and in whatever way the opportunity presented itself. Even among free Blacks, education and schooling were neither compulsory nor universal, and the pursuit of literacy was not necessarily restricted to children. The line between adult literacy and child literacy for African Americans during this period therefore cannot always be clearly drawn. Nonetheless, even a brief overview of the long and complex African American struggle for literacy explains in part why a written African American children's literature did not come into full flower before the twentieth century and underscores the cultural functions that reading and writing, including the creation of literature, have historically been expected to serve for African American youth.

UNFIT FOR SLAVERY: LITERACY ON THE PLANTATION

Among enslaved Blacks, literacy was highly prized because it could lead to liberation, not only in the literal sense, but also in the sense of self-determination or the ability to influence, if not control, one's destiny. On a plantation, literate Blacks could acquire information useful to themselves and the community. Knowing how to read and write could, for example, aid in planning and carrying out escapes. One historian reported, based on an analysis of advertisements for fugitives, that in Kentucky, of 350 runaways, approximately 1 in 5 were advertised as able to read, and about half of those could also write (Cornelius 1991, 9). Often those with some literacy skills became leaders within their communities and potentially dangerous to slaveholders, as was the case with the three most famous leaders of slave revolts: Denmark Vesey, Nat Turner, and Gabriel Prosser. Given the strong association between liberation and literacy, many Black people zealously pursued opportunities for learning, sometimes making heroic efforts at great personal risk to learn and teach themselves and each other.

Fear of the potentially liberating power of literacy was the impetus for some state governments to pass legislation outlawing the teaching of slaves. Although such laws would have been difficult to enforce on plantations, many slaveholders needed no outside authority to force adherence. In his autobiography, nineteenth century orator and abolitionist Frederick Douglass (1845/1987) sheds light on the fear that motivated many slaveholders to forbid the teaching of literacy:

Very soon after I went to live with Mr. and Mrs. Auld, she very kindly commenced to teach me the A, B, C. After I had learned this, she assisted me in learning to spell words of three or four letters. Just at this point of my progress, Mr. Auld found out what was going on, and at once forbade Mrs. Auld to instruct me further, telling her, among other things, that it was unlawful, as well as unsafe, to teach a slave to read. To use his own words, further, he said, "If you give a nigger an inch, he will take an ell. A nigger should know nothing but to obey his master—to do as he is told to do. Learning would spoil the best nigger in the world. Now," said he, "if you teach that nigger (speaking of myself) how to read, there would be no keeping him. It would forever unfit him to be a slave." (274)

For Douglass, the knowledge that literacy would unfit him for slavery only strengthened his determination to learn. As is well known, Douglass did became literate, escaped from slavery, and became famous as an abolitionist, civil rights activist, diplomat, and orator. Sometimes using trickery to learn from white school children, Douglass learned to read in spite of the risks involved.

Cornelius (1991) cites accounts of slaves being severely beaten or even killed for their literacy activity. She notes that the most common punishment for reading or teaching others to read was to amputate joints of the offenders' fingers (66). Nevertheless, slave testimony confirms the strong link between literacy and liberation perceived by numerous slaves. Thomas Jones, for example, suffered a severe whipping rather than reveal where he had hidden a book that he had obtained after several attempts, noting that he thought that learning to read and write would lead him to "freedom, influence and real, secure happiness" (Webber 1978, 135).

Those who were not taught by members of the slaveholders' families often learned from other enslaved men and women, and some taught themselves by studying printed matter they found in their environment, such as old newspapers or printed material used in the course of running the plantation or other businesses. The testimony of former slave Mandy Jones (Berlin, Favreau, and Miller 1998) provides a vivid picture of some of the paths to literacy on a southern plantation:

An'dey had pit schools in slave days too. Way out in de woods, dey *was* woods den, and de slaves would slip out o'de Quarters at night, and go to dese pits, and some niggah dat had some learnin' would have a school. De way de cullud folks would learn to read was from de white chillun. De white chilluns thought a heap of de cullud chilluns, and when dey come

out o'school wid deir books in deir han's, dey take de cullud chilluns, and slip off somewhere an' learns de cullud chilluns deir lessons, what deir teacher has jes' learned dem. Deir
was a yaller slave man named Gunn, an' his young marster taught him so good, dat atter
while he taught a pit school hisself. Dis Gunn had a boy named Henry, who learned in his
daddy's pit school, and atter de S'render, Henry Gunn had a school for de cullud chilluns.
He was my onlies' teacher, but I didn't learn much, I was too big to go to school, 13 years
ole, but I had to work in the fiel! We learned firs' de A B C, den l-o-g, log, d-o-g, dog, jes'
like dat, you knows how it goes, de Blueback speller. (206)

Jones's revealing testimony describes not only the way slaveholders' children were
sometimes the teachers of their parents' slaves, but also the way their lessons were
echoed by their students and then again by *their* students, demonstrating the
determination of some enslaved people to pass learning on to one another. It is also
interesting to note that the teaching activities of the slaveholders' children were as
secret as the pit school, another indication of the strength of some slaveholders'
opposition to literacy.

Another noteworthy reference in Mandy Jones's account is the Blue-back Speller,
which was mentioned as an instructional text in numerous learning-to-read accounts
by African Americans, both enslaved and free. Noah Webster's Blue-back Speller,
formally *The American Spelling Book* was first published in 1783 and was used
extensively throughout the next century, with as many as 24 million copies distrib-
uted (N. B. Smith 1965, 45). It was widely available in American households, and
some enslaved people were able to save enough to purchase their own copies.

The speller focused primarily on pronunciation, beginning with the alphabet
and proceeding to words of one, two, or three syllables. Word lists are followed by
practice sentences. The book also contained some fables, poems, realistic stories,
and dialogues, usually moralistic in tone. Thus, for many children, both Black and
white, the speller became their first "literary" text. In numerous slave testimonies,
as in that of Mandy Jones, references are made to progress through the speller.
(In a revised, 1880 edition, getting to l-o-g, log, d-o-g, dog took a student to
Lesson XIII on p. 25.) Not surprisingly, the other main text available for reading
and instruction was the Bible, which many enslaved people held in reverence, and
which would also have been widely available in nineteenth century homes.

RELIGIOUS AND ABOLITIONIST SCHOOLS FOR BLACKS

In contrast to plantation pit schools and secret learning, more than a few antebellum Black people learned to read and write in formal school settings established
both by free Blacks and by Whites. Early on, some Whites taught Blacks to read
out of missionary zeal. For example, under the auspices of The Society for the
Propagation of the Gospel in Foreign Parts (SPG), a missionary organization connected with the Anglican Church, Reverend Samuel Thomas established a school
for Blacks in Goose Creek Parish, South Carolina in 1695. The SPG also established
a school in New York in 1704, and another in South Carolina in 1743 (Woodson
1919/1968, 26–27; Cornelius 1919, 14). Other religious groups, including the
Puritans in New England, also taught slaves to read as part of their perceived
Christian duty. It is noteworthy that these groups were not particularly interested
in liberating slaves but in saving souls.

The Quakers, however, were one exception. Having concluded that slavery was
incompatible with Christianity, they taught Black people not only so that they could
secure their own salvation, but also so that they could be prepared for emancipation

and the responsibilities of citizenship. They opened schools for Blacks in a number of locales, including Virginia and North Carolina, as well as in New Jersey, New York, and Pennsylvania, where there was less opposition. They established a school for Blacks in Philadelphia as early as 1774, and by the turn of the century, at least seven such schools were in existence in that city (Franklin and Moss 1994, 100).

During the last quarter of the eighteenth century, several abolition and manumission societies also established schools for Blacks, particularly in New England and the mid-Atlantic states (Franklin and Moss 1994, 99–100). One of the better known such schools is the New York African Free School, which was opened by the Manumission Society in 1787. By 1820 there were 500 pupils enrolled in the school. The curriculum was fairly broad and academic, in contrast to that of schools concerned mainly with Bible literacy. A letter from a 15-year-old senior student, Isaiah Degrass, addressed to a convention of an abolitionist group in 1828, noted that the curriculum included "reading, writing, arithmetic, geography, navigation, astronomy, and map drawing" (Degrass 1828, 157). Along with the letter from Degrass, the principal of the New York African Free School sent to the Abolitionist Society some poems and letters written by other pupils in the school, certifying that the work was original and uncorrected. A poem from twelve-year-old Thomas Sidney (1828) illustrates the tone of most of the submissions:

On Freedom

Freedom will break the tyrant's chains,
And shatter all his whole domain
From slavery she will always free
And all her aim is liberty. (156)

Whether prose or poetry, all the students' writing addressed to the Abolitionist Society sounded the same notes: decrying the evils of slavery, calling for freedom for their brothers and sisters in chains, and thanking the convention-goers for their support for the abolitionist cause. Clearly, the pupils of this school were also initiated, in addition to a broad academic curriculum, into the use of literacy for political purposes, a tradition that has remained significant in African American history and literature.

BLACKS ESTABLISH SCHOOLS AND OTHER INSTITUTIONS OF SELF-HELP

Wherever concentrations of free Blacks existed in antebellum America, self-help became an important avenue to education and literacy. As might be expected, most formal schools for Blacks were to be found in urban areas, where there were fairly large communities of free Black men, women, and children. By 1860, thousands of free Blacks were living in cities like Philadelphia, New York, Boston, Baltimore, Charleston, and New Orleans, and 32,629 free Blacks were attending school in the United States and its territories (Franklin 1967, 230). These gains did not come without struggle. Despite their substantial numbers, Blacks were generally not permitted to attend free tax-supported schools until after 1840, when some states began to appropriate money for the education of Blacks. As a consequence, free Blacks often established their own schools, while at the same time agitating for public funds.

In the South, public education for Blacks was nonexistent, making self-help efforts even more critical. A notable example of a school launched by free Blacks was one established in 1803 in Charleston, South Carolina, by the Minors' Moralist Society, a group of seven free Black men, to educate and provide for the basic needs of "colored" children who were very poor or had been orphaned (Payne 1888/1968, 14). It began with fifty members, who paid an initial fee of $5 each and afterward a fee of 25 cents a month. The school served only about six pupils and lasted until 1847.

The students of such schools often became leaders in their communities, as exemplified by Daniel Alexander Payne, a free-born Black who attended the Charleston school around 1819–1821 and went on to become a bishop in the African Methodist Episcopal Church and president of Wilberforce University. As a young man of about nineteen, Payne established a school for Black children. Lacking textbooks for his pupils, he taught himself geometry and other subjects from whichever books he could find and in turn taught those subjects to his pupils, using the world of nature as his textbook and sometime classroom. His curriculum included map drawing, grammar, chemistry, and botany.

Some time after a local plantation owner discovered how well educated Payne's pupils were, a bill was introduced into the South Carolina legislature making it unlawful to teach a slave to read or write or to maintain a school or other place of instruction to teach either a slave or a free person of color to read or write (Payne 1888/1968, 27). The bill, which took effect on April 1, 1835, set the punishment for whites who broke the law at $100 and six months in prison and for free Blacks at fifty lashes and a $50 fine. It forced the closing of Payne's school and was a setback to organized efforts to provide educational institutions for Blacks in that state. Payne's story exemplifies the strivings of antebellum Blacks for education. It also provides evidence that people in power feared and strongly resisted the growth of a free, liberally educated population of African Americans since such a population would have constituted a major threat to the institution of slavery.

In the meantime, free Blacks were looking to education in general and reading in particular to provide refinement and a guide to clean living, especially for the young. In Philadelphia in 1832, a group of Black people organized the Philadelphia Library of Colored Persons to encourage Black youth to cultivate literary pursuits and to improve their minds (Fishel and Quarles 1967, 159). In New York the following year, the Phoenix Society, a Black self-help group, founded A Library for the People of Color. In a call for donations, printed in the *New York Observer*, Samuel Cornish (1833), co-editor of the nation's first Black newspaper and head of the Phoenix Society, noted the purpose of the library and the benefits he hoped would accrue from its use:

The objects of the institution are general improvement and the training of our youth to habits of reading and reflection. I need not tell you that, for the want of such institutions, many of the young and unthinking part of our colored citizens are led by those older than themselves to haunts of wickedness and vice. Many young men, yea! and old ones, too, spend their evenings in improper places, because they have no public libraries, no reading rooms, nor useful lectures, to attract their attention, and occupy their leisure hours. We hope to save such from ruin and lead them to habits of virtue and usefulness. (159–160)

Cornish went on to describe the plans for the library, which were to include three 1-hour classes on three evenings a week, during which someone would read aloud from preselected works, followed by group discussions. He also noted that the Constitutions of the Temperance and Moral Societies would be kept at the library, and that those causes would be promoted among the youth. The expectation was, then, that reading could not only educate, but could possibly save the young from depravity and immoral conduct. Cornish also mentions opening a "classic school for ten or twelve promising youth" to be connected with the library, indicating the desire for education well beyond the Bible literacy that may have been the goal of early missionaries. Among free Blacks, the foundation for a literate community and an educated citizenry began to be laid early in the history of the republic, as was the expectation that literature could provide a path to self-improvement as well as a moral compass for young people. The concept of literature providing a moral compass for youth is one that continues to influence some African American children's book authors as well as numerous other authors of children's books.

POSTWAR EDUCATION

When the Civil War ended, for many freed Blacks literacy was one of the first dreams to be pursued, second only to locating and reuniting with family members from whom they had been separated. In his autobiography, Booker T. Washington (1901/1965, 33–34), influential educator and founder of Tuskegee Institute, who was born into slavery, describes the magnetic power that literacy and education held for those to whom it had been so long denied:

Few people who were not right in the midst of the scenes can form any exact idea of the intense desire which the people of my race showed for an education. As I have stated, it was a whole race trying to go to school. Few were too young, and none too old, to make the attempt to learn. As fast as any kind of teachers could be secured, not only were day-schools filled, but night-schools as well. The great ambition of the older people was to try to learn to read the Bible before they died. With this end in view, men and women who were fifty or seventy-five years old could often be found in the night-school. Sunday-school was formed soon after freedom, but the principal book studied in the Sunday-school was the spelling-book. Day-school, night-school, Sunday-school, were always crowded, and often many had to be turned away for want of room.

The federal government had established the Freedmen's Bureau in 1865 to aid war refugees and former slaves in rebuilding their lives. One of the Bureau's charges was to establish schools to educate former slaves. Not only did they set up the kinds of schools Washington described, they also established or provided aid for Black colleges, among them Howard University and Hampton Institute. Northern missionaries and philanthropists also participated in the campaign to educate the freedmen. For example, Lydia Maria Child (1865), the writer and activist best known for the Thanksgiving song "Over the River and through the Woods," published *The Freedmen's Book*, at her own expense, the year the Civil War ended. It was intended for recently freed slaves and included work from several Black writers, such as Frederick Douglass and Phillis Wheatley, as well as biographies, simplified by Child, of figures such as Benjamin Banneker, Toussaint L'Ouverture, and John Brown. Although it also contained the work of White writers, including Child herself, and an excerpt from *Uncle Tom's Cabin*, this anthology highlighted the work of African Americans. It was a far cry from the Blue-back Speller, and a significant early step toward making African American literature accessible to a readership still in development. Postwar literacy efforts were also advanced by large numbers of teachers who came from the North to work in the new schools. Franklin and Moss (1994) report that four years after the end of the war there were about 9500 teachers in schools for former slaves in the South, and that by 1870, there were nearly a quarter of a million Black pupils in more than 4000 schools (230–231).

This phenomenon of a "whole race trying to go to school," as described by Washington, resulted in an immense and rapid increase in the literacy rates among African Americans following emancipation. By 1900, just three and a half decades after the Civil War, the percentage of Blacks who could read or write had risen to 60 percent (Jackson 1989, 295), and between 1870 and 1930 the literacy rate among African Americans rose from 19 percent to 84 percent (Franklin and Moss 1994, 408). Although the definition of literacy in these reports is unclear, it is apparent that by the end of the nineteenth century a substantial portion of Black Americans were able to read and write well enough to support a growing number of Black publications, some of which encased seeds of an African American children's literature.

NINETEENTH CENTURY BLACK PUBLISHING: THE FIRST BUDS OF AFRICAN AMERICAN CHILDREN'S LITERATURE

NEWSPAPERS AND PERIODICALS

A written African American children's literature may well have its beginnings in nineteenth century newspapers and periodicals launched by Black religious and secular organizations and by activist individuals. Black individuals and institutions had begun publishing newspapers and periodicals decades before the Civil War; the first Black newspaper in the United States, *Freedom's Journal*, began publication in New York in 1827, and the first magazine-type Black periodical was published in 1838 (Hutton 1993). Among the most famous antebellum newspapers was that of Frederick Douglass, the self-liberated former slave whose owner had recognized that literacy would "unfit him for slavery."

Not surprisingly, an important purpose, although not the only one, of many of the publications launched before the war was to protest slavery and agitate for abolition and human rights. Over the nineteenth century, these publications also came to function as voices of racial uplift, as shapers of a national Black community, as instruments for educating a Black citizenry, and as vehicles for self-definition, self-determination, and self-expression. To these ends, editors and writers frequently addressed materials to parents and children as part of the effort to educate and inform them and to promote what they saw as positive values.

Among the most notable nineteenth century Black publications are those of Black churches, whose interests and reach extended well beyond the religious needs of their members. One of the most active and far-reaching such institutions is the African Methodist Episcopal Church, which stands here as an exemplar. The A.M.E. Church, as it is commonly known, was founded in 1787, not because of conflicting religious doctrines, but as a social protest when a group of Black worshippers, led by Richard Allen and Absalom Jones, responded to racial discrimination by walking out of St. George's Methodist Church in Philadelphia.

Consequently, from its beginnings in the Free African Society formed by Allen and his associates, the A.M.E. Church was intended to serve not only the spiritual needs of people of African descent, but their civic, educational, material, and cultural needs as well. Publishing its own materials was integral to the effort to encourage the Black community to be independent and self-reliant, and the church was doing so as early as 1817 (Payne 1891/1969, 52). In 1852 it established *The Christian Recorder*, currently the oldest continuously published Black newspaper in the United States. In its explicit address to Black children and their parents, and in its apparent intention to function as a moral guide while appealing to children's interests, *The Recorder*'s child-related material can be considered a precursor to African American children's literature.

The Christian Recorder

Perusing issues of the *Recorder* published between 1854 and 1864 reveals that, in addition to being a forum for news and views related to the A.M.E. Church, the nation, and the world, it was a family newspaper, for "the Dissemination of Religion, Morality, Literature, and Science" as noted on its masthead. Church leaders such as Bishop Payne used the paper as a forum for reporting on the business of the church and for expressing their views, exhortations, and differences of opinion. It also attracted contributions from other prominent African Americans, including Frances E. W. Harper, Frederick Douglass, and Fanny Jackson Coppin. True to its multifaceted mission, the *Recorder* contained a variety of articles on matters as diverse as transplanting strawberries, indigestion, fashion, and rules and examples for living a good Christian life. Its commitment to literature was manifest in the inclusion of a substantial number of poems and stories, although its concomitant commitment to religion and morality meant that the literature was usually purposeful—a vehicle for instilling moral values and promoting religion as integral to everyday life.

Among the most prominent concerns of the paper during this period was family—marriage, parenting, and the welfare of children. An editorial entitled "Our Children" published in the August 17, 1854, issue states, "Perhaps there is no subject, at the time of the present crisis, that demands our attention more than the proper education and training of our children." The writer was concerned not only with moral and religious training, but also with the general education of African American children. Every child, the column declared, deserved regular and proper parental instruction, a trade by which he could earn a good living, and as good a literary education as the parents could afford. A later piece, "Wants of the Church—Education of Children," asserted that educating children was so important a duty that "Heaven is unprepared to acknowledge" parents as good Christians if they neglect to cultivate the minds of their children (March 19, 1855). Clearly, the A.M.E. Church viewed children as vital to the future of African America, and it used the *Recorder* as one means to educate both parents and their offspring.

Material for children in the *Recorder* appeared both in columns explicitly addressed to them, such as "The Child's Cabinet," and in features such as "The Family Circle." Many pieces were reprints from other religious periodicals and Sunday school tracts and were unlikely to have been written by African Americans but to have been chosen for their compatibility with the moral, religious, or literary views of the editors. There were also children's pieces from well-known White authors such as Lydia Maria Child, Harriet Beecher Stowe, Hans Christian Andersen, and Oliver Optic. Many other pieces, which were unsigned or unattributed or by writers who are not now well known, most likely were produced by the editors or other African American contributors.

Many of the stories addressed to children were moralistic or religious cautionary tales: "My first step to ruin," exclaimed a wretched youth as he lay tossing from side to side on the straw bed in one corner of his prison house, "My first step to ruin was going fishing on the Sabbath" (January 16, 1861). Most were unabashedly didactic, offering lessons in the conduct of life and reiterating Christian precepts. Children were particularly urged to be obedient to both God and their parents, to faithfully carry out whatever responsibilities they were given by either, and to forgive the transgressions of their companions. The familiar story "The Boy at the Dyke" (November 17, 1854) provided an opportunity to impress on children that God had given them a duty to occupy, and that they could not escape the obligation to carry it out. Another typical story, "Sounding Brass," which highlights the importance of forgiveness and charity, was reprinted from the *Tract Journal* in the February 10, 1861, *Recorder*. Bully Frank Burton has fun on Dick's purloined ice skates while Dick stands helplessly on the sidelines. When Frank falls through thin ice, however, it is Dick who rescues him, displaying a charitable heart, for which he receives an apology from Frank and high praise from his companions.

Some authors couched their lessons in colorful plots, familiar circumstances, and characters who were likely to attract children's interest. One writer, for example, invented the "Just-As-I've-a-Mind-To," a creature likened to a wild tiger, to warn of the perils of willfulness and obstinacy. When Will ignored warnings not to cross the ford because the water was too high, he fell off his horse into the strong current and was dashed to death among the rocks. "The Just-as-I've-a-Mind-To killed him as certainly as any loose tigress would have done. Children! Beware of it!" (April 12, 1862). In contrast, the July 12, 1862, issue included "The Wild Honeysuckle," an unsigned fairy tale. Sisters Laura, Lauretta, and Laurencia vie to become the surrogate daughter of the king, whose beloved only child, Angelina, has died. In a dream, Angelina instructs her father to choose, from among all the girls in the kingdom, the one with honeysuckle in her hair, and the king announces a search. While looking for flowers to wear for the king, Laura and Lauretta each in turn encounters and refuses to help a poor ragged woman who comes begging for food. But Laurencia shares her food and drink, and the woman, through her incantations, causes Laurencia to end up with the requisite honeysuckle and to be chosen as the king's new daughter. The inclusion of this secular fantasy tale with Cinderella and "toads-and-diamonds" motifs demonstrates that the *Recorder* went beyond the usual Sunday school literature of the day to include imaginative stories that were likely to appeal to children without explicit moral or religious lessons.

Poems for or about children in the *Recorder* ranged from the sentimental to the didactic to the nonsensical. "All Alone, My Baby Boy" (January 18, 1856) is a father's celebration of a child learning to walk, literally and figuratively, and an expression of the father's hopes for the child's future. It begins, "O' my precious baby boy,/ Father's pride and mother's joy." The first four verses address the paths the child should take in life; the last four describe the child's actual first steps, ending with:

Come, my darling, come to me,
Laughing, crowing in your glee:
See your father's beckoning arms
Wait to shield from hurts and harms:
Ha! You've started! Tripping, running,
Hands outstretched, and steps so cunning.

"Kind Little Children" (July 5, 1862) is a didactic verse by J. M. Crawford that describes two children who guide a blind man across the street. The poem then goes on to assert that every child can perform kind acts, such as cheerfully obeying one's parents and willingly performing needed tasks, and that doing so pleases both parents and God. In contrast, "The Kitchen Clock" (September 19, 1963) describes the clock and in the first verse asks, "Tell me what it says." In subsequent verses, the clock "says" that it is patient, truthful, active, and obliging, with each verse except the last ending with the refrain, "'Tick-tock—tick, tock'/ That is what it says." In the last verse, when the pointer reaches two, the clock changes its tune: "'ding-ding'—tick-tock"/ That is what it says." "The Kitchen Clock" exemplifies the attempt of some authors to appeal to young children by writing about a familiar everyday object without overtly hammering in a moral lesson or religious truth but still promoting certain virtues.

Given that the *Christian Recorder* was a church publication, and given the conditions under which Black people, free or enslaved, were living in antebellum America, as well as the objectives of the paper, neither the didactic tone nor the emphasis on moral and religious teachings is surprising. In that regard, the *Recorder*, in its writings for and about children, reflected the moralistic, evangelistic tone of the popular Sunday school literature of the day. What is of greater significance, however, is the existence of creative writing by Black writers addressed to Black children; this writing is in the form of poems and fictional stories designed not only to impart lessons in life and living, but also to entertain while doing so. Neither the prose nor the poetry was of lasting quality generally, but the *Recorder* was among the earliest publications to offer written stories and poems to a readership of Black children.

Other Nineteenth Century Newspapers

The A.M.E. Church also addressed children through at least one other publication. In 1858, under the leadership of Bishop Payne, the Church began publishing *The Repository of Religion and Literature and Science and Art*. A general interest magazine addressed to the public at large, the *Repository* was intended to provide information, to nurture the creative talents of African Americans, and to provide moral, intellectual, and spiritual uplift. True to its title, the *Repository* contained sections on various subjects, including music and poetry. The magazine also included a "Young Ladies' Lecture Room," a "Children's Room," and a series, written by Bishop Payne, called "Letters to Children about God" (Bullock 1981, 47–48).

Although Payne himself contributed a substantial portion of the material for the magazine, contributions also came from other editors and from writers outside the editorial staff, including a number of women, such as Sarah M. Douglass, a teacher at the Philadelphia Institute for Colored Youth (Mossell 1894/1971, 95), and Frances Ellen Watkins Harper, popular poet, essayist, and novelist. The *Repository* also published speeches and papers that had been delivered by lesser-known writers, many of whom were women. The inclusion of women is significant since the first stirrings of a secular, written African American literature addressed to children emanated from women writers. The magazine lasted only five years, but in its attention to women as writers and children as audience and the assumption of a natural affinity between the two, it stands as another representative of one of the roots from which an African American children's literature developed.

Hutton (1993) provides evidence that antebellum Black editors also used the secular press as a vehicle for the moral education of Black children and youth. She notes, for example, that Samuel Cornish's 1829 paper, *Rights of All*, which survived only for about a year, featured a Youth's Literary Column. Hutton also cites several examples of material from *The Colored American*, which existed from 1837 to 1841, pre-dating the *Recorder*. It was particularly concerned about young people. In fact, Hutton asserts that, once it started weekly columns addressed to youth, it devoted more column space to young people than any other Black newspaper before the Civil War (133). As an example of the tone of the youth-oriented material, she cites one story that stresses the importance of good sense and hard work. Entitled "The Robin and the Squirrel," it begins:

"A very pleasant day," exclaimed a handsome robin, as he finished his song one fine autumnal morning and observed a pert, facetious looking ground muck eyeing him very shrewdly. "How do you do, Mr. Squirrel? What do you remark in my appearance that attracts so much attention?" "I was thinking," replied the whiskered rogue, "what a pleasant life you lead Mr. Robin, who can sing so sweetly, and fly about the trees all day long, pecking a little of everything that suits your taste." "I think the same," observed the robin gravely . . . "and I cannot but pity your monotonous mode of living, who have always to trudge about on foot and can never gather but one kind of fruit at a time." (135)

Like the grasshopper in the Aesop fable of the grasshopper and the ant, the robin is unprepared for winter and has to be rescued by the squirrel, and as in the fable, the moral lesson is obvious. Overall, the stories for youth in *The Colored American* focused on promoting such values as being kind and caring, being obedient to parents, being respectful, fearing slavery, and working hard in school (Hutton 1993, 135).

Another youth-related category in the content of antebellum Black newspapers, as identified by Hutton, is a group of messages that report on children's school activities, programs, and exhibitions. Although not necessarily addressed exclusively to children, these reports are significant as demonstrations of the accomplishments and intellectual capacity of Black youngsters, in contradiction to the popular notion of Black inferiority as expressed in the literature of the time. They are also evidence of the faith the editors and writers placed in Black youngsters as the hope of the future. These kinds of reports would be echoed decades later, for essentially the same reasons, in the first twentieth century magazine for Black children.

LATE NINETEENTH CENTURY AFRICAN AMERICAN WOMEN WRITERS

The successful launching of a significant number of newspapers and magazines published by and for people of African descent in the nineteenth century substantiates the existence of a significant amount of literacy among the Black population, while the contents of the publications speak to the existence and growth of a Black middle class. The middle class in this context should be understood not only in economic terms, but also in terms of their strivings for respectability within their communities and beyond, in their participation in self-improvement activities, and in their concern for education for themselves and for Black children.

To a large extent these strivings influenced the content and tone of nineteenth century Black writing for and about children and youth. In Victorian America, responsibility for the social and moral education of children and youth rested with women, and much of the published material aimed at Black children was produced by Black women writers who, in post-Reconstruction nineteenth century Black America, became a significant social and literary force. The end of the nineteenth century and the early twentieth was the era of Black women who, on their own and through organized clubs and other institutions, sought to be of service to the masses of Black people, who were not yet very far removed from bondage. Active in postwar efforts to assist newly freed Black people with their educational and social advancement, Black women by the end of the century had entered a number of professions, including journalism, literature, medicine, law, and teaching (Mosell 1894/1971). Prominent Black women raised their voices, either in speeches or in writing, to protest racial and gender oppression, to assert their identities as women, and to demand women's rights. At the same time many of these women, both womanist[1] and traditionally feminine, tended to conform to expectations in their roles as mothers and keepers of the hearth. Their sense of responsibility to the young was expressed in the writing these women addressed to children, often in magazines and periodicals.

As was the case with *The Repository*, some periodical publications included pages or departments explicitly addressed to children, presenting potential opportunities for women writers. For example, I. Garland Penn (1891/1969), in his contemporaneous chronicle of late nineteenth century Black publishing, reports that in 1884, Lucy Wilmot Smith, a noted journalist, edited a children's column in *The American Baptist* of Louisville (378), and that Amelia E. H. Johnson was responsible for a "Children's Corner" in the *Sower and Reaper* of Baltimore, for which she created original pieces (424).

Not surprisingly, however, women's magazines were more significant as outlets for Black women's writing, including that intended to guide, educate, or entertain Black children. One such magazine, *Woman's World*, initiated in 1900 in Fort Worth, Texas, was advertised as containing "good stories, with colored men and women as heroes and heroines; special articles that are informing as well as entertaining; *special talks for girls; a page for children*, a household page with timely articles for the economical, studious housewife; a fashion page with latest Paris and New York styles illustrated; a department of flower-culture; and many other good things for pleasure and instruction" (Bullock 1981, 169, emphasis added).

One of the most influential nineteenth century Black women's magazines was *Our Women and Children Magazine*, a publication established in 1888 in Louisville, Kentucky, by two Baptist ministers, Charles H. Parrish and William J. Simmons. Penn (1891/1969) had high praise for the magazine:

Its purpose was the uplifting of the race, particularly our Afro-American women and children. Being devoted to this kind of work, it has done more than all the Afro-American papers together in bringing to the front the latent talent of our lady writers. Its columns have been open from time to time, to all our women, for articles on the particular questions which affect home, the mother and children. By the efforts of its editor [William J. Simmons] it has thus given to the world a bright array of female writers, upon different questions hitherto unknown to the literary world. (120)

Penn's comments are insightful. He identifies the goal of the magazine as racial uplift, an important and common goal of Black literary efforts at the turn of the century. He also explicitly links Black women's writing to the home, including children, and he recognizes the significance of their distinctive literary contributions. Even a century later Black women writers would continue to dominate the field of African American children's literature.

The various departments of the magazine were edited by a circle of women writers, among whom was Mary V. Cook, editor of the education department.

She was principal of the normal department and professor of Latin and mathematics at Simmons's school and an active civic leader, Baptist church leader, and speaker (Penn 1891/1969, 371–372). In 1887, she read a paper in Louisville before the National Press Convention, the title of which was "Is Juvenile Literature Demanded on the Part of Colored Children?" Cook (1887) referred to this speech in a later address about the place of women in the work of the Baptist Church:

> The field of juvenile literature is open. I said recently before the National Press Convention, held in Louisville, Kentucky, there are now published 24 secular papers and magazines in the United States for the children. . . . Of the religious journals there are 47. . . . Of this number, 71 secular and religious papers, there is not one so far as I know, edited especially for colored children. There is a little paper whose name does not appear on the list that is written for colored youth, being edited and controlled by Miss J. P. Moore of Louisiana.[2] (45–56)

Even though, in this reference, Cook focuses on periodicals, her speech for the National Press Convention is significant because it well may be the first recorded public call for an imaginative literature created for and addressed explicitly to an audience of Black children and thus is an important milestone in the development of an African American children's literature.

As if in answer to Mary V. Cook, Amelia Etta Hall Johnson, in the same year as Cook's call for Black juvenile literature, launched a magazine generally considered to be the first African American periodical for children. Johnson, the wife of a prominent Baltimore minister, was born in Toronto in 1858 and educated in Montreal. She wrote poems and short stories for various publications, including children's stories for *The National Baptist*, the organ of a White denomination, and one of the most widely circulated church-related journals in the country (Penn 1891/1969, 424). She also wrote for the aforementioned *Our Women and Children Magazine*, and, as noted, she edited a children's feature for a Baltimore paper. Johnson, then, is one of the first known African American writers to devote a considerable part of her creative efforts to producing imaginative literature for Black children. In 1887, she launched an eight-page monthly, called *The Joy*, as a forum in which Black writers, especially women, could publish original poems and stories for young people (Penn, 423–424).

A year after publishing *The Joy*, Johnson also launched a second magazine for children, *The Ivy*, which focused on Black history and was intended to encourage Black children to read (Penn 1891/1969, Shockley 1988). Neither magazine was still in existence by the time Penn's book was published in 1891, even though he indicates that both had been well received. In its emphasis on literary materials such as original stories and poems, *The Joy* may be the first secular publication produced by African American writers and devoted exclusively to imaginary literature for children. It is also significant that Johnson aimed specifically to provide opportunity for female writers, suggesting that she may have been as much womanist as she was a race or culture loyalist. In any case, her emphasis on women writers confirms once again the traditional strong cultural association between female writers and the creation of children's literature.

A Novel First

Arguably, Johnson's most significant achievement was becoming the first African American woman to publish, in 1890, a novel for children, entitled *Clarence and Corinne; or God's Way*. No elements of the novel other than its authorship by a

Black woman identify it specifically as African American children's literature. Its main characters are never physically described, although in the illustrations they appear to be Caucasian. Neither Black life nor identifiably Black people are at the center of this book; its literary roots lie in late nineteenth century Sunday school and reform literature. Nevertheless, Mrs. Johnson's achievement is highly significant, in part because it is one of the earliest novels by a Black American woman to be published in book form and in part because it represents a publishing breakthrough for a Black writer of children's literature. *Clarence and Corinne* was published by the American Baptist Publication Society, at the time one of the country's largest publishers (Penn 1891/1969, 424). Mrs. Johnson was the first woman and the first "colored author" to have a manuscript accepted by the Society.

Aimed at intermediate readers, *Clarence and Corinne* was a book for Sunday school libraries (Penn 1891/1969, 425). As such, it was didactic, moralistic, and strongly evangelical in tone. It fit well into one of the literary traditions of its times, reflecting the influence of the temperance movement that had come to prominence earlier in the century. *Clarence and Corinne* features a sister and brother who overcome poverty and adversity to find "God's way" to a comfortable adulthood and status as physician and teacher, respectively. Their drunken and abusive father abandons them on the sudden death of their mother when the children are nine and twelve years of age. The siblings, who are intelligent, hardworking, and devoted to each other, are separated, find homes over the years with various foster families, and are eventually reunited, having triumphed over hardship and misfortune by following God's plan. In the concluding chapter, we see Clarence and Corinne as adults, happily living together with their spouses in a large house in the neighborhood where they had lived in poverty as children.

Clarence and Corinne was well received by both the Black and White press. The Black press hailed it as an excellent story, its excellence attributed in part to its espousal of antialcohol, pro-Christian values, although it was also praised for its literary qualities. The Black press also saw *Clarence and Corinne* as an instance of racial uplift, a weapon in the fight against the racist belief that Blacks were incapable of creating literature. In issuing Johnson's book, the American Baptist Publication Society made a tacit statement to the effect that Blacks could produce literature comparable to what was available from White contemporaries producing a similar kind of writing. Penn quoted several admiring reviews from the White press, noting that positive reviews were unexpected from that source. He goes on to indicate that Mrs. Johnson had written the book to demonstrate that "colored people" could think on their own and that they lacked only opportunities to express those thoughts in public forums (1891/1969, 425–426). Mrs. Johnson's Black contemporaries understood well the importance of her entrance into the mainstream of late nineteenth century publishing for children. Given the historical association between the ability to write and membership in the human race that was part of the impetus for the development of an African American literature, this was a highly significant symbolic gesture.

Some White reviewers also praised the literary quality of *Clarence and Corinne*. Mainly, however, White reviewers were impressed by the fact of its author's race and gender. The *Missionary Visitor*, of Toulon, Illinois, for example, stated, "This, we believe, is our first Sunday School library book written by a colored author. Mrs. Johnson is the wife of a noted and successful Baltimore pastor, and in this book shows talent worthy of her husband" (Penn 1891/1969, 425). It is interesting to note that her talent is assessed in relation to her husband, an indication of the place that women held in the minds of some church leaders and of the importance of the growth of women's activism.

Although Johnson's novel demonstrated that she had considerable talent as a writer, the significance of *Clarence and Corinne* lies not in its literary quality, which does not place it among the all-time best in children's literature, but in its having been produced by a Black woman writer in the late nineteenth century and its acceptance by what was then a major publisher. Because of its moralistic tone, *Clarence and Corinne* has not outlived its era, and the same is true of its two successors, *The Hazely Family* (1894) and *Martina Meriden; or What Is My Motive?* (1901). Given its time and circumstance, however, it was a singular achievement and an important milestone along the path to a modern African American children's literature.

Other Children's Books by Black Women

A few other Black women activists also produced books for children before the end of the nineteenth century. Victoria Earle Matthews (1893), for example, was a journalist and social reformer who established the White Rose Mission, a home for "colored" working girls in New York City, which eventually became a settlement house. In 1893 she published a sixteen-page book for young people, entitled *Aunt Lindy: A Story Founded on Real Life*. It concerned an old Black woman who, after agreeing to nurse a sick stranger brought to her by the local doctor, discovers that the stranger is her former slave master, who had sold her children away. Her first impulse was to take revenge, but Aunt Lindy finds the spiritual strength to forgive "Marse Jeems" and nurse him back to health. From that time on, she and her husband Uncle Joel "never knew a sorrow." With its theme of forgiveness, *Aunt Lindy* clearly continues the tradition of moralistic stories to guide readers on the right path.

In 1890, another activist Black woman, Josephine Henderson Heard, published *Morning Glories*, a book of poems, "from a heart that desires to encourage and inspire the youth of the Race to pure and noble motives" (Preface). Heard's poetry resembles other Victorian era poetry, and if it was intended to inspire youth, it was not because she selected subject matter, language, or imagery that was particularly appealing to the young. Some poems are tributes to famous figures such as John Greenleaf Whittier and Frederick Douglass. As the wife of an A.M.E. bishop, she was also inspired to write religious poems and obituaries. Other topics include nature, love, and race. Nevertheless, Heard was a reasonably good poet, and her collection represents one of the early volumes of poetry by a Black author explicitly aimed in the direction of Black youth.

By the end of the nineteenth century, then, just thirty-five years after the Civil War, the seeds of an African American children's literature were sprouting. A tradition of story and song, including some tales and rhymes especially associated with children, had been created and passed on orally for several generations. About 60 percent of the African American population could read and write to some degree, and that percentage was growing rapidly, indicating that the development of a critical mass of young Black readers was well under way. Women writers had begun producing literature addressed explicitly to Black children, the first magazines for Black children had come and gone, and the first children's novel by an African American had been published.

Perhaps even more important were the functions that literacy, and, by extension, literature, had come to serve in the national Black community. Black literature, broadly defined, had functioned as self-affirmation, as a vehicle of protest, as a source of information about Black people and issues and events that affected Black lives, as an educational tool, as a means to inculcate moral and spiritual values in young and old alike, and as a path to racial uplift. Although by the end of the century there was an incipient move toward "purely literary" work for children, the tradition of literature as a purposeful enterprise had been well established and would influence the development of an African American children's literature as a literature of social action.

NOTES

1. Alice Walker (1984), in *In Search of Our Mother's Gardens* (New York: Harvest/HBJ), coined the term *womanist* to describe "a black feminist or feminist of color." A womanist is, among other things, "committed to the survival and wholeness of entire people, male and female." She encapsulates her definition in the famous line, "Womanist is to feminist as purple is to lavender" (xi–xii).

2. Joanna P. Moore (1832–1916) was a White Baptist missionary who conceived and created a number of "Fireside Schools" dedicated to helping African American women and children. *HOPE* was a newsletter begun in 1885 to provide reading material for the Fireside Schools. It was "full of Bible and testimonies of what the Bible has done for those who love and obey it. This paper started out to teach faith in God and love for one another. HOPE is the organ of the Fireside School. It is an interdenominational family magazine. Its object is to make home the best and happiest place in the world." *In Christ's Stead. Autobiographical Sketches,* http://docsouth.unc.edu/church/moore/moore.html#jmoore217.

BIBLIOGRAPHY OF BOOKS FOR CHILDREN AND YOUNG ADULTS

Sources other than books for children and young adults are documented in a reference list at the back of the book.

Heard, Josephine Henderson. 1890. *Morning Glories.* Digital Schomburg African American Women Writers of the 19th Century. http://digilib.nypl.org/dynaweb/digs-p/wwm9710/@Generic_BookTextView/129;pt=122.

Johnson, A. E. 1890/1988. *Clarence and Corinne; or God's Way.* New York: Oxford University Press.

———. 1894. *The Hazeley Family.* Philadelphia: American Baptist Society.

———. 1901. *Martina Meriden; or What Is My Motive?* Philadelphia: American Baptist Society.

Matthews, Victoria Earle. 1893/1998. *Aunt Lindy: A Story Founded on Real Life.* Repr. in *Afro-American Women Writers, 1746–1933: An Anthology and Guide.* Ed. by Ann Allen Shockley. Boston: G. K. Hall.

CHAPTER 2

For the Children of the Sun: African American Children's Literature Begins to Bloom

Although the roots of African American children's literature had been established by the end of the nineteenth century, its blossoming unfolded over several more decades. The first twentieth century milestone in African American children's literature was *The Brownies' Book*, a children's magazine published in 1920–1921 by W.E.B. Du Bois, the leading African American intellectual of his day. Although *The Brownies' Book* lasted only a short time, its spirit lived on. At least two of its regular contributors continued to write for children. In the last half of the 1920s, Effie Lee Newsome produced a regular children's page for *The Crisis*, the NCAAP magazine edited by Du Bois. Later she published a noteworthy volume of original poetry for young children, which included some of the poems she had published originally in the two magazines. Langston Hughes, the most famous of the Harlem Renaissance writers, contributed a variety of poems and other pieces to *The Brownies' Book* and, beginning in the 1930s, also produced a number of children's books.

Although *The Brownies' Book* was a remarkable development of the period, it was not the only one. Another African American intellectual giant, historian Carter G. Woodson, established his own publishing company and between the late 1920s and the early 1950s published a number of children's books about Black life and Black history, including a few books he wrote himself. The work of these pioneering individuals represents the first steps toward a canon of modern African American children's literature.

THE BROWNIES' BOOK

The Brownies' Book emerged out of a number of complex social and political circumstances. By the time it was launched in 1920, W.E.B. Du Bois had assumed the intellectual leadership that had been the province of the very influential and highly respected Black educator Booker T. Washington, who had died in 1915. Washington, who had been born into slavery, had espoused a strategy for advancing the race by postponing open agitation for social equality until Black people lifted themselves up through acquiring training in useful skills and trades and becoming economically self-reliant. Therefore, he promoted and supported vocational and industrial training schools for Blacks, even at the college level. Du Bois strongly opposed both Washington's social philosophy regarding equal rights and his over-emphasis on vocational and industrial training, particularly in higher education.

Born in 1868 in Massachusetts, Du Bois was a highly educated graduate of Fisk University; he also studied in Germany and in 1895 became the first Black scholar to earn a PhD from Harvard. He was a sociologist, writer, teacher, lifelong advocate for equal rights, and one of the founders of the National Association for the Advancement of Colored People (NAACP), an organization seeded in part by opposition to Washington's accommodationist views. Its founding purposes were to secure equal civil and political rights for all citizens and to end discrimination and violence against African Americans.

When the NAACP was launched in 1909, Du Bois became director of publications and research and thereby editor of its official organ, *The Crisis*. Beginning in October 1911, *The Crisis* had annually published a children's issue, which proved to be the most popular issue each year. In an editorial piece entitled "The True Brownies" in the October 1919 *Crisis*, Du Bois declared that the popularity of the children's number was fitting because "we are and must be interested in our children above all else, if we love our race and humanity" (Du Bois 1919, 285). He was concerned that the "kiddies," influenced by monthly reports in *The Crisis* of race riots and lynchings, might be learning hatred rather than activism. Between 1900 and 1919, 1,360 Black people were lynched, 76 in 1919 alone (Linder 2000). Du Bois had received a letter from a twelve-year-old stating that she hated "the white man as much as he hates me and probably more." Du Bois was appalled, but he understood well the dilemma that Black parents faced in trying to raise their children in a racialized society. "To educate them in human hatred is more disastrous to them than to the hated. To seek to raise them in ignorance of their racial identity and peculiar situation is inadvisable—impossible" (Du Bois 1919, 285). His alternative was to launch "a little magazine for children—for all children, but especially for *ours,* 'the Children of the Sun'" (286). It was to be published independently, but in cooperation with *The Crisis*, by Du Bois and Augustus Dill, who was the business manager for both publications.

If the founding of the NAACP was partly the result of impatience with Washington's social philosophy, *The Brownies' Book* was partly a reflection of Du Bois's contrasting vision of the ideal education for Black people. Du Bois resolutely demanded excellence in education for Black children, including a strong foundation in reading, writing, and especially thinking. He also encouraged the teaching of the humanities and sciences and believed that education for Black children should cultivate a spirit of sacrifice and aspirations to a life of service. He viewed education as a process of teaching certain values that are central to the development of character, such as moderation, courtesy, endurance, and a love of beauty (Aptheker 1973, x–xi).

In terms of higher education, at this point in his life Du Bois was also espousing his own strategy for elevating "the race." Unlike Washington, Du Bois did not believe that the masses of Black people could lift themselves by their own bootstraps, so to speak. He thought that advancement would come through the efforts of a cadre of liberally educated "exceptional men," the most able 10 percent of young Blacks, which he referred to as the Talented Tenth. Armed with an excellent education, they would in turn serve Black people as "race leaders," thereby taking the leadership of the national Black community out of the hands of Whites, whom Du Bois did not always trust to act in Blacks' best interests (Du Bois 1968, 236). By encouraging its readers to pursue the ideals of a broad and liberal education, Du Bois used *The Brownies' Book* to promote the development of future members of the Talented Tenth.

THE NECESSITY FOR *THE BROWNIES' BOOK*

A magazine with a mission, *The Brownies' Book* was a prime example of literature as social action. It was advertised in the October 1919 *Crisis* as follows:

It will be a thing of Joy and Beauty, dealing in Happiness, Laughter and Emulation, and designed especially for Kiddies from Six to Sixteen.

It will seek to teach Universal Love and Brotherhood for all little folk, black and brown and yellow and white. (Du Bois 1919, 286)

Although its primary audience was defined as "the children of the sun," in reaching out to all children, Du Bois prefigured the move toward multiculturalism in children's literature that would come decades later. In any case, *The Brownies' Book* was not intended merely as a pleasant diversion. In keeping with his educational philosophy and his concern for the "peculiar situation" of Black children, Du Bois made clear in the statement of goals for the magazine that *The Brownies' Book* would be guided by an explicit set of values and an underlying ideology:

Deftly intertwined with the mission of entertainment will go the endeavor:

(a) To make colored children realize that being "colored" is a normal, beautiful thing.
(b) To make them familiar with the history and achievements of the Negro race.
(c) To make them know that other colored children have grown into beautiful, useful and famous persons.
(d) To teach them delicately a code of honor and action in their relations with white children.
(e) To turn their little hurts and resentments into emulation, ambition and love of their homes and companions.
(f) To point out the best amusements and joys and worth-while things of life.
(g) To inspire them to prepare for definite occupations and duties with a broad spirit of sacrifice. (Du Bois 1919, 286)

To build a magazine on the perceived need—among others—for Black children to recognize themselves as normal, to learn about Black history, and to recognize their own potential was to indict both the sociopolitical environment and the instructional and literary texts available to children of the time. Although by 1920 English language children's literature had made great strides toward literary artistry and enjoyment, and away from the moralizing and piety that marked so many children's books of prior centuries, realistic Black American characters were mostly absent. England was experiencing a "golden age" with the flourishing of fantasy and fairy tales and fictional classics that were read on both sides of the Atlantic, such as *The Wind in the Willows* (Grahame 1908), *Peter Pan* (Barrie 1906/1980), and *The Tale of Peter Rabbit* (Potter 1903). In the United States, although well-known and long-lasting books such as *The Wizard of Oz* (Baum 1900) and *Rebecca of Sunnybrook Farm* (Wiggin 1903) had appeared at the turn of the century, children's book publishing as a distinct enterprise of the major publishers was just beginning to flourish.

The first mainstream publishing house to establish an independent children's department, Macmillan, did so in 1919, the year before *The Brownies' Book* was launched. Fewer than 500 new children's books were published in the United States in 1920 (Huck et al. 2001, 101), and it is safe to assume that very few, if any, were created by Black writers or featured realistic Black characters.

A Black presence, however, had been a part of establishment children's books and magazines, presumably aimed at a white audience, for decades. For the most part,

Blacks in those early materials were presented as plantation stereotypes, objects of ridicule or laughter, or faithful and comical servants to White children and their families. Even *St. Nicholas Magazine*, the premier children's magazine of its time, engaged in such stereotypes. It had been established in 1873 and in its pages had appeared the work of an impressive array of famous White authors, including Louisa May Alcott, William Cullen Bryant, Frances Hodgson Burnett, Lucretia Hale, Joel Chandler Harris, Robert Louis Stevenson, and Mark Twain. In 1920 it was still considered the nation's finest literary magazine for children. *St. Nicholas* may well have provided a model of a successful children's magazine in terms of its format and features, but if Du Bois had searched its pages the year before he published *The Brownies' Book*, he would have found ample motivation to develop a magazine with more uplifting content for and about the children of the sun.

Regarding Black children, the most striking feature of *St. Nicholas* is the veil of invisibility it confers on them and their lives. No pictures of "normal" Black children appear in any of the issues for that year except for one Black child who appears in a decoration representing children of various ethnicities or nationalities at the top of a puzzle page in the January 1919 issue (287). The one Black character who appears in the 1919 issues is Mammy in Chapter 6 of a serialized story called "Blue Magic," by Edith Ballinger Price. Mammy, who is the nurse to a young White boy cruising on a yacht on the Nile, speaks in the exaggerated dialect typically employed by White writers to show the ignorance and lack of intelligence of Black characters: "Lawdy, Lawdy! One of dem heathen men! Hyah, you! git out ob here! Did n' I allus says dis was a onnatchel lan'? I ain' nebbah seen such a onnatchel lan—nebbah! Oh, Massa Fen! honey chile, doan' let dat air E-gypshun critter tech you!" (July 1919, 246). The illustration shows Mammy as an overweight, dark-skinned woman wearing a white ruffled cap and a long white apron over an even longer plaid dress. It is telling that the only active Black character in a year's worth of issues is an adult whose function as a servant to a child "master" is taken for granted and whose function as a character is to provide comic relief. To the extent that *St. Nicholas* was typical, it indicates not only the dearth of suitable material connected to the lives of Black children, but also the persistent presence of stereotyped images of Blacks and assumptions of the natural superiority of whites that lingered in one form or another in children's literature through at least the first five or so decades of the twentieth century.

While *The Brownies' Book* functioned to lift the veil of invisibility and counteract false images and stereotypes in children's books and magazines, it also had an active agenda related to the development of Black children and what was commonly referred to as "the race," meaning a national Black cultural community. Implicit in its set of goals is the intention to foster self-esteem and race pride by offering young Black readers information about exemplary Black children, Black heroes, and Black achievements. The objectives also tacitly acknowledge a need to help Black children live successfully in a social atmosphere poisoned by racism. Implicit as well is a desire to direct Black child readers toward an education that would introduce them to "the worth-while things of life" and equip them for service and leadership. In setting out these aims, Du Bois identified Black children as a distinctive readership with unique needs brought on by the realities of growing up Black in the United States of the early twentieth century.

Du Bois saw no contradiction in his intent to interweave teaching and entertainment. The goals of *The Brownies' Book* reflect his attitude toward the functions of art/beauty and the relationship between beauty and truth. Du Bois (1995) saw art/beauty as inextricably tied to truth and goodness and rejected the notion of art for art's sake. "I am one who tells the truth and exposes evil and seeks with beauty to set the world right. That somehow, somewhere eternal and perfect beauty sits above truth and right I can conceive, but here and now and in the world in which I work they are for me unseparated and unseparable" (511). Indeed, Du Bois goes on to declare:

Thus all art is propaganda and ever must be, despite the wailing of the purists. I stand in utter shamelessness and say that whatever art I have for writing has been used always for propaganda for gaining the right of black folk to love and enjoy. I do not care for any art that is not used for propaganda. But I do care when propaganda is confined to one side while the other is stripped and silent. (514)

The Brownies' Book, consequently, is an example of art used in the service of social change, truth and goodness, aimed at setting the children of the sun on the path to love, enjoyment, and leadership.

CONTENTS OF *THE BROWNIES' BOOK*

Much of the credit for carrying out the vision that Du Bois set forth for *The Brownies' Book* belongs to Jessie Fauset, who was its literary editor and, for the second year, managing editor. An apt choice, Fauset was herself a well-educated member of the Talented Tenth, a Phi Beta Kappa graduate of Cornell, with a master's degree from the University of Pennsylvania. A writer who later published four novels, she had also studied at the Sorbonne and spoke fluent French. She is frequently cited as one of the important contributors to the Harlem Renaissance, both as an author and as a mentor to the young writers whose work she published in *The Crisis*. In addition to acquiring and supporting the work of the contributors to *The Brownies' Book*, Fauset personally contributed many of the pieces—poems, biographies, stories—that were published in the magazine.

Each issue of the magazine, which measured 8 × 11 inches, was about thirty-two pages long and contained poems, stories, biographical sketches, illustrations, photographs, and a number of featured columns. Month by month, Fauset and Du Bois provided Black children with a view of themselves and of Black people in general, as well as a perspective on the nation and the world, that was largely unavailable in any other publication addressed to young people. The dedicatory verse in the first issue, written by Fauset, indicates that the magazine was indeed intended to fill a void:

To children who with eager look
Scanned vainly library shelf and nook
For History or Song or Story
That told of Colored People's glory
We dedicate *The Brownies' Book*. (January 1920, 32)

This dearth of literature about "Colored People" was, even decades later, still one of the motivations for the creation of African American children's literature.

"The Judge": Wisdom from an Elder

"The Judge" was one of two columns in which the editors created a persona through which to address the readers directly. The column is usually ascribed to

Jessie Fauset, although Harris (1986, 141) noted that there is some argument about whether Fauset was actually the author. In keeping with Du Bois's and Fauset's views on education as a process of teaching values, "The Judge" was unabashedly didactic and made clear from the beginning that he would offer advice on the conduct of life, and that he expected the children to make a difference in the future:

I Am the Judge. I am very, very old. I know all things, except a few, and I have been appointed by the King to sit in the Court of Children and tell them the Law and listen to what they have to say. The Law is old and musty and needs sadly to be changed. In time the children will change it; but now it is the law. . . . It is my business—I, the Judge—to say each month a little lecture to Billikins, Billie and William, *and* their sisters . . . and also to listen very patiently while the *children* speak to me and to the world. (January 1920, 12) [italics in original]

In the "little lectures," "The Judge" explicitly focused on the behaviors and attitudes that needed to be developed if the children were to become the kind of adults who would change "the law," in other words to become race leaders. The column consisted of conversations between the Judge, the above-named children, who are six, ten, and fifteen, respectively, and William's older sister, Wilhelmina, who is sixteen. The children's ages, from six to sixteen, correspond to the ages of the children to whom *The Brownies' Book* was directed, and across the twenty-four issues, the conversations addressed some of the differing developmental needs and characteristics of children from early childhood to adolescence.

The October 1920 number provides an example of the tone of the Judge's voice. In this conversation, little Billikins is overjoyed because he is going to school. The older children sneer at his enthusiasm and express their displeasure at the "stupid business of going to school." The Judge speaks: "You know," he continues meditatively, stroking his wig, "the value of education consists not in what you take in but in what it brings out of you. If a person has to study hard to get his lessons and does it, he develops will power, concentration and determination, and these are the qualities which he carries out into life with him. That's what education is going to do for you, isn't it, Billikins?" (306).

The general thrust of the "The Judge" was to socialize, to provide instruction in the conduct of life for a cultured Black individual (Harris 1986, 139). Conversations grew out of life situations and centered on the kinds of behaviors, attitudes, and values that would be expected of a refined intelligent Black child or adolescent, such as appropriate manners and deportment, recognition of their parents' responsibilities and respect for their parents' decisions, participation in worthwhile recreational activities, selection of suitable reading matter, use of Standard English grammar, and appropriate ways to dress. In addition, "The Judge" also sought to move the young people toward becoming active and informed citizens, with knowledge about and positive attitudes toward Africa and people of African descent. Children who heeded the Judge's advice would become not only refined, but also knowledgeable about the world and about themselves as members of families, citizens of a democratic society, and African Americans with an obligation to make a positive difference in their world.

"As the Crow Flies": News of the World

While Fauset, in the guise of the Judge, offered wisdom, Du Bois cast himself as the Crow and offered world news in a column called "As the Crow Flies." If the Judge sought to socialize, the Crow aimed to politicize. The Crow, "black and O so beautiful" (January 1920, 23) flew over the earth and gathered news for the Brownies. Generally, the Crow reported first on news from around the world and then on what he found when he returned back home to the United States. The Crow emphasized news that was particularly relevant to people of color in the nation and in the world and at the same time broadened the horizons of his readers by bringing them news of global importance generally. In the February 1920 issue, for instance, the Crow reported: "Norway has adopted the prohibition of strong alcoholic liquors, by a vote of 428, 455" (63) and "Many of the most beautiful art treasures of Austria will be sold to obtain food for the starving." In the second part of the same column, when he returned to the United States, the Crow reported:

America has not ratified the Peace Treaty. The Senate, led by the stubborn Senator Lodge, does not want to sign the treaty unless the responsibilities of the United States in the new League of Nations are made very much smaller. The President, also stubborn, wants the treaty signed just as it stands. Most folk would like a compromise. (63–64)

As is evident, the Crow did not simply "report the facts." His political perspective was reflected in his selection of items and his interpretations of the news. "Colored" children growing up in a nation where lynching Black people was a regular occurrence needed to understand the larger world context in which the United States was operating. The Crow also did not hesitate to criticize directly the actions of the U.S. government. Du Bois saw constructive criticism not only as a right, but as part of the responsibility of citizenship: "There is no place like Home—none, none so good, none so bad: good because it belongs to Us; bad, because it is Ours to make better and this means Work and Eye-sight" (October 1920, 318, 320). In the February 1920 issue, for example, he criticized the treatment of Mexico:

Some folk are making continued effort to embroil Mexico and the United States in war. Mexico is a poor, struggling country, which the United States has grievously wronged in the past and deprived of territory. Today, many Americans own vast property there,—in oil, minerals, land, etc.—and they want to control the policy of Mexico, so as to make lots of money. (64)

The Crow also was interested in having the children of the sun make connections between themselves and the world's other people of color and between their struggles at home and those of oppressed people everywhere. Aptheker (1980) notes that, throughout the twenty-four Crow columns, Du Bois paid particular attention to women's rights; to labor issues; to the independence struggles of countries such as India, Egypt, and Ireland; and to the emergent Soviet Union. In his national news, the Crow also paid special attention to news about Black people and their activities and events that would be particularly relevant to them. In keeping with the magazine's expressed intention to provide information about the achievements of Black people, some of those items focused on accomplishments such as the opening of a Black hotel in Washington, D.C., and on commemorations of important achievers, such as Frederick Douglass.

Each international and national section of the column is introduced with a paragraph demonstrating the Crow's penchant for poetic language. The August 1920 column, for example, begins: "Midsummer! Dark green forests bow to light green waters; blue skies kiss golden suns; great sheets of rain swirl on brown and black lands. I love summer. My plumage is dead black and sleek and the whirr of my wide wings is heard from Minnesota to Georgia as I fly and peer and cry and scream" (234). This artistic touch supports Du Bois's claim to be "one who seeks with beauty to set the world right." The main purpose of the column, however, was to politicize readers of *The Brownies' Book* and to prepare them to be astute and socially progressive citizens of the nation and of the world.

Celebrating the Children: "The Little People of the Month," "Some Little Friends of Ours"

Although the entire *The Brownies' Book* magazine tacitly fostered self-esteem and race pride, "The Little People of the Month" column addressed that goal directly. This column, accompanied by photographs, celebrated the academic and creative achievements of Black children and youth who were themselves growing into beautiful and useful, if not necessarily famous, persons. For example, the March 1920 issue noted that "Leta B. Lewis is an 'A' pupil, in both conduct and proficiency. She's in the fifth term grammar school, at Omaha, Neb. During her entire school course, she has received only one 'B'" (20). The September 1920 issue celebrates an artist who is particularly noteworthy: "It's so wonderful to be an artist, and make pictures of beautiful flowers and trees and oceans and skies. . . . Well, at Boston, Mass., there's a Brownie, 14 years of age, who has won her second scholarship at the Museum of Fine Arts. Her name is Lois M. Jones, and she's an honor student of the High School of Practical Arts at Boston" (284). Lois Mailou Jones went on to become an acclaimed artist, professor at Howard University, and an illustrator of children's books.

Other "Brownies" were lauded for such accomplishments as winning oratorical contests, winning essay contests, having perfect school attendance, and making contributions to the welfare of the community. Looking back from the beginning of the twenty-first century, some of these achievements may appear rather ordinary, but they often were hard-won in the world of 1920. They most certainly ran counter to the prevailing images of Black children and their families in the books and other media of the day. That these Black children were doing so well in these endeavors was a demonstration of the intellectual potential of Black children. That their achievements were highlighted was an indication of the kinds of behaviors Black adults valued as well as an inspiration for other children.

Both July issues of *The Brownies' Book* were called Education Issues, and supplanting the "The Little People of the Month" column were features called "Graduates of 1920" and "Brownie Graduates." These sections were filled with photographs and brief profiles of African American high school graduates as well as reports of the numbers of such high school graduates nationally. It is a testament to the state of education for Black people that, in the early 1920s so few Black children were graduating from high school, relatively speaking, that the editors could write to "all high schools having colored graduates" (July 1921, 194) and either list the names of such graduates or name the schools across the nation from which Blacks were graduating and the numbers of Blacks graduating from each school. In 1920, there were "121 graduates from mixed high schools, 865 graduates from colored high schools, and 2029 graduates from colored normal schools—or a total of 3015 Brownie graduates, of each one of whom we are proud" (210). Among the graduates pictured in the July 1920 issue is one Langston Hughes, of Central High School in Cleveland, who would become one of the leaders of the Harlem Renaissance and one of the most important American literary figures of the century.

Another feature, titled "Some Little Friends of Ours" or some variation of that theme, offered photographs of Black children. Usually posed and apparently taken by professional photographers, the children were shown at their very best—well dressed, hair neatly styled. These photographs, sent by parents at the invitation of the editors, apparently were intended to celebrate the beauty and diversity to be found among Black children. In so doing, the editors provided a much-needed refutation of the images of Black children and Black people that were prevalent in the literature and popular culture of the day.

Voices of Readers: "The Jury" and the "Grown-ups' Corner"

The voices of readers were featured in the letters-to-the-editor column called "The Jury." Many of their letters indicate that Fauset was right in inferring that "colored" children were hungry for material about "Colored People's glory." The letters from "The Jury" also indicated that Black children were very much aware of racial discrimination and the racist environment in which they were living and looked to *The Brownies' Book* for ammunition to counter racist views of themselves and their people. George Max Simpson, of Toronto, wrote in the March 1920, issue: "Could you take time to suggest a small library for me? . . . I want to know a great deal about colored people. I think when I finish school I shall go to Africa and work there in some way. If I decide to do this I ought to know a great deal about our people and all the places where they live, all over the world, don't you think so?" (83).

"The Jury" also provided opportunities for children to relate their own accomplishments. In the July 1920 issue, there is a long letter from James Alpheus Butler Jr. of Tampa, Florida. He describes himself:

I am a colored boy, brownskinned and proud of it. I am 14 years old. My home is now in Tampa, but at present I am a second year student at the Florida A. & M. College. My father is a doctor and my mother a music teacher. I play four musical instruments: the violin, piano, clarinet and 'cello, but I like the violin best of all. I started playing the violin when I was six years old. Long ago I completed the Keyser violin method and have subsequently studied awhile in New York and also under a very strict German professor. I've been appearing in public with my violin ever since I can remember. (215)

His musical talents notwithstanding, Butler wants to be a writer, and the October 1920 and December 1921 issues of *The Brownies' Book* contain well-written realistic stories by this precocious teenager, undoubtedly part of the Talented Tenth. Other young readers also became contributors of poems, pictures, and stories, including, as we shall see, Langston Hughes.

The "Grown-ups' Corner" provided a forum for parents and other adult subscribers to express their support or criticisms of the magazine and to request the kinds of material they wanted to see. Mainly, the letters are laudatory and express gratitude for the magazine and its contents, which apparently filled gaps in typical school curricula and was a source of pride and inspiration for parents and children alike.

The Brownies' Book as Literature

Although *The Brownie's Book* was expressly intended to instill certain values and attitudes, it was at the same time a literary endeavor. It included nonfiction, realistic and fantasy stories, folktales, biography, plays, and poems that would compare favorably to the typical children's literature of its day. In part because of Du Bois's and Fauset's influence as editors of *The Crisis*, they were able to draw from an impressive group of participants in the Harlem Renaissance. Some of the best and best-known Black writers of the day—James Weldon Johnson, Georgia Douglas Johnson, Arthur Huff Fauset (Jessie Fauset's half brother), Nella Larsen Imes, and Langston Hughes—contributed to *The Brownies' Book*. Jessie Redmon Fauset and Du Bois both contributed pieces under their own names, as did Du Bois's daughter Yolande. Alongside material from this prestigious group, Fauset published stories, poems, and other works written by readers, such as the aforementioned James Alpheus Butler and a teenager named Pocohantas Foster.

A number of stories and plays in *The Brownies' Book* incorporate fantasy elements—fairies, elves, talking animals, dragons, magic, transformations, and the like. Often these stories and plays make their points very clear, and their morals reflect the values espoused by the editors. In the October 1921 issue, for example, there is a play called "The Dragon's Tooth" by Willis Richardson. The child characters, guided by the king's soothsayer, retrieve the secret of the future of good in the world, which is written on the tooth of an expired dragon. The secret, it turns out, "depends upon the growth of Love and Brotherhood. Liberty, Equality and Fraternity must rule the world in place of Inequality, Envy, and Hate." When asked how this future can be realized, the Soothsayer replies: "Children such as you must bring this good about. It must grow in your hearts until you are men and women, and as you grow you must spread the truth abroad" (278–279). The "lesson" of the play clearly echoes Du Bois's explicit intention to teach "Universal Love and Brotherhood" and his intention to inspire children to a life of service.

The magazine also served as a forum for original stories by some of its readers, who apparently also clearly understood its objectives. Pocohantas Foster, a reader who had written to the "Jury" column, for example, wrote a story promoting pride of identity. In "A Prize Winner," King Earth offers a prize to the "race" that had made the greatest advance. The four existing races were Winter, Spring, Summer, and Fall. Spring, Fall, and Winter, each represented by a queen, brought rich gifts symbolizing the progress of their races. Summer, however, was represented by "a little brown child about 10 years old" and "hosts of little barefoot brown children with sleeves rolled up and bare heads" and carrying no gifts but various farm implements. King Earth awards the prize to the little Queen of Summer because she had "learned the one thing that is greater than all,—the Spirit of Service." Foster ends her story this way: "Thus you see that the first prize ever given was won by a little brown child and little brown children have been winning prizes ever since that day" (August 1920, 244).

Realistic stories in the magazine provided a picture of the everyday lives of Black people in the early 1920s—mainly middle class, but from other socioeconomic strata as well. A story, for example, by James Alpheus Butler, the reader whose letter had been published in the July issue, showed his understanding of the idea that material wealth does not determine character, and that among Blacks the boundaries between socioeconomic classes should not constitute obstacles to friendship. In "An Elusive Idea," Marcus Cornelius Smith, a middle-class aspiring writer (not unlike James Alpheus Butler), meets and befriends "ragged and barefooted" 'Lias, who is struggling to help his mother make ends meet and has had his money stolen by a bully. Over an afternoon of fishing, Marcus and 'Lias become friends. All ends well when 'Lias forces the bully to return his money, and Marcus uses 'Lias as inspiration for a story that gets published (October 1920). Class differences between the characters are clearly marked, most obviously by the differences in their dialects: Marcus is a speaker of Standard English, 'Lias speaks a less-prestigious variety. Although Marcus seems a bit patronizing in his views of 'Lias, he is able to see beyond the surface to 'Lias's quick intelligence, his determination, his sense of duty, and his courage in facing and triumphing over the bully. Although the "lessons to be learned" from this story are fairly obvious, it is also a fairly well crafted tale, with its story-within-a-story frame and enough action to hold the attention of its readers.

The Brownies' Book also published a number of folk tales across its twenty-four issues. Most of the stories were either African in origin or could be traced to people of African descent. Prominent among them were animal tales such as the African American Brer Rabbit stories, but a variety of other kinds of stories were also included, such as an Annancy story from the West Indies and a story from the Cape Verde Islands, "Wolf and His Nephew." The folk stories, for the most part, were generally directed toward the goal of entertainment and, aside from the emphasis on valuing stories related to Africa and the African diaspora, were not overtly didactic.

The Brownie's Book contained numerous poems, produced by various writers, some of whom were or would become famous, such as Langston Hughes, James Weldon Johnson, and Georgia Douglass Johnson. Probably only a few of the poems, such as Hughes's "April Rain Song" (April 1921, 111), have passed the proverbial "test of time." Not unlike other poetry and verse for children produced at the time, *The Brownies' Book* poems frequently focused on nature and on topics thought to be of interest to children, such as everyday child activities. C. Lesley Frazier published this verse in the June 1921 issue:

Come on in, the water's fine,
Put away your fishing line,
Hang your pants up next to mine—
Come on in! (173)

Some poems dealt with the holidays that occurred during the month of publication. Some were addressed to Brownie children, as in "Slumber Song," by Alpha Angela Bratton (November 1921, 315):

Close those eyes where points of light
Shine like stars through the velvet night,
Brownie Boy.

A goodly portion of the poems also addressed topics such as race pride and the beauty of Black children. Some were sheer nonsense, indicating that Fauset did not forget the declared intention of the magazine to deal in happiness and laughter. One of the most frequently published of *The Brownies' Book* poets, Mary Effie Lee (Newsome), would go on to produce a book of children's poetry a couple of decades after the demise of the magazine.

True to its goal of making "colored" children "familiar with the history and achievements of the Negro race," *The Brownies' Book* introduced its readers to "colored" achievers from a variety of fields through numerous biographical sketches. Subjects included Harriet Tubman, Katy Ferguson, Crispus Attucks, Phillis Wheatley, Benjamin Banneker, Samuel Coleridge-Taylor, Alexander Pushkin, and

Denmark Vesey. These pieces usually made clear those aspects of the person's life that were, in the view of the author, worthy of emulation. A biographical sketch of Paul Cuffee, for example, honors him not only for his achievements as a sailor, but also for his service to his people. It also makes clear the desirability of maintaining connections with Africa.

After Cuffee had thus gratified the wish of his heart,—the desire to ride the seas,—he bent every effort toward satisfying his other ruling passion,—that is, his ambition to help his fellowman. The people in whom he was most deeply interested lived in two widely separated lands,—in Massachusetts and in Africa. (February 1920, 38)

Almost all the subjects were Black men and women who had achieved some degree of fame, but as a general rule, whether the subjects were White or Black, male or female, well known or little known, they were committed to service, to helping or advancing the race. They were exemplars of the "broad spirit of sacrifice" with which *The Brownies' Book* sought to imbue its readers.

The magazine also included a number of other features, both to amuse and to provide information. "Playtime" included games, some of which are challenging word or math games, dances, and nursery rhymes with actions, songs, and puzzles. Frequently, the games had an international focus, such as the Mexican games "arranged" by Langston Hughes in the January 1921 issue. An international perspective suffused the magazine, with places such as the Caribbean, Africa, and Scandinavia represented in story, song, games, or expository material. Several pieces were translated from Spanish or French. Other features of *The Brownies' Book* included information on science, geography, and other such topics of general knowledge. It also included a few works by Robert Louis Stevenson and other non-Black writers.

Even a cursory look through the issues of *The Brownie's Book* reveals that presenting nonstereotyped visual images was an important aspect of the magazine. Photographs of attractive Black children, youth, and adults abound, reflecting a cross-section of African American physical features (e.g., skin coloring, hair texture). They often showed Black people engaged in what might today seem ordinary activities: at the library, as members of a Boy Scout troop; taking part in activities at Black colleges; participating in a protest parade; participating in scouting. Given the goals of the magazine, however, it is likely that the photographs were carefully chosen to be exemplary. The cover art and the illustrations throughout *The Brownies' Book* were drawn by some of the young Black artists whose work became highly respected over the next decade, most notably Laura Wheeler, Marcellus Hawkins, and Hilda Wilkinson. Their depictions of Black people reflected warm affection and an apparent appreciation for the beauty of their subjects. Through the art and the photographs, Du Bois and Fauset sought to offer the Brownies a public view of themselves as normal, attractive, and appealing people, contrary to the prevailing images of the day.

In her comprehensive study and analysis of *The Brownies' Book*, Harris (1986, 207) identified eight themes that were developed in the fiction and poetry published in the magazine. These themes emphasized activism and service, character values, and pride in race and culture. They were clearly connected to the expressed goals of the magazine, and the writers, in tailoring their work to fit those goals, sometimes appeared to make literary considerations secondary. As a consequence, the quality of the literature was uneven, but a substantial portion

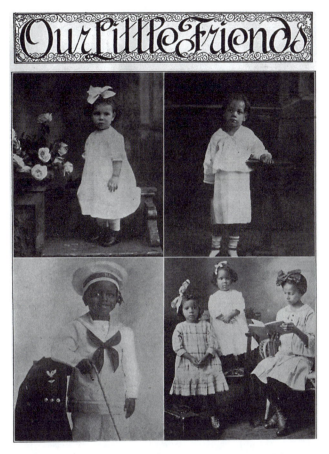

Page from the June 1921 *The Brownies' Book*. Celebrating
African American children.

of the selections would likely have been very appealing to the presumed primary
audience.

In addition to the explicitly expressed thematic emphases, a number of subthemes were also developed within the magazine, many of which remain significant
in contemporary African American children's literature. For example, even though
the importance of family is not explicitly stated as one of the values the magazine
sought to inculcate, it is, not surprisingly, an important theme in the stories, especially in the sense that parents are held up as a source of wisdom that should be
obeyed. Internal, in-group attitudes toward skin color are broached in a number
of stories, bringing to light—sometimes in tacit agreement with, sometimes in
opposition to—the popular association between beauty and light skin and straight
hair. The issue of class and attitudes toward Black people with less money and less
formal education than middle-class protagonists is also raised, usually upholding
the idea that character is more important than economic status. In the fiction
and poetry, as well as the nonfiction, the columns, and the information pieces,
self-pride and pride in identity are emphasized through such devices as advocat-
ing "colored dolls" for Brownie children. The similarity that will be seen between
the thematic emphases in contemporary African American literature and those of

Cover of the June 1921 issue of *The Brownies' Book*.

The Brownies' Book may be attributed not to a conscious imitation of the latter, but to the perception among writers a couple of generations later that many of the social and literary conditions that had spurred the creation of *The Brownies' Book*—for example, the dearth of books about Black children, the distortion and omission of Black history and Black achievement from school curricula, the inaccurate or caricatured visual or literary images of Black people—had changed but little since the 1920s.

SIGNIFICANCE OF *THE BROWNIES' BOOK*

In light of the prevailing social and political climate, Du Bois and his associates had set about to create a new literature and a new image of and for the Black child. Thus, the twenty-four issues of *The Brownies' Book* collectively constitute a literary and artistic "cultural family album" for the children of the sun. It affirmed them as "normal and beautiful" children in a literary world that most often either ignored their existence or offered them portraits of themselves mainly as plantation pickaninnies. It connected them with the larger national and international Black community and introduced them to Black people—young and old, living and dead—whose achievements were worth noting and worth emulating. Recognizing its dual audience of parent and child, it provided opportunities for parents to participate in the shaping of the magazine and offered some tacit advice about how to deal with the responsibilities of parenting. It also provided a forum for the children of the sun to express their own views and reflect on their own lives. It was as well a forum in which some of the best African American writers and artists of the day participated in the creation of a remarkable literary milestone in the history of African American children's literature.

The final issue of *The Brownies' Book* was published in December 1921. For the two years of its existence, it had sought to educate, politicize, socialize, enculturate, and at the same time entertain its readers. In conceiving and creating *The Brownies' Book*, Du Bois and his associates had called for a literature that would be "adapted to colored children, and indeed to all children who live in a world of varied races" (December 1921, 354). Explicit in the stated objectives of the magazine, and implicit in the magazine's content, was the proposition that literature "adapted to colored children" was to be a literature with a mission, literature as social action. It aimed to counter the effects of racism on Black children and their self-image, to foster race pride, to counter prevailing negative images and stereotypes of Black people, to promote certain positive values and behaviors, and to inspire a sense of responsibility to the race as a whole. In a sense, like the nineteenth century writings addressed to Black children in secular and religious periodicals, *The Brownies' Book* can be viewed as a vehicle for racial uplift. The significance of *The Brownies' Book* was that it affirmed the need for a distinctive African American children's literature, provided a model of what such a body of literature might be like, and articulated through its expressed mission an ideological stance that constituted a foundation on which such a literature could be built.

CARRYING ON THE TRADITION: TWO LEGACIES OF *THE BROWNIES BOOK*

The Brownies' Book lasted for only two years and for twenty-four issues. In their "Valedictory," published in the December 1921 issue, Du Bois and Dill announced that they were discontinuing the magazine for financial reasons. They had as many as 3,500 subscribers but needed at least 15,000 to keep up with their expenses. They were $3,000 in debt and were not optimistic that they could generate enough subscriptions soon enough to continue publishing (354). The main pool of prospective subscribers—educated, middle-class Blacks—was still relatively small in the United States of 1921, and it would be nearly half a century more before an African American children's literature would fully blossom into a distinctive feature of the children's literature landscape. *The Brownies' Book* died about the time that the Harlem Renaissance was born, but even though the Renaissance produced an outpouring of African American literature, very little of that literature was directed to children. At least two regular *Brownies' Book* contributors, however, continued to advance the burgeoning field of African American children's literature after its demise: Mary Effie Lee Newsome and Langston Hughes. The latter became famous; the former has been nearly forgotten.

MARY EFFIE LEE/EFFIE LEE NEWSOME

Mary Effie Lee (later Effie Lee Newsome) was, if not the first, certainly one of the first twentieth century African American women to devote the bulk of her literary career to writing for children. Mainly a poet, but something of a naturalist as well, she contributed several poems and one nature study to *The Brownies' Book* over the two years of its existence. Born in 1885, Lee was the daughter of Benjamin Franklin Lee, the A.M.E. bishop who succeeded Daniel Alexander Payne as president of Wilberforce University and who was editor of *The Christian Recorder* from 1884 to 1892. She married an A.M.E. bishop, and although she spent some time in Birmingham, Alabama, much of her adult life was spent in Wilberforce, Ohio. Lee was a keen observer of the natural landscape around her. She particularly loved birds, and the nature study she published in *The Brownies' Book* was on the topic "Birds at My Door" (April 1920, 105).

Her poems also were most often about nature, although some were devoted to celebrating children and their everyday lives and activities. For example, in the May 1920 issue of *The Brownies' Book*, she published "Mount Ice Cream," a verse in the voice of a small child:

Mumsie, I had the sweetest dream!
I fought I lived on Mount Ice Cream,
And wif a silver spoon for shovel,
I 'stroyed that mountain without trouble! (253)

Beginning in March 1925, using the pen name Effie Lee Newsome, she wrote "The Little Page" for *The Crisis*, which was still under the editorship of W.E.B. Du Bois. The column appeared regularly, although not in every issue, until June 1929. It was an attempt to continue to address and engage the audience that had been served by *The Brownies' Book*, and it subtly carried on some of the ideals of that publication. Newsome's column primarily featured her original poems and a "Calendar Chat," which was frequently accompanied by her own pen-and-ink illustrations. The calendar chats were mainly written nature sketches, usually featuring a plant, animal, insect, or bird that might be associated with the month or the season of publication. Frequently, she recalled a childhood experience or described some of the flora and fauna in and around her home in Wilberforce. The sketches were generally intended to be informative as well as entertaining, including not only material about nature, but also references to literature, myth, and history, evidence of her liberal educational background. She had studied at Wilberforce, Oberlin, and the University of Pennsylvania. She often made a special effort to allude to the works of people of color, alongside allusions to "classic" Western literature and art. For example, the November 1926 "Calendar Chat" reads in part:

Dunbar in his poem "Sympathy" said that he could imagine what must be the feeling of the caged bird as he listens to the free birds singing about him, taunting in their boundless liberty.

You have read so much of the great Italian painter Da Vinci. You have seen many prints from his Mona Lisa, or La Gioconda, as the mysteriously-smiling lady is sometimes called. . . . But have you remembered that this same Da Vinci who painted Mona Lisa, The Last Supper, Madonna of the Rocks—this same Da Vinci, who was a sculptor, a military engineer, a writer of masks and pageants, the musician who took his home-manufactured silver harp to the court of Milan, mathematician, mineralogist—what not—this same imposing courtier in his long rose-colored robe used to buy caged birds whenever he was able and set them free, and watch them with great joy flying into the turquoise skies of Italy? I shall write you a rhyme about Da Vinci, so that when you read of his art you will think of his *heart*. [italics in original] (25)

Newsome also included in "The Little Page" some imaginative stories, often featuring Mother Gardner, a matronly figure through whose voice Newsome could inform readers about nature and offer wisdom about life. Many of the stories included personified plants, animals, or seasonal objects such as kites. A few, such as "On the Pelican's Back" (August 1928, 264), "Jonquil and Goldfish" (April 1927, 50), and "Spider and Amber" (January 1929, 11) offer fable-like lessons about self-esteem, self-pride, and endurance. In their focus on such values, the stories reflected the emphasis on identity and pride emphasized in the stated goals of *The Brownies' Book*.

Newsome, however, was primarily a poet. Many of her poems focused on nature as well—cardinals, winds, ladybugs, butterflies and the like— but others focused on everyday childhood experiences. A number were about play, and a few were humorous, or nonsensical such as "Old Commodore Quiver," which would easily amuse contemporary young children:

Old Commodore Quiver
Went down to the river
Old Commodore Quiver of Gaul.
He sailed from the shore,
But what he went for
He hadn't a notion at all,
No, he hadn't one notion at all. (*The Crisis* January 1928, 8)

Many of the nature poems from "The Little Page" and those from *The Brownies' Book* were included in her one book of poetry, *Gladiola Garden*, published in 1940 by Associated Publishers. Not only was Lee/Newsome one of the few African American writers in the 1920s who devoted most of her work to a child audience, she was among the first African American poets to produce a body of original poems primarily for children.

LANGSTON HUGHES

One of the most important legacies of *The Brownies' Book* is that in its pages appeared the first nationally published poems of Langston Hughes, the most famous son of the Harlem Renaissance and one of America's most highly respected poets. When *The Brownies' Book* was first published in 1920, Hughes was just turning eighteen. His picture and notice of his high school graduation appeared in the July 1920 issue of *The Brownies' Book*, as did a letter he had written to the editor: "It might interest you to know that I have been elected Class Poet and have also written the Class Song for the graduates. I am, too, the first Negro to hold the position since 1901, when it was held by the son of Charles W. Chesnutt" (July 1920, 206).

Hughes was not only aware of *The Brownies' Book*, but he was also familiar with the work of its founder and editor. In a 1965 memorial tribute to Du Bois, Hughes (1965, 11) noted: "My earliest memories of written words are those of Du Bois and the Bible. My maternal grandmother in Kansas, the last surviving widow of John Brown's raid, read to me as a child from both the Bible and *The Crisis*. And one of the first books I read on my own was *The Souls of Black Folk*." It is no wonder then, that *The Brownies' Book*, with Du Bois as editor and its policy of encouraging readers to submit material for publication, appealed to the young Hughes as a possible venue for his poems.

In January 1921, two of his poems, "Fairies" and "Winter Sweetness," appeared in *The Brownies' Book*. "Fairies" is a whimsical little musing about the wonder of fairies weaving garments from dream dust and creating wings from the "purple and rose" of memories. "Winter Sweetness," on the other hand, captures in four lines both a charming image of a small house in winter and the accent on the beauty and self-esteem of Black children that was a part of the magazine's reason for being. A snow-covered house is likened to sugar and at the window is a "maple-sugar" child, connecting the brown sweetness of maple sugar to the figurative sweetness of a Black child. The appearance of these two poems preceded by six months the publication, in the June 1921 issue of *The Crisis*, of "The Negro Speaks of Rivers," which is frequently cited, even by Hughes himself, as his first nationally published poem (Hughes 1940, 72).

Over the course of the year 1921, Fauset published six more of Hughes's poems in *The Brownies' Book*, including the well-known "April Rain Song." In the same issue in which the first two poems appeared, Hughes "arranged" descriptions of three Mexican games for the "Playtime" section. His experience living in Mexico with his father was also the basis for two nonfiction pieces in later issues, "In a Mexican City" and "Up to the Crater of an Old Volcano." In the July 1921 issue, there was a play, "The Gold Piece." For the November 1921 issue, Hughes contributed a story called "Those Who Have No Turkey," which slyly contrasted the innocent generosity of a country child to the uptight concern with middle-class propriety of the aunt with whom she spends Thanksgiving. Thus, *The Brownies' Book* was an important outlet for the early work, in various genres, of the talented poet, essayist, playwright, novelist, and short-story writer who would become the most prolific writer of the Harlem Renaissance and one of America's foremost literary artists.

By the time his first book for children appeared, Hughes was an established literary presence and had already published four books of poems and a novel. His poems had also been published in a number of magazines, including both the most influential Black magazines of the day and important magazines with a largely White readership. Among the readers of his poems were a White librarian, Effie Lee Power, and her youthful patrons at the Cleveland Public Library. In 1931, Power, the library's director of work with children, requested that Hughes compile a selection of his poems that would be suitable for young people (Rampersad 1986, 197). Hughes gathered 59 poems, which were published the following year by Knopf under the title *The Dream Keeper* (Hughes 1932). It was a landmark publication of African American poetry for children, one of the first children's books by an African American writer to be published by one of the major New York publishers.

The Dream Keeper

Because of its significance as a landmark, because it set a new standard for artistry in African American literature for young people, and because a number of the poems in the book have become classic, it is informative to examine the contents of *The Dream Keeper*. It was divided into five sections, which collectively exemplify the range of Hughes's early poetry. The first section, "The Dream Keeper," contains the poems that seem most directly addressed to children or to speak in a voice closest to that of a child. Included here are four poems that were composed for a child audience since they were first published in *The Brownies' Book*: "Fairies," "Winter Sweetness," "Autumn Thought," and "April Rain Song." With the possible exception of the reference to a "maple sugar child" in "Winter Sweetness," the poems in this section are not overtly race conscious but are about such topics as a winter moon, seasons, hopes, and dreams. This section includes three of the best-known and most often anthologized poems in American children's literature: "Dreams" ("Hold fast to dreams"), "Poem" ("I loved my friend"), and the afore-mentioned "April Rain Song" ("Let the rain kiss you"). The second group of poems, "Sea Charm," reflects, as the section title implies, Hughes's experiences on the sea and abroad.

The poems in the other three sections, "Dressed Up," "Feet o' Jesus," and "Walkers with the Dawn," are deeply rooted in Hughes's experience as an African American and in his profound love for ordinary Black people. It is this expression of the dis-tinctiveness and inherent value of Black culture and Black life that was the declared aim of Hughes and the other young literary artists of the Harlem Renaissance. "Dressed Up," which includes five blues poems, opens with an instructive preface, "A Note on Blues." The other poems in this section, although not in blues form, are generally about the topics associated with the blues—love, loneliness, pain—but tempered with the recognition that, in the words of a spiritual, "trouble don't last alway." Hughes was among the first, if not *the* first, twentieth century literary artist to celebrate the blues and jazz as artistic forms and to dip into this Black music as a way to shape his writing. He was certainly the first to offer work based on these forms to a child audience.

The poems in "Feet o' Jesus" also dip into Black culture but move from the secular to the sacred, from the cabaret to the church. This section includes eight poems, six of which echo the Black church in terms of their religious themes and their forms and structure. Hughes captured in poetic form the diction of songs and prayers and testifying that might be heard on Sunday mornings and week-night prayer meetings in many Black churches. The other two poems, "Baby" and "Lullaby," both are addressed to children. In "Baby," an adult, presumably a mother, warns Albert not to play in the road. "Lullaby" is a quiet night poem that celebrates a "little dark baby."

The final section of *The Dream Keeper*, "Walkers with the Dawn," contains poems that express Hughes's pride in being Black and that honor Black people as individuals and as a people. The general mood is hopeful, uplifting, and forward-looking. "The Negro Speaks of Rivers," written when Hughes was just out of high school and crossing the Mississippi River on a train bound for Mexico, has become a classic expression of pride in a racial/cultural heritage. Some of Hughes's best-known and best-loved poems—"Mother to Son," "Dream Variation," "My People," "Aunt Sue's Stories"—are included in this section. The poems celebrate the history of Black people from Africa through and beyond slavery and then look to the future. "I, Too," another of his famous poems, asserts Black people's claim to a scornful nation and expresses faith that the future will bring change. The book ends with "Youth," the poem Alain Locke, professor and influential Harlem Renaissance intellectual, cited in his 1925 anthology, *The New Negro*, as expressing the essential outlook and attitude of the young artists of the Harlem Renaissance, marching toward the future, with the past "a night-gone thing."

Hughes's Manifesto: Free within Ourselves

The views of Hughes and the other "New Negroes" were not without opposi-tion. One of the controversies during the Harlem Renaissance was related to the extent to which the full range of Black life was an appropriate subject for literature. If Black life was to be portrayed, in the view of some "old school" conservatives, then it should be respectable, middle-class Black life, which would demonstrate that Blacks could be easily integrated into mainstream America. Also, some Black intellectuals thought it important that Black writers move outside the boundaries of race to create literature that emulated and measured up to the most-valued literature in the Western tradition.

Even among the young Renaissance writers there was not unanimity. In a statement that continues to resonate with some African American writers, acclaimed poet Countee Cullen (1924) argued that he was not interested in being identified as a "Negro poet":

If I am going to be a poet at all, I am going to be POET and not NEGRO POET. This is what has hindered the development of artists among us. Their one note has been the concern with their race. That is all very well, none of us can get away from it. I cannot at times. You will see it in my verse. The consciousness of this is too poignant at times. I cannot escape it. But what I mean is this: I shall not write of negro subjects for the purpose of propaganda. That is not what a poet is concerned with. Of course, when the emotion rising out of the fact that I am a negro is strong, I express it. But that is another matter. (*Brooklyn Eagle*, February 10, 1924)

Langston Hughes took issue with Cullen's views, interpreting them as devaluing Black life and culture as literary subjects. While Hughes ably demonstrated his own ability to create "nonracial" poetry, he saw Black life and Black culture as vital sources for his art, and in an article, "The Negro Artist and the Racial Mountain," Hughes (1926, 201) declared, "So I am ashamed for the black poet who says, 'I want to be a poet, not a Negro poet,' as though his own racial world were not as interesting as any other world." He ended the essay with the stirring declaration:

We younger Negro artists who create now intend to express our individual dark-skinned selves without fear or shame. If white people are pleased we are glad. If they are not, it doesn't matter. We know we are beautiful. And ugly too. The tom-tom cries and the tom-tom laughs. If colored people are pleased we are glad. If they are not, their displeasure doesn't matter either. We build our temples for tomorrow, strong as we know how, and we stand on top of the mountain, free within ourselves. (202)

With this essay, Hughes in effect created a manifesto for the young Black artists of the Harlem Renaissance and offered inspiration for new generations of Black writers and artists.

By the time he started writing for children, Hughes had become acutely aware of the necessity for a literature addressed specifically to the needs of African American children. In a piece published in *The Children's Library Yearbook* of 1932, Hughes lambasted the kind of material available about and for Black children in textbooks and in "booklets on Negro themes." "The need today," he declared, "is for books that Negro parents and teachers can read to their children without hesitancy as to the psychological effect on the growing mind, books whose dark characters are not all clowns, and whose illustrations are not merely caricatures" (1932a, 109). Given his awareness of the clowns and caricatures that populated so much of the material available for children, he was understandably wary about the artwork for *The Dream Keeper*. The illustrator was Helen Sewell, a White artist who would go on to create the original illustrations for some of Laura Ingalls Wilder's Little House books. Hughes had begged Sewell to avoid the typical stereotyped images of Blacks and expressed a desire for beautiful images that Black children would not be ashamed to associate with themselves. Hughes admired the drawings (Rampersad 1986, 235). In 1994 Knopf published a new edition of *The Dream Keeper* (1932/1994), illustrated by a young, highly praised Black artist, Brian Pinkney. Pinkney's remarkable black-and-white scratchboard drawings make the poems seem fresh for a new generation of readers while remaining true to the emotions of the poems and the race pride and affection for the common Black folk that permeate them.

In *The Dream Keeper*, Hughes produced the first known twentieth century collection of original African American poems selected (or written) with children expressly identified as the target audience.[1] Like *The Brownies' Book*, *The Dream Keeper* included material that was "race conscious" in that it incorporated aspects of Black culture—music and religious expression—and expressed race pride and racial self-love. As did *The Brownies' Book*, Hughes also took an integrationist stance in the sense of representing the Negro as "the darker brother" in the American family. And as in *The Brownies' Book*, some of the poems in *The Dream Keeper* reflect experiences and emotions that easily cross cultural or racial boundaries. Unlike *The Brownies' Book*, however, *The Dream Keeper* is not didactic in its intent. The poems do not talk down to children, partly because many of them were not written specifically with a child audience in mind. The poems are essentially literary pieces expressing cultural and political themes. If one of the criteria for becoming a classic is timelessness, then in *The Dream Keeper* Hughes created one of the first classics of African American children's literature.

With one exception, it would be two decades before Hughes published another children's book. Between 1952 and 1960, he produced five books for the Franklin Watts First Book series: *The First Book of Negroes* (1952), *The First Book of Rhythms* (1954), *The First Book of Jazz* (1955), *The First Book of the West Indies* (1956), and *The First Book of Africa* (1960). He also wrote three collective biographies on Blacks, *Famous American Negroes* (1954), *Famous Negro Music Makers* (1955), and *Famous Negro Heroes of America* (1958) all for Dodd, Mead. The titles reflect Hughes's intense interest in the history and culture of Black people and his personal interest in Black music. In creating these nonfiction works, Hughes continued the tradition, as expressed by Du Bois in his goals for *The Brownies' Book*, of making children "familiar with the achievements of the Negro race." That goal has remained one of the most important underlying motives for the creation of African American children's literature.

CARTER G. WOODSON: EDUCATION THROUGH LITERATURE

Historian Carter G. Woodson also pursued the goal of acquainting Black children, indeed all children, with knowledge and understanding of the history and achievements of Black people in Africa and in the Americas. Known as "the father of modern Black history," Woodson was one of the most highly regarded scholars of his day. The son of former slaves, he earned a PhD from Harvard in 1912. In 1915, he established the Association for the Study of Negro Life and History and the next year became the founder and editor of its official quarterly, the *Journal of Negro History*, to which W.E.B. Du Bois was an early contributor. Woodson is also credited with establishing, in 1926, Negro History Week, which grew over the years into Black History Month. As an author, he may be best known for his book, *The Miseducation of the Negro* (1933/1972), in which he denounced the inadequacies of an educational system in which Black children were taught that they were inferior and deprived of opportunities to learn about Black history and achievement and to develop pride in themselves and their cultural group. He called for comprehensive curricular reform to make it possible for Black children to develop to their fullest potential.

In an effort to address the dearth of information available to Black youngsters, Woodson published a number of books for children and youth. In 1921, the second year of *The Brownie's Book*, Woodson founded Associated Publishers, which issued several books on Black history and culture for school-aged readers. Woodson himself wrote a number of the books, including *The Negro in Our History* (1922) for high school and college students, *Negro Makers of History* (1928) for elementary students, *African Myths, Together with Proverbs* (1928), and *African Heroes and Heroines* (1939).

Associated Publishers also issued, over the next few decades, a number of children's books by authors other than Woodson, including folklore collections, biographies, and poetry. It was Woodson's company that published Effie Lee Newsome's book of poems, *Gladiola Garden* in 1940. Several of the children's books from Associated Publishers were illustrated by the renowned artist Lois Mailou Jones, who had been featured in *The Brownies' Book* when she was in high school. During a period when African American children's literature was less than plentiful, these works helped to fill a void. True to the mission of educating young African Americans about their history and heritage, some of the books include features usually associated with instructional texts, such as end-of-chapter questions and grade-level designations.

Nevertheless, Woodson's contributions should not be underestimated or undervalued. Like Du Bois, Woodson recognized a need for books that told the story of African and African American contributions to the world and contradicted the misinformation and negative stereotypes perpetuated in the popular literature and informational texts of the time. Like Du Bois, he set about to fill that need. In the 1920s, in particular, Woodson's books were among the few that did so. It was not until the 1930s that Langston Hughes and Arna Bontemps moved African American children's literature into the mainstream or, in Bontemps's terms, the front line of children's book publishing.

NOTE

1. The poems in *Little Brown Baby*, a selection of Paul Laurence Dunbar's work for young people, were composed earlier, but the book was not published until 1940. Paul Lawrence Dunbar. *Little Brown Baby*, edited by Bertha Rodgers (New York: Dodd, Mead, 1940).

BIBLIOGRAPHY OF BOOKS FOR CHILDREN AND YOUNG ADULTS

Sources other than books for children and young adults are documented in a references list at the back of the book.

Barrie, James. 1906/1980. *Peter Pan in Kensington Gardens*. Illus. by Arthur Rachham. New York: Buccaneer Books.

Baum, L. Frank. 1900/1956. *The Wizard of Oz*. Chicago: Reilly and Lee.

Dunbar, Paul Lawrence. 1940. *Little Brown Baby*. Edited by Bertha Rodgers. New York: Dodd, Mead.

Grahame, Kenneth. 1908. *The Wind in the Willows*. New York: Scribner's.

Potter, Beatrix. 1902. *The Tale of Peter Rabbit*. New York: Warne.

Hughes, Langston. 1932. *The Dream Keeper*. Illus. by Helen Sewell. New York: Knopf.

———. 1932/1994. *The Dream Keeper*. Illus. by Brian Pinkney. New York: Knopf.

———. 1952. *The First Book of Negroes*. New York: Franklin Watts.

———. 1954. *Famous American Negroes*. New York: Dodd, Mead.

———. 1954a. *The First Book of Rhythms*. New York: Franklin Watts.

———. 1955. *Famous Negro Music Makers*. New York: Dodd, Mead.

———. 1955a. *The First Book of Jazz*. New York: Franklin Watts.

———. 1956. *The First Book of the West Indies*. New York: Franklin Watts.

———. 1958. *Famous Negro Heroes of America*. New York: Dodd, Mead.

———. 1960. *The First Book of Africa*. New York: Franklin Watts.

Newsome, Effie Lee. 1940. *Gladiola Garden*. Washington, DC: Associated Publishers.

Wiggin, Kate Douglas. 1903/1986. *Rebecca of Sunnybrook Farm*. New York: Penguin.

Woodson, Carter, G. 1922. *The Negro in Our History*. Washington, DC: Associated Publishers.

———. 1928. *Negro Makers of History*. Washington, DC: Associated Publishers.

———. 1928. *African Myths, Together With Proverbs*. Washington, DC: Associated Publishers.

———. 1939. *African Heroes and Heroines*. Washington, DC: Associated Publishers.

CHAPTER 3

Breaking New Ground: Arna Bontemps and Some of His Contemporaries

In the three-and-a-half decades between 1930 and 1965, only a few African American writers were focusing on books for children. Nevertheless, during this period an African American authorial presence and perspective became an important element of American children's literature. The most prominent African American voice of the era was that of Arna Bontemps, whose writing for children, along with that of Langston Hughes, is one of the most important legacies that the Harlem Renaissance left to African American children's literature. Although Bontemps's work was dominant in this period, there were also other important advances in the development of African American children's literature.

It was at this time that poetry selected or created especially for children by African Americans began to appear in anthologies and volumes of original poems by individual poets. Some of those poets, such as Countee Cullen and Gwendolyn Brooks, focused their major work mainly outside the field of children's literature, and although their output of children's poetry was important, it was limited in quantity. African American picture books also began to appear during this era, thanks mainly to the work of Ellen Tarry. A few African American writers, most notably Jesse Jackson and Lorenz Graham, also began to publish children's fiction in which characters confronted the racism and discrimination that are inescapable aspects of growing up Black in the United States. It is noteworthy that, beginning in the early 1930s, African American children's book authors were published by the major children's book houses, with their access to a wide distribution network and a broad national readership.

THE WORK OF ARNA BONTEMPS

No other African American children's book author of the 1930s, 1940s, and 1950s was as prolific, as versatile, and as highly regarded by children's literature critics as Arna Bontemps. Over the course of his forty-year career as a children's book author, he produced about sixteen books, including contemporary realistic novels, historical fiction, fantasy, picture books, a poetry anthology, a book of Black history, and a number of biographies. His writing for children across so many genres broke new ground and helped to establish African American children's literature in the mainstream of children's book publishing. Although children's literature scholar Violet Harris (1990, 548) justifiably labeled Bontemps "the contemporary 'father' of African American children's literature," it should also be noted that children's books were only one aspect of Bontemps's literary career.

A poet, novelist, historian, playwright, and biographer, Bontemps was a highly respected member of the cadre of young Harlem Renaissance literary artists. His first book for children, *Popo and Fifina: Children of Haiti* (1932/1993), was written in collaboration with Langston Hughes, whom he had met in Harlem in 1924, just after Hughes returned from a trip abroad as a seaman. They would become lifelong friends and correspondents, but at the time of their initial meeting, Hughes was the more famous of the two, and their relative positions in that regard never changed. Yet, by the time Langston Hughes published his third book for children in 1952, Arna Bontemps had written, individually or in collaboration, almost a dozen books for young people. His nonfiction history, *The Story of the Negro* (1948), had been selected as a Newbery Honor Book; an essay of his had been published in the prestigious *Horn Book*, and the same issue carried a biocritical piece on his life and work (Rider 1939).

Arna Bontemps was born in Alexandria, Louisiana, in 1902, just eight months after Langston Hughes. As a young aspiring writer, he was drawn to Harlem by the presence of the community of young Black writers and artists who were creating the Harlem Renaissance. Married in 1926, he and his wife would become the parents of six children, a circumstance that would be an important influence on Bontemps's decision to write children's books. Bontemps's marriage and fatherhood made him unique among the Harlem Renaissance writers and was the source of the insights into children and family that informed the characterizations in his children's books. Providing for his family was also the likely motivation for Bontemps to work at careers other than writing. By 1932, when his first children's book was published, Bontemps was teaching at a Seventh Day Adventist school in Huntsville, Alabama. Later he would study at the Graduate Library School at the University of Chicago and in 1943 would become the librarian at Fisk University in Nashville, where he remained for more than two decades.

It was during his stay in Alabama that Bontemps collaborated with Hughes to produce *Popo and Fifina* (1932/1993). Bontemps noted that the collaboration had resulted because "Langston had the story and told it to me; I had the children! So we worked together" (Hopkins 1974, 49). Hughes, unmarried and childless, had lived in Haiti for three months in 1931 and observed the conditions under which the Haitian poor lived and worked. *Popo and Fifina* describes the life of a family who move from the country to Cape Haiti (Cap-Haitien). Popo, who is eight, his sister Fifina, who is ten, along with their parents and their baby sister, Pensia, walk to town, their belongings on the backs of two burros. Papa Jean finds work as a fisherman, while Mamma Anna and the children keep busy adjusting to town life—collecting water from the communal fountain, washing clothes in the stream, securing food, and collecting fuel. Popo is apprenticed to his uncle to learn woodworking. Their life is not all work, however; Mama Anna and the children go to visit her family in the country; Papa Jean makes a red star kite for Popo, and he and Fifina enjoy glorious afternoons flying the kite on the beach. Papa Jean and Uncle Jacques take their families on a picnic to the lighthouse, where they are drenched in a rainstorm. Back home in town, a rainbow appears, a symbol of a new beginning.

Popo and Fifina is a quiet episodic story, with little plot, but it offers a glimpse of daily life in a setting that was probably unfamiliar to its presumed audience.

The assumption of unfamiliarity possibly led the authors to slip into offering more information than is necessary in a book of fiction, but Bontemps and Hughes seem intent on presenting this Haitian family, not as exotic curiosities, but as an ordinary family going about their lives as best they can. Though the characters are economically poor, that is not what defines them as people; they are not down-trodden. They maintain strong family ties; the parents are firm but loving in their dealings with the children; the children contribute to the family's well-being but have time and space to be children. This is not a tourist-eye view of the island; the story reveals life as the tourists seldom see it. Bontemps and Hughes make the family seem real and engage readers in the characters' lives. In this family, readers can recognize something of themselves, regardless of their geographical, economic, or chronological distance from the Haiti of that time.

Part of the richness of the book lies in the lyrical language of some passages, not unexpected from two accomplished poets:

The sunshine was like gold. The little dusty white road curved ribbon like among the many hills. It was overhung with the leaves of tropical trees. On the warm countryside there was no sound but the droning of insects and the sudden crying of bright birds. There was no hurry or excitement. And the burros' lazy steps set the speed for the little band of travelers. (1)

The book is further enhanced by the black-and-white illustrations of E. Simms Campbell, an African American artist who later became a well-known cartoon-ist, famous for his work for *Esquire*. Campbell's attractive and realistic images are noteworthy as alternatives to the comic pickaninny images that passed as por-traits of Black children in many children's books of the day. As co-author, Hughes (Rampersad, 1986, 235) must have been particularly pleased with Campbell's art-work in light of his plea for beautiful images for *The Dream Keeper*, which was published the same year as *Popo and Fifina*. Campbell's illustrations may also be significant because they make *Popo and Fifina* the first children's book written by Black authors and illustrated by a Black artist to be published by one of the major publishers of children's books.

Viewed in the context of its times, *Popo and Fifina* was an important achieve-ment. It served as counterpoint to the negative images of Black people and Black life that were popular in the children's books of the day. It carried into mainstream children's literature some of the ideological, philosophical, and psychological val-ues that were so important to *The Brownies' Book* and to the Harlem Renaissance: an appreciation for Pan Africanism, an appreciation for the life and culture of ordi-nary Black folk, a desire to provide children with accurate information about Black people, and a sense of self-love and race-pride. It stayed on the Macmillan list for twenty years and was reissued in 1993 by Oxford University Press.

AN URBAN NOVEL: *SAD-FACED BOY*

In a letter to Langston Hughes, Bontemps (Bontemps 1980, 47) mentions his hope that he had produced "the first Harlem story for children." If *Sad-Faced Boy* (1937) is not the first such story, it is undoubtedly the first to receive widespread attention. In its Harlem setting, and in its use of affectionate humor and the informal vernacular of Black people of its day, it is the precursor to the early Harlem novels of Walter Dean Myers, the African American writer who, decades later, would become one of the most highly respected creators of urban stories for children and young adults. Incidentally, among picture-book enthusiasts, *Sad-Faced Boy* will also be noted as the first book illustrated by Virginia Lee Burton, who would go on to fame as the creator of the beloved *Mike Mulligan and His Steam Shovel* (1939) and *The Little House* (1942), winner of the 1943 Caldecott Medal.

For *Sad-Faced Boy*, which appeared in 1937, Bontemps drew on his experiences both in Alabama and in Harlem. Based on an actual incident, it is the story of Slumber and his two brothers Rags and Willie, who hop a train in Alabama and make their way to Harlem and the home of their uncle. The boys earn their keep by doing chores for Uncle Jasper Tappin, who is building superintendent, and in their spare time explore the wonders of New York City. Their adventures include rides on the subway, taking part in a big parade, and being evicted from the library when their exuberance over the adventures of the Gingerbread Man becomes too loud. Eventually, with Slumber's harmonica, a drum for Willie, and a guitar for Rags, they form the Dozier Brothers Band and earn money playing outside downtown theaters during intermission. Soon, however, their season in New York draws to a close as the boys, summoned by the memory of ripe persimmons, decide it is time to return to Alabama and home.

The boys' odyssey to New York and back is related with warmth, humor, and sympathetic affection. They are realistically drawn, even while their story is told with a bit of the flair of a tall tale. In contrast to the Black characters in many of the children's books popular at the time, they are not caricatures; they are the resourceful, if naïve, heroes of their own story, not comic relief. Although *Sad-Faced Boy* fulfills one of the expressed aims of *The Brownies' Book*—"to make colored children realize that being 'colored' is a normal, beautiful thing"—it does so without moralizing and is entertaining besides.

Sad-Faced Boy is also marked by Bontemps's use of an informal, southern Black vernacular. In that regard, it is significant as one of the first successful published attempts by an African American writer to capture the cadences of that speech variety in a fictional novel for children. Bontemps was able to do so with a minimum of unconventional spellings and without the peculiar syntax that authors often used to ridicule Black characters (see Chapter 4 for examples). Bontemps had first used this dialect in *You Can't Pet a Possum* (1934), which is set in the South, but in *Sad-Faced Boy* we have an excellent example of his skill in representing the everyday speech of ordinary Southern Black people without much formal education. For example, here is part of the dialog as the boys arrive at Uncle Jasper Tappin's door:

"Uncle Jasper Tappin must be moved somewheres else," Willie said, almost ready to cry. "No, I think he still lives here," Rags told him. "Keep on knocking, Slumber." . . . "Well, you scamps!" an old cracked voice said. "Was you trying to break my door down, knocking like all that?" "No, sir," Slumber answered. "We wasn't aiming to break the door." . . . "Whose boys is you all? I ain't never seen you before, has I?" (19)

Although decades later this dialect seems dated, Bontemps's ear was well tuned to the speech of undereducated rural southern Blacks of the 1930s.

AN ANTHOLOGY OF AFRICAN AMERICAN POETRY: *GOLDEN SLIPPERS*

Another of Arna Bontemps's groundbreaking contributions to African American children's literature was *Golden Slippers* (1941), the first comprehensive anthology of poetry for children and youth featuring Black poets. It contains 109 poems by twenty-nine different poets, who are profiled in an appendix. Divided into fourteen sections, the collection is wide ranging. It includes traditional rhymes and spirituals, poems about work and play, sleeping and awakenings, romance and religion, people and places, joy and sadness. There is also variation in form and style. Some poems reflect Black folk or musical expression, such as the blues poems, spirituals, and work songs; others reflect more traditional or conventional poetic styles and forms. Many reflect the spirit of racial pride and racial unity that characterized the Harlem Renaissance, and some recognize the racial dilemmas that challenged Black people and America itself.

The Harlem Renaissance is well represented in the anthology by Claude McKay, Countee Cullen, Langston Hughes, Jessie Fauset, James Weldon Johnson, Arna Bontemps, and others. Many of the poems are classics of Black literature, such as Hughes's "Mother to Son" and "Dreams" and James Weldon Johnson's "The Creation," as well as his lyrics for "Lift Every Voice and Sing," which became known as the national Negro anthem. Paul Laurence Dunbar, who died before the Harlem Renaissance, is also represented, both with some dialect poems and with his Standard English "Dawn." Included, too, are a number of poems by Mary Effie Lee Newsome. Aside from the traditional play rhymes, Newsome's poems are the ones in the anthology most clearly and concretely directed to children. The inclusion of seven of her poems in this important anthology is recognition of her contribution to African American children's poetry.

In his careful selection of poems, Bontemps made available to young audiences a treasury of poets and poetry they might not otherwise have encountered. Many of the poems are timeless and continue to appear in anthologies more than fifty years later. Others are less well known but still hold up well. In bringing to American children a selection of the best of Black poetry, Bontemps made an extraordinary contribution to the advancement of African American children's literature and to children's literature in general. It would be more than a quarter of a century before a similar anthology would be produced.

AFRICAN AMERICAN HISTORY: *THE STORY OF THE NEGRO*

In addition to poetry, Bontemps had a strong interest in history and in telling the African American story to children. This interest developed in part because of the dearth of material on African Americans available to him as a child. An avid reader, he early developed a curiosity about African American history and culture. Failing to find his own reflection in books on the library shelves and finding that his schooling distorted or denied him knowledge of his heritage, he was compelled to discover the facts for himself and to help set the record straight. This commitment in turn motivated him to write children's books and, later, to become a librarian (Jones 1992, 45).

Bontemps's nonfiction history, *The Story of the Negro* (1948), was cited as a 1949 Newbery Honor Book, making it the first book by an African American author to be so recognized. Dedicated to Langston Hughes, the book uses as its epigraph Hughes's classic poem, "The Negro Speaks of Rivers." Bontemps begins his history with the arrival of twenty Blacks at Jamestown in 1619. From there, he takes the reader back to Africa and gives an overview of the continent and its history, stressing the diversity to be found among its peoples and the precolonial achievements of African nations and individuals. The story continues with a brief history of slavery, a description of the middle passage, and the history of Haiti's fight for independence. The rest of the book is devoted to the story of Black people in the United States, from slavery to the time of the book's publication. The section on slavery is titled "The Bondage," but the emphasis is on the fight for freedom and on freedom fighters, including Gabriel Prosser, Denmark Vesey, and Nat Turner, leaders of famous slave revolts. Throughout the book are the stories of extraordinary Black individuals who are to be admired for their courage and their contributions. A special feature is the appended chronology juxtaposing events in Black history and comparable dates in world history. It makes clear that the history of Black people neither began nor ended with slavery.

The book is distinguished not only for its scholarship, but also for the quality of the writing. Bontemps's craft and power as a storyteller is evident from the opening paragraph:

The story begins with a mystery—a ship without a name. It flew the Dutch flag and had the appearance of an armed trader, but that doesn't say much. Appearances were not to be trusted at sea in 1619. The vessel may have been sailing under false colors. She may just as well have been a slave ship or a privateer. Whatever her name or nation, however, her deeds are known and recorded.

This is the ship that brought the stolen Africans to the young colony at Jamestown. (*The Story of the Negro*, 1948, 3)

In citing *The Story of the Negro* as a Newbery Honor Book, the children's literature establishment honored both the story Bontemps told and his literary artistry. Bontemps, however, was disappointed that it had not won the "first prize," the John Newbery Medal. In a letter to Langston Hughes, he notes: "Knopf just wired to congratulate me on the fact that *The Story of the Negro* was mentioned as a runner-up for the Newbery Medal (the Pulitzer of the juveniles), but near misses don't make me happy. I'd like a jackpot, a bullseye, or something—*sometime*" (Bontemps 1980, 252). As it turns out, only three African American writers of children's fiction hit the "bull's-eye" in the twentieth century—Virginia Hamilton, Mildred Taylor, and Christopher Paul Curtis.

HISTORICAL FICTION: *CHARIOT IN THE SKY*

As librarian at Fisk, Bontemps was eager to relate the story of the famed Fisk Jubilee Singers, who introduced Negro spirituals to the concert stage. *Chariot in the Sky* (1951) is the fictionalized story of the first Fisk Jubilee Singers. It is also the story of a young man's search for liberation and empowerment and as such is a precursor to a goodly portion of the African American children's historical fiction of the late twentieth century. Much like the newer historical fiction, *Chariot* put a human face on slavery and challenged the distorted and stereotyped images of antebellum free Blacks, enslaved Blacks, slave life, plantation slavery, and ex-slaves after the war.

Caleb, the protagonist of *Chariot*, was born enslaved. After emancipation and an unsuccessful attempt to locate his parents, he makes his way to the Fisk School in Nashville, where he earns money for his fees by teaching in a country school. A talented singer, Caleb joins the choir that becomes the Fisk Jubilee Singers. When Fisk is about to fold for lack of money, the choir sets out on a fund-raising tour. At first their singing of classical European music receives excellent reviews but very little money. The turning point comes one night when they astonish a meeting of Congregational ministers at Oberlin with an impromptu rendering of the spiritual "Steal Away." The rest of the tour brings in enough money to save the school.

In addition to deftly weaving accurate historical information throughout the book, Bontemps deals with themes that would recur in many later books set in the era of slavery and Reconstruction, themes such as the importance of family ties, the importance of literacy and education, the linking of literacy and liberation, and the deep-seated desire for freedom. For example, he has an elderly slave recount to Caleb the legend of the Africans who could will themselves to fly back to Africa. This well-known tale is the title story in Virginia Hamilton's groundbreaking collection of Black folktales, *The People Could Fly* (1985), and appears in a number of collections and works of historical fiction. The flying motif is also present in a number of fictional African American works for children, including contemporary works such as Faith Ringgold's *Tar Beach* (1991). Bontemps anticipates the resurgence of the emphasis on Africa and connections to Africa that would mark African American children's literature of the 1960s and 1970s. Referring to an African drum given to him by a sailor, Caleb's father says, "Africa is where we come from—our people, way back yonder." "It do me proud to say we come from Africa" (30). When Caleb is sold off to Chattanooga, his father sends the drum with him, a tangible tie to his family and to his heritage.

Chariot also touches on the issue of class differences among Black people. The mother of a girl that Caleb admires likes Caleb well enough until she realizes that he might have a romantic interest in her daughter. She thinks an ex-slave is not good enough for her free-born child. Within-group social conflicts or tensions based on status, color, and socioeconomic class have plagued Black people since slavery, and that issue continues to be explored in contemporary African American literature for both adults and youth.

In creating this novel of historical fiction, Bontemps led the way toward extending accounts of the history and accomplishments of Blacks into the realm of literary fiction. By personalizing the story and making it that of a realistically drawn, sympathetic, and strong young man, Bontemps made it both appealing and accessible. In terms of its thematic emphases, *Chariot* could easily have been a model for the historical fiction novels that were produced decades later about enslaved Black people and their lives immediately after slavery.

A BIT OF SURREALISM: *LONESOME BOY*

In an article in *The Horn Book*, Bontemps (1966) identified what he saw as a recurring motif in his work, "the lonesome boy" theme, which he perceived as at least partly autobiographical. The clearest expression of that theme is his 1955 novella, *Lonesome Boy*, a surrealistic story of a boy called Bubber and his trumpet. From the time Bubber first learned to play the trumpet, his grandpa warned him, "You better mind how you blow that horn, sonny boy. You better mind" (1). Despite repeated warnings from Grandpa, Bubber continued to play his horn whenever and wherever he was moved to do so. Eventually, he left home and found his way to the city. There, he played as much and as often as the trumpet called and the music inside him commanded, until one day he received a strange invitation to play at what turned out to be the devil's ball. When he found himself after the ball sitting alone in a pecan tree, he knew it was time to go back home.

Lonesome Boy is an ambiguous tale, open to various interpretations. It has the ring of a folktale, especially in the beginning with Grandpa's repeated "You better mind." It also echoes many folktales in its plot involving a young country boy going off to the city to seek his fortune and his manhood and in the circularity of his journey, a pattern that also holds in *Sad-Faced Boy*. In the development of African American children's literature, *Lonesome Boy* is significant for its innovation. No book of original African American children's fiction published up to that time had offered a similar combination of the real and the bizarre, or woven together folk elements and aspects of Black culture such as jazz into a unique artistic expression. In that regard, it would remain unrivaled until the advent of Virginia Hamilton in the late 1960s. *Lonesome Boy* was reissued by Beacon Press in 1988. Unlike *Sad-Faced Boy*, which is clearly of a past era, *Lonesome Boy* has weathered well; forty years after its publication, it retains its freshness. It is Bontemps's most lasting work for young people and, arguably, his best.

TALL TALES AS PICTURE BOOKS

Bontemps also cowrote three folk-like stories with Jack Conroy, a White writer he met while working in Chicago. The central characters of *The Fast Sooner Hound* (1942), *Slappy Hooper, the Wonderful Sign Painter* (1946), and *Sam Patch, the High Wide and Handsome Jumper* (1951) are all White. They are of interest here, however, because they demonstrate something of the breadth of Bontemps's contributions to children's literature. The tales read like American tall tales, with characters capable of extraordinary feats. They are also notable because Bontemps is one of the few modern Black writers of children's books to have had books published unrelated to African Americans or African American themes. That he was able to do so fifty years ago suggests the degree to which Bontemps, who was listed as first author, was established as an important writer of children's books.

If W.E.B. Du Bois laid the foundation of twentieth century African American children's literature, then Arna Bontemps built much of the ground floor. His work carried on and refined some of the traditions that had begun with *The Brownies' Book*—a focus on pride in Black racial/cultural heritage, a pan-African perspective, and an effort to acquaint children with Black heroes and Black history. Beginning in the 1950s, Bontemps published biographies of famous Black figures such as George Washington Carver, Frederick Douglass, and Booker T. Washington. This focus on acquainting young readers with the achievements of Black leaders and heroes was a tradition that had begun at least as early as the 1920s and continues to the current time.

Bontemps's authentic rendering of informal Black vernacular in children's fiction, his choice of Harlem as a setting for a children's novel, his creation of a comprehensive anthology of Black poetry for children, his artistic use of fiction as a means to make a historical event engaging to youthful readers—all may have been firsts in the development of African American children's literature as created by Black Americans. Certainly, being the first African American writer to have a book selected both as a Newbery Honor Book and a Jane Addams Award (for the 1955 edition) winner attests to Bontemps's standing as a writer in mainstream American children's literature. Bontemps interjected a Black perspective on Black subjects, Black themes, and Black traditions, many of which were carried over from adult African American literature into American children's literature, an arena in which such a perspective was sorely needed.

AFRICAN AMERICAN CHILDREN'S POETRY IN THE 1940s AND 1950s

The African American children's poetry of the 1940s and 1950s is marked more by its variety than by any apparent common purpose or sense of mission. Only about a handful of such poetry books was published during this period in any case. One was a selection of poems that had been written in the late 1800s and early 1900s. The others were collections of original poems on various topics. Unlike the poetry to come in the late 1960s and 1970s, there is surprisingly little that is overtly race conscious or culturally conscious in these collections. The exception was the selection of Paul Laurence Dunbar's poetry in a book for children entitled *Little Brown Baby* (1940).

PAUL LAURENCE DUNBAR

At the turn of the twentieth century, Paul Laurence Dunbar had been the premier Black poet in America. He was born in 1872 and died in 1906, four months before his thirty-fourth birthday. Although he wrote novels and short stories, and although more than two-thirds of his poetry was written in Standard English, Dunbar was best known for his dialect poems reflecting the life of Blacks living in or not long removed from the rural South. He grew up in Dayton, Ohio, and was not a speaker of the dialect he used in his poems; his dialect poems, according to the book's introductory biographical sketch, derived from stories his mother, an ex-slave, told him about the plantation life she had known as a child.

Little Brown Baby was compiled by Bertha Rodgers and illustrated by Erick Berry, an Englishwoman who apparently specialized in creating or illustrating children's books featuring Africans or African Americans. The publisher claims that this was the first gathering in book form of the Dunbar poems most appropriate and appealing to children. That this publication came more than three decades after his death attests to the enduring popularity of Dunbar's work.

Almost all of the twenty-five poems in *Little Brown Baby* are dialect poems (e.g., "Little brown baby wif spa'klin' eyes."). The poems in *Little Brown Baby* center for the most part on rural or plantation good times—music, food, courting, nature, family life and love, leisure. Having grown up on his mother's stories, Dunbar was attuned to the oral tradition and the folk culture of an earlier generation. Strongly rhythmical, Dunbar's poems beg to be read aloud or recited. Although his idyllic images have been criticized for a lack of realism, the poems carry a certain charm, and they make their subjects seem like real individuals. The title poem, for example, is a warm evocation of a loving bedtime interaction between a father and his child. The emotions in "Little Brown Baby" are timeless; more than a century after its composition, it still carries the ring of truth. Many of Dunbar's dialect poems have been beloved for generations and have been memorized and recited over the years in countless Black churches, homes, and community settings. The importance of this collection is that it made the work of this famous and beloved poet widely available to children.

A more accurate sense of Dunbar's work, however, must extend beyond his dialect poetry. In "The Poet," which is not included in this collection, Dunbar himself characterized his dialect work as "a jingle in a broken tongue" and lamented that, although he wrote poems that he considered to have greater depth, it was these "jingles" that received all the praise. In *I Greet the Dawn*, Ashley Bryan (1978), artist and poet, gathered a selection of Dunbar's poems that stress his poems in Standard English. These poems reflected the style of the formal poetry popular in Dunbar's day and the influence of poets he admired, such as Keats, Tennyson, and Shelley. Bryan's collection includes two of Dunbar's best-known poems, "Sympathy" ("I know why the caged bird sings") and "We Wear the Mask," both dealing with the tensions brought about by being Black in a racialized society. Even though most of Dunbar's work was not addressed to children, much of it is accessible to them, and in that regard, Rodgers's collection helped to bring him into the canon of African American poetry for children. It would take both collections, however, to give children a reasonably accurate picture of the work of this important African American poet.

POETRY FOR ELEMENTARY SCHOOLS: ASSOCIATED PUBLISHERS

Associated Publishers, Carter G. Woodson's company, the publishing arm of the Association for the Study of Negro Life and History, was particularly interested in enriching school curricula by making them more inclusive, particularly of work by and about African Americans. To that end, they published, among other things, two books of poetry, one aimed at preschool, kindergarten, and intermediate grades and the other designated for second-grade readers. Neither, however, is particularly focused on any distinctive African American cultural themes, but on what Du Bois might have meant by "the best amusements and joys and worthwhile things of life" (Du Bois 1919, 286).

Effie Lee Newsome, who had created the "Little Page" for *The Crisis*, published a collection of her poems, entitled *Gladiola Garden*, in 1940. In one of her early "Calendar Chats" (December 1925), Newsome had noted that the "gaudily dainty and exquisite flowers, the gladioluses" (89) had first been found in Africa. Thus, the aptly chosen title of her book hints at both the primary intended audience and Newsome's appreciation for the beauty of children of African descent. Nevertheless, even though all the children shown in the illustrations are clearly Black, only one or two of the poems hint at any consciousness of racial themes or African American culture. Subtitled "Poems of Outdoors and Indoors for Second Grade Readers," the book consists mainly of verses about nature and natural phenomena, although a substantial number also feature children and their emotions and everyday activities. Thus, it is for the most part the illustrations, rather than the poems themselves, that link this work specifically to African American children.

As were a number of children's books from Associated Publishers, *Gladiola Garden* was illustrated by Lois Mailou Jones, the award-winning and highly respected African American artist who had studied in Boston and in France and who taught for a number of years at Howard University. Jones did freelance work for Associated's publications for children and adults for almost thirty years. Unfortunately for the field of children's literature, however, she never received the recognition in mainstream children's publishing that her work as illustrator of children's books warranted. Her black-and-white drawings for *Gladiola Garden* continue *The Brownies' Book* tradition of portraying Black children as attractive individuals with diverse physical characteristics. Many of her drawings of insects, birds, trees, flowers, and other natural objects could stand alone as art pieces.

The poems in *Gladiola Garden* are all rhymed and metered. Newsome was fond of figurative language, and at her best she offered fresh visual imagery that would appeal to children—fireflies as gold confetti in the night sky, spiders dressed in black velvet, grasshoppers wearing goggles. A few poems also display welcome touches of humor. Many of the verses are lyrical, written in the first person; Newsome was adept at capturing a child's voice and reflecting a child's perspective. Creating 163 rhymed and metered verses aimed specifically at seven-year-olds would not come easily to many writers, however, and some of Newsome's verses suffer from the effort to find suitable rhymes and from unvaried meter. In some cases, the language seems trite rather than lively or vivid. Fifty years after their publication, some poems that would have captured some of the daily experiences of children of the 1920s and 1930s have become dated. On the other hand, the best of these verses would still be appealing to many contemporary children. A selection of her best poems is available in *Wonders: The Best Children's Poems of Effie Lee Newsome* (Newsome 1999). As has been mentioned, Newsome is probably the first twentieth century African American woman poet to devote the bulk of her writing career to creating work for children.

The other poetry book from Associated Publishers, *The Picture-Poetry Book* (1935) by Gertrude Parthenia McBrown, was aimed at young children. Full of fairies and other such "little folk" and featuring child life indoors and out, McBrown's verses are for the most part undistinguished. The significance of the book lies in its very existence as a poetry collection featuring Black children in the mid-1930s and in the lively, realistic black-and-white illustrations by Lois Mailou Jones.

COUNTEE CULLEN

A contemporary of Langston Hughes and Arna Bontemps, Countee Cullen was considered one of the most brilliant poets of the Harlem Renaissance. Educated at New York University and Harvard, Cullen was the poet who had declared that he did not want to be known as "a Negro poet." Ironically, however, some of his best-known poems—"Yet Do I Marvel" ("To make a poet black") and "Incident" ("Once riding in old Baltimore")—are the race-conscious ones. "Incident," a poem about a Black child and his encounter with racism, is often included in contemporary anthologies of poetry for children. His two books for children are in a much lighter mood.

In 1940, Cullen published an excellent example of his nonracial poetry, *The Lost Zoo,* a collection of narrative verses about some imaginary animals who were left off Noah's Ark. "Coauthored" by Christopher Cat, *The Lost Zoo* opens with a prose introduction, "A Word about Christopher," in which the narrator tells Christopher about his afternoon trip to the zoo, and Christopher reveals that a number of animals that previously existed cannot be found in a zoo since they had been left off the ark for one reason or another. Cullen was teaching French and English at a junior high school at the time, and supposedly these poems were cautionary tales aimed at improving the behavior of his students.

The first group of poems tells of Noah's invitations to the animals and the written responses of a few who had special requests (e.g., L. E. Phant wishes not to room with mice). The next set of poems relate the stories of the animals of the "lost zoo," such as the wakeupworld, the squilliligee, the sleepabitmore, and the hoodinkus, and reveal the reasons they were not among those who sailed on the ark. The poems are complete with rhymed footnotes from Christopher Cat. Although there is a certain Seuss-like quality to his animal names and characteristics, Cullen's skill as a poet shines through these highly crafted verses along with the humor. The poems are accompanied by Charles Sebree's striking watercolor portraits of the animals, both real and imaginary, rendered in vivid colors. Sebree was a well-known African American artist from Chicago.

The Lost Zoo is unique in twentieth century African American children's poetry. Although fairies and such magical creatures appear frequently in some early work, Cullen stands alone among African American poets in his creation of a set of imaginative, original, talking animals, presented in a unique voice, and displaying both humor and the craft of an accomplished poet. Christopher Cat also appears in a second Cullen book for children, *My Lives and How I Lost Them* (1942), in which Christopher, who is on his ninth life, explains how he lost the other eight.

GWENDOLYN BROOKS

The other accomplished adult writer who produced an important book of poetry specifically for a child audience during this period was Pulitzer Prize-winning poet Gwendolyn Brooks. In 1956, Harper published *Bronzeville Boys and Girls*, her collection of thirty-four poems about Black children. The title of each poem is the name of a child living in Bronzeville, a Black community on Chicago's south side. Although some of the poems could be set anywhere, the focus on urban life is an important feature of the book and one of the ways it contrasts to *Gladiola Garden*.

Like *Gladiola Garden* and *The Picture Poetry Book*, however, the poems in *Bronzeville Boys and Girls* do not place Blackness or Black culture in the foreground, although it is by no means absent. In the urban Black community of Bronzeville, blackness is, in a sense, taken for granted. The illustrations—black-and-white sketches—are all of Black children. The closest the text of any poem comes to a direct reference is "Gertrude," in which the speaker declares that hearing Marian Anderson sing makes her feel "STUFFless." There is no use of Black English vernacular. Blackness is manifest in signs such as the name Bronzeville, certain of the children's names, and expressions such as the echo of the spiritual "Swing Low, Sweet Chariot" in the first two lines of "Skipper": "I looked in the fish-glass/And what did I see."

The poems capsulize a variety of childhood experiences and express genuine and sometimes intense child-like emotions. Several of the poems are frequently anthologized and, after a half century, can be considered classics among contemporary American children's poetry. For example, Keziah, who has "a secret place"; Cynthia, for whom the snow is achingly beautiful; Andre, who dreamed of having to choose his own parents; and Lyle, who has moved seven times, have become familiar companions in classrooms in which children's poetry is taken seriously and enjoyed.

During this period, which included the Great Depression and World War II, only Effie Lee Newsome emerged as an African American poet whose main body of work was directed to children. The period was also graced, however, by the publication of collections of accessible poems by famous and accomplished African American poets who wrote mainly for adults. It would not be until the Black Arts Movement of the 1960s and 1970s, however, that African American poets would again publish collections of original poetry for children and a group of African American children's poets would begin to emerge.

PICTURE-BOOK BEGINNINGS

Historians of American children's literature usually cite Wanda Gag's *Millions of Cats*, which was published in 1928, as the first American picture storybook. In the next few decades, the growth of picture storybooks would be phenomenal, but African American writers and artists were not well represented in the genre until the late 1960s.

In the mid-1940s, however, Ellen Tarry became one of the first African American writers to produce picture storybooks about African Americans for young children in an urban setting and among the first African American writers to emphasize positive relationships between Black characters and White ones. Her focus on integration can be attributed to her own philosophy of hope: "When we are united, there will be no door in America marked 'colored' or 'white.' Instead there will be the third door—free from racial designations—through which all Americans, all of God's children will walk in peace and dignity" (Tarry 1955/1992, 304).

Tarry's entry into the field was almost accidental. She had joined the Negro Writers' Guild in New York City and through that connection met the famous poet and novelist Claude McKay. At a meeting, she overheard McKay haughtily rejecting the opportunity to write children's stories: "I'm Claude McKay, I don't want to write any *little* stories! Let Miss Tarry have it" (1955/1992, 133). "It" was a scholarship, designated for an African American with experience as both a writer and a teacher, to study with Lucy Sprague Mitchell at what eventually became Bank Street College (134).

Tarry produced her first picture book under the mentorship of Mitchell, an influential proponent of progressive education, and Margaret Wise Brown, the author of the famous and much loved *Good Night, Moon*, who was also working at the bureau. Mitchell believed that children's stories should reflect their everyday world—the here and now—and, to some extent their language patterns and vocabulary (Mitchell 1921). Tarry's first picture book, and her favorite (Hopkins 1969, 281), *Janie Belle* (1940), is based on an actual incident. It is a lively story about a "colored baby," a foundling who is rescued and adopted by Nurse Moore. The pictures indicate that the only obviously "colored" character is the baby; aside from the plot line, the main feature of the book is the language, which, with its patterns, its rhythms, and its choice of vocabulary (e.g., Dr. Great, Dr. Big, Dr. Little) displays the influence of Mitchell's theories. Interestingly, some Southern readers found the book offensive because the "colored" baby is adopted by a White nurse (K. C. Smith 1999).

In 1942, Tarry moved to Viking where, under the editorship of May Masse, the well-known and highly respected children's book editor, she published her second book, *Hezekiah Horton* (1942). Also based on real life, it tells the story of a young Black boy whose main passion is cars. One day, as he sits on the stoop watching and wishing, a White man drives up in a red car that was finer than even Hezekiah could imagine. The man befriends Hezekiah, takes him and some of the neighborhood boys for a ride, and promises to return another day. The book was illustrated by Oliver Harrington, a well-known Black cartoonist, and thus *Hezekiah* became one of the first picture storybooks to be both written and illustrated by African Americans and published by one of the major New York children's book publishers. Tarry and Harrington also published a sequel, *The Runaway Elephant*, in 1950.

Masse also brought Tarry together with Marie Hall Ets, a White artist and social worker, with whom Tarry collaborated to create her most highly regarded children's book, *My Dog Rinty* (1946), a popular picture book illustrated with black-and-white photographs. Ets was unaware of the existence of any picture book featuring urban Black children. She wanted to produce one, and Tarry had the Harlem connections. Masse insisted on having the book illustrated with photographs (K. C. Smith 1999), and Tarry was able to convince suspicious Harlemites to allow the Allands, a couple of White photographers to take the pictures. Its satisfying plot, its engaging young hero, and its realistic portrait of Harlem in the 1940s made *Rinty* a landmark picture book in African American children's fiction.

My Dog Rinty features David, a young African American boy, and his badly behaved dog, Rinty, who causes trouble all over the neighborhood. When David's father decrees that Rinty must be sold, a Black "society woman," Mrs. Mosely, buys him and takes him to obedience school, where all his bad behavior is eradicated except his attempts to chew holes in rugs and dig up floorboards. Rinty, it seems, is a valuable mouser; invariably, the place where he tries to dig is the place where mice are hidden. Through the kindness of Mrs. Mosely, Rinty is reunited with David, and soon Rinty's services as a mouser are in demand all over the community, in all the places where he was previously unwanted. He and David have become Harlem's Pied Pipers.

Although the story is fictional, the book shows real people and places. For example, Augusta Baker—highly respected librarian and storyteller and friend of Ellen Tarry's—is shown in the 135th Street Branch of the New York Public Library telling a story. (Although Bader [1976, 378] identifies a man shown reading to children in the library as Spencer Shaw, another revered librarian/storyteller, Shaw himself, in a hallway conversation with me in June 2000 at the annual meeting of the American Library Association in Chicago, denied that he is the man pictured.) During the 1940s, Harlem embraced the full socioeconomic spectrum of the Black community from the poor to the wealthy, and this diversity is reflected in both the photographs and the text. With one or two possible exceptions, all of the pictured people are Black—including the nuns, the owners of small businesses, and the newspaper editor. A number of important community institutions and establishments, such as the Hotel Theresa and Harlem Hospital, are also featured. David delivers flowers to the building where Joe Louis lives on Sugar Hill. Thus, the book presents a realistic picture of the Harlem of the 1940s.

Tarry and Ets's book also embraces many of the values characteristically embedded in African American fiction for children. It features a close-knit and loving family headed by a strong father. The mention of Joe Louis and the choice of Fred-Douglass as the first name of one of David's brothers suggest the importance of Black heroes. Adults outside the family are shown as caring and fair, even when they are angered by Rinty's behavior. Mrs. Mosely, the woman who bought Rinty and who is clearly better off financially than David's family, pays David to walk Rinty, exemplifying how people in the community interacted across economic class lines and one of the ways adults outside the family contributed to the welfare of the children in the community.

High value is placed on reading and literacy. In the first photograph of the family, every child is engaged with reading or writing. Father is reading the newspaper. Only Mother is not reading, but as she works on her sewing, she appears to be helping David with his book. On Friday afternoon, it is Mother who suggests that David and his brother and sister "go to the library and listen to the story-hour lady tell those nice stories from books." Idealistic though this portrayal may be, it is not very different from the depictions of Black families that appear in later African American children's books.

Critic Barbara Bader (1976) points out that *My Dog Rinty* might be called a "semi-documentary" and assesses its significance: "Showing the social range in a community, any community, from hardship to decency to comfort to luxury . . . ; indicating that the poor in old buildings live poorly; suggesting a concrete solution, that the buildings be replaced: all this was novel in a picture book in 1946" (378). Thus, *My Dog Rinty* is important not only in the history of African American children's literature but also in American children's literature in general. To the extent that it is a "semidocumentary" offering an accurate picture of a Black community and a solution for a social problem, it is both a good story and an instance of African American literature as a social action.

Another picture book featuring a Black family and illustrated with photographs was *My Happy Days* (1944), published by Associated Publishers. The text was written by Jane Dabney Shackelford, a schoolteacher who wanted to show what she considered a typical middle-class African American family with happy intelligent children guided by intelligent, hard-working, cultured parents. Clearly, *My Happy Days* is a book with an agenda, an attempt to counter popular portrayals of Black families and Black life and provide guidance for Black children and their families. Artistic considerations are secondary to the book's mission, and the language is stilted. The photographs, however, provide a detailed portrayal of the life of an idealized, very light-skinned, straight-haired, middle- or uppermiddle-class Black family in the 1940s. Mother, with her sweet smile and gentle voice, never scolds. She keeps the house spotless, prepares healthy food, and reads to the children at night. Dad is a radio patrolman who drives a squad car and helps children answer their questions by looking in the encyclopedia. This genteel "average" family is actually rather well off financially compared to many Black families of the time and appears to espouse the same values as does the Judge in *The Brownies' Book*. In other words, this is very much a refined "colored" family that serves as a model of what at least one segment of the Black population thought Black people should be or of the image of Black people they wished to display to the public.

THE REALITY OF RACISM ENTERS AFRICAN AMERICAN CHILDREN'S BOOKS

As far back as 1919, W.E.B. Du Bois had acknowledged, in his announcement of the launching of *The Brownies' Book*, that relations between Black children and White children were likely to be difficult. He declared as one of the major thrusts of the magazine that it would "seek to teach Universal Love and Brotherhood for all little folk, black and brown and yellow and white." He also listed among his objectives teaching the children of the sun "delicately a code of honor and action in their relations with white children" and seeking "to turn their little hurts and resentments into emulation, ambition and love of their homes and companions" (Du Bois 1919, 286). One can infer that the "little hurts and resentments" referred to the effects of having to confront racist remarks and incidents. It is safe to assume that other African American creators of children's literature were aware of the same issues but chose, with a few exceptions, to focus their writing either on life among Black people or on nonracial topics, such as the natural world. One exception, Ellen Tarry, chose to write about positive relationships between Black children and White adults in some of her picture books. Another exception was

Chariot in the Sky, Bontemps's 1951 historical novel in which including some racial issues in the period following the Civil War was unavoidable.

CALL ME CHARLEY

Call Me Charley (1945) by Jesse Jackson (not to be confused with the Rev. Jesse Jackson of civil rights fame) was the first African American children's novel to directly confront racial conflict in a then-contemporary Northern setting. Set in suburban Columbus, Ohio, the novel is also significant for its nearly all-White cast. Charles Moss lives in Arlington Heights, where his parents work for Doctor Cunningham, Mrs. Moss as a cook, Mr. Moss as a chauffer. Charley is the only Black child in the community. His job as a paperboy leads, early in the book, to his critical encounter with George Reed, who wears his racism like a banner, and Tom Hamilton, whose parents wrap themselves in the mantle of liberalism. George's greeting is "Move on, Sambo." To which Charley replies, "My name is Charles. Charles Moss." When George insists on Sambo, Charley repeats: "My name is Charles. Sometimes I'm called Charley. Nobody calls me Sambo and gets away with it" (7–8).

The rest of the plot concerns Charley's attempts to win acceptance in the community. Tom befriends Charley, which often places Tom in a difficult position since he also tries to remain friends with George. Charley encounters several other instances of racism, from the principal's initial refusal to accept him in school, to the director's refusal to give him a part in the school play, to the town leaders' refusal to award him a pass to the community swimming pool—the prize he and Tom win in a contest.

Although Charley never gets a pass to the pool, the other problems are solved by the intervention of White friends and benefactors—Dr. Cunningham and the Hamiltons. Mrs. Moss understands the power of White privilege, telling Charley "a word from a white man travels around the world while a colored man is just trying to get someone to listen to him" (21) and is grateful for the support of the Cunninghams. The Hamiltons act out of their belief that (White) people with privilege and clout need to take responsibility for helping those less fortunate: "Some people don't like colored people and don't want to give them a chance. And that's where their friends have to stand up for them" (131). Given this expression of a sense of "noblesse oblige" by Mrs. Hamilton and Mrs. Moss's gratitude and optimism, it is likely that the book anticipated an audience of both Black and White readers. Charley's mother sums up one of the book's themes as it relates to Black readers: "As long as you work hard and try to do right, you will always find some good [White] people like Doc Cunningham or Tom and his folks marching along with you in the right path. And fellows like George may come along too, sooner, or later" (156).

Jackson saw himself as asking for "a very small advance" in race relations—the right of Black people to be called by their own names, to be recognized as individuals (Lanier 1977, 333). At the time *Call Me Charley* appeared, it was one of the very few contemporary novels for children written by African American writers and published by mainstream publishers. By placing the main character and his family in an otherwise all-White social environment in which he must fight discrimination and gain acceptance, Jackson introduced the African American children's novel of racial conflict. In their focus on interracial relationships, *Call Me Charley* and its sequels, *Anchor Man* (1947) and *Charley Starts from Scratch* (1958), resemble a number of works, published from the 1940s through the mid-1970s, generally by White writers, that constitute a set of ideologically related books referred to elsewhere as "social conscience" books (Sims 1982b) since their main purpose seemed to be to engender empathy or sympathy for Black children facing racial discrimination in housing or schooling and to promote tolerance for racial desegregation or integration. Jackson's early work also fit snugly into the Intercultural Education Movement, which was prevalent at the time and which influenced many White writers to produce books featuring African American characters.

Jackson went on to write two young adult novels—*The Sickest Don't Always Die the Quickest* (1971) and *The Fourteenth Cadillac* (1972)—that tie more closely into the growing trends in African American children's literature. Thirty years after *Charley*, Jackson would attribute the perspective of his early novels to the influence of White editors, asserting they reflected the perspectives of White authors writing for a White audience, while his later works were guided by an English editor with a more egalitarian viewpoint (Lanier 1977, 339). Nevertheless, while his later books have been nearly forgotten, it is *Call Me Charley* for which Jesse Jackson is best remembered.

LORENZ GRAHAM

Another African American writer known in part for his focus on race relations is Lorenz Graham, author of *South Town* (1958) and its sequels *North Town* (1965), *Whose Town?* (1969), and *Return to South Town* (1976). These books follow David Williams and his struggles and triumphs as he overcomes numerous obstacles to become a physician and eventually fulfill his dream of practicing medicine in the small Southern town where he grew up. In contrast to Jackson's Charley Moss, David Williams is not concerned about being accepted by Whites in a White community but with having the freedom to live the life he chooses as a young Black man. David is placed solidly at the center of a strong Black family with a well-developed sense of their own dignity and a determination to maintain their independence.

South Town is based on Graham's experiences living and working in Virginia. It reveals the oppressive social conditions and injustices under which Black people in the 1940s and 1950s were forced to live. Segregation in public facilities was legal, and unwritten laws supporting white supremacy prevailed. David's dream of becoming a doctor is considered "uppity," and eventually his family is forced to move out of South Town because powerful Whites saw to it that his father was unable to find a job. Moving north would presumably also provide better educational opportunities for David. In North Town, however, although the family is not faced with legal segregation, David has to confront racism and bigotry nevertheless. By the time of the third novel, the civil rights movement was in full swing, and one of the issues the Williams family faces is deciding the best way to bring about change in social and economic conditions—nonviolent protest or "any means necessary." In the final novel, David returns home to begin practicing medicine and discovers that, although many positive changes have been made in South Town, the battle against racism has not yet been won. It is a hopeful ending, but a realistic one.

That the Town books were groundbreaking is borne out by Graham's experiences with editors as he was trying to get the books published. It took about twelve years to get *South Town* into print because the publisher who had originally contracted to issue it believed that the American public of the mid-1940s would not accept Black characters who did not fit the stereotype of the day. They thought the Williams family was too "American"–dignified, intelligent, just like everybody else—to be believed. Even in the late 1950s when the book was finally published, the editor sought expert verification that the social conditions in the South were as Graham described them. Clearly, children's book publishers were not used to seeing books in which a strong Black family confronted racism and were unwilling to challenge the images of Black people that prevailed in American society at the time (Graham 1988).

Graham did not set out to be a writer. Although he was born in 1902, the same year as Langston Hughes and Arna Bontemps, he did not make his way from California to New York in the early 1920s to join the young artists fomenting the Harlem Renaissance. The son of an A.M.E. minister, Graham chose to teach at a mission school in Liberia, where he worked from 1925 to 1929. It was his experience in Africa and in France that motivated him to choose writing as a career and to commit to promoting the message that "people are people" (Graham 1988, 119). "People are people" became his mantra, and the Town series makes clear that, for Graham, it was not an empty platitude; he was asserting that all people are equally deserving of basic human rights and equal treatment under the law.

Graham's first books endeavoring to show that people are people were set in Africa. Aware of the popular American images of Africa and Africans as primitive and exotic, and having learned first-hand that such a view was grossly inaccurate, Graham wanted to foster a truer picture. On his return to the United States, however, he discovered that there were virtually no children's books available in which Africans were presented realistically. Unable to convince anyone else to remedy that situation, he decided that he himself had to "write books that would make Americans know that Africans were people" (Graham 1973, 186). As was the case with *South Town*, however, his first work about Africa was rejected by a publisher because the editor thought that American readers would not accept Graham's depiction of Africans as ordinary human beings rather than primitive savages.

Graham refused to compromise, however, and his first book for children, *Tales of Momolu* (1946), published a decade and a half later, was a fictional depiction of the everyday life of a ten-year-old African boy in a Liberian village. Twenty years later, he would write a sequel, *I, Momolu* (1966). In 1975, at a period when African American children's literature was the object of a great deal of attention, Momolu reappeared in the picture book, *Song of the Boat* (1975), in which he helps his father replace the canoe he lost in a fight with an alligator. In all three books, Momolu is recognizable as an ordinary boy, living an ordinary life; the main difference between him and American readers is the setting.

Graham's sojourn in West Africa also led to the noteworthy books that are his unique contributions to African American children's literature. In 1946, Reynal and Hitchcock published Graham's *How God Fix Jonah*, a collection of Bible stories told, like *Song of the Boat*, in the vernacular English of Liberians. In the 1970s, five of the stories were published as single stories in picture-book format. They were retellings of the birth of Jesus Christ (*Every Man Heart Lay Down*, 1970), the Great Flood (*God Wash the World and Start Again*, 1971b), the parting of the Red Sea (*A Road Down in the Sea*, 1970), David and Goliath (*David He No Fear*, 1971a), and the Prodigal Son (*Hongry Catch the Foolish Boy*, 1973). The stories beg to be read aloud:

Long time past
Before you papa live
Before him papa live
Before him pa's papa live— (Graham 1971, n.p.)

These transformations of familiar Bible stories into the language and imagery of West Africans recall the way African American slaves used some of the same material to create the Negro spirituals. In both cases, people of African descent adapted and imbued material from the Judeo-Christian tradition with their own style, rhythm, and meanings and turned it into a unique art form.

It is little wonder then, that Graham's book would find favor with W.E.B. Du Bois, who devoted a chapter in *The Souls of Black Folk* (1903/1969) to what he called the "sorrow songs." Du Bois wrote the foreword for *How God Fix Jonah*, which was not originally published as juvenile literature, and praised its artistry: "This is the stuff of which literature is made" (ix). Four years after the publication of *How God Fix Jonah*, W.E.B. Du Bois would marry Lorenz Graham's sister Shirley, who herself produced a number of children's biographies of famous African Americans, such as George Washington Carver, Frederick Douglass, and Booker T. Washington. Lorenz Graham's connections to W.E.B. Du Bois circle back to the genesis of twentieth century African American children's literature, a reminder of the ways in which various threads are woven together to form that literary tradition.

The first two-thirds of the twentieth century were marked by slow, but significant, progress toward an African American children's literature. Early in the century, one strand of literature aimed at African American children was spearheaded by literary and intellectual leaders with a sociopolitical agenda—to use literature as a vehicle for countering the popular literary stereotypes of Blacks and as a means to foster self-esteem in Black children by affirming their humanity and acquainting them with Black history, African American cultural traditions, and Black heroes. By the 1930s, there was emerging a strand of African American children's literature in which the didactic function became subordinate to more general literary and artistic goals—to illuminate Black life and Black lives and explore and comment on the human condition.

At the same time, depictions of Black life were still subject to the perspectives and whims of some White editors and publishers, whose views of African lives and African American life were shaped by popular stereotypes and whose image of American readers was limited to the one they saw in the mirror. Nevertheless, by the 1950s literature by and about African Americans had become a part of the American children's literature landscape. One cannot, however, ignore the fact that most of the Black-inclusive children's literature produced for the first two-thirds of the century was neither written by Black writers nor illustrated by Black artists. During that period, one of the motivations for the development of an African American children's literature, in fact, was the existence of a body of literature in which Black characters functioned at best to evoke laughter in the presumably White readership of children's books and at worst to perpetuate blatant racial stereotypes.

BIBLIOGRAPHY OF BOOKS FOR CHILDREN AND YOUNG ADULTS

Sources other than books for children and young adults are documented in a reference list at the end of the book.

Bontemps, Arna. 1934. *You Can't Pet a Possum*. New York: Morrow.
———. 1937. *Sad-Faced Boy*. Boston: Houghton Mifflin.

———. 1941. *Golden Slippers: An Anthology of Negro Poetry for Young Readers.* New York: Harper and Brothers.

———. 1945. *We Have Tomorrow.* New York: Knopf.

———. 1948/1955. *The Story of the Negro.* New York: Knopf.

———. 1951. *Chariot in the Sky: A Story of the Jubilee Singers.* New York: Holt, Rinehart and Winston.

———. 1955. *Lonesome Boy.* Boston: Houghton Mifflin.

Bontemps, Arna and Jack Conroy. 1942. *The Fast Sooner Hound.* Illus. by Virginia Lee Burton. Boston: Houghton Mifflin.

———. 1946. *Slappy Hooper, the Wonderful Sign Painter.* Illus. by Ursula Koering. Boston: Houghton Mifflin.

———. 1951. *Sam Patch, the High Wide and Handsome Jumper.* Illus. by Paul Brown. Boston: Houghton Mifflin.

Bontemps, Arna and Langston Hughes. 1932/1993. *Popo and Fifina.* Illus. by E. Simms Campbell. New York: Oxford University Press.

Brooks, Gwendolyn. 1956. *Bronzeville Boys and Girls.* New York: HarperCollins.

Brown, Margaret Wise. 1947. *Goodnight Moon.* Illus. by Clement Hurd. New York: Harper and Row.

Bryan, Ashley, ed. 1978. *I Greet the Dawn: Poems by Paul Laurence Dunbar.* New York: Atheneum.

Burton, Virginia Lee. 1939. *Mike Mulligan and His Steam Shovel.* Boston: Houghton Mifflin.

———. *The Little House.* 1942. Boston: Houghton Mifflin.

Cullen, Countee. 1940. *The Lost Zoo.* Illus. by Charles Sebree. New York: Harper Brothers.

———. 1942. *My Lives and How I Lost Them.* New York: Harper Bros.

———. 1991. *The Lost Zoo.* Illus. by Brian Pinkney. New York: Silver Burdett.

Dunbar, Paul Laurence. 1940. *Little Brown Baby.* Ed. by Bertha Rodgers. Illus. by Erick Berry. New York: Dodd, Mead.

Gag, Wanda. 1928. *Millions of Cats.* New York: Coward McCann.

Graham, Lorenz. 1946. *How God fix Jonah.* New York: Reynal and Hitchcock.

———. 1946. *Tales of Momolu.* New York: Reynal and Hitchcock.

———. 1958. *South Town.* Chicago: Follett.

———. 1965. *North Town.* New York: Thomas Y. Crowell.

———. 1966. *I, Momolu.* Illus. by John Biggers. Claremont, CA: Graham Books.

———. 1969. *Whose Town?* New York: Thomas Y. Crowell.

———. 1970. *Every Man Heart Lay Down.* Illus. by Colleen Browning. New York: Thomas Y. Crowell.

———. 1971a. *David He No Fear.* Illus. by Ann Grifalconi. New York: Thomas Y. Crowell.

———. 1971b. *God Wash the World and Start Again.* Illus. by Clare R. Ross. New York: Thomas Y. Crowell.

———. 1973. *Hongry Catch the Foolish Boy.* Illus. by James Brown, Jr. New York: Thomas Y. Crowell.

———. 1975. *Song of the Boat.* Illus. by Leo and Diane Dillon. New York: Thomas Y. Crowell.

———. 1976. *Return to South Town.* New York: Thomas Y. Crowell.

Hamilton, Virginia. 1985. *The People Could Fly.* Illus. by Leo and Diane Dillon. New York: Knopf.

Jackson, Jesse. 1945. *Call Me Charley.* New York: Harper.

———. 1947. *Anchor Man.* New York: Harper and Row.

———. 1958. *Charley Starts from Scratch.* New York: Harper and Row.

———. 1971. *The Sickest Don't Always Die the Quickest.* New York: Doubleday.

———. 1972. *The Fourteenth Cadillac.* New York: Doubleday.

McBrown, Gertrude Parthenia. 1935. *The Picture-Poetry Book.* Illus. by Lois Mailou Jones. Washington, DC: Associated Publishers.

Newsome, Effie Lee. 1940. *Gladiola Garden*. Illus. by Lois Mailou Jones. Washington, DC: Associated Publishers.

———. 1999. *Wonders: The Best Children's Poems of Effie Lee Newsome*. Illus. by Lois Mailou Jones. Compiled and introduced by Rudine Sims Bishop. Honesdale, PA: Boyds Mills Press.

Ringgold, Faith. 1991. *Tar Beach*. New York: Crown.

Shackelford, Jane Dabney. 1944. *My Happy Days*. Washington, DC: Associated Publishers.

Tarry, Ellen. 1940. *Janie Bell*. Illus. by Myrtle Sheldon. New York: Garden City Publishing.

———. 1942. *Hezekiah Horton*. Illus. by Oliver Harrington. New York: The Viking Press.

———. and Marie Hall Ets. 1946. *My Dog Rinty*. Photos by Alexander and Alexandra Alland. New York: The Viking Press.

———. 1950. *The Runaway Elephant*. Illus. by Oliver Harrington. New York: The Viking Press.

CHAPTER 4

"Give Them Back Their Own Souls": Change and the Need for Change

Both the need for an African American children's literature and the importance of the work of Black writers in the 1930s, 1940s and 1950s come into sharp focus when understood in light of the demeaning popular depictions of Black characters in White-authored books during those three decades and for at least a century prior to that time. From as early as the nineteenth century until as late as the 1950s Black people were repeatedly represented as subhuman, often comical caricatures, not only in literature, but also in films, advertisements and commercial logos, and in popular everyday objects such as ashtrays and salt and peppershakers. The pervasiveness and enduring popularity of these stereotypes, which reflected the prevailing racial, social, and political attitudes of their day, provided important motivation for the development of an African American children's literature that would contradict those images and counteract their effects by providing children realistic images of Black people as normal human beings. Langston Hughes articulated the seriousness of the situation in a 1932 article: "Faced too often by the segregation and scorn of a surrounding White world, America's Negro children are in pressing need of books that will give them back their own souls. They do not know the beauty they possess" (Hughes 1932, 110).

Paralleling the efforts of Hughes, Arna Bontemps, Ellen Tarry, Jesse Jackson and other African American writers during these decades were the efforts of a few enlightened White writers who wrote against the prevailing negative images. Often motivated by social idealism or by developments such as the intercultural education movement, these authors eschewed obvious physical and linguistic stereotypes, and created books that featured Black characters as normal human beings. Although many of these books were praised, many were also somewhat flawed, particularly when viewed in retrospect. Those flaws, along with the abundant demeaning portrayals of Black characters, led African American librarians and other professionals to develop and publish criteria by which to assess critically books about Black characters and to continue to call for an African American literature that had the power to give Black children "back their own souls."

It was not until the late 1960s, however, that a substantial body of such literature began to emerge. At that time, several social, political and economic circumstances came together to act as catalysts for the launching of the canon of contemporary African American children's literature. The 1960s was a decade of turbulence, marked by antiwar protests, assassinations, and violent reactions to nonviolent activism. All across the nation, compelling events, including urban uprisings, focused urgent attention on the injustices and inequities suffered by African Americans and the frequently violent resistance to the prospect of African Americans being fully integrated into American society. Black people had been agitating for basic human and civic rights for long years before the 1960s, but in that decade, the struggle, brought into the national living room by television, became impossible to ignore. Consequently, both the national mood and the sociopolitical context were fertile soil for the cultivation of an African American children's literature through which Black writers could "express [their] individual dark-skinned selves" (Hughes 1926, 202) and provide for children a narrative of Black people's journey across the American hopescape as they saw it.

THROUGH A GLASS, DARKLY: A CENTURY OF BLACK LITERARY STEREOTYPES

For the most part, the dominant images of Black people in children's literature in the latter part of the nineteenth century and the first four or five decades of the twentieth century were not essentially different from the popular stereotypes found in adult literature. In a classic and frequently cited article, "The Negro Character as Seen by White Authors," Sterling Brown (1933), highly respected African American poet, scholar, and critic, analyzed the manner in which Blacks were portrayed in books written by Whites and published in the century between 1832 and the early 1930s. Brown noted seven major stereotypes that formed the picture of Black life generated by those writers: the Contented Slave, the Wretched Freeman, the Comic Negro, the Brute Negro, the Tragic Mulatto, the Local Color Negro, and the Exotic Primitive. Almost all of Brown's seven stereotypes also appeared in some variation in Black-centered literature for children, but the two that seem to have had the most resounding echoes in children's literature are the Local Color Negro and the Comic Negro. The local colorists specialized in presenting their versions of Black customs, superstitions, and speech, usually in an author-created dialect that was not only inaccurate and exaggerated, but difficult to read. The Comic Negro flourished in children's books from the turn of the century until the 1950s. This character was both someone to laugh at and someone who was always laughing since contented slaves had no cares or woes. Among the main attributes of the Comic Negro were a grandiose name, exaggerated physical features, loud clothes, bluster, wild-eyed cowardice, and the use of big words that he did not understand (190).

Children's book authors are no less vulnerable to the dominant social attitudes of their time and place than authors who write for adults. In her notable study, *Image of the Black in Children's Fiction* (1973), Dorothy Broderick analyzed a sample of children's books published between 1827 and 1967, recommended by standard references in the field of librarianship. Her book is replete with examples of the recurrent images that constitute the representation of Blacks that White writers sketched for children until the recent past. They mainly mirrored the ones that Brown discovered in his 1933 study, with some variations and adjustments attributable to the younger audience and to changes over time in the social and political climate since the 1930s.

Although her sample included books by Black authors, the overwhelming majority of the books Broderick analyzed were produced by White writers, and because they all were recommended in respected sources, she asserted that the image presented in those books was the image of Black people that the White establishment sanctioned for White children (1973, 6). One of the most remarkable of Broderick's findings is that, in the nineteenth century children's literature she examined, with two exceptions, all the Black characters in the books she analyzed were adults. These adults were either slaves or servants, present in the books to serve the needs of the White children and their families, and to provide comic relief. These caricatures reinforced for White children a sense that Whites were always and in all ways superior to Blacks, and that this was a normal and natural condition. For much of the past century and a half, the dominant literary portrait of Black people in children's books has been that delineated by White writers looking "through a glass darkly," unwilling or unable to transcend the prevalent racist or, at best, paternalistic attitudes of their day.

TOPSY AS PROTOTYPE

When Black *children* began to appear in children's books written for Whites, the main deviation from the stereotypes that Brown identified in adult literature was the addition of the stereotyped Black child, the plantation pickaninny, a variation on the Comic Negro. Both Brown and Langston Hughes identify Topsy, the character in *Uncle Tom's Cabin* (Stowe 1852/1982) as the literary model for the pickaninny in children's books. Topsy was eight or nine years old when she arrived at the St. Clare plantation, having been purchased by Tom's putative master as a gift to his Vermont cousin Miss Ophelia and as a challenge to her hypocritical criticisms of Southern slave owners. This is Topsy:

She was one of the blackest of her race; and her round shining eyes, glittering as glass beads, moved with quick and restless glances over everything in the room. Her mouth, half open with astonishment . . . displayed a white and brilliant set of teeth. Her woolly hair was braided in sundry little tails, which stuck out in every direction. (240)

Miss Ophelia is aghast, so the amused St. Clare orders Topsy to perform:

"Here, Topsy," he added, giving a whistle, as a man would to call the attention of a dog, "Give us a song now, and show us some of your dancing."
   The black, glassy eyes glittered with a kind of wicked drollery, and the thing struck up, in a clear shrill voice, an old negro melody, to which she kept time with her hands and feet, spinning round, clapping her hands, knocking her knees together in a wild, fantastic sort of time, and producing in her throat all those odd guttural sounds which distinguish the native music of her race; and finally, turning a somerset or two, and giving a prolonged closing note, as odd and unearthly as that of a steam-whistle, she came suddenly down on the carpet, and stood with her hands folded, and a most sanctimonious expression of meekness and solemnity over her face, only broken by the cunning glances which she shot askance from the corners of her eyes. (241)

That such a description would appear in a book that was antislavery and presumably sympathetic to Black people is an indication of the pervasiveness of taken-for-granted racist assumptions that were woven into the social fabric of this nation. Although *Uncle Tom's Cabin* was an important weapon in the fight against slavery, it also helped to perpetuate some of the longest-lasting stereotypes in the literary history of the United States. Abolitionist sentiment clearly could not be equated with antiracist attitudes.

LITTLE BLACK SAMBO

The most famous turn-of-the-century Black child character in children's books, however, was not a plantation pickaninny but a product of British imperialism known as Little Black Sambo. *The Story of Little Black Sambo* (Bannerman 1899) appears to be set in an imaginary India where anthropomorphic tigers thrive. The illustrations in the "authorized American version" (1899/no date) do, however, incorporate the exaggerated physical features associated with plantation and minstrel stereotypes. Enough has been written about *Little Black Sambo* to fill several chapters (e.g., Yuill 1976, Martin 2004), and it is not my intention to offer yet another lengthy critical analysis. It should be noted, however, that the purportedly East Indian setting notwithstanding, its use of the term *Sambo*, which was derogatory even at the time of its publication; its implicit ridiculing of African names (Mumbo, Jumbo); its caricatured illustrations; and its representations of Black people as primitives with enormous appetites who are also enamored of bright colors all reinforced racist notions about Black people. The craft that Bannerman displayed in creating the plot, with the child's satisfying triumph over the tigers, and her skilled use of an economical language that would appeal to young readers/ hearers of the story cannot overcome the racism, even though it may be unconscious racism, that influenced and, on some level, informed the book. Nevertheless, it remains in the minds of many a classic of English language children's literature. Recent retellings (Lester 1996; Bannerman 1899/1996, Bannerman 1899/2003) that seek to skirt around the racism of the original and preserve its story qualities attest to the book's staying power.

PICKANINNIES APLENTY: EPAMINONDAS, NICODEMUS, KOKO, AND FRAWG

It is possible that the book that introduced and helped to popularize the pickaninny as a main character in American children's books was *Epaminondas and His Auntie* (1907/1938) by Sara Cone Bryant. Bryant took a folk story, the "Lazy Jack" story with a "fool" motif, and turned it into a plantation tale. Not only was the main character a pickaninny, however, with exaggerated red lips, a grandiose name, and braids sticking out all over his head, but his mammy and his auntie were perfect plantation stereotypes, complete with exaggerated features and head rags. In reality, of course, the credit for the visual images in *Epaminondas* goes to the illustrator, Inez Hogan, who carried on the form in her Nicodemus stories of the 1930s, which would remain popular for at least two decades, into the 1950s. By the 1930s the comic pickaninny was a sanctioned image of the Black child in mainstream children's literature, and the term itself was commonly used. The first of the Nicodemus stories, *Nicodemus and His Little Sister*, appeared in 1932, the same year as *The Dream Keeper* (Hughes 1932) and *Popo and Fifina* (Bontemps and Hughes 1932/1993) to which it presented a stark contrast in images. If the jacket ads are to be believed, the Nicodemus books, of which there were ten, received favorable reviews in major newspapers such as *The New York Times* and *The Philadelphia Inquirer*. No matter how affectionately the characters were viewed in their time, however, they were merely extensions of the comic Negro of the plantation. Their images, their language, and their actions were designed to draw laughter.

One of the most offensive of the 1930s books was *Frawg* (1930) by Annie Vaughan Weaver. Frawg lives on an Alabama plantation with his brothers John, Bush, and Shine; his sisters Viney, Iwilla (short for "I will arise and go to my Father") and Evaleena; and his dog Buckeye. The book opens and closes with images of Frawg and watermelon. In between are four comical adventures. The humor comes from the characterizations of the family as lazy, mischievous, and not too bright; from the caricatured images, and most notably, from the language spoken by the characters, including the dog, who has apparently acquired the dialect of his owners. Carrying a bucket of six worms on the way to a fishing expedition, Buckeye the dog complains: "Wait jes' er minute, chillun, tell I resses er lil spell. Dese wums is de heavies' things I ever toted" (16).

Frawg included an afterword by Hugh Lofting, of Dr. Dolittle fame. He endorses Vaughan's authority, stating that she really knows "coloured" people, having been brought up among them (127–128). In fact, much of the assumed authority of White authors to present the stereotypes they created came from their claim to *know* Black people from having lived with them, generally on the family's plantations. However, most such writers "knew" Blacks only as servants or menial workers, and were hardly likely to view them as social or intellectual equals. It seems not to have occurred to these writers that, given the inequality inherent in their relationship with Blacks, they were unlikely to have the faintest idea what the lives of their subjects were really like, or that they were prepared to see only the ways in which Black people seemed different from themselves—odd, quaint, comical.

Another book in which the White southern author claims special knowledge of her Black subjects is *Narcissus an' de Chillun: Final Adventures of Those Plummer Children* by Christine Noble Govan (1938). Govan is a master at creating the "local color Negro." On the title page is a sketch of a pickaninny running barefoot, looking for all the world like Topsy. Narcissus is a maid, the mother of twins named Sears and Roebuck. Their language is every bit as strange as that of literary plantation slaves. The characterizations are replete with the "standard" comic stereotypes: flashing White teeth, grinning, a "raggedy" dog, fear of "ha'nts," funny names, simplistic though fervent religious beliefs, a fondness for big words they cannot pronounce, and a fondness for chicken.

Govan states in her introduction:

I have tried to give a good idea of the negroes [*sic*] of that time and how we felt towards them. Their stories and songs, their laughter and quarrels, their praise and their scoldings were as much a part of our lives as the food we ate. They took great pride in us and only scolded us for our own good. Each one wanted her "White folks' chillun" to shine the best. Like the simple good times we had outdoors, the kindly old darkies are dying out. Their patience and service will never be forgotten by those who knew them, and I wanted my own children to see them as we did. (xii)

The fact that the book was published by a major publisher means that not only Mrs. Govan's children, but numerous American children were offered her perspective on the "kindly old darkies." If by the end of the 1930s, the "darkies" were beginning to die out, their literary demise has been slow and painful.

The pickaninny was still popular as late as the 1950s. *Stories of Little Brown Koko* (Hunt 1951), for example, entertained White readers with the antics of a little boy and his mother. Koko was in essence an object of ridicule—an eye-rolling, head-scratching imp with a voracious appetite, especially for chocolate cake and watermelon. When his "big round eyes" were not rolling, they were frequently "bugged way out on stems." He and his Mammy spoke a made-up language that adds to their portrayal as comic characters who exist merely to amuse White children with supposedly superior intellects, habits, and values:

Why Mammy! Where 'bouts air my new first reader book, nohow?" asked Little Brown Koko as he picked up his lunch pail.
   "Lan'-sakes-alive-ter-goodness! I doesn't know, shore," answered his nice, good, ole, big, fat, black Mammy just sweeping away for dear life. "Where 'bouts did you-all put hit las' night, honey-chile? (18)

The narrative was reinforced and extended by the illustrations, which show Koko and his Mammy with large white lips, large white eyes, and a preference for bright red. It is the popularity of such portrayals, even through the middle of the twentieth century, that has made contemporary Black librarians, critics of children's literature, and Black parents sensitive to any portrayals of Black children that echo these images, or appear to portray Black children in a similar light.

As the work of Brown and Broderick makes clear, from fairly early in the nineteenth the century and for a century or more beyond, the popular images of Black people in mainstream children's literature consisted of a set of sanctioned stereotypes designed to entertain White children and reinforce their position of assumed social and racial superiority, making it crucial for African Americans to develop a literature that would contradict those images and offer Black children a dignified vision of themselves. Although it would take some time for this literature to develop, changes in the ways White writers and artists portrayed Blacks in children's literature did come gradually, and were affected by at least three developments— recognition by the children's literature establishment of a Black child readership, criticisms and protests by Black professionals, and the advent of the intercultural education movement.

SIGNS OF CHANGE

RECOGNIZING THE BLACK CHILD AS READER

By the 1930s, some authors and children's literature professionals had begun to recognize Black children as readers and to call for books that would be suitable and appealing to them. One White writer who had pioneered even earlier in efforts to provide realistic and affirming literature featuring Black children was Mary White Ovington. Born in Brooklyn just after the Civil War ended, and imbued from childhood with liberal and Unitarian ideals, Ovington became a Socialist, a feminist and a social reformer. One of the founders of the NAACP and an admirer of W.E.B. Du Bois, Ovington was, in fact, chairperson of the board of the NAACP at the time *The Brownies' Book* was in existence. Her background and her work with the NAACP may have made her especially aware of the dearth of acceptable books for and about Black children. In any case, she wrote two novels, *Hazel* (1913) and *Zeke* (1931), and co-edited *The Upward Path: A Reader for Black Children* (1920).

In the preface to *Hazel* (1913/1972), Ovington makes clear her intentions and her presumed primary audience. Referring to her years of experience with "these soft-eyed, velvet cheeked" friends, she asserts that she wrote the story for Black children, believing that they might yearn to see themselves and their lives reflected in books for a change. She also expressed the hope that the book might awaken sympathy in any White girls who might read it (v–vi). Thus, Ovington's expressed goal was to make the Black characters in her books visible as ordinary human beings, with ordinary life problems, and the capacity and will to solve those problems.

Hazel is the story of an eleven-year-old girl who, after she and her widowed mother fall on hard times in Boston, spends a winter with her paternal grandmother in Alabama. Hazel finds life in the South quite different from life in Boston, but with Granny's help, she adjusts, learns some important lessons about life, and regains her health. She returns to Boston better for the experience both physically and mentally. In the context of early twentieth century American children's literature, *Hazel* was unusually realistic. It recognized racial discrimination as problematic. It portrayed the Tyler social circle as being socially, educationally, and culturally the equal of their White neighbors, and recognized class differences among Blacks. It granted dignity to all of its important Black characters, even though it also included two "no-account" Black men as minor characters. It maintains that wisdom is not the exclusive possession of people with formal education, and suggests thematically that having greater advantages than others gives one the opportunity, even the obligation, to help those less fortunate. From the vantage point of the late twentieth century, *Hazel* seems dated in the stances it assumes towards racial issues, probably reflecting the social realities of its day. Whatever its flaws, however, *Hazel* is notable as a counter to the minstrel and plantation images of Blacks in most of the literature of the day, and possibly unique as a turn-of-the-century novel in which working class or middle class Black children could have seen something of themselves reflected.

Ovington and Pritchard's reader for "colored children," *The Upward Path*, was published in 1920. It was an anthology of poems, stories, sketches, and speeches from Black writers. Representing a wide range of Black thought, it included contributions from Phillis Wheatley, Paul Laurence Dunbar, Booker T. Washington, W.E.B. Du Bois, Jessie Fauset, William Wells Brown, Charles W. Chesnutt, James Weldon Johnson, and others. Later, Ovington also plucked one of the minor child characters from *Hazel* and developed him into the title character of a young adult novel, *Zeke* (1931). As was the case with *Hazel*, all of Ovington's works for children were invariably welcomed as affirming contributions to children's literature about Blacks.

As a challenge to the prevailing literary treatment of Black characters in children's books, Mary White Ovington's work was a harbinger of things to come. By the early 1930s, the professional library establishment and some enlightened writers and artists had begun to pay attention in print to Black children as readers and to realize that their needs were not being met. The *Children's Library Yearbook* of 1932 carries two pieces of note. An article by Ruth Theobald, "Library Service for Negro Children," reported on the status of such services and discussed issues such as the lack of library services available to Negroes living in the South, the inadequate number of trained Negro librarians nationwide, and the need for reliable information about the reading interests of Negro children. Her reference list indicates that the American Library Association (ALA) had been reporting on library services to Negroes for more than a decade before the 1932 yearbook, although that attention had little apparent effect on the production of African American children's literature.

Theobald called for books that would not be too difficult, and in which "the Negro child may be able to identify himself satisfactorily with the story he reads" (1932, 116). Appended to her article was a list of seventeen recommended

"Books About Negro Life for Negro Children," presumably meeting her criteria. Mary White Ovington's three books were included, as were collective biographies by Arthur Fauset, Elizabeth Ross Haynes, and Carter G. Woodson, a book on the life and works of Paul Laurence Dunbar, and Langston Hughes's newly published *The Dream Keeper* (1932). Of the remaining nine, four were set in Africa. The others were *Little Black Sambo* (Bannerman 1899), *Frawg* (Weaver 1930), and three Joel Chandler Harris collections of Uncle Remus stories. Theobald concedes that *Sambo* and *Frawg* might be troublesome to older children, although she asserts that younger children enjoy both books. The list is a revealing commentary on the state of American children's books about Black people, particularly contemporary Black children, in the early 1930s.

Although Bader (1976) cites the Theobald list as the first widely circulated recommended bibliography of books about the Negro (373), the same yearbook also carried a second list of recommended books, created by Langston Hughes (1932). Well aware of the dearth of suitable books about and for Black children, Hughes took the opportunity to criticize the kinds of children's books available at the time:

So far, the children's booklets on Negro themes, other than the folk-tales, have been of the pickaninny variety, poking fun (however innocently) at the little youngsters whose skins are not white, and holding up to laughter the symbol of the watermelon and the chicken. Perhaps Topsy set the pattern; Sambo and the others came along—amusing undoubtedly to the white child, but like an unkind word to one who has known too many hurts to enjoy the additional pain of being laughed at. (109)

Hughes suggests five books on Negro life that he feels are suitable, four of which overlap the Theobald list: two of the collective biographies and Ovington's two novels. In addition, he recommended a book on Haitian kings. It is noteworthy that the books about Sambo, Frawg, and Uncle Remus do not appear on Hughes's list. Hughes sees Black children oppressed by racism and in danger of losing their very souls and calls for literature in which they can see reflections of the beauty of their own humanity. Theobald, on the other hand, while recognizing the lack of suitable literature, describes in a classically paternalistic tone "Negro" children, and Black people in general, as underdeveloped and dependent: "The Negro child, by his friendliness, his responsiveness, his happy spirit, his childlike dependence, enlists our aid. What we do for him will find recompense in the worthy development of his race" (Theobald 1932, 119). The difference in perspective between Hughes and Theobald not only accounts for the differences in their lists but also is an intimation of the controversies over suitable books for and about Black children that would erupt publicly in the decade to follow.

As more librarians and authors responded to the growing demand for realistic books by and about true-to-life Black children, more White authors and artists entered the arena and more changes began to occur. One case in point is that of Ellis Credle (Bader, 143, 375), whose Black-inclusive books exemplify some of the changes beginning to take place in the late 1930s and early 1940s. In the span of four years, Credle published three books that featured Black characters. The first, *Across the Cotton Patch* (1935) was a typical plantation story, with Black twins named Atlantic and Pacific who spoke the expected "Negro dialect." The second, *Little Jeemes Henry* (1936), which might be called a transition book, included both visual, linguistic and character stereotypes and a portrayal of a resourceful and attractive little boy with hard-working and responsible parents. By the time of the third book, *Flop-Eared Hound* (1938), Credle and her publisher were aware of the growing controversy over dialect and visual images. The characters did not use "Negro dialect" and the book was illustrated with photographs (Bader 1976, 375).

Since photographs avoid one of the more objectionable aspects of books about Blacks produced in this period by White writers, a number of books illustrated with photographs appeared around this time. One such book is *Tobe* (1939) by Stella Gentry Sharpe. *Tobe*, which was quite popular when it was published, chronicles the daily life of a Black farm family. Although the language of *Tobe* is stilted and reads like a primer (Here are Mother and Daddy./ On Sundays they go to church./ They do not go to school.), the photographs are remarkable for a book of the time, as is the dignity with which the family and their life are represented. Stilted as the language is, however, it employs Standard English grammar and vocabulary and thereby avoids controversy by eliminating the objectionable plantation dialect that had been commonly used to represent the speech and imply at best, ignorance and at worst, stupidity in Black characters in children's books.

BLACK LIBRARIANS TAKE A STAND

A controversy played out in the pages of *Publisher's Weekly* in 1941–1942, revolving around the use of dialect, demonstrates that change did not come easily and highlights the entry of African American librarians into the public conversation and their willingness to assert their authority as experts on Black life and literature. In the August 30, 1941 issue of *Publisher's Weekly*, Eva Knox Evans, a writer and a teacher in the kindergarten at Atlanta University described an experience she had with her five-year-old "colored" kindergarten students. At the time, *dialect*, or *Negro dialect* in particular, referred to the made-up spellings, ungrammatical constructions, and misused or made-up vocabulary that were characteristic of many popular books about Blacks. Negro dialect as used in books of the time marked its speakers as illiterate, ignorant, and often comical. It was a mainstay of the creators of literary "local color Negroes," and many writers were reluctant to relinquish it. Evans had written *Araminta* (1935), a collection of stories about a little "colored" city girl, a speaker of Standard English, who visits her grandmother in the country. Evans had read the manuscript to the children in her class as it developed, so she was puzzled when, on seeing the pictures in the finished book, they were surprised to learn that Araminta was "colored" since she didn't "talk colored." When reminded that they did not talk colored either, the children agreed, but declared that *in books* colored people do. Evans went on in her article to bemoan the fact that these children had been conditioned not to expect to see themselves reflected in books in any realistic way. She also pointed out that Negro dialect was hard to read and had become passé in any case and recommended a number of well-written and appealing books about Negro children that did not use dialect.

In a special feature, "Negro Dialect in Children's Books" (October 18, 1941), *Publishers' Weekly* printed indignant responses from three White women from Tennessee—a bookstore owner, a librarian, and Christine Noble Govan, author of the books featuring the twins Sears and Roebuck. They argued that books incorporating dialect—and pickaninnies—were extremely popular, even among Black children; therefore, it must follow that they were readable and appealing.

The bookseller declared that pickaninnies "are in all truth among the cutest of God's creatures!" (1556). Both the bookseller and the librarian cited Annie Vaughn Weaver's *Frawg* (1930), Inez Hogan's Nicodemus stories, and Christine Govan's books as among the best and most popular. Govan invoked the authority of her own first-hand knowledge of Negroes to declare that while Evans may have been accurate in rendering the speech of the children *she* was teaching, those children were not representative of Negroes in general. Govan's defensive reaction suggests that Evans had touched a sensitive nerve. She rejected the idea that her books ridicule Blacks and more than once declared her genuine affection and sympathy for "the negro." She and her fellow protesters also argued for dialect as a means of conveying the folk flavor of a people's speech and a means of preserving cultural traditions. Ms. Govan even went so far as to invoke Black singers of spirituals and Black writers such as Langston Hughes and Arno Bontemps as examples of artists who employed dialect.

The final published response to the Evans piece came from a group of seven Black librarians and teachers, including Charlemae Hill Rollins of the Chicago Public Library (Poole et al. 1942). They decried the inaccuracy of the dialect used by Weaver and Govan and its inapplicability to contemporary Negroes, as well as the tendency to ascribe the same language patterns to all Negroes. They also pointed out the fallacy in claiming that books that are purchased from bookstores or borrowed from a public library necessarily reflect children's tastes, when in fact the purchasers and many of the borrowers are probably adults. They disclaimed any similarity between what Bontemps, Hughes, and other Black artists had done in rendering the flavor of Black speech and the books created by Govan, Weaver, and others. Finally, they maintained that, good intentions notwithstanding, Black children are harmed—embarrassed and humiliated—by portrayals such as Ms. Govan's.

This controversy suggests that a segment of the children's literature community had both an emotional and a financial stake in maintaining the stereotypes of Blacks with which they had become comfortable. The Black librarians' entry into the fray served notice that Black teachers and librarians had an equal stake in fostering change. These controversies have their roots in the social history of the nation, in the differing functions that Black literature has been called on to serve for different readers and writers, and in the struggle of Blacks to assert their own voices and make them heard.

THE INTERCULTURAL EDUCATION MOVEMENT AND BOOKS ABOUT BLACK PEOPLE

By the 1940s, an intercultural education movement, a precursor to the current multicultural education movement, was under way in the United States. It aimed to decrease tensions among racial, ethnic, and religious groups while raising the self-esteem of minorities and integrating them into the American mainstream (Olneck 1990, 147) The Service Bureau for Intercultural Education was founded in New York City in 1934. Initially concerned with assimilating new immigrants, by the mid-1940s the emphasis in intercultural education had shifted to a concern with race relations. A major race riot in Detroit in 1943, in the middle of the war years, and a number of outbreaks in other cities led to a flurry of interest in interracial relations and an increased emphasis, in the field of education, on positive books about Blacks as well as White ethnic and religious groups (Montalto 1982).

Many advocates of intercultural education believed that, if people belonging to different racial and ethnic groups could get to know or know about one another, tensions would be erased, tolerance would be increased, and minority groups would become truly integrated into American society. Children's books were considered to have great potential as vehicles to help children to develop positive attitudes toward others and increase the self-esteem of Black and other so-called minority or ethnic children. Articles with titles such as "Intercultural Books for Children" (Trager 1945) and "Books that Build Better Racial Attitudes" (Breed 1945) began to appear in education and library journals. They offered lists of books recommended for their potential to "further better, wiser, more understanding, more democratic human relations" (Trager 1945, 138). One of the characteristics of children's literature about Blacks produced as part of the intercultural education movement was that Black people were portrayed as realistic human beings rather than caricatures. A second was that Blacks in books were beginning to be portrayed as a part of the larger American society, whether as one distinct piece of a mosaic or as part of the proverbial melting pot. Important books by two White writers exemplify this trend.

FLORENCE CRANNELL MEANS: REFLECTING THE AMERICAN MOSAIC

Florence Crannell Means was well known and highly respected for her fiction featuring members of groups representing the diverse peoples of the United States. The daughter of a Baptist minister, Means had many opportunities to interact with people from diverse backgrounds who had been guests in her parents' home. She came to see American society as a mosaic and wrote about her attempts to "grow race friendship while trying in the compass of a shelf of books to make a mosaic of young America" (Means 1940, 40). To that end, she wrote books about girls of several so-called minority groups.

One of her most highly regarded books was *Shuttered Windows* (Means 1938), a novel in which a young woman, following the death of her mother, journeys from Minneapolis to an island off the coast of South Carolina to spend time with her great grandmother and attend a local girls' boarding school. A high school senior and talented musician used to a comfortable life and a well-equipped city school, Harriet is at first appalled by the economic conditions and the lack of formal education she finds on the island. Although she loves Great Grandmother, she fears that she cannot possibly achieve her life goals living on the island. However, she grows to appreciate and value the island people and to recognize that she can not only achieve her personal goal as a musician, but also serve others by becoming a teacher and thereby help to "uplift the race."

Unlike the creators of the plantation and local color stories, Means acknowledged the difficulty of trying "to interpret other peoples" (1940, 40) and asserts that "the writer must herself deeply know the people she's writing about. *She must go to them—when they are of her day*—and *be of them as well as among them*" (35, emphasis added). *Shuttered Windows* grew out of a visit Means made to Mather School to gather background information for a series of short stories to be written for a church publication. At the end of her visit, a group of the girls requested that Mrs. Means "write a book about us, M'm. Like we were white girls" (Means 1940, 40), underscoring the dearth of fiction featuring characters other than Whites. To make the book as accurate as possible, Means read the manuscript aloud to two senior English classes at the school and made revisions based on their comments (Andrews 1946, 20). In a further bid for accuracy, Means also wrote to Arna Bontemps to seek help with handling the Gullah dialect (Vandergrift 1993). Viewed in light of its historical context, *Shuttered Windows* is an exceptional book. The character of Harriet is well drawn and believable of Harriet's (and by extension, African Americans') proud heritage and presents a sense of the linguistic, educational, and socioeconomic diversity to be found among African Americans. It gives a reasonably accurate sense of the islanders' Gullah dialect without appearing to ridicule its speakers.

Shuttered Windows is dedicated to Mather School, and presumably African Americans constitute one of the projected audiences for the book. In one sense, Means took it on herself to give literary voice to a group she saw as having little opportunity—or power—to make their own voices heard. In making Harriet an outsider, a Northerner, however, Means also gave herself an opportunity to present the school and the island as it might be seen by a White middle-class reader, who might also be considered an "outsider." Writing two years after the publication of *Shuttered Windows*, Means had this to say about the importance of books about the American mosaic: "Children of today's varied racial groups—wouldn't it change something if Rabbit-Girl, Willie-Lou, O Mitsu San, Priscilla, were to understand each other better? If Priscilla could see why some of these are backward and slow of adjustment?" (1940, 35). The identification of some groups as "backward and slow of adjustment" is an unconscious revelation of the extent to which such attitudes were a part of the White national consciousness. Even a White person of goodwill, such as Means, was not immune to them. The assumption that it is Priscilla who needs to understand the conditions that lead to people becoming backward and slow of adjustment implies that the Priscillas of the nation are a primary audience for these books. It is this emphasis on understanding cultural groups other than one's own that places Means's work in the intercultural movement and differentiates it to some extent from much of the writing for children that comes from African American authors.

MARGUERITE DE ANGELI AND *BRIGHT APRIL*

Books about African Americans that were produced as part of the intercultural education movement often tried to achieve their goals by showing that many Black people were just like White Americans. In their attempts to promote understanding, they were often not much concerned with a focus on or challenge to racism as an institution or a societal affliction but on racism represented as the prejudices of individuals that can be overcome with knowledge. This perspective is exemplified by the work of writer and artist Marguerite de Angeli, who is probably best known today for her illustrated collection of Mother Goose rhymes, which has become a standard. She created books about children of White ethnic and religious groups—Polish, Amish, Pennsylvania Dutch, Mennonite, Quaker—as well as *Bright April* (1946), a book about a young Black girl living in Philadelphia during World War II.

For its sympathetic portrayal of an attractive contemporary middle-class urban family and their encounters with racial discrimination, *Bright April* (de Angeli 1946) is considered a landmark book in American children's literature. It is also notable because it explicitly—through the characters' dialogue—espoused the values and ideals of the intercultural education movement: differences between people are only superficial, skin deep so to speak; prejudices against individuals can be mitigated by getting to know them as people; every American subgroup has made contributions to the larger American culture; "to be unkind to anyone because of his race or religion is neither Christian nor American" (24).

Bright April presented an idealized Black family of the 1940s: April's father is a postman; her sister is in nursing school; her adult brother Ken, who had studied architecture at college, is away in the army; her teenaged brother Tom is infatuated by drums and the noise of drumming; an uncle teaches music at a famous school in New York; her mother does not work outside the home. They live in a racially integrated neighborhood in Germantown, a section of Philadelphia; April attends an integrated school, has both Black and White friends, and belongs to an integrated Brownie troop. Most of the book is devoted to giving a sense of the family as "typically" American—close-knit, loving, thrifty, hard working, and clean (especially clean; there are at least ten references to their cleanliness—on pages 12, 17, 22, 23, 27, 28, 49, 60, 65, and 84—a tacit commentary on commonly held stereotypes of the time). Given her emphasis on the Bright family's embracing of middle-class American values and mores, it is likely that de Angeli was attempting to persuade a White audience to accept them, and by extension other Blacks in the same mold, as part of the larger American "family."

For the Bright family, racism and discrimination are facts of life. Papa has been passed over for a promotion for which he was the best-qualified candidate; Ken complains about being restricted to performing menial work in the military in spite of his college education. The major conflicts arise when April has two encounters with racism. A Brownie Scout scoffs at the idea that April could become a hat designer and "the boss of a big store on Chestnut Street" (41). Another girl, Phyllis, refuses to sit next to her at a Brownie picnic on April's tenth birthday. In the first case, the Brownie leader tells April that she must "be so well trained that you will be able to take your place in the world. You may find you will have to go somewhere you don't want to go in order to be a greatest service. Perhaps by the time you are grown up you can go anywhere you want to go" (42). In the second instance, the leader reminds April that the Brownie motto, "Do Your Best," means "allowing for the thoughtlessness of others as well as trying to be thoughtful yourself. It means forgiving because someone else doesn't know what she is saying" (78). Furthermore, Phyllis is a lonely, motherless child who has not had the benefits of scouting. In the end, Phyllis becomes April's friend because she, Phyllis, realizes that they have shared interests, that April is as clean as she, and that the major difference between them is superficial—their skins are different colors. At home, April's mother reinforces the idea that knowledge will drive away prejudice, ending the book with the Bible quotation: "Ye shall know the TRUTH, and the truth shall make you free!" (88).

Clearly, the book was not without its flaws. The African American characters, attractive though they are, have a "color-me-brown" look; that is, they look very much like de Angeli's White characters, particularly the children, who also resemble each other. It is difficult to believe the opening episode of the book, in which nine-year-old April, who attends a racially integrated school, learns for the first time that she is brown. From the distance of half a century, one might wish that less of the responsibility for being acceptable, accepting, and forgiving had been placed on April's shoulders, and that the book had been informed by a deeper understanding of the nature of racism. Nevertheless, at a time when literary pickaninnies were still popular, de Angeli's *Bright April* was a welcome antidote.

TWO IS A TEAM: DISMISSING DIFFERENCE

Another landmark book that appeared in the 1940s was Lorraine and Jerrold Beim's *Two Is a Team* (1945), usually cited as the first American picture book to portray a friendship between a White child and a Black child in which the two are on equal footing. In that regard, it was a major step forward. *Two Is a Team* was also the first children's book illustrated by Ernest Crichlow, a well-known African American artist who later illustrated several other children's books, the best known of which is Dorothy Sterling's *Mary Jane* (1959), a book about school integration. *Two Is a Team* is usually noted for its reliance on the illustrations as the only clue to the racial identities of the characters. In other words, race is treated as if it has no more significance than hair color or eye color.

Ted and Paul, who are the same age and the same height, play together every day after school. Paul suggests they pool their resources and make a coaster. Unable to agree on the best way to go about the task, each boy stalks off and makes his own. When they try to race each other, their poorly made carts cause them to continually crash into neighborhood residents. Obliged to pay for the damage, the contrite boys agree to share a job delivering groceries. For that they need a wagon, so they pool the resources from their individual coasters to make one good wagon and earn enough to pay their debts. Friends again, they have a good time driving their wagon down the hill.

Part of the significance of *Two Is a Team* is that it takes the focus on inclusion in a new direction, representing a move from the mosaic to the melting pot. It celebrates the boys' sameness and refuses to recognize—in the written text—the one socially significant physical difference between them and thereby hints that the difference is not neutral, but undesirable. At a time when Black fighters were helping to "make the world safe for democracy" while suffering discrimination and segregation in the armed forces, a "color blind" society may have seemed like an important advance in human relations, and *Two Is a Team* was highly praised by both Black and White children's literature specialists and critics.

Ten years earlier, Eva Knox Evans had omitted any mention of race or color in the text of *Araminta* (1935), and that fact, coupled with her refusal to employ what then passed for a literary "Negro dialect," had resulted in her pupils' surprise when they saw the book for the first time. It is interesting that, during the prepublication readings to her kindergartners, Evans thought they would recognize themselves, in the absence of any textual or visual clues, simply on the basis of the character's activities. "I made her exactly like the real life Aramintas that I knew. Everyday I read them a new account of Araminta's doings, and every day I got a new suggestion for something else that she might do. . . . She was real and alive and kin to them. And I felt that she was so real that I need not mention in the text that she was colored" (1941, 650). That the children did not imagine Araminta as "colored" is both a testament to the rarity of true-to-life Black children in American children's literature of the time and evidence of one possible effect of ignoring racial/cultural identity as an aspect of a Black character. It is also a further testament to the existence of at least two parallel threads in children's literature written by Whites about Blacks: one attempting to portray and illuminate the specifics of Black life and Black lives and cultures, the other attempting to integrate Black people into American children's literature, and implicitly into American society, by ignoring or de-emphasizing those specifics.

REACHING OUT TO TEACHERS:
WE BUILD TOGETHER

If the interculturalists were to reach children and mold or change their attitudes through books, then they would also have to reach teachers, who were an important influence on children's reading and access to books. The National Council of Teachers of English (NCTE) provided one pathway to the classroom through its membership of several thousand elementary, high school, and college teachers. In the spirit of the intercultural education movement, NCTE published an annotated bibliography, *We Build Together: A Reader's Guide to Negro Life and Literature for Elementary and High School Use* (WBT; 1941/1948/1967). It was edited by Charlemae Hill Rollins, one of the Black librarians who had responded to the *Publishers' Weekly* controversy. Rollins was then a children's librarian in Chicago, and she would go on to become one of the most active and highly respected librarian leaders in the field of children's literature. The publication signaled the intention of African American children's literature professionals to affect, through the wide-reaching influence of NCTE, the kind of Black-inclusive literature that was chosen and read in classrooms around the nation.

The influence of the intercultural education perspective on WBT is evident in the references made in the introduction to "using literature to advance democracy," promoting "more democratic attitudes among boys and girls," and making available "books which help young readers live together." The nod to the intercultural movement aside, however, the declared purposes of the bibliography were (1) "to present the underlying principles which we as Negroes feel should guide a teacher in choosing books for young people" and (2) "to list in a systematic fashion many books now available which depict Negro life honestly and accurately" (1941, 3) This list, then, was in some sense a declaration of the rights of Black professionals to define the ways in which Black people should be represented in children's books, to artistically re-create literary Black people in their own image, and to protect Black children from ridicule and damage to their self-esteem.

There would be two subsequent editions of WBT, one in 1948, one in 1967. The three editions of the bibliography constitute a chronicle of change in children's literature about African Americans over the quarter century between World War II and the civil rights movement of the 1960s. In the twenty-six years between 1941 and 1967, the number of Black-inclusive books Rollins deemed suitable for children (Grades 1–9) had about quadrupled. The first edition of WBT included about 200 titles, only 59 of which were recommended for children younger than high school age. The 1948 edition included 500 titles, 90 of which were recommended for elementary and junior high school use. In the interim between the second and third editions, American society was profoundly affected by a number of events, including the Supreme Court order to desegregate schools, major events in the civil rights movement, and the Watts riots. By 1967, the numbers of children's books including Black characters had increased sufficiently that the editor could be selective and could eliminate adult books for high school students, which had been very prominent in the first edition. The third edition included only about 244 entries (some books appeared more than once), but all were suitable for elementary and junior high school.

In the time between the first and last editions of WBT (Rollins 1941/1967), White-authored children's literature about African Americans had, in general, shifted focus from Blacks as subjects for the amusement of White children to Black characters as instruments for helping White children to develop democratic ideals, although there had been and continued to be exceptions. Writing in the introduction to the third edition about the period following World War II, Rollins asserts the importance of integrating Negroes into American life and contends that the best way to do so is for Americans to understand and accept Negroes as fellow human beings. She argues that making available suitable books about Blacks is one of the most effective means for helping children to gain this understanding (1967, x). One significant consequence of this emphasis on using children's books as a vehicle for integrating Black people fully into American life and accepting Black people as fellow human beings was that a substantial portion of black-inclusive fictional books became outward looking, *about* Black people, primarily addressed to non-Blacks.

Black readers were not so much ignored, however, as taken for granted. While it was assumed that White children needed to learn about the humanity and the ordinariness of Black people as well as their "contributions" to the larger society, it was also assumed that Black children would be interested in books in which they could find reflections of themselves and their lives, and that they needed to discover something of their own history, culture, and the inspiring achievements of individual Black people. The many biographies, autobiographies, and historical works on the list were intended to meet the needs of both audiences. Black authors appear on the list mainly as writers of nonfiction: history, poetry, biography, and autobiography.

Societal changes were also reflected in the themes, topics, and other aspects of the texts of children's books about Blacks. This is particularly true of fiction for children, 90 percent of which was created by White authors. In general over the three editions, the focus of Black-inclusive children's literature shifted from rural to urban settings, from the South to more varied settings within the United States, from a substantial number of books set outside the United States to a preponderance of books set within the United States. In the books on the lists, Black characters had advanced from Little Black Sambo to Peter of *The Snowy Day* (Keats 1963). A substantial portion of the recommended picture books and fictional books feature friendships between White children or youth and Black children or youth, or they have Blacks as minor characters in a White child's story. Another notable aspect of the 1967 edition is the number of books, such as *Two Is a Team* (Beim and Beim 1945), in which only the pictures indicate that the main character (or any character) is Black, an apparent attempt to diminish or ignore the social significance of both race and culture. Thus, even though they had become more visible in children's literature overall, Black characters frequently appeared as part of an interracial cast of characters, or they were portrayed as the American "Everychild."

In creating these bibliographies, then, Rollins and her colleagues were attempting to create in the minds of White teachers and children a new image of Black people in the United States. That Rollins was conscious of White readers as a primary audience for the lists and for the titles that were included on them is indicated by this explanation, quoted from the introduction for the 1967 edition, for the inclusion of *Little Black Sambo* in the first edition: "Because *Little Black Sambo*, written and illustrated by Helen Bannerman (1901) has both pictures and text which have given great delight to white children the world over, it was included in the earliest list" (xvii). The third edition, as did the second, omits *Sambo* and explains why it is offensive to so many people.

The presumption of a predominantly White audience was also a presumption of ignorance about the ways in which books had been and continued to be offensive to Black readers. Consequently, from 20 to 30 percent of each of the three editions of WBT is taken up with a discussion of guidelines or criteria for judging children's books about Negroes. Four themes dominated the criteria: (1) a call for accurate representation—both in illustrations and in text—of Black people as realistic human beings with human physical features and characteristics; (2) the obligation to reflect Black language patterns accurately and to avoid offensive terminology; (3) the importance of portraying relationships between contemporary Blacks and Whites based on an assumption of equality; (4) the desirability of not stressing differences of class, race, color, education, or religion in any unfavorable way (1948, 4).

These criteria developed as much out of the goals and functions that the books were expected to fulfill as the need to challenge the ways Black people were being portrayed in the popular literature of the day. With some refinement and revisions, this set of criteria would become, over the next few decades, a standard guide for assessing the suitability of children's books about Blacks. Their longevity underscores the effect of the differing ideological and political perspectives that inform and drive the creation of American children's literature about Blacks and the differing expectations about the functions such literature is to serve.

A comparison of the selection criteria listed in the first edition of *We Build Together* (Rollins 1941) and the goals of *The Brownie's Book* of two decades earlier provides a clear demonstration of some of those different expectations and the different audiences each publication was trying to reach. Both lists are reminders of the extent to which children's literature in general and specifically Black-inclusive literature are expected to fulfill a didactic function. Although *The Brownies' Book* claimed to be open to all readers and to teach "Universal love and brotherhood," its face was in reality turned toward "the children of the sun." Its expected outcomes, which have to do with building self-esteem in Black children and educating them about their history and heritage, as well as instilling particular cultural and social values, are explicitly expressed. *We Build Together*, in contrast, faces outward to address those—publishers, teachers, writers, artists—who had the power to affect the ways Black people were portrayed and perceived by the larger White society. This is not to suggest that WBT ignores Black readers, but that its main purpose is to promote books that persuade readers to accept Black people as fellow human beings and fellow citizens of a democracy.

By the time the third edition of WBT was published in 1967, the need for an African American children's literature was well established. Librarians such as Ruth Theobald and Charlemae Hill Rollins had called attention to the scarcity of suitable books about Black people and Black lives. Interculturalists and others had made a case for such books as important vehicles for promoting democratic ideals among children. In addition to African American writers such as Arna Bontemps, White authors such as Florence Crannell Means had demonstrated that there was a readership for books that featured Black characters. The continued call for accurate or realistic representations of Black characters and Black lives, however, indicates that the available children's literature about African Americans did not adequately represent the perspectives of African Americans. It was near the end of the 1960s that African American children's literature began to blossom in the light of a society undergoing a sociopolitical sea change.

CHANGING TIMES: CATALYSTS FOR THE EMERGENCE OF CONTEMPORARY AFRICAN AMERICAN LITERATURE

Among the major developments in the late 1960s and early 1970s was a marked upsurge in the numbers of children's books about African Americans. One incentive for this increase came from the federal government when, in 1965, President Lyndon Baines Johnson, as part of his attempt to wage War on Poverty and create "The Great Society," signed the Elementary and Secondary Education Act (ESEA). It made available large sums of money for the purpose of equalizing educational opportunity and improving school achievement for educationally disadvantaged children from low-income families, vast numbers of whom were African American. Part of this effort was focused on providing materials and resources that reflected the life experiences of these children in an effort to make schooling seem more relevant to their lives. Since a substantial portion of ESEA funds was available for the purchase of trade/library books, children's book publishers began to try to meet the needs of school districts—and to benefit from those federal funds—by producing more books that featured African Americans. The demand for such books also helped to open the doors of the major publishing houses to more African American writers and artists, enhancing the potential for the development of a body of African American children's literature.

NANCY LARRICK: "THE ALL-WHITE WORLD OF CHILDREN'S BOOKS"

Although Black librarians and others had been protesting for decades the long-standing failure to include African Americans in children's literature in any substantial and authentic way,[1] it was the timely publication of Nancy Larrick's "The All-White World of Children's Books" in 1965 in *The Saturday Review* that caught the attention of the American public. In this article she identified the nearly complete omission of African Americans in children's books as "one of the most critical issues in American education" (63). Larrick was an influential educator, author of a parents' guide to children's reading, and respected expert in children's literature. Following up on the charge by Whitney Young, then director of the Urban League, that the publishing industry, including trade book publishers, omitted Negroes from their books for children, Larrick conducted a survey of children's book publishers. Her analysis revealed that of the more than 5000 children's books published by 63 publishers during 1962, 1963, and 1964, only 349 or 6.7 percent included any Negroes, and only four-fifths of 1 percent were about contemporary Negroes. Moreover, she reported that, with rare exceptions, the few available books that included African Americans were mediocre at best. Larrick argued that integrating American schools and American society meant integrating the curriculum, including the literature offered to America's children.

A number of editors in the Larrick survey had expressed their willingness to publish books that featured African Americans, but with the caution that such books must include Negroes or deal with the problems faced by Negroes in a way that was "natural" and not forced. Ironically, this concern echoes that of African Americans who, since Du Bois's *Brownies' Book*, had been calling for literature in which African American children could see images of Black people as normal human beings. Publishers and critics such as Ruth Hill Viguers (1966), editor of the *Horn Book*, rightly objected to analyses that amounted to a mechanical counting of Black images but seemed unwilling to confront the deeper problem that Larrick labeled "White supremacy" in children's literature. They were, on some level, defending literature as an art form and rejecting the idea that children's books should be used as a weapon in a battle for social justice. The objection to contrivances is on target, but the defense of literature as art failed to come to grips with the ways books, as art forms, reflect the social and cultural contexts in which they are created. A history of omission and ridicule had made mainstream children's literature a source of as much pain as pleasure for African American readers, and advocates for change were counting on books as one way to help change the prevailing social context.

THE COUNCIL ON INTERRACIAL BOOKS FOR CHILDREN

Larrick was also a founding member of the Council on Interracial Books for Children (CIBC), an organization that vigorously carried on the fight for change. Although the CIBC did not limit its concerns to African American children's literature, it began there and had an important impact on people who were creating, publishing, and reviewing children's books about African Americans. Active for about twenty years, from the mid-1960s to the mid-1980s, the CIBC was a controversial and sometimes confrontational organization, incorporated in 1965.

According to Elinor DesVerney Sinnette (1999), the highly respected African American librarian who was also one of the organizing members of the council, it was founded in response to the dearth of good children's books about African Americans. She and poet Lilian Moore, concerned about the lack of such materials in the private school their children attended as well as in the public schools of New York City, were actively involved in efforts to bring about change. When Moore's son returned from a summer as a volunteer in the Mississippi Freedom Schools in 1964 incensed by the unavailability of books by or about African Americans for the Black children in those schools, she took the issue to a meeting of children's book writers. From that meeting came the decision to create an organization "committed to changing the all-white world of children's literature into one representative of a multiracial society" (Chambers 1971, 24). Although initially almost all the council leaders were White, eventually Beryl Banfield, an African American, became president and remained in that position for several years.

In its official periodical, which was launched in 1966, the council announced its aims:

We believe books can do much to create the will and enlarge the capacity to achieve an integrated society. Our aim is therefore to encourage the writing, production, and effective distribution of books to fill the needs of non-White and urban poor children. Through such books, we think all American children will gain a fuller awareness and a keener understanding of one another. (*Interracial Books for Children* 1967, 9)

Like the interculturalists, then, the council initially saw books as a weapon in the battle for integration. Unlike the interculturalists, however, the council also maintained a strong and active commitment to social justice. Two of its major thrusts were to promote the work of so-called minority writers and artists and to help such writers and artists gain access to the publishing industry.

Acting on its belief that books "on interracial subjects" should not be written mainly by White writers, the council sponsored a contest for minority writers. At first, it was for African Americans; the initial announcement in *Interracial Books for Children* offered "three $500 prizes for the best children's books by Negroes" in three age categories: 3 to 6, 7 to 11, and 12 to 16 years of age (Winter 1967, 12). The winning manuscripts were made available to publishers. By the time of the third contest, so much interest had been generated and so many members of other underrepresented groups had made inquiries that eligibility was expanded to include Afro-Americans (no longer Negroes), "American Indians, and Americans of Spanish-speaking origins" (Summer 1969, 1). The fourth contest added Asian Americans. In focusing on these groups, the council anticipated the move toward multiculturalism in children's literature.

The results of the early contests were highly significant for African American children's literature. Winning manuscripts became the first published children's books of Walter Dean Myers, Kristin Hunter, Sharon Bell Mathis, and Mildred D. Taylor, all of whom went on to become important contributors to African American children's literature. Clearly, the contest was successful in providing an incentive for Black writers and an invaluable service to their publishers. Nonetheless, the council was nothing if not controversial. Its first president, Brad Chambers (1971, 23), for example, challenged publishers to impose a five-year moratorium on using White writers and artists to create books about minorities. Among the more provocative pieces in the newsletter were re-readings of classics through antiracist lenses. Not only did the council criticize such traditional classics as *The Story of Dr. Dolittle* (Lofting 1920), *Mary Poppins* by P. L. Travers (1934), and the much-loved *Story of Little Black Sambo* (Bannerman 1899), however; they also criticized acclaimed contemporary books such as Newbery winners *Sounder* (Armstrong 1969) and *The Slave Dancer* (Fox 1973) and Jane Addams Award winner *The Cay* (Taylor 1969). Furthermore, the criticisms were not couched in polite language or the conventional language of literary criticism.[2] Rather, they foregrounded race, gender, class, and other such sociocultural factors, leading many children's literature professionals to view the council's criticisms as nonliterary, political, and inappropriate. The council, however, with a strong belief in the power of books to sway young minds, insisted on the legitimacy of criticism that examined books for what they called antihuman values as well as literary ones.

Given the council's view of many classic and acclaimed books as racist and sexist, they sought to raise the level of awareness of teachers and others. To that end, the CIBC published a list of "10 Quick Ways to Analyze Books for Racism and Sexism" (1974 *Bulletin* 5, no. 3). Reprinted as a flier, it was widely circulated and to some extent helped to institutionalize the examination of racism and sexism as critical criteria in the evaluation of children's books. Although the council's guidelines were not limited to books about Blacks, in part they overlap the guidelines that Rollins and her committees established back in the 1940s, indicating that progress had been slow at best.

The council's guidelines, for example, focus on stereotypes in illustrations, and true to its interracial focus, they also assert a need to assess the ways Black characters are portrayed and situated in relation to Whites. They suggest that readers consider such issues as tokenism and the extent to which "minority" characters are self-reliant rather than dependent on Whites. They also call for an assessment of the potential effect of the book's underlying ideology on children's self-image. In addition, the guidelines concern themselves with the author's background and the cultural perspective he or she brings to the work.

Underlying these criteria was the assumption that books about people of color would continue to be written and published by Whites, whose worldview—what the guidelines called a "single ethnocentric perspective"—had dominated children's literature and informed, if not determined, authors' attitudes toward and treatment of Black characters and themes. This assumption has maintained at least partial validity throughout the remainder of the twentieth century; that is, White writers—whatever their perspectives—would continue to create, if not the majority, then a substantial portion of books about African Americans. Although the council cannot be given sole credit—or blame—for creating the tensions that continue to surround that circumstance, it certainly stimulated much of the debate.

One goal of the foregoing activities—government funding, individual advocacy, organizational action—was to improve the quality of education for poor and disadvantaged students, including Black children. Another was to desegregate the all-White world of children's books. A third was to promote social justice through children's books. Associated mainly with people of goodwill from outside the Black community, their main impact was to raise national awareness of the need for children's literature by and about African Americans and thereby help to spur an increase in the visibility of African Americans in children's books and help pave the way for a body of modern African American children's literature to develop and thrive.

THE BLACK ARTS MOVEMENT

The emergence of modern African American literature in the late 1960s also coincided with and was influenced by interrelated social, artistic, and political happenings within the national African American community, among which was the Black Arts Movement. Larry Neal, one of its major theorists, made clear that the movement was political and nationalistic as well as artistic:

The Black Arts Movement is radically opposed to any concept of the artist that alienates him from his community. Black Art is the aesthetic and spiritual sister of the Black Power concept. As such, it envisions an art that speaks directly to the needs and aspirations of Black America. In order to perform this task, the Black Arts Movement proposes a radical reordering of the western cultural aesthetic. It proposes a separate symbolism, mythology, critique, and iconology. The Black Arts and the Black Power concept both relate broadly to the Afro-American's desire for self-determination and nationhood. Both concepts are nationalistic. One is concerned with the relationship between art and politics; the other with the art of politics. (1994, 184)

In literary works emanating from the Black Arts Movement, orality was paramount, and poetry was king, although drama was situated close to the throne, and other genres were also represented. Black artists who embraced the movement were expected to create works that would speak to Black people about issues affecting them, and the Black urban masses were both inspiration and audience for Black arts productions. Black arts literature was marked by the tendency to incorporate and improvise on the linguistic and musical tastes, styles, and forms characteristic of young Black urbanites. One goal of the movement was to change the ways Black life and images were portrayed and presented to Black people. To that end, the concept of "Black is beautiful" was a rallying cry, and Africa was a source of both pride and inspiration.

Black arts proponents also advocated independent publishing as one instrument of self-definition and cultural and artistic self-determination. As a result, a number of magazines and at least two important Black publishing companies, Broadside Press and Third World Press, were established in those years. Mainly, the publications of these enterprises were aimed at adult readers, but they did produce some works for children. Broadside Press in Detroit published two children's poetry books, one by Sonia Sanchez and one by Gwendolyn Brooks, both of whom were well known for their adult works. Its first children's book, which sold for $1.00, was *Frank* by Carolyn Thompson (1970); it was a thin, wordless paperback, illustrated with pencil sketches. Frank is a teenager who starts smoking marijuana out of boredom, graduates to shooting heroin, then spirals downward until he eventually dies of an overdose. A provocative yet affecting work, it was fairly widely distributed. Third World Press, founded by poet Don L. Lee (now Haki Madhubuti), also published several books for children, including Gwendolyn Brooks's *The Tiger Who Wore White Gloves* (1974), a poetic picture book about being satisfied to be oneself. Drum and Spear Press, a small Washington, D.C., company, published Eloise Greenfield's first book, *Bubbles* (1972) (later reissued as *Good News*), and thus launched the career of one of the most important creators of African American children's literature.

A number of prominent writers and artists from the Black Arts era have been significant contributors to African American children's literature whether or not they explicitly expressed their affinity with the movement. Nikki Giovanni, for instance, one of the most prominent young revolutionary poets early in the Black Arts Movement, produced a number of poetry books for children, even while she continued to publish her works for adults. Other African American writers and artists, especially those who came to prominence in the 1970s such as Lucille Clifton and John Steptoe, also appear to have been influenced by movement ideas, as indicated by their commentaries on their writing.

The extent of the influence of the Black Arts Movement on African American children's literature is difficult to trace, in part because some of the movement goals overlapped some earlier expressions of the goals of African American children's literature. For example, both Du Bois and the Black arts proponents were interested in speaking to the needs of Black America/Black children, and both saw a relationship between art and politics. In any case, both the early Black literature for children and the literature of the movement were seen as instrumental, that is, as vehicles for influencing attitudes and educating and acculturating readers/listeners. In both cases, Black artists and writers were seen as teachers as well as creators. The tendency to view children's literature in part as a pedagogical tool has historically been an important influence on the themes and topics Black writers have chosen to highlight in their work addressed to children.

Concomitant with the Black Arts Movement, some Black theorists called for a Black aesthetic, a means of evaluating and criticizing Black art that took into account its having grown out of the distinctive cultural experiences of Black people. Black aesthetic theorists rejected the idea of a criticism based on the concept of "universal" literature, perceiving universal as a code for "white, Western." Critic Addison Gayle justified the idea of a Black aesthetic: "Unique experiences produce unique cultural artifacts, and art is a product of such cultural experiences. To push this thesis to its logical conclusion, unique art derived from unique cultural experiences mandates unique critical tools for evaluation" (1997, 1876). The call for a Black aesthetic, in other words, was a call for a set of evaluative criteria that would reflect the distinctiveness of Black cultural experience and that could be used to assess the productions of Black artists and writers.

Possibly the clearest expression of a Black aesthetic for children's books was relayed to me by Tom Feelings, the "dean" of African American picture book artists, whose views on his art were firmly grounded in the ideology of the Black Arts Movement.[3] In an informal conversation at a 2002 meeting, Feelings related that he,

George Ford, and a few other Black artists and writers had come together in the 1970s to work on improving the overall quality of literature and the arts for Black children. He provided me with a copy of an unpublished handout for a 1975 workshop on Black children's literature. The handout laid out a list of suggested criteria for critical evaluation of Black children's books.

One part of the criteria had to do with artistic effectiveness; the other was labeled "Essentials of Black Expression" and amounted to the articulation of a Black aesthetic for children's books. The Black expression criteria suggested that a work be examined to ascertain whether it (1) reflects the simultaneous consciousness of pain and pleasure prevalent in Black life; (2) communicates the unconquerable strength and dignity that constitutes our positive affirmation of life and that we continually strive to pass on to our children; (3) contains those juxtapositions that give tension to Black expression (e.g., poor but a slick dresser, unschooled but wise); (4) appeals to the audience on an emotional level and is intellectually stimulating; (5) demands participation and involvement from the reader; (6) invokes some of the rituals that characterize Black relations; (7) vibrates with Black people's innate need to create the unique twist that gives new life to old forms; (8) includes some evidence of the "dance consciousness" inherent in our lives and in our art (i.e., the intervals are just as expressive as the notes); (9) embodies in the written word all the life and vigor of our rich oral tradition. Aspects of this aesthetic appear in a substantial portion of the children's literature created during the 1970s and beyond, most evidently in illustrations, but also in texts. These qualities, to the extent that they appear in the literature, are in part what makes African American children's literature a distinctive body of work.

The Black Arts Movement declined in the 1970s. Although the movement had a significant impact on the literature of its day, its ideology was not universally embraced. Some of the writing and the language in which it was couched was considered shocking by some critics and some of the poetry unworthy, that is, not well crafted by any standards. Also, some African American writers found the movement too prescriptive. Some rejected the very idea of a separate Black aesthetic and embraced the idea of African American literature as one distinctive component of American literature, created with a sensibility informed by the experience of being Black in America. Nonetheless, whether directly or indirectly, the Black Arts Movement left its mark on twentieth century African American children's literature.

MOVING TOWARD SELF-EMPOWERMENT

THE CORETTA SCOTT KING AWARD

By the end of the 1960s, modern African American children's literature was gaining a foothold, but the children's literature establishment was slow to appreciate its quality, as indicated by the near absence of African American writers on the lists of winners of prestigious awards. The first time an African American writer had been recognized by a Newbery Award committee was in 1949, when Arna Bontemps's *The History of the Negro* was named a Newbery Honor Book. Twenty years later, Julius Lester's *To Be a Slave* (1968) was the second, but up to that time—1969—no African American writer had been awarded the Newbery Medal. Out of a chance conversation deploring the absence of African American writers and artists on the lists of winners of the two most prestigious awards in the field grew the Coretta Scott King (CSK) Award.

In 1969, the year following the death of Dr. Martin Luther King Jr., librarians Mabel McKissack and Glyndon Greer, along with publisher John Carroll, formed an organizing committee and launched the award. Intended to commemorate the life and work of Dr. King and to honor his widow, the award calls attention to the work of African American writers and artists. It is given to "authors and artists of African descent whose distinguished books promote an understanding and appreciation of 'the American Dream'" (H. Smith 1994).

The first award, appropriately for a biography of Dr. King, was given in 1970 at a meeting of the New Jersey Library Association, but it took another dozen years before it became an official award of the ALA, administered until recently by the Coretta Scott King Task Force of ALA's Social Responsibilities Round Table. (Currently, the task force is affiliated with the Ethnic and Multicultural Information Exchange Round Table [EMIERT].) In the interim, however, the task force continued to name winners and to present the award at a breakfast held during the annual meeting of the ALA.

In spite of the declared intention of the award to encourage and honor writers and artists of African descent, twice in the first decade at least three of the CSK honor book authors were not African American but were presumably honored for their promotion of the ideals embodied in the award. This contradiction notwithstanding, however, the award has been overwhelmingly successful in meeting its goals. The annual breakfast now attracts several hundred enthusiastic conferees. It has called attention to the work of writers and artists who might otherwise be ignored, and it has also honored the work of African American writers and artists who are widely considered major figures in the field. Its criteria, as listed on the EMIERT website, overlap those of the other major awards in terms of their attention to literary quality and also are distinctive, not only in their focus on African Americans and Black experience, but also in paying attention to "titles which seek to motivate readers to develop their own attitudes and behaviors as well as comprehend their personal duty and responsibility as citizens in a pluralistic society" (EMIERT 2005). This criterion echoes the goals set out by W.E.B. Du Bois early in the century. Even though the selection committees for the CSK award are purposefully racially integrated, I would argue that, given its genesis and the works that have been honored, the CSK award is another example of African American professionals attempting to define what African American children's literature should be and to reassert the function of children's literature as a socializing agent.

JUST US BOOKS

Throughout the twentieth century, Black critics and activists—from W.E.B. Du Bois and Carter G. Woodson to Augusta Baker and Charlemae Rollins—have asserted a need for literature in which Black children could see their lives reflected in a realistic way and from which they could learn about their heritage and absorb certain cultural values. As Black arts proponents asserted, the most likely means to achieve that end would be to establish publishing companies committed to producing the desired kind of literature.

With the exception of Du Bois and Woodson, however, few African Americans set out to publish and distribute such literature for children. Critics and activists in children's literature have instead tried to influence the major publishing houses, whose finances and market access give them the power to make a difference if they so desire. Those African Americans who did establish small presses were, like Du

Bois and Augustus Dill with *The Brownies' Book*, often unable to sustain profitability over a long term.

The most successful such venture in contemporary times has been Just Us Books (JUB), an independent publishing company established by Cheryl and Wade Hudson. Even though JUB was not established until 1988, it is an example of the impulse toward self-empowerment that resulted in the independent presses of the Black Arts era. JUB is distinct, however, in its commitment to literature for children and youth.

The Hudsons were initially motivated by the lack of literature in which their daughter could see reflections of her physical self, her environment, her life experiences. Their first response was to write their own materials and try to sell them to mainstream publishers, who rejected the books on the basis of their belief that there was no market for books aimed at young Black readers and featuring Black experiences. Undaunted, the Hudsons started their own publishing company and launched their first books, a series for young children featuring the AFRO-BETS Kids introducing concepts such as letters, numbers, and shapes. From there, the company's list has expanded to include picture books, novels (chapter books), biographies, and nonfiction for children aged from 2 to 12. As well, the company has developed a "stable" of writers and artists, some of whom were already well known and others who are finding in JUB opportunities that might be limited in large, bottom-line-oriented houses owned by multinational corporations.

The list of key factors that JUB uses to determine which manuscripts to accept constitute, in essence, the underlying philosophy and ideology of the company, which, not surprisingly, echoes the ideology that underlies much of African American children's literature. In addition to considerations such as strong characters and attractive graphics, the guidelines include references to positive images, positive perspectives, accurate information, cultural authenticity and cultural specificity, self-affirmation, and a range of African American lifestyles and values, including "respect for our ancestors." In an unabashed recognition of an underlying didactic intent, the final key ingredient calls for "a vehicle that opens the windows of knowledge, information, and self-discovery" (http: www.justusbooks.com).

In articulating its philosophy, JUB reaffirms the need for a distinctive African American children's literature and indicates that such a literature should provide information, affirmation, and empowerment. Like *The Brownies' Book*, JUB clearly targets the "children of the sun" as its primary audience. Further, the guidelines reaffirm the function of story as a vehicle for teaching, for passing on cultural values, as well as entertainment. The principal concern is that in their books African American children see an accurate reflection of themselves and their lives and culture.

A NEW MANIFESTO?

Among the prominent African American writers who began publishing children's books in the late 1960s and early 1970s was Eloise Greenfield, who declared, "There's a desperate need for more Black literature for children, for a large body of literature in which Black children can see themselves and their lives and history reflected. I want to do my share in building it" (1990, 98). In a 1975 article in *The Horn Book*, Greenfield published what can be seen in retrospect as a "manifesto" for contemporary African American children's literature, a declaration of its principal objectives and of its implicit underlying philosophical or ideological stance. Unlike Langston Hughes in his 1926 "manifesto," Greenfield does not claim to speak for a cadre of writers; she writes in the first person singular. Nonetheless, she artic-ulates a set of goals and intentions that permeate much of the African American children's literature of the last quarter of the twentieth century. In their emphasis on self-esteem, on Black history and achievements, on finding positive solutions to problems, and on the merits of the arts, including literary art, Greenfield's goals bear a striking resemblance to the declared intentions that Du Bois set out for *The Brownies' Book* more than a half century earlier.

Table 2
The Brownies' Book and Eloise Greenfield: African American Children's Literature: A Manifesto?

Goals/Purposes	Eloise Greenfield: I want to:	The Brownies' Book: Intertwined with entertainment will be the endeavor to:
To develop an appreciation for worthwhile things	give children a love for the arts share the feeling I have for words	point out the best amusements and joys and worthwhile things of life
To build children's self-esteem	encourage children to develop positive attitudes toward them selves. . . to love themselves	make colored children realize that being "colored" is a normal, beautiful thing.
	reflect back to children and reinforce the positive aspects of their lives	
To help children overcome negative experiences; learn positive problem solving	present children alternative methods for coping with the negative aspects of their lives and inspire them to seek new ways of solving problems . . .	turn their little hurts and resentments into emulation, ambition and love of their homes and companions
		teach them a code of honor and action in their relations with white children
To pass on knowledge of Black history/heritage, Black achievements-with a view to preparing for the future	give children a true knowledge of Black heritage, . . . that they may develop a sense of direction for the future	make them familiar with the history and achievements of the Negro race
	allow children to fall in love with genuine Black heroes and to be outstanding in ability and in dedication to the cause of freedom.	make them know that other colored children have grown into beautiful, useful, and famous persons
		inspire them to prepare for definite occupations and duties with a broad spirit of sacrifice.
To reinforce the importance of family ties	give children an appreciation of the contribution of their elders	
	reflect the strength of the Black family	
	Source: The Horn Book 1975, 51, 6, 624–6	*Source: The Crisis,* 1919, 6, 286

That these goals are fundamental to so much of African American children's literature is an indication of the extent to which the literature is seen as a tool for teaching, for enculturating, and for socializing Black children. Their long-standing prevalence indicates that many Black adults who write and publish materials about and for Black children perceive that the conditions out of which these goals and purposes arose have not changed substantially over the course of the twentieth century.

Prior to the 1960s, progress in African American children's literature had been driven by the work and the vision of a relatively few committed individuals, such as W.E.B. Du Bois and Arna Bontemps. Describing that progress, therefore, could be accomplished in a fairly linear fashion. Once social, political, and economic circumstances combined to foster an increase in the quantity of available children's books by and about African Americans, the literature began to grow in several genres simultaneously.

To a large extent, however, the development of post-1965 African American children's literature has also been driven by the work and vision of a core group of writers and artists whose work has shaped the body of that literature. The following chapters are organized around the genres of poetry, picture books and their illustrations, and contemporary and historical fiction. Within those genres, the focus is on important writers and artists, the major thematic threads that run through their work and through similar work of others, and the important ideological or philosophical ideas that appear to underlie the creation of the literature.

NOTES

1. See, for example, Baker, Augusta, 1944–1945, "Books for Children: The Negro in Literature," *Child Study* 22: 58–63, Baker, Augusta (1969), "Guidelines for Black Books: An Open Letter to Juvenile Editors." *Publisher's Weekly* 96: 131–133, and Rollins, Charlemae Hill, Ed., 1941, *We Build Together*, Chicago: National Council of Teachers of English.

2. Isabel Suhl (1985), a 1969 issue of the *Bulletin*, had this to say about the Dr. Dolittle books by Hugh Lofting:

As a result of careful examination of four of the most popular of these books, I charge that the real Dr. Dolittle is in essence the personification of the Great White Father Nobly Bearing the White Man's Burden and that his creator was a white racist and chauvinist, guilty of almost every prejudice known to modern white Western man, especially to an Englishman growing up in the last years of the Victorian age. (151) Suhl, Isabel. "The 'Real' Doctor Dolittle." Reprinted in *The Black American in Books for Children: Readings in Racism.* Ed. Donnaroe MacCann and Gloria Woodward (151–161). Metuchen, NJ: Scarecrow Press.

3. Steele, Vincent, Tom Feelings: A Black Arts Movement, *African American Review* 32 (1): 119–124.

BIBLIOGRAPHY OF BOOKS FOR CHILDREN AND YOUNG ADULTS

Sources other than books for children and young adults are documented in a reference list at the back of the book.

Armstrong, William. 1969. *Sounder.* New York: Harper.
Bannerman, Helen. 1899. *The Story of Little Black Sambo.* London: Grant Richards.
———. 1899/no date. *The Story of Little Black Sambo.* The only authorized American edition. Philadelphia: Lippincott.

———. 1899/1996. *The Story of Little Babaji*. Illus. by Fred Marcellino. New York: HarperCollins.

.———. 1899/2003. *The Story of Little Black Sambo*. Illus. by Christopher Bing. New York: Handprint Books.

Beim, Lorraine and Jerrold Beim. 1945. *Two Is a Team*. Illus. by Ernest Crichlow. New York: Harcourt Brace.

Bontemps, Arna. 1948. *The Story of the Negro*. New York: Knopf.

Bontemps, Arna and Langston Hughes. 1932/1993. *Popo and Fifina*. Illus. by E. Simms Campbell. New York: Oxford University Press.

Brooks, Gwendolyn. 1974. *The Tiger Who Wore White Gloves*. Chicago: Third World Press.

Bryant, Sara Cone. 1907/1938. *Epaminondas and His Auntie*. Illus. by Inez Hogan. Boston: Houghton Mifflin.

Credle, Ellis. 1935. *Across the Cotton Patch*. New York: T. Nelson and Sons.

———. 1936. *Little Jeemes Henry*. New York: T. Nelson and Sons.

———. 1938. *The Flop-Eared Hound*. New York: Oxford University Press.

de Angeli, Marguerite. 1946. *Bright April*. New York: Doubleday.

Evans, Eva Knox. 1935. *Araminta*. New York: Minton, Balch and Co.

Fox, Paula. 1973. *The Slave Dancer*. New York: Orchard.

Govan, Christine Noble. 1938. *Narcissus an' de Chillun: Final Adventures of Those Plummer Children*. Boston: Houghton Mifflin.

Greenfield, Eloise. 1972. *Bubbles*. Washington, D.C.: Drum and Spear Press.

Hamilton, Virginia. 1967. *Zeely*. New York: Macmillan.

Hogan, Inez. 1932. *Nicodemus and His Little Sister*. New York: E. P. Dutton.

———. 1941. *Nicodemus Laughs*. New York: E. P. Dutton.

Hughes, Langston. 1932b. *The Dream Keeper*. New York: Knopf.

Hunt, Blanche Seale. 1951. *Stories of Little Brown Koko*. Illus. by Dorothy Wagstaff. Chicago: American Colortype Co.

Keats, Ezra Jack. 1962. *The Snowy Day*. New York: Viking.

Lester, Julius. 1968. *To Be a Slave*. New York: Dial.

———. 1996. *Sam and the Tigers*. Illus. by Jerry Pinkney. New York: Dial Press.

Lofting, Hugh. 1920. *The Story of Dr. Dolittle*. New York: Frederick A. Stokes.

Means, Florence Crannell. 1938. *Shuttered Windows*. Boston: Houghton Mifflin.

Ovington, Mary White. 1913/1972. *Hazel*. Freeport, NY: Books for Libraries Press.

———. 1931. *Zeke*. New York: Harcourt.

Pritchard, Myron T. and Mary White Ovington, compilers. 1920. *The Upward Path: A Reader for Colored Children*. New York: Harcourt, Brace and Howe.

Sharpe, Stella Gentry. 1939. *Tobe*. Chapel Hill: University of North Carolina Press.

Sterling, Dorothy. 1959. *Mary Jane*. New York: Scholastic.

Taylor, Theodore. 1969. *The Cay*. New York: Doubleday.

Thompson, Carolyn. 1970. *Frank*. Detroit: Broadside Press.

Travers, P. L. 1934. *Mary Poppins*. New York: Harcourt.

Weaver, Annie Vaughan. 1930. *Frawg*. New York: Frederick Stokes Co.

CHAPTER 5

African American Poetry for Children: Soft Black Songs

Given the purposeful nature of African American children's literature, it should not be unexpected that contemporary African American children's poetry has been, for the most part, poetry on a mission. Like African American literature in other genres, it has been influenced, if not driven, by the social, political, and cultural contexts out of which it has arisen. It began to flower during the late 1960s and early 1970s and has continued to flourish in the gardens of multicultural education. Earlier African American poetry for children, such as that published by Effie Lee Newsome and Countee Cullen in the 1940s, often focused on nature or nonsense, but beginning in the late 1960s the poetry took a more serious turn for the most part. Although it is not without humor or lightness, the dominant impulse of late twentieth century African American children's poetry has been to affirm the worth and beauty of Black children and their lives.

The main body of post-1965 African American children's poetry has been produced by fewer than a dozen poets. Early in the 1970s, the influence of the Black Arts Movement can be seen in the children's work of poets such as Sonia Sanchez, Nikki Giovanni, and artist Tom Feelings. From then until the end of the twentieth century and beyond, it was the work of Lucille Clifton and Eloise Greenfield that essentially defined contemporary African American children's poetry. The other major African American children's poet is Nikki Grimes, who also published her first children's poetry collection in the 1970s but did not come into her own as a children's poet until the 1990s. The 1990s also saw the publication of new poetry books from a few others, including Joyce Carol Thomas and Angela Johnson. Since 1965 few African American males have published poetry for children, but Ashley Bryan and Walter Dean Myers, who are better known as artist and novelist, respectively, are important exceptions.

In the late 1960s, in spite of the prominence of poetry in the Black Arts Movement, few African American poets were creating poetry addressed specifically to children and youth. One response to that circumstance was to publish anthologies or collections of poems that were not necessarily created for young people but that were accessible to them. Two important such collections appeared during that time. In 1968, Arnold Adoff, who would go on to become a highly acclaimed anthologist and poet, published an anthology of poems by Black Americans, the successor to Bontemps's *Golden Slippers* (1941), which had been published nearly three decades earlier. *I Am the Darker Brother* (1968) was aimed at an audience of middle school or older youth. It featured well-known Black poets, almost none of whom had written specifically or primarily for a child audience. Adoff had started collecting the poems for use with the students he was teaching in New York City since the anthologies in use at the time generally did not include the work of many Black poets. The collection served as an excellent young people's introduction to the African American poetic tradition. It was reissued in 1997 with twenty-one additional poems and nineteen additional poets, a testament to the upsurge in interest in poetry over the nearly three decades since the first edition.

The other important late 1960s collection was *Don't You Turn Back* (1969), a selection of Langston Hughes's poems compiled by Lee Bennett Hopkins and illustrated with striking woodcuts by Ann Grifalconi. It was a timely publication since Hughes had died in 1967 and an important one since he was one of the most revered African American poets. Not surprisingly, more than half the poems in *Don't You Turn Back* also had appeared in *The Dream Keeper* (1932), the collection put together decades earlier by Hughes himself, but there are 18 other poems as well. Although both the Adoff anthology and the Hopkins compilation served to bring the work of important African American poets to a new generation, neither represented the work of new poets who wrote primarily with a child audience in mind. Such poets are relatively scarce, even early in the twenty-first century, and as a result the body of African American children's poetry is relatively small compared to other genres, such as picture books.

THE BLACK ARTS MOVEMENT AND BEYOND: POETRY AS SOCIAL ACTION

The first post-1965 African American poetry aimed specifically at a child audience was inspired by the Black Arts Movement with its political bent, its revolutionary rhetoric, and its glorification of things Black and African. For the most part, the Movement poets published for an adult audience, but a few children's books reflect its influence.

One of the clearest examples of the style of Black Arts poetry for children is Sonia Sanchez's collection, *It's a New Day* (*Poems for Young Brothas and Sistuhs*) (1971). Published by Broadside Press, the Detroit-based independent Black publishing house known for its focus on poetry, the collection contained fourteen poems. In typical Black Arts fashion, they emulate the rhythms and sounds of the urban Black speech of the time, incorporate elements of or influences from Black music, and incorporate some grammatical features of Black vernacular, such as distinctive uses of the verb *to be* (e.g., "we be singen"). Sanchez also experiments with unconventional spellings (e.g., "yo" for "your," "u" for "you," "-en" for " -ing" as in "singen") to represent pronunciation. Slash marks within lines create interest and emphasis. Organized in "sets," as in jazz music, Sanchez's poems lovingly celebrate Black children as the hope of the future. The first poem in the collection, "to Morani/Mungu" is typical, with lines such as

the world
awaits yo/young/blackness

It is in the voice of a mother addressing her sons, promising her support and love as they become the leaders/activists of a new tomorrow. The other poems envision the new day of the title, a day when, as the final poem imagines, Black people will possess and inhabit a new land. Although these poems are, as the subtitle indicates, *for* Black youngsters, they seem mostly directed *at* young people; the sensibility remains that of an adult, even in the poems that purport to speak in the voice of a child or youth. This is in keeping with the Black Arts ideological stance and its instrumental view of poetry. Where better to begin to create a new day than with young people? Sanchez continues writing and is a well-respected poet, although her work is generally considered appropriate for adults and older youth.

NIKKI GIOVANNI: POET OF THE PEOPLE

Some time in the late 1960s or early 1970s, Nikki Giovanni was crowned, in the popular Black media, the Black Princess of Poetry. Because of the "revolutionary" sentiments expressed in many of her early poems, she was for a time considered one of the major voices of the Black arts movement. Giovanni, however, refused to be restricted to particular subjects and themes and so eventually lost favor with some Black Arts critics, who insisted that poetry must always serve the cause. She never lost favor, however, with the large audiences who continue to attend her readings and lectures.

In a way similar to Langston Hughes, Giovanni has been a poet of the people. She made a number of recordings, including the once-popular album *Truth Is on Its Way*, which features the poet reading her own works, accompanied by a gospel choir. This mixture of music and poetry echoes the fusion of visual and verbal art that is an important tenet of the Black Arts Movement. Although she may be best known for her poetry for adults, Giovanni has published, as of this writing, four books of her own poetry for young people. In addition, two of her poems, "Knoxville, Tennessee" and "Genie in the Jar" have been published as picture books of the same names (in 1994 and 1996, respectively).

Ego-tripping and other poems for young people (1973) provides an excellent overview of Giovanni's early poetry and the variety of its concerns. It expresses a number of personal emotions; it displays Giovanni's knack for satirical twists and humor; it addresses racism and expresses often-angry responses to it. And, like much of the poetry of the times, it is steeped in the language, music, and other aspects of popular culture prevalent among many young Black people of that era. Many of the poems in *Ego-tripping* embrace the Black cultural and political struggle of the 1960s and praise some of the more militant activists such as H. Rap Brown and the Black Panthers. Some of those poems, such as "poem for Black boys" ("Ask your mother for a Rap Brown gun") have an angry tone. Others are more sad than angry, and still others address more personal issues.

A selection of previously published work, the book contains some of Giovanni's most popular poems, including the title poem, which she referred to as a "sassy hands on the hips poem" (Janeczko 1991, 87). "Ego-tripping" exemplifies the affinity of Black arts poetry for the oral discourse popular among urban Black people of the time. It reflects in particular the popularity of "rapping," a type of oral performance, used especially by Black males, that is a forerunner of contemporary popular rap/ hip-hop music. Full of hyperbole and braggadocio, the poem retells history from the perspective of a mythological Black woman who claims to have been involved in the creation of much of the ancient world and its resources, from the Sphinx to the Nile to diamonds and uranium. *Ego-tripping* also includes Giovanni's signature poem, "Nikki-Rosa," with its famous line "Black love is Black wealth."

Giovanni declares in this poem that she does not want white biographers to write about her because she fears they will see only that the family is lacking in material wealth and miss what is most important, the family love that nurtures the soul. This concept is highlighted by a number of African American writers as a counter to some of the prevailing attitudes and misunderstandings about Black family life.

Black music is a very important aspect of *Ego-tripping* and in much of Giovanni's other early poetry, both in terms of its influence on the rhythms and structures of the poems and as a central topic or the source of important allusions in many of the poems. "Revolutionary Music," for example, addresses the impact of the popular music of the times and celebrates the names of the groups (e.g., Temptations, Supremes) who produced it. "The Geni in the Jar" is a tribute to singer Nina Simone. There are numerous references to performers popular at the time, such as James Brown, Aretha Franklin, Ray Charles, and Sly and the Family Stone.

Giovanni's poetry sometimes shouts and sometimes whispers; it moves between the political and the personal, the silly and the serious. Her first collection of poems written expressly for children, *Spin a Soft Black Song* (1971), is in the main a celebration of children and childhood. It was the first such collection by an African American poet since Gwendolyn Brooks's *Bronzeville Boys and Girls* (1956). A number of the poems in the book were responses to requests from the children with whom Giovanni worked in the Reading Is Fundamental (RIF) program to "write a poem about me" (Copeland and Copeland 1994). Others grew out of the memories that she and the illustrator Charles Bible recalled from their own growing up years. Like the poems in *Bronzeville Boys and Girls*, the poems in *Spin* focus on childhood concerns and treat the Black cultural context as a given. The title of the book is taken from "dance poem," which insists that Black children must learn to dance to their own music and "spin a soft black song." A number of the poems in *Spin* speak in the imagined voices of babies and children. Giovanni asserts that in these poems she was trying to provide a voice for children whose voices are often not heard. "What I really wanted to do in this collection was show a respect for children. I thought they deserved a voice and that these particular youngsters especially deserved somebody to write about their thoughts and feelings" (Copeland and Copeland 1994, p. 143).

Giovanni also has a playful side, as demonstrated in *Vacation Time* (1980). A number of the poems in this collection are nonsense rhymes (e.g., "Never tickle a prickled pickle"), a rarity in African American children's poetry of the time. Others describe everyday events and natural phenomena such as stars and rainbows. Attempting to capture the interests and feelings of eight-year-old children, these poems are a far cry, in tone and in subject matter, from Giovanni's angry revolutionary poetry of the sixties. There is little or no political commentary or reference to Black cultural themes or topics. In fact, of the children pictured by the artist Marisabina Russo, only a few are Black. Although these rhyming verses do not display Giovanni's strengths as a poet, it is noteworthy that she is one of the few modern Black writers of poetry for children who risked, during that period, trying to capture the silly side of eight-year-olds.

Although some of her poetry written expressly for children addresses social, political, and cultural issues, and does so with wit and bite and some pride, much of it is a celebration of children and childhood. Rendered mainly in rhythmical free verse (1980's *Vacation Time* is the main exception), often named for particular individuals, Giovanni's poems for children express the variety of emotions that are a part of growing up, both as African Americans and as children more generally.

Although the contrasting moods and tones of her poetry may seem contradictory, they might better be seen as different facets of a quick-witted, independent spirit, a poet who keeps her fingers on the pulse of the ordinary people for whom she writes.

"DUALING" ARTS: FUSING THE VISUAL AND THE VERBAL

Black artists must rethink the whole idea of "art." Their work must be given back to the people it comes from. The visual arts must be fused with the rest of our art forms—poetry, drama, dance, and music—in order to give direction and life-giving force to Black people.

Tom Feelings (1972, 67)

One of the goals of the Black Arts Movement was to have Black artists reclaim the public image of Black people, that is, to promote the idea—among Black people—that contrary to long years of derogatory portrayals and negative associations with blackness, Black is beautiful. In that regard, the work of artist Tom Feelings, who was the "dean" of contemporary African American children's book artists, is one of the most enduring legacies of the ideology of that movement in the field of children's literature. The quotation above comes from his memoir *Black Pilgrimage* (1972), in which he described the experiences in the 1960s that helped to shape his life and profoundly affected his ideological stance and his development as an artist. The pilgrimage of the title is both his literal journey from Brooklyn to the American South to Ghana and back home and his symbolic journey of self-discovery and affirmation of his African heritage: "I am an *African*, and I know now that Black people, no matter in what part of the world they live, are one African people" (50).

Although Feelings was not a poet, he was the catalyst for the creation of an important, if small, corpus of African American poetry for children. Acting on his belief that visual art should be integrated with other art forms, Feelings commissioned poets to create text in response to his drawings. The drawings in the books were selected from numerous pencil or pen-and-ink sketches Feelings made of Black people in the United States, in West Africa, and in Guyana. Each of the books includes a note explaining the techniques used to reproduce the art and enhance the drawings with color, usually tones of sepia and gray. In his drawings of women and children, Feelings reflects back to viewers the warmth and beauty he sees in Black people. In a kind of silent call-and-response, the poems both echo the images and add their own distinctive voices to create interactive works of art.

Something on My Mind (Feelings 1978) is a collection of poems composed in response to portraits of African American children, usually in urban settings. In an unconventional gesture, the artist is listed as the "author" of the book, with the poet Nikki Grimes credited in the manner usually reserved for illustrators: "Words by Nikki Grimes." Each of the nineteen lyrical poems in this work takes on the voice of a pictured child or teenager. The poems match the mood of the drawings. They speak, in the first person, of the emotional experiences of growing up—the longings, the loneliness, the endless waiting. A few of the poems employ informal Black vernacular, but most do not. The first poem reveals children's awareness of the challenges of living in a racialized society; the children dream of a place in which Black children could just feel at home—perhaps Africa. There are also poems about relationships with family members and with friends. Interestingly, these are not portraits of happy-go-lucky children but of thoughtful young people who appear to be taking life rather seriously because, Feelings would likely have argued, growing up Black and whole in the racialized social context of the United States is serious business.

The drawings in *Daydreamers* (Greenfield 1981) are similar, although the age range of the pictured children is wider, from toddlers through young adults. The poet this time is Eloise Greenfield, who saw daydreams in the faces of the children and youth. Her response is a single interpretive poem, its lines interspersed among the drawings, which sometimes form a montage across a double-page spread. Unlike Grimes's lyrical first-person poems, Greenfield's poem speaks in the third person, describing what she imagines are the thoughts behind the pensive faces. The poem celebrates Black children but does not speak in a child's voice.

A third collaboration, *Black Child* (1981) was produced with Joyce Carol Thomas. In keeping with Feelings's belief that art should be made accessible, *Black Child* was an inexpensive paper-covered booklet published by an entity called Zamani Productions. It was intended, as Thomas notes in her brief introduction, to "celebrate the beauty and promise of the children" of the sun, particularly in the wake of a series of killings of Black children in Atlanta. As in the Grimes collection, the poems in *Black Child* take on the voices of the pictured children, who are identified by their places of residence (Guyana, Ghana, Senegal, United States), highlighting Feelings's contention that Black people everywhere are an African people. Thomas's poems, a number of which were subsequently published in later collections of her work, express the strength of spirit, the pride, and the hope that the poet sees projecting from the faces of the children.

Soul Looks Back in Wonder (Feelings 1993) was the first book Feelings produced in full color. The young people in these drawings are mainly older youth, "standing between childhood and adulthood," as Feelings notes in the introduction. For this work, Feelings sought out a number of Black poets, each of whom composed a poem in response to one of the drawings. Many of the contributing poets are well known, although not commonly associated with work for children—Margaret Walker, Haki Madhubuti, Eugene B. Redmond, for example. There is a never-before-published poem by Langston Hughes, composed years earlier to accompany the art Feelings had produced for a CORE (Congress on Racial Equality) poster. Numerous references to Africa and African heritage and roots celebrate the ties among African peoples and celebrate Africa as a source of creativity and strength for young people who are, in Feelings's view, endangered in our times.

In *Now Sheba Sings the Song*, Maya Angelou (1987) responds to a set of Feelings's drawings of Black women. Although Angelou gets top billing on this book, it is very much like the others in that her interpretive poem is a response to drawings made long before the poem itself was composed. Unlike the others, it is not a tribute to children, but a powerful and sensuous celebration of Black womanhood. As such, its primary audience is likely to be found among teenagers and adults rather than children.

These books represent Feelings's attempt to translate into picture books his belief that artists should work together collaboratively. He believed that in his drawings he had shown "both bright hope and despair, beauty, and the ugliness of oppression, the complete truth" (1972, 70). He wanted his art and the poetry that accompanies it to be a mirror in which Black children and parents would see the beauty and warmth he found in them, often beneath a layer of sadness. The resulting books are praise songs for Black children and Black women, sometimes expressing adult hopes and aspirations, sometimes taking on a child's perspective. Speaking both to children and adults, this unique set of books constitutes a note-worthy double-voiced affirmation of the concept of Black is beautiful.

"WHO LOOK AT ME?"

> I came back to Brooklyn and looked at the faces again, right outside my door on Putnam Avenue. They were the same faces. Had I really looked at them before? Had I seen the beauty in them? And if I hadn't, growing up with them, drawing them, who had?
>
> Tom Feelings (1972, 32)

> We do not see those we do not know. Love and all varieties of happy concern depend on the discovery of one's self in another. The question of every desiring heart is, thus, *Who Look at Me?* In a nation suffering fierce hatred, the question—race to race, man to man, and child to child—remains: *Who Look at Me? We answer with our lives.* Let the human eye begin unlimited embrace of human life.
>
> June Jordan (1969)

Although Feelings's work is the best-known exemplar, in the field of African American children's books, of fusing poetry and visual art to create new works that comment on Black experiences, it was not the first. Poet June Jordan had asked a similar question in the title of her long interpretive poem *Who Look at Me* (1969). Feelings's recognition that Black people in America suffered a peculiar invisibility echoes Jordan's statement in the epigraph, published three years earlier. *Who Look at Me* appeared at a historical moment when its challenge to America—to make the effort to actually *see* Black Americans—was especially timely. The text is interlaced with historical and contemporary paintings of Black people in America. Although the title page states that the book is "Illustrated with twenty-seven paintings," the paintings most certainly came first, and since many sections of the poem are directly connected to the paintings near which they are placed, it would be more accurate to say that the poem "illustrates" the visual art.

The paintings in *Who Look at Me* (Jordan 1969) were selected from a collection assembled by author Milton Meltzer. Created by various artists, both Black and White, including Charles Altson, Winslow Homer, and Andrew Wyeth, the paintings constitute a brief visual history of Black life in America, and the accompanying poem comments on this history and the relationship of African American lives to American racial attitudes. The poem itself is sparsely punctuated, syntactically idiosyncratic, and frequently enigmatic. It speaks in a number of different voices and expresses, among other things, pride, sorrow, anger, and love. A challenging text, it nevertheless makes a strong visual and verbal impact.

Well beyond the decline of the Black Arts Movement, poetry created in response to visual art has continued to appear in a surprising number of collections of African American children's poetry, although newer versions have been less overtly steeped in the political ideologies of the Black Arts Movement. Eloise Greenfield (1988b), for example, wrote a series of poems to accompany the paintings of Mr. Amos Ferguson, a Bahamian painter. Greenfield has also written poems to accompany the paintings of Jan Spivey Gilchrist, who has illustrated a number of Greenfield's collections. Nikki Grimes has also published a collection of poems in response to photographs, *It's Raining Laughter* (1997).

Walter Dean Myers, who is best known for his young adult novels, wrote his own poems to accompany selections of the vintage photographs he collected over a number of years. His first collection, *Brown Angels* (1993), features turn-of-the-century photographs of African American children. It was followed by *Glorious Angels* (1995), which features antique photographs of children from around the world, and *Angel to Angel* (1998), which honors mother-child relationships with old photographs of African American mothers and children. Myers's original poems range from nonsense verse to "nursery rhymes," to a call for adults to celebrate the children in our lives, to poems that speak in the voices of children. Particularly in the first book, a number of the poems also celebrate racial/cultural pride and the physical beauty of "dark and precious" Black children.

This fusion of art forms, in which poems respond to visual images, constitutes an important strand of African American children's poetry. Whether the poets speak to children or take on the voices of children, the effect is to affirm their physical selves, give expression to their emotions, and celebrate their lives. Well beyond the Black Arts Movement, which was steeped in political rhetoric, African American children's poetry seems intent on achieving some of the same effects: affirmation of their selfhood, emotional expression, and illuminating and validating the everyday lives of children whose physical images and life experiences have been consistently devalued by omission from the literature available to them in schools and libraries.

AFRICAN AMERICAN CHILDREN'S POETS: CELEBRATING THE CHILDREN

Recognizing the invisibility of Black children in literature and perceiving a crucial need for literature that affirms Black children and their worlds, poets Lucille Clifton, Eloise Greenfield, and Nikki Grimes have dedicated their craft to fulfilling that need. In so doing, they have given voice to children whom they felt have too long been voiceless in American children's literature. The overwhelming majority of the books produced by these three women have been either in picture book format or profusely illustrated. Although illustrations are not unusual in American books of children's poetry, the art is particularly significant in these works because of the focus on affirming the beauty and normalcy of ordinary black children and their worlds.

THE WORLD OF EVERETT ANDERSON

The first important collection of contemporary African American children's poetry for young children was Lucille Clifton's *Some of the Days of Everett Anderson,* which appeared in 1970. It introduced Everett Anderson, a six-year-old with a dactylic name that repeats its melody throughout the poems. It was the first in a series of eight books about Everett Anderson, who lives in an urban housing project. Through the seven books published before 2000, he grows two or three years and has to come to terms with his mother's remarriage, the birth of a baby sister, making friends with a girl, and the death of his father, along with numerous more ordinary events and occasions. In an echo of Giovanni's "Nikki-Rosa," Clifton identified one of her underlying purposes for creating the books: "What I wanted to show through Everett Anderson was that being poor just means you don't have any money. Not having any money has nothing to do with character. One does not have to be poor in spirit because he is poor economically" (1981, 36–37).

The Everett Anderson books, then, like much of African American children's literature—perhaps like *most* literature for children—are not intended solely to entertain but to impart some guidelines for living. This is not, however, to suggest that the books are in any way "preachy."

Part of what Clifton (1981, 32) was trying to do was to carry out what she described as the job of a writer: "to authenticate their [Black children's] own world." In her attempt to authenticate the worlds of the nation's Everett Andersons, Clifton focuses on affirming their selfhood, articulating and respecting their feelings and emotions, and emphasizing the importance of relationships, particularly within a family. *Some of the Days* (1970) is full of affirmations of Everett—his joys and fears, his wishes and dreams, and his own irrepressible self. In "Wednesday Noon Adventure," the phrase "Who's black" is repeated like a chant at the beginning of each verse, emphasizing the importance and naturalness of that aspect of his identity. It is as much a part of him as his name. In a reprise of the "black" motif, Clifton repeats the word again in each verse of "Sunday Morning Lonely," a poem that laments the absence of Everett's father, whose back is "broad and black" and whose side is "black and wide." In the February verse in *Everett Anderson's Year* (1974), Clifton compares Everett Anderson in the snow to vanilla and chocolate ice cream, once again making positive associations with his physical blackness.

Clifton has said that all of her children's books "are about love in a family" (1981, 35), and these books exemplify that concern. In the early books, Everett Anderson has a cozy one-to-one loving relationship with his single working mother, who makes time for the two of them whenever she can. In the course of the series, he struggles with his emotions as his mother dates and eventually marries Mr. Perry and gives birth to Baby Evelyn. The poems in *Everett Anderson's 1, 2, 3* (1977) and in *Everett Anderson's Nine Months Long* (1978) express the variety of feelings he experiences—from jealousy to anger to acceptance—as his life changes and he moves from being one of two to one of four.

Everett Anderson's father is a persistent presence throughout the series, even though he no longer lives with Everett and his mother. At least one poem in each of the books refers to him. Everett loves and misses his father, and those feelings complicate his response to Mr. Perry. When Mama marries Mr. Perry, Everett chooses to keep his (father's) name, Anderson. In the penultimate book of the series, *Everett Anderson's Goodbye* (1983), Mr. Anderson has died, and Everett experiences the five stages of grief. In the end, Everett comes to the conclusion that the certainty of his father's love will sustain him. At a time when many African Americans complained that Black males were too frequently mischaracterized as irresponsible, Clifton presented a family in which two Black men were behaving in loving and responsible ways.

For all their underlying seriousness, the rhyming poems are often lively and lighthearted, and many are subtly humorous. The rhythms vary, making them pleasant to the ear, and Clifton has a knack for expressing complex ideas in clear, spare, often sententious language that a child can understand. A number of the poems, too, are about ordinary pleasures and activities—a Halloween costume, playing in the snow, refusing to use an umbrella. Everett Anderson has been portrayed by three different artists: Evaline Ness in the first two books, Ann Grifalconi in the rest, and Jan Spivey Gilchrist in a reissue of *Everett Anderson's Christmas Coming* (1971/1991). Although each book can stand alone, as a group they constitute a sensitive portrait in verse of a typical, ordinary but exceptional young African American boy and the loving family of which he is a part.

The Everett Anderson books represent an important advance in African American children's poetry, in part because the picture book format and the brief, deceptively simple poems make them accessible to primary age children, for whom precious little African American poetry was available at the time. In addition to her picture books, Clifton also writes highly respected poetry for an adult audience. In fact, that has been her primary occupation. She was, for example, Poet Laureate of Maryland from 1979 to 1982. Many of Clifton's poems for adults are accessible and appealing to young adults and are anthologized in collections intended for middle and high school students. Much like her Everett Anderson verses, her poems frequently focus on family in both a personal and a community sense. She also celebrates her African heritage, the legacy of her great-great-grandmother Caroline, who told her daughter, the first Lucille/Lucy in the family, "Get what you want, you from Dahomey women." Clifton also celebrates and explores her roles as woman—mother, daughter, sister, wife, friend—and the intersections of those roles with race. Many of her poems address issues of race and culture and historical oppression. She frequently expresses optimism, determination, pride, love, and a strong sense of continuity. One of her most frequently anthologized poems in collections for young people is "listen children," in which she expresses her belief in a strong cultural unity, declares that "we have always loved us," and urges children to "pass it on." As she notes in her lyrical memoir, *Generations* (1976b), Clifton believes that "Lines connect in thin ways that last and last, and lives become generations made out of pictures and words just kept" (78). Focusing on the everyday and extraordinary experiences of ordinary humans, Clifton's poetry is, in the truest sense, life affirming.

ELOISE GREENFIELD: ACCENTUATING THE POSITIVE

I'm trying mostly to reflect the lives that African American children know they lead. These lives are not very much depicted by the media. What I want to do is give a balanced view of life and of family life, which will include negative but also positive aspects. In general, I think we see just the negative. This needs to change. This must change.

Eloise Greenfield (Janeczko 1991, 97)

Like Lucille Clifton, Eloise Greenfield writes poetry that is about authenticating the world of Black children or, as she puts it in the epigraph, "reflecting the lives that African American children know they lead." Her poetry, therefore, is always set in a Black cultural context, within which she focuses on everyday things and events and relationships in children's lives. One of her goals, which she shares with Clifton and Giovanni, is to portray Black families who refuse to allow themselves to be defined by the level of their income. About her first book, she notes: "And I wanted to write about things that children love, about childhoods where there may or may not be much money, but there's so much fun" (1997, 631). This desire to provide a truer picture of the lives of Black children living in poor economic conditions, to affirm the fullness of their lives, has been an important motivator for a number of African American creators of children's literature.

By virtue of her longevity in the field and the quality of her work, Eloise Greenfield is the doyenne of African American children's poetry. Between 1978 and 1998, she published five notable collections of original poetry for children: *Honey I Love and Other Love Poems* (1978), *Under the Sunday Tree* (1988b), *Nathaniel Talking* (1988a), *Night on Neighborhood Street* (1991), and *Angels* (1998). In addition, she has published single poems in picture book format, board books consisting of single poems for very young children, and "Let's Read Aloud" books geared to beginning readers. In recognition of the significant contribution her poetry has made to the world of children's literature, Greenfield was awarded the 1997 NCTE (National Council of Teachers of English) Excellence in Poetry Award for the body of her work, the first African American to be so honored.

Greenfield's highly acclaimed first poetry collection, *Honey I Love and Other Love Poems* (1978), has become a modern classic. It consists of sixteen poems that celebrate the numerous everyday people and things there are to love: family, laughter, words, friends, heroes, music, and oneself. The importance of love is a common theme in African American children's literature, expressed in Giovanni's famous line from "Nikki-Rosa," "Black love is Black wealth" and echoed in this book's epigraph from a Sharon Bell Mathis novel: "It's a love place. A real black love place." The poems in *Honey I Love* are about topics as diverse as playing dress-up, riding on the train, a girl running to meet her mother, playing peek-a-boo with a baby, and the heroic deeds of Harriet Tubman. The title poem, with its captivating rhythm and rhyme, celebrates small things—the Southern lilt in a cousin's speech, playing under the "flying pool" made by a water hose, playing with dolls, a train ride, a family car ride, and a quiet moment with a mother. These poems also exemplify Greenfield's remarkable ability to capture and express the sensibilities of children and to relate their concerns in a childlike voice. Almost all of the poems in this collection are first-person, lyrical poems representing Black children imagining, wondering, enjoying, and reflecting on commonplace experiences and events. In her focus on the ordinary, Greenfield accentuates the normality of Black children's lives, recalling Du Bois's goal in *The Brownies' Book* to make "colored" children know that they are normal. By highlighting particular details of the everyday lives of Black children, Greenfield also affirms their very humanity.

Reflecting Greenfield's determination to portray a balanced view of the lives of Black children, the seventeen poems in *Night on Neighborhood Street* (1991) together form a quasi narrative that describes the events of one evening on a city street. Not everything or everyone on the street is happy or admirable—one poem portrays an encounter with a drug dealer (whose temptations the children reject) and another a family struggling financially while the father is out of work. For the most part, however, the poems are about often-pleasant, ordinary experiences such as street games, a new baby, family bedtime rituals, and a sleepover. As the children who live on the street confront situations both familiar and new, they experience a wide range of emotions—fear, pride, sadness, joy, loneliness, and love. The book closes on a tranquil note with the title poem, in which a parent's trumpet solo announces that night is settling onto the street.

As was the case with Giovanni, Langston Hughes, and several other African American poets, a number of Greenfield's poems owe some debt to various forms of Black music. Greenfield is a jazz enthusiast, for example, and many of the poems in *Honey I Love* (1978) echo jazz rhythms. This connection is highlighted in a 1982 recording of Greenfield and a group of six children reading, reciting, or singing the poems, accompanied by jazz musicians. In part, the recording is intended as a child's introduction to jazz. It is an extraordinary blend of words, music, and rhythms, an exemplar of the sort of melding of Black art forms that Tom Feelings and others were calling for in the early 1970s.

Nathaniel Talking (Greenfield 1988a) taps in to the contemporary interest in rap music as well as the traditional blues. In both cases, Greenfield has incorporated the musical form into the poetry itself. In the tradition of Langston Hughes and a number of other Black writers, she composed two twelve-bar blues poems, "My Daddy" and "Watching the World Go By." At the end of the book, she includes an explanation of the form and an invitation to readers to create their own twelve-bar blues poem. In "Nathaniel's Rap," a rhyming, fast-moving rap that frames the collection, nine-year-old Nathaniel declares that he has something on his mind that he wants people to listen to. Greenfield's curtsy to rap recognizes contemporary music's powerful appeal to young people, lends a certain legitimacy to rap as a form of poetry, and continues the tradition of incorporating oral discourse and folk art into African American literature.

Greenfield also integrates into her poetry, though sparingly, other oral discourse traditions from the Black community. The signature line of the title poem in *Honey I Love* (1973) reflects her infatuation with the expression, "Honey, let me tell you" that, as she noted (Bishop 1997, 631), had not yet become cliché in the late 1970s but was still in wide use among African American women. The Harriet Tubman poem echoes informal African American syntactic and semantic structures: "Harriet Tubman didn't take no stuff." The repeated use of the syntactic negative emphasizes Tubman's determination *not* to be a slave. The grammatical strategy (negate every element that can be negated in a sentence) accurately reflects linguists' descriptions of the syntax of urban Black vernacular speech. Greenfield's use of such linguistic forms and structures helps to situate her poetry within a social and cultural context many African American children will recognize as their own.

The poems in *Nathaniel Talking* (Greenfield 1988a) show a nine-year-old Black boy in a rather contemplative mood, another attempt to balance the usual portrayals of such children as always physically active, interested mainly in athletics. His name, Nathaniel B. Free, expresses an important cultural value and is tied to a line from the book's epigraph, taken from a Joyce Carol Thomas poem: "I am a root/that will be free." The poems in the collection delineate Nathaniel's observations about life from his young perspective. There is a strong focus on people and relationships with friends and family, but also serious thinking about issues relevant to him: his future, what kind of person he is, and what kind of man he will be. *Nathaniel Talking* stands as a reminder that intellectual activity is a valued aspect of African American life and culture, even though its expression may take unique forms.

Greenfield (1975) has explicitly stated that one of her purposes in writing for children is to awaken them to the beauty of words and to instill a love for the arts. One of the best-known poems in *Honey I Love* (Greenfield 1973) is "Things," which celebrates the lasting power of words, and specifically poetry, in contrast to the relatively ephemeral nature of mere things. Greenfield's attention to the beauty of language highlights an aesthetic dimension within the ideological stances that underlie and help to typify African American children's literature. This dimension, an important aspect of African American children's literature from at least as early as *The Brownies' Book*, is frequently either de-emphasized or only tacitly recognized in discussions of the literature.

Greenfield's emphasis on the importance of the arts is also apparent in her willingness to create poetry in response to the work of visual artists. Her second collection of original poems, *Under the Sunday Tree* (1988), consists of poems written to accompany paintings by Mr. Amos Ferguson, a Bahamian artist whose work depicts the lives of local islanders. These poems are a slight departure from Greenfield's more typical emphasis on the ordinary lives of African American children. Nevertheless, the work is set in a Black cultural context and reflects a sense of kinship among people of the African diaspora. Some of the poems address typical Greenfield themes and topics—family, love, relationships, and dreams. Others paint vivid word pictures that extend and enrich Ferguson's visual images of the sights and experiences associated with island life. In these poems, for example, water lilies compose visual music, and boats ride the water's wings; repetition and clipped words and phrases evoke the urgency with which firefighters carry out their mission to save lives and property. Greenfield's fascination with words is readily apparent in this collection.

Greenfield's love of language is also apparent in two of her most recent collections, *I Can Draw a Weeposaurus* (2001) and *In the Land of Words* (2004). *Weeposaurus* introduces a young artist who paints pictures, both visual and in the form of poetry, of the unusual dinosaurs she imagines. *In the Land of Words*, which contains both previously published and new poems, is a collection that celebrates the very existence of words, imagining that there could actually be a place where words live. Both these books reflect Greenfield and her illustrator in a light mood, providing a balance to the more serious tone of many of her poems and a glimpse of her lighter side.

Greenfield is one of the very few African American poets who have devoted their careers entirely to writing for children. Her careful attention to her craft has brought her well-deserved acclaim. Greenfield is a keen observer of children and their life journeys, and her poetry appeals because of its strong rhythms and its accurate reflections of their emotions and their voices. Her poetry, like Clifton's, authenticates and affirms the lives of Black children while it also transcends real and imagined cultural and racial divides.

NIKKI GRIMES: REFLECTIONS OF HER WORLD

> When I was growing up, I rarely found beautiful images of myself in the pages of a book, and that's precisely why I chose to write books for young people like me. I wanted them to meet girls like Zuri and Danitra in *Meet Danitra Brown*, like LaTasha in *Come Sunday*, boys like Damon, and men like Blue in *My Man Blue*. These were people from my neighborhood, from my world. People who walked and talked the way I did, who danced the way I danced, and who worshipped the way I worshipped. These were people whose stories I knew and wanted to tell, people who looked and felt like me.
>
> Nikki Grimes (2000, 33)

As is evident from the quotation in the epigraph, Grimes's poetry carries on the tradition of Greenfield and Clifton, reflecting a commitment to making visible and authenticating the worlds of ordinary African American children. Although the first was published in 1978, the rest of Grimes's poetry books for children have been published since 1990 (most after 1995). In the decade and a half between 1978 and 1993, she was not inactive; she published adult poetry and children's books in other genres and followed a number of other creative interests, including photography, music, and fiber art. But, she has found a home in children's poetry. In spite of that fifteen-year hiatus, in terms of both quantity and quality, she is well on her way to becoming the early twenty-first century's predominant African American voice in children's poetry. As of the end of 1999, Nikki Grimes had published nine collections of poems for a child audience and an alphabet book in rhyme. In 2006, she became the second African American poet to be awarded the NCTE Excellence in Poetry Award.

She addresses many of the same themes and topics as Clifton and Greenfield: family relationships, friendships, childhood experiences, and love. For example, one of Grimes's collections, *Hopscotch Love* (1999b), echoes the theme of Greenfield's classic *Honey I Love* (1973), although its target audience is a bit older. Subtitled "A Family Treasury of Love Poems," the collection of twenty-two lyrical poems mainly celebrates the ways family members express their love for each other, such as a son making a Christmas valentine card for his mother, a grandmother baking a grandchild's favorite cake. One poem evokes Malcolm X, whose public image is that of a fierce activist, to remind us that he was also a devoted husband who wrote mushy poems to his wife. In *Stepping Out with Grandma Mac* (2001b), Grimes highlights the loving relationship between a rather unconventional grandmother who is gruff on the outside and her granddaughter, who comes to know and understand the loving heart beneath Grandma Mac's facade.

Friendship is a particularly important theme in Grimes's work. Her best-known book prior to 2000, the Coretta Scott King Honor Book *Meet Danitra Brown* (1994), celebrates the friendship between Zuri and Danitra, two young African American girls. The voice is that of Zuri, who introduces readers to her purple-wearing friend Danitra, the most "splendiferous" girl in town. Since 2000, Zuri and Danitra have appeared in two subsequent books, *Danitra Brown Leaves Town* (2002) and *Danitra Brown, Class Clown* (2005). *My Man Blue* (1999c) is a cycle of poems, in picture book format, about the friendship that develops between a young boy and a surrogate father. Blue, who is a childhood friend of Damon's working mother, had lost his own son to the streets and is determined that the same thing does not happen to Damon. He takes the boy under his wing and teaches him some of what he needs to know to become a strong, self-confident, sensitive man.

Many of Grimes's poems focus on celebrating children and giving voice to their emotions and their struggles with growing up as well as their dreams. A number of them successfully capture the voices of young people around middle school age and the emotional highs and lows of their friendships and budding romantic relationships. Many of her poems are lyrical, expressed in the first person. Frequently, her poems express and validate the strong emotional highs and lows that are a part of growing up. Some are direct straightforward descriptions of experiences common to young people, inviting them to see those experiences in a new light. In *It's Raining Laughter* (1997), Grimes focuses on celebrating Black children—their names, their physical attributes, their energy, their joy. *A Dime a Dozen* (1998) attends to the range of emotions and experiences that can accompany growing up in a difficult family situation and the hopes and dreams and love that can ensure that a young person maintains the strength to remain whole. In *Shoe Magic* (2000), Grimes lightheartedly uses the idea of stepping into magic shoes as a metaphor for following one's dreams by stepping into various roles and careers. Her focus on the everyday lives of children also includes attention to their spiritual lives, in *From a Child's Heart* (1993), a book of prayers, and on the experience of worship in a Black church in *Come Sunday* (1996).

In general, Grimes's poetry moves between free verse and the artful use of rhyme, especially in her work for younger readers, although she employs various poetic forms. In *A Pocketful of Poems* (2001a), each single or double page includes both free verse and a haiku about the topic at hand. She also enjoys word play, as in the poem "Words," from *Hopscotch Love* (1999b), in which she notes the sweets-based names people often bestow on those they love—Sugar, Honey, Sweetie Pie, and the like—and suggests that, with all that sweetness, love just might lead to cavities. In *C Is for City* (1995), she takes the opportunity presented by an alphabet book to incorporate a great deal of alliteration and assonance into the verses. Grimes also creates some vivid sensory images and apt metaphors. In "Sister Love," for example, from *Hopscotch Love*, a woman with sons and "a girl shaped whole in her heart" wants to adopt only one of a pair of sisters. Her cycle of poems in *Aneesa Lee and the Weavers Gift* (1999a), is in fact an extended metaphor that not only examines the weaving of cloth, but also likens the process to weaving together a family

Even though most of Grimes's children's poetry has been published since 1990, her work has been spurred by her recollection of a childhood deprived of the pleasure of finding in books people who not only looked like her, but whose life experiences were similar to hers. It is not surprising then that Nikki Grimes continues in the tradition of Greenfield and Clifton, trying to fill a void, using her poetry as a vehicle to make visible and to celebrate the lives of ordinary Black children.

"NEW" VOICES: CONTINUING AND EXTENDING THE TRADITION

A few "new" African American poets have entered the field since 1990 and, to some extent, taken the poetry in new directions. Some of these poets are new only in the sense that they are coming to poetry from other genres of children's literature or they are new to poetry aimed at children or young adults. In any case, their work is helping to shape the African American children's poetry of the early twenty-first century. Joyce Carol Thomas, for example, is not new to children's poetry; she re-entered the field in the 1990s. Like Nikki Grimes and Eloise Greenfield, Thomas had produced one of the earlier collaborative picture books with Tom Feelings. Continuing the tradition of celebrating and authenticating the lives and experiences of Black children, Thomas has published at least three cycles of poems in picture book format: *Brown Honey in Broomwheat Tea* (1993), *Gingerbread Days* (1995), and *Crowning Glory* (2002). *Brown Honey* and *Gingerbread Days* each contains twelve poems, the first centered on an unnamed young girl whose mother compares her to brown honey and whose father says she is the "sweetwater of his days." *Gingerbread Days*, with a poem for each month, is centered on a young boy and his relationships with members of his family. Thomas's lyrical and eloquent poetry is full of vivid imagery and metaphorical language that invests the poems with layers of meaning. What is new about these two books is that, in addition to her focus on family relationships and on affirming Black children as gifts to be cherished, she also celebrates the ties to both African and Southwestern U.S. pioneer ancestry. Unlike much of the work of other African American poets, which tends to assume urban settings, Thomas's poetry reflects the influence of her Oklahoma background with its references to broomwheat, yellow flowers, horses, and Oklahoma cowboys. The third book, *Crowning Glory*, is a collection of poems about Black girls' and women's hair and the various ways it is worn and adorned. It celebrates the versatility of Black hair, asserts its claim to beauty, and honors the mothers and grandmothers, sisters, and friends who bond over the experience of dealing with each other's hair.

Another important book of poetry published in the 1990s by an author with a long history in children's books was Ashley Bryan's *Sing to the Sun* (1992). One thing that makes this book distinctive is that it is one of the few collections of original children's poems by an African American male poet. As has been pointed out, throughout the last third of the twentieth century, creating African American poetry for children has been mainly an enterprise of African American women. Bryan's book is also distinctive for its having been self-illustrated and for the Black Caribbean flavor of both the poems and the paintings. The rhythmical poems celebrate everyday people, everyday things, everyday sights—a granny, a storyteller, an artist, a "braided beaded lady," flowers, birds, the sun, and the moon. Both in pictures and in words, they evoke island images and experiences, such as hurricanes and frangipani trees. Many express emotions, from joy to the sadness of leave-taking. For all their focus on ordinary life, the poems are set in a Black cultural context. Like Hughes and Greenfield, for example, Bryan includes a blues poem. The final poem, "Ancestry," pays tribute to African ancestry and references Black spirituals. The specificity of Bryan's poems ensures that they transcend their cultural context even while celebrating it.

Another important Black male writer, Walter Dean Myers, known for his young adult novels, has also written some well-received poetry in recent years. *Harlem* (1997) is a poem in picture book format, illustrated by Myers's son Christopher. It pays homage to the community he loves, its sights and sounds and the life experiences of the people who call Harlem home. Myers also composed a collection of poems for young adults, *Here in Harlem* (2004), in which each poem is in the voice of a Harlem resident. Inspired by Edgar Lee Masters's *Spoon River Anthology* (1916), the poems honor the everyday people Myers could imagine passing a Harlem street corner. Together, they form a vivid portrait of a community.

One poet who represents the voice of a newer generation is Angela Johnson, the versatile award-winning creator of several picture books and novels. As of this writing, she has published a very powerful collection of poems called *The Other Side: Shorter Poems* (1998). These poems relate the reminiscences of a fictional young woman who grew up in Shorter, Alabama, a small town that is about to be torn down to make room for a dog track. Summoned by her grandmother, the fourteen year-old, who has moved away, visits the town with her mother one last time and writes of the people, places, and events that shaped her childhood and the feelings she experiences as she recollects them. While earlier poets such as Greenfield and Clifton were overtly concerned with serving perceived needs of Black children, Johnson expresses no such explicit sense of mission. Johnson's voice and her vision are unique and, it appears in these poems, highly personal. In the poem that is also the preface, she equates poetry to "immediacy" and "sudden impact." That immediacy and impact is felt in the spare, rich, and expressive poems in this slim volume. Nevertheless, the vision and the truth of these poems are grounded in the particulars of a specific African American cultural setting. Its evocations of "longing, loss, hope and absurdity" are played out in the racialized American context that is manifest in Ohio as well as Alabama. This is a distinctive collection of poems for older readers, crafted by a gifted writer who is one of the major voices in late twentieth and early twenty-first century African American children's literature.

As we have moved into the twenty-first century, a number of newer poetic voices have joined the chorus of African American poetry for children or young adults. One of the noteworthy writers already known in adult publishing is Marilyn Nelson, Connecticut Poet Laureate (2001–2006), whose first book published for the young adult market was named a Newbery Honor Book. *Carver* (2001) is a remarkable biography of the African American scientist George Washington Carver. Nelson has since published two history-based cycles, *Fortune's Bones* (2004), a tribute to a slave whose bones had been preserved by his doctor owner, and *A Wreath for Emmett Till* (2005), a tribute to the young Chicago teenager who was murdered for allegedly whistling at a White woman. Nelson's sophisticated poems are a powerful means to convey the effects of historical events on the hearts and minds of the people who have lived through them.

Tony Medina, another poet who is new only to children's books, has published two picture book collections to date. In *Da Shawn Days* (2001), a young boy, through a series of poems, introduces readers to his life, the people who are close to him, and what it is like to live in "the hood." Medina's poems in *Love to Langston* (2002) are all written from the point of view of the poet Langston Hughes and reveal some of the important events and moments in his life.

Among those making their poetry debut was Jaime Adoff, son of Virginia Hamilton and Arnold Adoff, whose first book of poetry was *The Song Shoots Out of My Mouth: A Celebration of Music* (2002). Aimed at young adults, but in picture book format, the twenty-four poems in this book capture the rhythms of various kinds of music and celebrate the joy to be found in listening to or making music. The book received the 2003 Lee Bennett Hopkins Poetry Award. Hope Anita Smith's *The Way a Door Closes* (2003), which won the Coretta Scott King New Author Award, is a cycle of poems that describes a young boy's emotional ups and downs as his family works its way through a difficult time. The entrance of these newer voices into the field of African American children's poetry is a welcome sign of the ongoing vitality of the genre.

Beginning in the 1950s with Brooks's *Bronzeville Boys and Girls* (1955) and continuing until the end of the century, rarely have African American poets focused outside the hearts, minds, and sociocultural environments of Black children. Prominent within the poetry are references to individual children—from the titles of all the poems in *Bronzeville Boys and Girls* to Nikki-Rosa, to Everett Anderson, to Nathaniel B. Free, to Danitra Brown, to Blue—naming names is important to these poets. As might be expected, these books are also full of appealing portraits—painted, drawn, or photographed—of Black children and families, holding up a mirror in which they can see themselves validated. In a sense, the poetry makes visible in the literature the formerly invisible child and gives voice to those whose voices had not been previously heard. The themes and topics addressed in this poetry are much the same as those addressed in other genres of African American children's literature: pride in identity and heritage; the importance of family and other human relationships; and the centrality of love as a fundamental need, binding tie, and source of richness in one's life. Within the context of those cultural concerns, the poetry also addresses topics common in children's literature in general—observations of everyday life, expressions of emotions and feelings, and the joys and trials of growing up. Also woven through the body of the poetry are references to Black music, Black history, Black achievers, and Black achievements, in keeping with the perceived need to acquaint American children, both Black and non-Black, with that part of American history that may not be part of common cultural knowledge. Thus, modern African American children's poetry, like most African American children's literature, functions both as an artistic expression intended to illuminate and sometimes entertain and as literature with a purpose.

BIBLIOGRAPHY OF BOOKS FOR CHILDREN AND YOUNG ADULTS

Sources other than books for children and young adults are documented in a reference list at the back of the book.

Adoff, Arnold, ed. 1968/1997. *I Am the Darker Brother: An Anthology of Modern Poems by Black Americans.* New York: Simon and Schuster.

Adoff, Jaime. 2002. *The Song Shoots out of My Mouth: A Celebration of Music*. Illus. by Martin French. New York: Dutton.

Angelou, Maya. 1987. *Now Sheba Sings the Song*. Art by Tom Feelings. New York: Dial.

Bontemps, Arna. 1941. *Golden Slippers: An Anthology of Negro Poetry for Young Readers*. New York: Harper and Row.

Brooks, Gwendolyn. 1956. *Bronzeville Boys and Girls*. Illus. by Ronni Solbert. New York: HarperCollins.

Bryan, Ashley. 1992. *Sing to the Sun*. New York: HarperCollins.

Clifton, Lucille. 1970. *Some of the Days of Everett Anderson*. Illus. by Evaline Ness. New York: Holt.

———. 1971. *Everett Anderson's Christmas Coming*. Illus. by Evaline Ness. New York: Holt.

———. 1991. *Everett Anderson's Christmas Coming*. Illus. by Spivey Gilchrist. New York: Holt.

———. 1974. *Everett Anderson's Year*. Illus. by Ann Grifalconi. New York: Holt.

———. 1977. *Everett Anderson's 1, 2, 3*. Illus. by Ann Grifalconi. New York: Holt.

———. 1978. *Everett Anderson's Nine Months Long*. Illus. by Ann Grifalconi. New York: Holt.

———. 1983. *Everett Anderson's Goodbye*. Illus. by Ann Grifalconi. New York: Holt.

Feelings, Tom. 1972. *Black Pilgrimage*. New York: Lothrop, Lee and Shepard.

———. 1978. *Something on My Mind*. Words by Nikki Grimes. New York: Dial.

———, compiler and illustrator. 1993. *Soul Look Back in Wonder*. New York: Dial.

Giovanni, Nikki. 1971. *Spin a Soft Black Song*. Illus. by Charles Bible. New York: Hill and Wang.

———. 1973. *Ego-tripping and Other Poems for Young People*. Illus. by George Ford. New York: Lawrence Hill and Co.

———. 1980. *Vacation Time*. Illus. by Marisabina Russo. New York: William Morrow.

———. 1994. *Knoxville, Tennessee*. Illus. by Larry Johnson. New York: Scholastic.

———. 1996. *Genie in the Jar*. Illus. by Chris Raschka. New York: Henry Holt.

Greenfield, Eloise. 1978. *Honey I Love and Other Love Poems*. Illus. by Leo and Diane Dillon. New York: Harper and Row.

———. 1981. *Daydreamers*. Pictures by Tom Feelings. New York: Dial.

———. 1988a. *Nathaniel Talking*. Illus. by Jan Spivey Gilchrist. New York: Black Butterfly Press Children's Books.

———. 1988b. *Under the Sunday Tree*. Illus. by Mr. Amos Ferguson. New York: Harper and Row.

———. 1991. *Night on Neighborhood Street*. Illus. by Jan Spivey Gilchrist. New York: Dial.

———. 1998. *Angels*. Illus. by Jan Spivey Gilchrist. New York: Hyperion.

———. 2001. *I Can Draw a Weeposaurus*. Illus. by Jan Spivey Gilchrist. New York: Greenwillow.

———. 2004. *In the Land of Words*. Illus. by Jan Spivey Gilchrist. New York: Amistad.

Grimes, Nikki. 1993. *From a Child's Heart*. Illus. by Brenda Joysmith. Orange, NJ: Just Us Books.

———. 1994. *Meet Danitra Brown*. Illus. by Floyd Cooper. New York: Lothrop, Lee and Shepard.

———. 1995. *C Is for City*. Illus. by Pat Cummings. Honesdale, PA: Boyds Mills Press.

———. 1996. *Come Sunday*. Illus. by Michael Bryant. Grand Rapids, MI: Eerdmans.

———. 1997. *It's Raining Laughter*. Illus. by Myles Pinkney. New York: Dial.

———. 1998. *A Dime a Dozen*. Illus. by Angelo. New York: Dial.

———. 1999a. *Aneesa Lee and the Weaver's Gift*. Illus. by Ashley Bryan. New York: Lothrop, Lee and Shepard.

———. 1999b. *Hopscotch Love*. Illus. by Melodye Benson Rosales. New York: Lothrop, Lee and Shepard.

———. 1999c. *My Man Blue*. Illus. by Jerome Lagarrigue. New York: Dial.

———. 2000. *Shoe Magic*. Illus. by Terry Widener. New York: Orchard.

———. 2001a. *Pocketful of Poems*. Illus. by Javaka Steptoe. Boston: Clarion.

———. 2001b. *Stepping Out with Grandma Mac*. Illus. by Angelo. New York: Orchard.

———. 2002. *Danitra Brown Leaves Town*. Illus. by Floyd Cooper. New York: Amistad/ Harper.

———. 2005. *Danitra Brown, Class Clown*. Illus. by E. B. Lewis. New York: Amistad/ Harper.

Hughes, Langston. 1932. *The Dream Keeper*. Illus. by Helen Sewell. New York: Knopf.

Hughes, Langston. 1997. *The Dream Keeper*. Illus. by Brian Pinkney. New York: Knopf.

———. 1969. *Don't You Turn Back*. Ed. by Lee Bennett Hopkins. Illus. Ann Grifalconi. New York: Knopf.

Johnson, Angela. 1998. *The Other Side: Shorter Poems*. New York: Orchard.

Jordan, June. 1969. *Who Look at Me*. New York: Thomas Y. Crowell.

Medina, Tony. 2001. *Da Shawn Days*. Illus. by Gregory Christie. New York: Lee and Low.

———. 2002. *Love to Langston*. Illus. by Gregory Christie. New York: Lee and Low.

Myers, Walter Dean. 1993. *Brown Angels*. New York: HarperCollins.

———. 1995. *Glorious Angels*. New York: HarperCollins.

———. 1997. *Harlem*. Illus. by Christopher Myers. New York: Scholastic.

———. 1998. *Angel to Angel*. New York: HarperCollins.

———. 2004. *Here in Harlem*. New York: Holiday House.

Nelson, Marilyn. 2001. *Carver*. Asheville, NC: Front Street.

———. 2004. *Fortune's Bones*. Asheville, NC: Front Street.

———. 2005. *A Wreath for Emmett Till*. New York: Houghton Mifflin.

Sanchez, Sonia. 1971. *It's a New Day (Poems for Young Brothas and Sistuhs)*. Detroit: Broadside Press.

Smith, Hope Anita. 2003. *The Way a Door Closes*. New York: Henry Holt.

Thomas, Joyce Carol. 1981. *Black Child*. Illus. by Tom Feelings. New York: Zamani Productions.

———. 1993. *Brown Honey in Broomwheat Tea*. Illus. by Floyd Cooper. New York: HarperCollins.

———. 1995. *Gingerbread Days*. Illus. by Floyd Cooper. New York: HarperCollins.

———. 2002. *Crowning Glory*. Illus. by Brenda Joysmith. New York: Joanna Cotler/ HarperCollins.

CHAPTER 6

African American Picture Books Take Shape: Authenticating the Worlds of Black Children

Picture books, with their combination of verbal and visual art, would seem to be an obvious choice of weapon for Black writers and artists engaged in a battle over what kind of images of Black people are presented to children. After all, one major impetus for the development of an African American children's literature was to contradict the plantation and minstrel-like visual representations of Black people that had become entrenched in popular culture and had spilled over into children's books. But unfortunately, in the decades when Nicodemus, Koko, and their ilk were flourishing, there were not enough readily available picture books written or illustrated by African Americans to effectively contradict those images. In the period between 1930 and 1960, only a few African American writers were focusing on writing for children, and even fewer were successfully producing and publishing picture books. Thus, the African American picture book, like other modern African American children's literature, did not begin to come into its own until the late 1960s.

As used here, the term *picture book* refers to the genre of children's literature in which pictures and written text are interdependent; the two art forms working together tell the story or relate the content. Usually, twenty-four to thirty-two pages in length, picture books are most often aimed at young children, but many picture books are appropriate for older readers, some for all ages. Alphabet books and other concept books, as well as wordless books, are also considered picture books. Currently, every genre of children's literature—fiction, nonfiction, biography, folktale—is being produced in picture book format, but my interest here is mainly in picture storybooks, fictional narratives in which a major part of the story is carried in the pictures. That is, the illustrations are not simply static representations of specific events or moments in the story, but they extend the text, fill in gaps, and help to tell the story. Thus, the role of the picture book illustrator is as important as that of the writer.

Given a working definition of African American children's literature as that created for children and youth by and about African Americans and given the role of the illustrations in a picture book, the definition of *African American picture books* becomes complicated. Since the number of published African American author-artists—those who create both written text and visual art for a picture book—has been relatively small, picture books featuring African Americans have most often been created by two different individuals, who may or may not both be African American. That is, some texts created by Black writers have been illustrated by artists who are not Black, and some Black artists have illustrated texts created by writers who were not Black, making labeling somewhat problematic. Labels notwithstanding, however, my emphasis throughout this volume is on African American writers and artists and the literature they create for children.

The discussion of picture books therefore is divided into two parts of two chapters each. The first two picture book chapters focus on written texts created by African Americans, the next two on the work of African American illustrators. Although the discussion of picture book texts includes some attention to a number of books set in the past, it generally excludes picture books about the slave experience, which are examined with historical fiction, and poetry books in picture book format, which are discussed in the poetry chapter. Folklore and nonfiction are for the most part beyond the scope of this book; therefore, little attention is given in this chapter and the next to picture book versions of folktales from Africa and the Americas or to picture book biographies and other nonfiction in picture book format.

For the two decades between the late 1960s and the late 1980s, the development of the modern African American picture storybook was led by the foundational work of three individuals: John Steptoe, Lucille Clifton, and Eloise Greenfield, all of whom started publishing children's books in the late 1960s or the early 1970s. Through their picture books and their declared purposes and goals, these writers and artists epitomized some of the major thematic thrusts that characterize African American picture books, particularly during the first two decades. Sadly, Steptoe died in 1989. By that time Clifton and Greenfield were concentrating on their poetry. Clifton's first post-1989 picture book did not come until 2001; Greenfield published several poetry books, but only one or two picture storybooks in the 1990s. Fortunately, by the end of the 1980s several other writers and artists had entered the field and had begun to broaden the scope of African American picture book texts. Although the majority of African American picture books produced in the 1970s and 1980s were realistic, reflecting the daily lives of ordinary Black children, particularly urban children, there was some attention to playfulness and to fantasy as a means both to entertain and to make a point. The last decade of the century, which is discussed in the next chapter, saw the entry of still more new voices into the field.

THE MODERN AFRICAN AMERICAN PICTURE BOOK EMERGES

The emergence of the modern African American picture book was heralded by the publication of two critically acclaimed books about African Americans. From the perspective of the children's literature establishment, the landmark modern picture book featuring an African American child was *The Snowy Day* (1962), written and illustrated by White author/artist Ezra Jack Keats. Peter, the main character, was the American Everychild in a brown face and a red snowsuit, playing in new-fallen snow. Keats's illustrations for *The Snowy Day* won the 1963 Caldecott Medal, the first time a book with an African American child as main character had been so honored. The award cited Keats for his effective use of collage to elevate the simple story of a young boy's adventure in the snow into an artistic achievement. According to Keats, it was the first full-color American picture book to feature a Black child. Because of the prestige the Caldecott Medal carries, it demonstrated that ordinary, "normal" Black children could be acceptable (read profitable) subjects for picture books and thus helped to make major publishing houses more welcoming to African American picture books.

The second precursor of the modern African American picture storybook was the first major picture book by an African American published by a mainstream press in the 1960s. It was Jacob Lawrence's *Harriet and the Promised Land* (1968), a biographical tribute to Harriet Tubman, the famous "conductor" on the Underground Railroad. Part of its significance lies in its continuing a tradition in African American children's literature—providing information about and celebrating the historical achievements of African American heroes and "sheroes," which has been an important aspect of African American children's literature at least since *The Brownies' Book*. *Harriet and the Promised Land*, however, is particularly significant because of the stature of its creator and the dramatic illustrations, which work in harmony with the poetic text to elevate the book to a work of art. Jacob Lawrence was one of America's most prominent and highly respected artists, famous in part for several narrative series of paintings centering on Black history and Black heroes. Lawrence's series on the Great Migration, and Harriet Tubman, Frederick Douglass, John Brown, and Toussaint L'Ouverture, have all been adapted into picture books.

Harriet and the Promised Land is biography, history, poetry, story, and visual narrative in one remarkable package. The text is a rhymed contemporary ballad—spare, rhythmical verse accessible to a young audience, but appropriate for people of all ages. The striking feature of the book, however, is Lawrence's art, rendered in the signature style that he called "dynamic cubism"—strong colors and distorted figures that express emotional and symbolic meanings. The North Star appears in every night scene, a constant guide and a symbol of freedom. Harriet's hands and feet are sometimes exaggerated in size, emphasizing her strength and hard work. Harriet indeed often appears larger than life. Faces also are expressively drawn, their shapes and the white lines that form eyes and teeth against very dark brown skin giving an almost skeletal appearance. The overall impression, however, is of Harriet's caring, her strength, her determination, her hope, and her triumph. This powerful, deceptively simple picture book won high praise from critics. *The New York Times*, for example, named it a Best Illustrated Book for 1968. But, at that time many Black parents, teachers, and librarians were searching for realistic and appealing images of Black people in books for children and were disturbed by Lawrence's expressionistic style and impatient with what seemed to them ugly images in the book. Reissued in 1992, it is nevertheless a singular achievement, a bequest for children from a preeminent American artist.

Notwithstanding the stature of *Harriet's* creator and the popularity of *The Snowy Day*, however, the breakthrough contemporary African American picture story was *Stevie*, which was published just before the nineteenth birthday of its creator, John Steptoe, in 1969. In an unprecedented move, *Life* published both the entire text and all of the pictures from *Stevie*—in full color—in the August 29, 1969, issue, the week before Harper was to officially release the hardback edition. *Stevie's* landmark status derives from its true-to-life story, its effective use of an informal Black spoken language, and the freshness and quality of Steptoe's art. It also marks the debut of the first African American picture book author-artist to emerge in the field of contemporary African American children's literature.

The story itself is simple. Robert's mother agrees to keep little Steven during the week while his mother works. Robert is jealous of his mother's attention to Stevie and considers him a nuisance, but when Stevie is gone, Robert misses him. Set in an urban working-class African American neighborhood and with an all-Black cast of characters, the text and pictures portray something of the life of ordinary Black city children and offer a glimpse of two families working together to provide satisfactory and trustworthy child care for working parents. Robert and Stevie engage in common daily activities—eating corn flakes for breakfast, playing "cowboys and Indians" on the stoop, playing in the park, eavesdropping on grown-up conversations. Robert expresses attitudes that would be typical of an only child who is suddenly confronted with being "big brother" and part-time babysitter, especially to someone from outside the family. At the same time, however, his affection for little Stevie is apparent as he reminisces about their time together. In that sense, the story carries a certain "universal" appeal; its theme echoes the emotions of children across many social and cultural divides.

Steptoe was very clear, however, about his intended audience. In the article that accompanied *Stevie*'s initial publication, he is quoted as saying, "The story, the language, is not directed at white children. I wanted it to be something black children could read without translating the language, something real which would relate to what a black child would know" ("I Am a Painter" 1969, 59). The language of *Stevie* needs no translation for Black urban children because it reflects the informal vernacular that would have come naturally to Robert and Stevie and others in a community such as theirs. It incorporates some grammatical features associated with a Black urban dialect, such as the double negative (e.g., "And my momma never said nothin' to him," n.p.), as well as certain discourse styles (e.g., "And so Stevie moved in, with his old crybaby self"). The importance of the language lies in its reflection of a Black oral narrative style; that is, the vernacular linguistic features are present not only in the dialogue among characters, but also in the narration itself. This narrative style is a feature of a significant number of contemporary African American literary texts for children, and its use in *Stevie* is a milestone in that canon.

Unlike most recent picture books, in which illustrations appear on every page, *Stevie* includes just six full-color paintings, for which Steptoe also received critical praise. The artwork in *Stevie* has been compared to that of Rouault because of its use of vivid colors and heavy black outlines. The expressionistic illustrations, drawn with marker and painted over with pastels, bring to life the details of the urban setting and the warmth and comfort of Robert's home. Every illustration shows a person or persons, revealing the characters, their relationships to each other, their emotions, and the mood of the story. Moreover, the characters are clearly portrayed as African Americans; they are not "color-me-brown" images identifiable as Black only by their skin color. Steptoe wanted his readers to see themselves in his work.

Growing up in Bedford-Stuyvesant in the 1950s and 1960s, Steptoe had been unable to find children like himself in the books available to him then. In one interview he noted, "What I try to create are all the things I didn't have as a kid that I would have liked to read" (Steptoe 1987). His statement is an implicit indictment of the historical omission from American children's literature of life experiences familiar to urban African American children. A number of Steptoe's early books therefore reflected a decidedly urban African American cultural environment.

In fact, a substantial portion of the picture books produced by African American writers in the 1970s had urban settings. By that time, uprisings in a number of large American cities had called the nation's attention to the failure of urban schools to adequately educate the children of the Black citizens and other people of color who inhabited the cores of those cities. Part of the response had been increased attention to producing textbooks and trade books that were considered relevant to the lives of children living in inner cities. Indeed, "relevance" became an important byword in discussions of appropriate texts for so-called disadvantaged urban children.

REALITY, RELEVANCE, AND "BLACKNESS": BEYOND *STEVIE*

Steptoe's second book, *Uptown* (1970), exemplifies the focus of African American picture books of the 1970s on reflecting the realities of urban life, especially for Black boys. Set in Harlem, *Uptown* follows John and his "main man," Dennis, as they walk through their neighborhood, talking of what they might be when they grow up. As they observe or remember past encounters with junkies, dashiki-wearing Brothers, teenagers, hippies, and karate experts, they imagine what it would be like to walk in each of their shoes for a while. Although the boys' consideration of the possibility of becoming junkies or hippies raised some eyebrows, *Uptown* succeeded in reflecting the reality of life for some Black urban children, those least likely to have been visible in previous children's books.

The urban reality is mirrored further by the boys' language. The first-person narration, like that in *Stevie*, reflects the grammar of informal Black urban speech, but also reflects the Black teenage jargon of the day. John declares, for example, "When I get big, I'm gonna be turnin' out with some clothes. I'm gonna have me on a pair of green gators, some bad silks, and a couple of Blye knits." Although many teachers and librarians would have found the vocabulary unfamiliar and would likely have questioned its appropriateness for elementary school settings, the language adds an air of authenticity to the book's portrayal of young Black urban boys imaginatively trying on roles—in the neighborhood, outside school—as they anticipate growing into manhood.

Steptoe's use of Black vernacular language, his identification of and with his audience, and his emphasis on African connections all echo the stance of Black arts movement proponents. The almost-19-year-old was quoted in the *Life* article that accompanied Stevie, "I have never felt I was a citizen of the U.S.A.—this country doesn't speak to me. To be a black man in this society means finding out who I am. So I have got to stay on my own, get out from under induced values and discover who I am at base. One thing I know: at the base there is blackness" ("I Am a Painter," 59).

In *Birthday* (1972), Steptoe explores, through the eyes of a young Black boy, what it might be like to live in a Black nation, to be surrounded by "blackness." Javaka Shatu celebrates his eighth birthday in Yoruba, an imagined rural Africanized town established by Black families who had left the "old America." The entire community participates in this important celebration. The townspeople, including children, address each other as "Brother" and "Sister," and all is peace and harmony in this self-sufficient utopia. Although Steptoe asserted that the setting of *Birthday* is "no particular place," the illustrations—as well as the name Yoruba—strongly suggest an African setting. The town buildings reflect African architectural styles. The clothing worn by people in the community is also African in style, and Steptoe incorporates elements of African design into some of the paintings. His political stance is also evident in both *Birthday* and *Uptown*. In *Uptown*, for example, they speak of "nice Black power things" in a bookstore window, in which a "Free the Panthers" sign is also visible. Steptoe uses the same device in *Birthday,* a sign in Yoruba proclaims, "Nation time has come."

Over time, Steptoe expanded the range of settings and themes in his writing. As his two children, Bweela and Javaka, grew, they became characters in a couple of intimate father-and-children family stories—*My Special Best Words* (1974) and *Daddy Is a Monster . . . Sometimes* (1980)—at a time when responsible single Black fathers were rarely found in picture books. Later, he moved beyond his familiar urban environment to retell and illustrate a Native American legend, *The Story of Jumping Mouse* (1984). As a picture book artist, Steptoe demonstrated an exceptional range and variety in technique, medium, style, and use of color. His work moved from the intense colors and expressionistic art of his early books, through experimentation with silkscreen and photographs, into naturalistic pencil drawings and full-color naturalistic paintings. His crowning achievement was *Mufaro's Beautiful Daughters* (1987), a painstakingly researched and lushly illustrated adaptation of a southern African tale, which contains both a "Cinderella" and a "toads-and-diamonds" motif. Steptoe's full-color realistic paintings for *Mufaro* received well-deserved critical acclaim; it was named a Caldecott Honor book and won a Boston Globe-Horn Book Award for illustration.

The emergence of John Steptoe as the first major contemporary African American picture book author-artist is one of the signal developments in modern African American children's literature. In the twenty years between the publication of *Stevie* and Steptoe's untimely death in 1989, Steptoe wrote and illustrated eleven of his own books, including one novel, and he illustrated five picture books written by others. He understood the demands of a picture book as an art form, and building on his intimate knowledge of growing up in a Black urban neighborhood, he fulfilled his commitment to make Black urban children visible in picture books and to make their voices heard. In identifying Black children as his primary audience in his early work, he echoed Du Bois's historical intention to publish literature for all children, but mainly for "ours, the children of the sun," an indication of the persistence of the idea that Black children need a literature of affirmation.

AUTHENTICATING THE WORLD OF BLACK CHILDREN: LUCILLE CLIFTON'S PICTURE STORYBOOKS

As noted in the chapter on poetry, Lucille Clifton expressed the concept of affirmation as "authenticating" the world of Black children, which she saw as the job of a Black writer. Between 1970 and 1979, counting the Everett Anderson series, Clifton published fourteen picture books, more than any other African American writer in those years, making hers the predominant voice in African American picture books of that decade. As a critically acclaimed and award-winning poet, Clifton is particularly adept at creating the sort of concise and economical texts that characterize excellent picture books, which because of length constraints and the requisite interplay between text and visual art, often have much in common with poetry.

Part of authenticating the world of African American children is providing them with information that allows them to understand their connections to others like themselves, to take pride in belonging to a particular social/cultural group. In that regard, some of Clifton's work helped to fill what was perceived as an unacceptable void—the lack of attention to Black history in children's books and in school curricula. This concern is particularly evident in two of her early books, *All Us Come Cross the Water* (1973a) and *The Black BC's* (1970). *The Black BC's* was written in response to questions raised by Clifton's own six children. In this primer on Black culture and history, organized as an alphabet book, Clifton used both short verse and expository prose to inform readers about significant people, places, and events—from Africa to Zenith. She placed particular stress on the contributions Black people have made to American life and culture. Don Miller's realistic black-and-white illustrations include a number of portraits of actual persons, providing a visual confirmation and extension of the factual information in the text.

All Us Come Cross the Water, which was illustrated by John Steptoe, also focuses on helping Black children understand something about their history and their roots in Africa. *All Us* relates Ujamaa's search for his ancestral roots, prompted by his teacher's request for the students to tell where they are from. Ujamaa knows that Big Mama, his "Mama's Mama's Mama," is an important source of family history. She informs him that her people came from Whydah in Dahomey in 1855, a detail that reflects Clifton's actual family roots and that helps to make African ancestry more concrete and specific than the more typical vague tie to the vastness—and for most American children, the strangeness—of the African continent. In a conversation with his "grown man friend" and mentor Tweezer at the Panther Book Shop, Ujamaa learns a bit about slavery from an African American perspective. Tweezer speaks of his grandfather having left his name in Africa when he was stolen to be enslaved and of the importance of names and naming: "Reckon he figure if they ain't got his name they ain't really got him" (n.p.). Big Mama and Tweezer help Ujamaa understand that Black people are all one people, with roots on the African continent. Concepts such as these, coming from within the family and the community, can have the effect of empowering young Black readers with knowledge that will enable them to survive psychologically in a society that often treats them as if they have no worthwhile history and are themselves less worthy than others.

Like Steptoe's *Uptown* (1970), Clifton's *All Us Come Cross the Water* (1973a) also implies that school is not likely to be a source of accurate information about African American history or Africa. In both stories, the source of such information is within the Black community—Black bookstores or Black people who function as elders/mentors. The implication is that, to the extent that knowledge is power, it is the Black family and community that are the source of empowerment for Black children. Another interesting feature of *All Us* is the characterization of the African American teacher as lacking in knowledge about Africa and insensitive to the importance of naming. (She calls Ujamaa Jim.) It is an example of an early—and in picture books, relatively rare—concern with class differences within the Black community, with the middle-class teacher made to appear like an outsider, a representative of the larger society that miseducates Black children.

Another aspect of authenticating the world(s) of Black children is to represent that world as "normal" by making it the setting for stories about familiar experiences involving people like those they know. For Clifton, as for Steptoe, this has meant, among other things, incorporating the variety of language and discourse styles that would be heard in that world, both those styles that do and those that do not conform to the grammatical rules of Standard English. *All Us Come Cross the Water* (1973a), *My Brother Fine with Me* (1975), and *Three Wishes* (1976) exemplify Clifton's use of first-person narration rendered in a language that reflects informal speech common to many African Americans. *My Brother Fine*, for instance, begins, "My brother Baggy, he gonna run away. He say he tired of Mama and Daddy always telling him what to do" (n.p.). Others of Clifton's books, such as *Don't You Remember?* (1973c), have a third-person narration that is rendered pretty much in Standard English grammatically even though it also incorporates features of a Black oral vernacular.

Clifton (1981, 36) also asserted that she writes about "poor children." To authenticate the world of poor children often means embedding in the story some of the details of living without abundant financial resources. For example, eight-year-old Johnetta, in *My Brother Fine with Me*, takes care of her five-year-old brother in the summer months while both parents work. The same is true of Johnetta's friend Peaches, who cares for a younger sister. In *Don't You Remember?* (1973c), a 15-year-old boy has dropped out of school to take care of his four-year-old sister while their parents work. The Everett Anderson books include many details of life in the projects for a single working mother and her child. In *Everett Anderson's Year* (1974), for instance, Everett's plan to make a cake for the Fourth of July is thwarted because they do not have enough sugar, and payday is a still a few days away. In *Amifika* (1977), a little boy and his mother live in two rooms and must make space for his father, who is returning home from the military. Except in *Amifika*, these details are not central to the story lines; they are matter-of-fact aspects of the lives of these children. None of these stories, including *Amifika*, is a story about being poor *per se*, and Clifton points out that such things have nothing to do with character. Certainly, being poor is not synonymous with being Black, but in the 1970s the intent of Clifton and others was to make visible in books a population that was underrepresented in American picture books. Whatever the socioeconomic circumstances of the characters, however, part of authenticating the world of Black children in fiction is weaving into the story the details of the cultural, social, and physical setting.

Another aspect of authenticating the world of Black children is Clifton's declared focus on family love. Ten of Clifton's fourteen 1970s picture books center on family relationships. *Good, Says Jerome* (1973d) for example, is a dialogue in verse in which a young boy shares his fears about moving—fears of monsters, a new place, a new school, even death—with his older sister, who unfailingly offers compassion and reassurance. The text of *Jerome* is as much poetry as the Everett Anderson texts and could as easily be discussed in the poetry chapter, but the point to be made here is the focus on the loving relationship between the siblings. Even in that context, however, Clifton weaves in a point about cultural identity and racial pride. "What's black?" Jerome asks. To which his sister replies in part, "It's a feeling inside about who we are/and how strong and how free" (n.p.).

As the mother of six children, Clifton was well aware of the ups and downs of the relationship between siblings. In *My Brother Fine with Me* (1975), former only child Johnetta relates the story of her brother Baggy's running away. At first she is happy to help him "get his stuff together," but when he has left, she realizes how much she misses him. Like *Stevie* (Steptoe 1969), *My Brother Fine* explores a familiar theme, set in a very specific cultural context. As has been pointed out, Johnny's speech patterns are identifiably Black. Other aspects of the text also help to identify the unmistakable African American cultural context—such as Baggy's deciding "he a Black man, a warrior" and his choice of a (hair) pick as one of the two essential items he needs to take with him when he runs away. The main point, however, is that Johnny comes to realize how much she cares for her little brother. Ultimately, it is a book about love in a family.

Although the main theme of *All Us Come Cross the Water* (1973a) concerns heritage, racial/cultural pride, and unity, it also focuses on family. With the Big Mama character in that book, Clifton became one of the first contemporary African American writers to represent in picture books an African American extended family that includes more than two generations living in the same household. Grandparents, great-grandparents, great-aunts and -uncles, and similar elderly relatives have major supporting—and often starring—roles in a substantial portion of African American picture books, especially those produced in the 1980s and 1990s. This emphasis on the roles and function of elders as integral and important members of the family is one of the characterizing features of African American children's literature.

The focus on the importance of family and on the loving relationships among various family members is very significant in African American children's literature. It is in part an attempt to contradict popular and historical misperceptions about African American families—especially those with few monetary resources—as fractured and unstable. In contrast to that image, African American writers stress the significance of the family as a source of love, stability, comfort, support, knowledge, and wisdom. This emphasis on valuing family ties, an echo of one of the important cultural themes identified by Webber (1978) in his study of the slave quarter community, reflects an important cultural attitude that many African American authors attempt, through their stories, to pass on to young readers.

While Clifton dwells mainly in the territory of the family, in a couple of books she also explores the topic of friendship. Clifton's *Three Wishes* (1976) relates how a young girl learns, with the guidance of her mother, the value of friendship. In *The Boy Who Didn't Believe in Spring* (1973b), King Shabazz leads his friend Tony Polito on a search for signs of spring. That Tony is Italian and not African American was significant at a time when few Black writers included White people as main characters in their picture books. Clifton recognized that there is racial diversity in some urban neighborhoods and chose to represent that reality in this book. What was important to her, she noted, was that, in contrast to a number of the "integrated" picture books of the time, the African American child in her story was the leader (Sims 1982a).

For Clifton, the name of the main character in *The Boy Who Didn't Believe in Spring*, King Shabazz, was another aspect of "authenticating" the world of Black children. By giving her characters names (and nicknames) of the kind that might be commonly found in a Black cultural context (e.g., Ujamaa, Amifika, Zenobia, Johnetta [a girl named after her father], Peaches, Victorious, Jamilla), Clifton calls attention to and validates this aspect of African American culture. Titles and forms of address are another example of this validation. "Big Mama," "Mama," "Ma'am" (as in "yes, ma'am), "girl" (as in "But, Jamilla, girl"), and "man" are familiar forms of address that abound in Black families, neighborhoods, and homes.

With her picture books, Clifton helped to expand the canon of children's literature with a body of stories that authenticates the very real cultural context in which Black urban, mainly poor, children live their lives. This authentication is realized through weaving into the texts and illustrations Black rhetorical styles, realistic details of everyday living, a focus on family and family relationships, and cultural traditions. Like Steptoe, Clifton identified her primary audience as Black children. Nonetheless, her stories invite readers to explore and learn about that which is "important, and real, and basic, and true" (Clifton 1981, 36) for humans across cultural divides.

AFFIRMING AFRICAN AMERICAN CHILDREN'S LIVES: THE WORK OF ELOISE GREENFIELD

In her "manifesto" article, Eloise Greenfield (1975b) identified what was "important, and real, and basic, and true" for her as a writer for children—appreciation for the arts and for language, self-love, a focus on the positive, effective problem solving, knowledge of Black heritage and acquaintance with Black heroes, respect for elders, and recognition of the strength of the Black family. These values are manifest in various ways in a substantial portion of African American literature for children and are therefore in some sense foundational. Greenfield expressed these values as those she hoped to instill in children through her writing. To that end, she has written in a number of genres, including picture book biographies, memoir, novels, and most notably, poetry. Beginning in the 1970s, she also created at least ten picture storybooks as well a couple of concept books for young children.

Greenfield's first book, *Bubbles* (1972), was originally published with a spiral binding by a fledgling Black publisher in Washington, D.C., called Drum and Spear Press. A small celebration of literacy, the book centers on a boy trying to find someone to listen to the good news that he has learned to read. When his mother is too busy to stop and listen, he shares his news with his baby sister. In keeping with Greenfield's expressed desire to share her love of words, it is fitting that her first book celebrates a child's excitement about being able to read words and his recognition of the promise and potential embedded in that act.

Greenfield also expressed a desire to give children a love for the arts and that goal, combined with her concern for positive images, suggests that she would take particular interest in the illustrations for her picture books. Greenfield has insisted from the beginning on Black artists to illustrate her work, presumably in part because she believes that African American artists can likely be counted on to portray Black people with dignity. Some of her early picture books provided opportunities, therefore, for emerging African American artists. The 1977 remake of *Bubbles* as *Good News* marked the debut of Pat Cummings, whose career became well established in the 1980s. *She Come Bringing Me that Little Baby Girl* (Greenfield 1974), illustrated by John Steptoe, received a 1975 Boston Globe-Horn Book Honor Award for Illustration. At least one critic saw Steptoe's illustrations for *She Come Bringing Me* as an example of his best work (Bradley 1991). It was also one of Greenfield's books that became the first illustrated picture book of Floyd Cooper, who went on to become a very prolific and popular illustrator. Ultimately, Greenfield formed a close collaborative relationship with Jan Spivey Gilchrist, who has illustrated all or almost all of Greenfield's books since the late 1970s and whose career has grown along with Greenfield's.

As was the case with Clifton's works for children, family is central in Greenfield's picture storybooks, which usually feature a young child coping with a familiar childhood problem or concern. These books focus on what she refers to as the strength of the Black family. In *She Come Bringing Me that Little Baby Girl* (1974), for example, Kevin overcomes his jealousy of the new baby and gains a new perspective on his role as big brother, aided by his uncle, who relates that he was once a big brother, and that his little sister grew up to be Kevin's mother. When Tyree in *First Pink Light* (1976) insists on waiting up to greet his father, who has been away seeing after Tyree's grandmother, his mother arranges for Tyree to feel victorious even though he ends up asleep. *I Can Do It by Myself* (1978), co-written by Greenfield and her mother, Lessie Jones Little, features a young boy who successfully navigates his way to and from the store, past a scary dog, to get a birthday present for his mother. In *Me and Neesie* (1975a), Janell has an imaginary friend who disappears when elderly Aunt Bea comes to visit and Janell goes off to school and meets new friends. In all these situations, the young child solves his or her problem supported by the love and guidance of parents and other adults.

Another thread woven through Greenfield's picture books is a focus on engendering in children an appreciation for their elders. In *Me and Neesie* (1975a), Aunt Bea is a revered visitor in Janell's home. Although the elder in *First Pink Light* (1976) is offstage so to speak, it is mentioned simply as a matter of fact that Tyree's father has spent a month taking care of his mother. In some of Greenfield's books, a special close relationship between grandparent and grandchild is central. In *Grandmama's Joy* (1980), for example, Rhondy is being raised by her grandmother, who is facing difficult times financially. It is Rhondy who helps her grandmother remember that their love for each other is what is most important. Tamika, in *Grandpa's Face* (1988), is frightened when she discovers that, as an actor, her beloved grandfather is capable of expressing anger or hate. She needs to be reassured that his acting has nothing to do with his love for her, which will endure. In *William and the Good Old Days* (1993), after his grandmother becomes ill, William reminisces about the good times they had enjoyed together and hopes for more good times to come. The importance of intergenerational relationships as a thematic emphasis in African American picture books, as well as the more general focus on family, suggests again that Greenfield's concerns as expressed in her 1975 article are shared across a number of African American writers (Greenfield 1975b).

John Steptoe, Lucille Clifton, and Eloise Greenfield established the contemporary African American picture book, and for the two decades between 1969 and 1989, their work constituted the most significant portion of that canon. In addition, carrying out their explicit intentions to focus on realistically reflecting African American urban life, on authenticating the worlds of Black children, and on affirming them and their lives, they delineated a set of thematic concerns that would be reflected in African American children's literature across the rest of the twentieth century.

OTHER SIGNIFICANT DEVELOPMENTS IN THE FIRST TWO DECADES

Although the writing of African American picture books of the 1970s and 1980s was dominated by the realistic stories of Steptoe, Clifton, and Greenfield, it should be noted that these themes were also evident in the works of a few other African American writers, such as Ianthe Thomas and Ray Prather, who also produced picture books during that period. Prather is most notable as another of the few African American author-artists, although he apparently stopped doing picture books after the 1970s. In the 1970s and early 1980s, Thomas published at least five well-received picture books about young children and their relationships with siblings, parents, and other adults, but then she too disappeared from the field. Although they did not sustain long careers in the children's literature or produce large numbers of children's books, they were part of the effort to make visible and to redefine and recast the written and visual images of Black people in children's books.

Of greater significance are two books from the 1970s and 1980s that have become "classic" or near-classic African American picture books. The first was *Cornrows* (1979), written by Camille Yarbrough, whose career spans theater, dance, film, and music. *Cornrows* incorporates a number of thematic concerns that are significant in African American children's literature—pride in African and African American heritage, intergenerational connections, the celebration of oral communication, and concerns with African American children's self-esteem. Its presentation of those themes, however, is innovative and unusual, combining story and verse, the historical and the contemporary, fiction and information.

The 1979 publication of *Cornrows* was timely since it appeared in the same year that Bo Derek wore her blond hair cornrowed in a very popular film, causing some media to label the hairstyle "Bo braids." In that regard, Yarbrough's book served to place the hairstyle in its historical context. In *Cornrows*, a great-grand-mother and her granddaughter braid the hair of her two great-grandchildren, all the while informing them of the African origins and the possible symbolic mean-ings of the hairstyles. Using both narrative prose and a rhythmic, poetic chant simi-lar to today's hip-hop, Great-Grammaw and Mama connect cornrows to the spirit of African peoples and invite the children to name their hairstyles after African Americans and Africans who made significant contributions to Black culture and history. Carole Byard's black-and-white drawings for *Cornrows,* which earned a Coretta Scott King Award for Illustration, portray not only the family of the story, but also scenes and artifacts from African and African American history. Byard also includes images of famous African Americans who are named in the text. The drawings very effectively reflect the spirit that Great Grammaw evokes. *Cornrows* is also significant as a precursor to a group of late-century African American chil-dren's books focusing on Black children's hair.

The other classic of the era is Valerie Flournoy's *The Patchwork Quilt* (1985), which was illustrated in full color by Jerry Pinkney. It is the best-known and prob-ably most enduring example of one of the major thematic emphases in African American picture books, particularly in the 1990s: honoring the elders in intergen-erational stories. Tanya's grandmother has decided to make a quilt from patches cut from clothing that had belonged to various members of the family. Each piece represents a family story, and Grandma helps Tanya realize the importance of pre-serving those memories. When Grandma becomes ill, Tanya takes over most of the work on the quilt, and once Grandma recovers, she has only to put the finishing touches on her masterpiece.

The Patchwork Quilt is significant in part because it exemplifies a number of characteristics typical of the African American intergenerational stories that would proliferate in the 1990s. Quilts constitute an important component of African American cultural history, and in teaching Tanya to quilt while recalling family stories, Grandma functions as a source of wisdom, knowledge, family history, and cultural history. Grandma commands, and is freely given, respect. At Christmas, "All Grandma's sons and daughters and nieces and nephews came to pay their respects" (n.p.). When Tanya's worried mother tries to move the feisty Grandma from her favorite spot by a drafty window, she cajoles, "Grandma, please. . . . You can sit here by the heater." Grandma replies: "I'm not your grandmother; I'm your mother. . . . And I am going to sit here in the Lord's light and make my masterpiece." Grandma's reference to the Lord's light is an example of the expres-sions of spirituality or religious beliefs that appear fairly frequently, particularly as part of the characterization of elders. Though she demands respect, Grandma is also loved and loving, and it is clear that she and Tanya are especially close. Special relationships between young children and grandparents or other relatives two or three generations older are another important feature of the African American "grandparent" stories.

The first two decades of modern African American picture books also saw the development of a strand of such books that do not highlight or foreground African American culture or heritage, although they reflect the life experiences of many Black children, particularly middle-class Black children. The work of Jeanette Caines and Pat Cummings, who illustrated two of Caines's books, exemplify this strand.

Although Caines did not produce a large number of picture books, her work added some newer topics to African American picture books featuring families. Some of Caines's books, while focusing on family relationships, are also "topical" books that deal with issues such as divorce or adoption through the eyes of African American children.

Her first picture book, *Abby* (Caines 1973), features a little girl who delights in hearing the story of her adoption and who needs reassurance that her brother loves her. *Daddy* (1977) concerns the relationship between a young girl and her divorced father. Two of Caines's books focus on special relationships within a family. *Window Wishing* (1980), one of the earlier intergenerational stories, features an unconventional sneaker-wearing grandmother who makes her grandchildren's vacations fun. *Just Us Women* (1982), in my view the best of Caines's picture books, relates the story of a leisurely trip taken by an aunt and a niece to visit relatives in the South. Illustrated by Pat Cummings, it is a warm story celebrating the special role that aunts can play in girls' lives. Few Black writers at the time were pitching their work for preschoolers, but Caines did so in *I Need a Lunch Box* (1988), which concerns a young boy who, although he is not yet old enough for school like his sister, wants very much to have his very own lunch box. *Lunch Box* incorporates elements of a concept book about color. As the narrator dreams of a different color lunch box for each school day, Pat Cummings's art enhances the concept book effect by infusing the illustration for each day with the appropriate color.

In the 1980s, Cummings established herself as both an author and an award-winning illustrator. As has been noted, she entered the field in 1977 as the illustrator of a reissue of Eloise Greenfield's first book. When she published *Jimmy Lee Did It* in 1985, she emerged as the second major African American author-artist to produce several original realistic picture storybooks. *Jimmy Lee Did It* (1985) was a harbinger of things to come in the way of Cummings's original stories. Based on her own childhood family memories, it follows Angel as she tries to solve the mystery of how the invisible Jimmy Lee gets by with all the misdeeds for which her brother Artie blames him. Cummings's sense of humor comes through in both her rhyming text and her lively art. In a period when many African American writers and artists were intent on the sociocultural functions that could be served by their art, Cummings chose to emphasize humor, playfully relating and slightly exaggerating experiences common to many middle-class American children, adding a welcome touch of playfulness to the genre of African American picture books. Cummings sees her work in a "universal" framework, stories with themes or other elements to which children can relate across cultural boundaries. Although she established herself as an illustrator in the late 1970s and the 1980s, most of her work as an author-artist was published in the 1990s.

As will be noted, some of Pat Cummings's original stories include enough exaggeration to place them on the edge of fantasy, a genre that has attracted only a few African American children's book writers. In *C.L.O.U.D.S.* (1986), however, Cummings created her own unique fantasy, a celebration of imagination and creativity. Chuku works for the department of Creative Lights, Opticals, and Unusual Designs in the Sky (C.L.O.U.D.S.). Assigned to the skies over New York, he creates spectacular images with clouds, inspired by a girl who pays close attention while most New Yorkers never bother to look up. When Chuku is reassigned to a "better" post in the tropics, he defies the rules and loses out on the "promotion," much to his satisfaction, since New York has become his briar patch. Although Chuku is an African name, and both the supervisor and Chuku appear to be African American in terms of their facial features, they are actually painted blue. *C.L.O.U.D.S.* is a unique contribution to African American picture books.

FANTASY IN AFRICAN AMERICAN PICTURE BOOKS OF THE 1970s AND 1980s

Although the focus in African American picture books in the 1970s was overwhelmingly on reflecting the realities of urban life, there was also some attention to fantasy, humor, and story purely as entertainment. One notable early example, Walter Dean Myers's *The Dragon Takes a Wife* (1972), was a humorous takeoff on the traditional knight-slays-dragon tale. In Myers's story, it is Harry, the flute-playing dragon, who must defeat the knight in order to win a wife. Unsuccessful after a number of tries, he seeks help from Mabel Mae Jones, an attractive and very hip, afro-wearing Black fairy. Mabel Mae is quite inept as a fairy, but when she transforms herself into a dragon she so inspires Harry that he is able to vanquish the knight, marry Mabel Mae, get "a good job in the post office," and live happily ever after. The reference to the post office is recognizable to African American adults as a sly indirect reference to a time when job discrimination was overt and rampant, and such a civil service position was the closest most African Americans, even those with college degrees, could come to a job high on the socioeconomic ladder. Such indirection, known among African Americans as signifying, is frequently found in African American literature.

Mainly, however, what turns this parody into an African American tale is Mabel Mae's speech, which is decidedly Black and urban. "What's bugging you Baby?" is her initial greeting to Harry. Her rhyming spells are also straight out of the Black urban discourse styles of that time: "Fire, be hotter/And hotter than that!/ Turn Harry on/So he can burn that cat!" (n.p.). Because such jargon is ever changing, the written text shows its age, but the humor holds up surprisingly well. Even though the expressions may be dated, the meanings are clear three decades later. The thread of whimsy and humor that is represented by Mabel Mae was a welcome nod to playfulness, which remained an important, but relatively muted, component of African American picture books throughout the rest of the century.

It is interesting to note that Myers received a substantial amount of hate mail regarding his recasting of the European fairy tale as a hip urban tale (W. D. Myers 1979). Apparently, the objection was not to his reversing the knight-slays-dragon motif, but to his appropriating the traditional European fairy tale by making the fairy an Afro-wearing, Black-vernacular-spouting, sassy Black woman. It is particularly interesting in the context of a field in which non-Black writers feel free, even compelled, to dip into African and African American literary and cultural traditions to create books that they consider to have universal appeal.

Often in a playful mood in his early work, Myers drew on African American folk traditions to create *Mr. Monkey and the Gotcha Bird* (1984), a story made up to entertain his young son on a long plane ride. *Gotcha Bird* involves a clever trickster monkey who uses his wits to outsmart others. It is written in a kind of patois reminiscent of some Caribbean English:

"Gotcha!" Gotcha Bird grab Monkey by he tail.
"Loose that tail, Gotcha Bird!" Monkey say. "I plenty danger!"
"You no danger to Gotcha Bird. You supper."

In order to save himself, Monkey helps Gotcha Bird catch and eat fish, turtle, and hare. But when Gotcha Bird is taken in by Monkey's claim that he also can trick Lion, it is Gotcha Bird who becomes supper. In this story, Monkey calls to mind the signifying monkey, an important figure in African American folklore.[1]

In some cases, fantasy was used in the service of relaying a message to readers, usually about self-esteem. *An Enchanted Hair Tale* (DeVeaux 1987), for example, celebrates the beauty of dreadlocks and is, like *Cornrows* (Yarbrough 1979), an exemplar of the focus on African Americans' hair that would appear in several end-of-the-century picture books. As in the realistic picture books, the theme of engendering pride in African Americans' ties to Africa is an important thread in some fantasy picture books. Mildred Pitts Walter's *Brother to the Wind* (1985), illustrated by Caldecott winners Leo and Diane Dillon, is an original story set in an unspecified African location. It is essentially a literary folktale about a boy who, with the help of Good Snake, manages to fulfill his dream of flying. According to the jacket blurb, Walter had been inspired by a visit to Nigeria to write a story that would incorporate African beliefs and symbols and would also be accessible to an American child. In *The Black Snowman* (Mendez 1989), a magic kente cloth brings to life a snowman created from dirty city snow. The snowman informs Jacob, a discouraged, self-hating, and cynical African American boy, about his proud African ancestry. With the help of the kente cloth and the snowman, Jacob finds the courage to rescue his younger brother from a fire, as well as the inner strength to restore his sense of self-worth and pride in his identity. Carole Byard's color illustrations not only portray the warmth of the family relationships that are at the core of the book, but also make visible the African ancestors invoked by the Black snowman. Books such as these fit easily into the African and African American tradition of using story as a vehicle for instruction or transmitting values.

In the hands of Patricia McKissack, an accomplished storyteller and writer, fantasy became a vehicle for infusing family stories, family history, and African American history and culture into African American picture books. Her 1980s trilogy of picture book fantasies, which contains some elements of African American folk culture, also embraces a "womanist" element in that each of the three main characters is a strong, empowered, young Black girl.

Flossie and the Fox (McKissack 1986), in which a young girl outwits a pretentious, fancy-talking fox intent on stealing her basket of eggs, is based on a story told to McKissack by her grandfather. It has been compared to "Little Red Riding Hood," but the resemblance to that tale goes only as far as the encounter in the woods between a young girl and a conniving animal. Flossie is not taken in for a moment by the fox, and she needs no woodsman to rescue her. She is in control during the whole encounter, making the vain fox prove that he is indeed a fox before she will consent even to be frightened: "I aine never seen a fox before. So why should I be scared of you and I don't even-now know you a real fox for a fact?" (n.p.). Set in what appears to be nineteenth century rural Tennessee, *Flossie* is kin to the Black folktales, very popular during the slave era, in which characters that appear to be weak or helpless overcome or outsmart stronger or more powerful characters by using their wits (e.g., Brer Rabbit and friends). McKissack's story also highlights power-related class differences by contrasting the formal and pompous language of the fox—"Are you saying I must offer proof that I am a fox before you will be frightened of me?"—to Flossie's "down home," not formally educated but very effective, way of talking, making Flossie's triumph all the sweeter.

Inspired by a photograph of McKissack's grandparents, *Mirandy and Brother Wind* (1988) is a wonderfully imaginative tale about a young girl who tries to capture the wind to be her dance partner so she can win first prize in the junior cakewalk. Brother Wind resists capture, but Mirandy is persistent, and in the end she and her partner dance away with the prize. The author's note explains the origins of the cakewalk and thereby helps to situate the tale in an African American historical and cultural context. Jerry Pinkney's rich watercolor illustrations, full of eye-catching detail and a quintessential rendering of a personified Brother Wind, earned a well-deserved Caldecott Honor citation.

The final book in McKissack's trilogy is *Nettie Jo's Friends* (1989), in which Nettie Jo seeks help from her animal friends to find a needle so she can sew a new dress for her doll to wear to Cousin Willadeen's wedding. Although Nettie Jo helps each animal with his or her problem, they are all too busy to help her. Her generosity pays off, however, when the animals realize the error of their ways and return to repay her kindness. *Nettie Jo's Friends* is an example of an entertaining story that also encourages certain behaviors or attitudes, in this case the idea that one good deed deserves another. One important feature of McKissack's trilogy is her portrayal of young Black girls, particularly Flossie and Mirandy, as determined problem solvers who use their wits or the resources available in their families and communities to meet challenges and accomplish their goals. McKissack had this to say about her reasons for writing the trilogy:

The reason I wrote Flossie, Mandy, and Nettie Jo is that I wanted Black kids to see a book with a picture of a beautiful black child on it—be it male or female—and say, "Oh, there's me in a book." And feel good about it. I wanted to have a little girl who was sharp and smart, learning a bit about her history and a little bit about our language. That's why I wrote those books. (Bishop 1992, 72)

Given the 1970s focus on urban Black children, with a particular emphasis on boys, McKissack's emphasis on empowered Black girls was particularly welcome.

By the end of the 1980s, some of the noteworthy authors and artists who would become prominent in the next decade had published their first children's books. One important 1980s publishing debut is that of Elizabeth Fitzgerald Howard, who ushered in what would become a major emphasis in the next decade, fictionalized family histories. While McKissack in her trilogy wove parts of her family history into fanciful stories, Howard chose to relate hers as realistic fiction. Her two 1980s books, *The Train to Lulu's* (1988) and *Chita's Christmas Tree* (1989), are based on the childhood experiences of Howard and her sister, their cousin Chita, and other relatives or stories related by family members. The 1980s also saw the debut of Angela Johnson, who would go on to become a critically acclaimed creator of picture books, novels, and poetry. Perhaps in a sense, the important thing about the 1980s in African American picture books is that the decade was a harbinger of things to come.

NOTE

1. For discussions of the signifying monkey and its significance in African American folk culture, see Roger D. Abrahams, *Deep Down in the Jungle: Negro Narrative Folklore from the Streets of Philadelphia*. First Rev. Ed., (Chicago: Aldine Publishing Co. 1970) and Henry Louis Gates, *The Signifying Monkey: A Theory of Afro-American Literary Criticism* (New York: Oxford University Press, 1988).

BIBLIOGRAPHY OF BOOKS FOR CHILDREN AND YOUNG ADULTS

Sources other than books for children and young adults are documented in a reference list at the end of the book.

Caines, Jeanette. 1973. *Abby*. Illus. by Steven Kellog. New York: Harper and Row.

———. 1977. *Daddy*. Illus. by Ronald Himler. New York: Harper and Row.

———. 1980. *Window Wishing*. Illus. by Kevin Brooks. New York: Harper and Row.

———. 1982. *Just Us Women*. Illus. by Pat Cummings. New York: Harper and Row.

———. 1988. *I Need a Lunch Box*. Illus. by Pat Cummings. New York: Harper and Row.

Clifton, Lucille. 1970. *The Black BC's*. Illus. by Don Miller. New York: Dutton.

———. 1973a. *All Us Come Cross the Water*. Illus. by John Steptoe. New York: Holt.

———. 1973b. *The Boy Who Didn't Believe in Spring*. Illus. by Brinton Turkle. New York: Dutton.

———. 1973c. *Don't You Remember?* Illus. by Evaline Ness. New York: Dutton.

———. 1973d. *Good, Says Jerome*. Illus. by Stephanie Douglas. New York: Dutton.

———. 1974. *Everett Anderson's Year*. Illus. by Ann Grifalconi. New York: Holt.

———. 1975. *My Brother Fine with Me*. Illus. by Moneta Barnett. New York: Holt.

———. 1976. *Three Wishes*. Illus. by Stephanie Douglas. New York: Holt.

———. 1977. *Amifika*. Illus. by Thomas DiGrazia. New York: Dutton.

———. 2001. *One of the Problems of Everett Anderson*. Illus. by Ann Grifalconi. New York: Holt.

Cummings, Pat. 1985. *Jimmy Lee Did It*. New York: Lothrop, Lee and Shepard.

———. 1986. *C.L.O.U.D.S.* New York: Lothrop, Lee and Shepard.

DeVeaux, Alexis. 1987. *Enchanted Hair Tale*. Illus. by Cheryl Hanna. New York: Harper.

Flournoy, Valerie. 1985. *The Patchwork Quilt*. Illus. by Jerry Pinkney. New York: Dial.

Greenfield, Eloise. 1972. *Bubbles*. Illus. by Eric Marlow. Washington, D.C.: Drum and Spear Press.

———. 1974. *She Come Bringing Me that Little Baby Girl*. New York: Harper.

———. 1975. *Me and Neesie*. Illus. by Moneta Barnett. New York: Thomas Y. Crowell.

———. 1976. *First Pink Light*. Illus. by Moneta Barnett. New York: Harper.

———. 1977. *Good News*. Illus. by Pat Cummings. New York: Putnam.

———. 1980. *Grandmama's Joy*. Illus. by Carole Byard. New York: Philomel.

———. 1988. *Grandpa's Face*. Illus. by Floyd Cooper. New York: Philomel.

———. 1993. *William and the Good Old Days*. Illus. by Jan Spivey Gilchrist. New York: HarperCollins.

Howard, Elizabeth Fitzgerald. 1988. *The Train to Lulu's*. Illus. by Robert Casilla. New York: Bradbury.

———. 1989. *Chita's Christmas Tree*. Illus. by Floyd Cooper. New York: Bradbury.

Keats, Ezra Jack. 1962. *The Snowy Day*. New York: Viking.

Lawrence, Jacob. 1968. *Harriet and the Promised Land*. New York: Simon and Schuster.

Little, Lessie Jones and Eloise Greenfield. 1978. *I Can Do It by Myself*. Illus. by Carole Byard. New York: Thomas Y. Crowell.

McKissack, Patricia. 1986. *Flossie and the Fox*. Illus. by Rachel Isadora. New York: Dial.

———. 1988. *Mirandy and Brother Wind*. Illus. by Jerry Pinkney. New York: Knopf.

———. 1989. *Nettie Jo's Friends*. Illus. by Scott Cook. New York: Knopf.

Mendez, Phil. 1989. *The Black Snowman*. Illus. by Carole Byard. New York: Scholastic.

Myers, Walter Dean. 1972. *The Dragon Takes a Wife*. Illus. by Ann Grifalconi. New York: Bobbs-Merrill.

———. 1984. *Mr. Monkey and the Gotcha Bird*. Illus. by Leslie Morrill. New York: Delacorte.

Steptoe, John. 1969. *Stevie*. New York: Harper and Row.

———. 1970. *Uptown*. New York: Harper and Row.

———. 1972. *Birthday*. New York: Holt, Rinehart and Winston.

———. 1974. *My Special Best Words*. New York: Viking.

———. 1980. *Daddy Is a Monster . . . Sometimes*. New York: J. B. Lippincott.

———. 1984. *The Story of Jumping Mouse*. New York: Lothrop, Lee and Shepard.

———. 1987. *Mufaro's Beautiful Daughters*. New York: Lothrop, Lee and Shepard.

———. 1988. *Baby Says*. New York: Lothrop, Lee and Shepard.

Walter, Mildred Pitts. 1985. *Brother to the Wind*. Illus. by Leo and Diane Dillon. New York: Lothrop, Lee and Shepard.

Yarbrough, Camille. 1979. *Cornrows*. Illus. by Carole Byard. New York: Coward, McCann and Geoghegan.

CHAPTER 7

African American Picture Books Expand: Celebrating the Past, Reflecting the Present

By the last decade of the twentieth century, a national emphasis on multicultural education and multicultural children's literature had opened spaces for more African American writers to enter the field, resulting in a substantial increase in the number of books featuring Black children. By the end of the century, at least four dozen African American writers were publishing picture books, and in the 1990s the output of African American picture books more than tripled that of the 1980s. This increase in quantity has meant a widening of the range of African American experiences reflected in picture books. Judging from their comments about their work and the nature of their picture book texts, however, many African American writers, across time and across two generations, subscribe to the same or a similar set of general goals and purposes, which are reflected in a core set of thematic and stylistic concerns and features that recur across the body of African American picture books.

The dominant themes in the picture books of the 1990s had to do with families and family histories, with many books revisiting the past, honoring the proverbial bridges that carried African Americans across the troubled waters of segregation and discrimination. As in the 1970s and 1980s, a few writers, such as Angela Johnson, Faith Ringgold, and Elizabeth Fitzgerald Howard, stand out because of the quantity and quality of their work, because they took common thematic concerns in new or different directions, or both. As in the 1970s and 1980s, there was also a strand of 1990s picture books that included elements of fantasy and folklore. African American folktales and folk culture continued to be a rich source on which to build new stories, and by the end of the century there was also an incipient move toward a body of original fantasies not directly traceable to the African American folk tradition.

THE FAMILY IN AFRICAN AMERICAN PICTURE BOOKS

It is not surprising that family is a common focal point in American picture books for young children since the family is the social institution that is most central to their lives. What distinguishes the body of African American picture books in that regard is the degree to which family dominates the genre and which aspects of family life are highlighted. Parents are a strong presence in these books, and a number of the stories are about interactions between child and parent. In books about siblings, the focus is often on family unity and on the responsibility siblings have for and to each other. Intergenerational stories and extended families are very prominent in African American picture books. In these books, whether the plot features children interacting with parents, siblings, grandparents, or members of their extended families, the focus is almost always on the ties that bind the family together. This emphasis on family echoes the cultural value placed on the family as a resource, a source of support, an educational institution, and instrument of survival that Webber (1978) and others described as a crucial aspect of life for enslaved African Americans and that has continuing salience in African American life and culture. For African American writers, it reflects both their own experiences and the ideals and values they wish to share with children.

One of the most notable new African American writers of the last decade of the twentieth century—and beyond—is Angela Johnson, whose picture books almost always center on family relationships. Between 1989 and 2000, Johnson published fourteen picture storybooks, more than any other African American writer during that period, making hers the predominant voice of the decade. For the most part, Johnson and her contemporaries seem much less compelled to focus on economically poor urban dwellers than did earlier writers such as Lucille Clifton. The families in Johnson's picture books tend to be middle-class, two-parent families. The settings may be urban, suburban/town, or rural, reflecting the diverse realities of contemporary African Americans. Unlike many earlier works, Johnson's picture book texts tend not to emphasize distinctive aspects of African American language, history, or heritage or to focus on aspects of racial or cultural identity or racial/cultural pride, although her stories are grounded in her own experience as a Black woman: "I am an African American woman. I write out of my history. I write out of my personal past. My stories are universal and I happen to be African American. Who I am is what I write. . . . I was given the freedom to write universal stories with African American kids in them" (2003). Being African American is treated in her books as a given, echoing the expressed intent of Du Bois's magazine decades earlier to make African American children know that being who they are is "a normal, beautiful thing."

Angela Johnson's family stories frequently emphasize the ties that bind both across and within generations. Three of them—*Do Like Kyla* (1990a), *One of Three* (1991), and *The Wedding* (1999)—focus on relationships between sisters, told from the point of view of the youngest. In *Do Like Kyla*, the narrator spends the day imitating older sister Kyla until bedtime, when Kyla turns the tables. Older siblings in such a situation often find the younger one's actions annoying, but Kyla is remarkably loving and patient. In *One of Three*, the older sisters Eva and Nikki are also usually patient and caring, but sometimes having little sister tag along does not fit their plans. In those cases, the unnamed narrator and her sympathetic parents form a different and equally satisfying set of three. In *The Wedding*, Daisy relates the bittersweet experience of being the flower girl in her sister's wedding. Although she enjoys the festivities and celebrates the occasion along with the family, she also is somewhat saddened by the knowledge that marriage means that Sister will be leaving home. In these stories, Johnson continues to emphasize the prominent theme that Clifton labeled "love in a family," stressing the positive aspects of the relationship between siblings.

Like a number of other African American writers, Johnson also celebrates intergenerational relationships, such as that between grandparent and child and between aunts and their nieces or nephews. In *When I Am Old with You* (1990b), for example, the narrator is a young boy in dreadlocks fantasizing that he and his grandfather can be old together, doing exactly those things that they are enjoying now. As is true with most of the African American picture books featuring grandparents, the relationship between the grandfather and grandson is an especially close and loving one. The two books that feature aunts each have a touch of the unusual. In *The Girl Who Loved Snakes* (1993a), Ali falls in love with snakes and discovers that the only one in the family who shares her enthusiasms is one of her four aunts. The title character in *The Aunt in Our House* (1996) appears to be White. The narrator and his sister are apparently biracial, the aunt is the sister of their artist father, and their mother is an African American weaver. No explanation is given for the aunt's coming to live with the family, and her racial background is not a factor in the plot; what is important is that the children find that the sun shines brighter and they are warmer in winter since she became a part of the household. Along with Caines's *Just Us Women*, Johnson's books are some of the few that focus on the special relationship between children and their parents' sisters.

At least three of Johnson's picture books—*Tell Me a Story, Mama* (1989), *The Rolling Store* (1997), and *Down the Winding Road* (2000)—focus on passing down family stories. They feature a parent or a grandparent and children who have heard the stories so often that they can take the lead in the telling. Thus, both the storytelling tradition and the stories themselves are preserved and passed on to a new generation. These books weave past and present together, exemplifying one of the important emphases in African American picture books of the 1990s—looking backward with a view to keeping alive the stories that help young readers understand and appreciate their cultural and familial roots.

Although Angela Johnson began her career writing picture books, she has also written award-winning novels and books of poetry. Her penchant for poetry is evident in the texts of her picture books, which are, for the most part, first-person narratives, told in the voices of young children. But, their voices are not so much realistically childlike as they are lyrical, expressing themselves poetically and with abundant imagery: "The Aunt came to stay/on a Sunday when the backyard buzzed with bees/and Sister and me sat in the wildflowers,/waiting for her" (1996, n.p.). And, from *The Leaving Morning* (1992): "The leaving happened on a soupy, misty morning, when you could hear the street sweeper. Sssshhhshsh" (n.p.). Her poetic prose is one of the distinctive characteristics of her work.

Angela Johnson's strong focus on family continues the thematic threads woven into African American picture books by older writers like Clifton and Greenfield and taken up by many others. At the same time, her books expand the range of life experiences that are mirrored in contemporary picture books about African Americans. Her stories tend to highlight relationships and children's feelings and emotions, rather than action-filled plot lines, and are well suited to the lyricism of her narration. Given the recognition she has received for her picture books, poetry, and novels, Johnson seems destined to be one of the premier writers of early twenty-first century African American children's literature. In 2003, she became the second African American writer of children's books to receive a MacArthur Fellowship, often referred to as a "Genius Award."

Johnson's focus on intergenerational relationships is echoed in a substantial portion of African American picture books of the 1990s. In fact, the most prominent family members of the 1990s family books were elders—grandparents, great-aunts and -uncles, great-great-aunts—all of whom are shown interacting with young children, with whom they share a special relationship. As was true of the grand-mother in Flournoy's 1985 classic *The Patchwork Quilt*, the highly respected elderly relatives in these books function as wise teachers, counselors, family and cultural historians, and special companions to the young. Almost all the elders in these books are women, but a few loving grandfathers (e.g., in A. Johnson's *When I Am Old with You*, 1990b) and at least one great-uncle also are portrayed. For example, the grandfather in Belinda Rochelle's *When Jo Louis Won the Title* (1994) weaves together family history with the story of the triumph of heavyweight boxing champion Joe Louis to reveal the origin of his granddaughter's name, Jo Louis, thus empowering her to meet with strength and pride the challenge of being the new girl in school. In this case, Grandfather acts both as counselor and family historian.

That the emphasis on grandparents is culturally significant is borne out by the number of different African American authors who have produced books that focus on grandparent-grandchild relationships. Grandparents appear in 1990s books by Dolores Johnson (*Your Dad Was Just Like You*, 1993), Eloise Greenfield (*William and the Good Old Days*, 1993), Evelyn Coleman (*The Glass Bottle Tree*, 1995), Irene Smalls (*Louise's Gift*, 1996), Jacqueline Woodson (*We Had a Picnic This Sunday Past*, 1997), Karen English (*Just Right Stew*, 1998), and Sandra Belton (*May'naise Sandwiches and Sunshine Tea*, 1994), among others. A shared sensibility is also indicated by the similarities in the characterization of these grandparents.

As a group, the elders in these picture books are portrayed as integral to the family unit and vital sources of wisdom and knowledge who have earned the love, respect, and appreciation of the entire family. Whether sharing family stories, sharing secrets, teaching and learning, having fun together, solving problems together, or simply being together, the individuals in these twosomes are clearly among the most important people in each other's lives. In the author's note for *Things I Like about Grandma* (1992), Francine Haskins captures the essence of the relationship between African American children and their elders as portrayed in these books: "It's a special relationship. It's teaching, telling, giving, and bonding. It's learning family histories and traditions, things that have been passed from generation to generation. It's building the foundation—giving the child a basis to grow on and come back to. It's love shared" (n.p.). These books exemplify the continuing salience of Clifton's early emphasis on writing about love in a family and Greenfield's expressed desire to give children an appreciation of the contributions of their elders.

SLICES OF CONTEMPORARY MIDDLE-CLASS AFRICAN AMERICAN LIFE

Some African American writers of the 1990s contributed to expanding the thematic range of contemporary realistic African American stories by focusing on familiar everyday childhood experiences rather than on relationships between family members. While most of these stories involve family members—responsible adults are nearly always present—they tend to emphasize the child's problems or concerns and often to focus on children's lives just outside the boundaries of home. Many of these "slice-of-life" books are similar to most of Angela Johnson's in that they do not highlight distinctive aspects of African American culture, even though they are set in a Black or predominantly Black cultural milieu. Like the family stories, stories of this type have been created by a number of different writers, most of whom published fewer than five such books in the 1990s.

Brian Pinkney's *JoJo's Flying Side Kick* (1995), for example, features a young African American girl who, with the help of her grandfather, among others, conquers her fears and manages to pass a test in her Tae Kwon Do class. This story seems to have evolved from Pinkney's own interests; he has a black belt in Tae Kwon Do. Although Tae Kwon Do is not a common topic in picture books, JoJo's dilemma and her emotions are easily recognizable to anyone who has had to face a difficult challenge. What the book does have in common with many African American picture books is that the grandfather plays a prominent role in the story as a member of the household and as someone who gives important advice and support. Pinkney also drew on his interest and expertise as a drummer to create *Max Found Two Sticks* (1994), in which a young boy, fascinated with drums and drumming, uses two sticks to turn almost everything around him into a drum and receives a special gift when an exciting marching band passes by in a parade through his neighborhood.

Even though Pat Cummings's stories often involve family situations, they tend to emphasize the humor in those situations. *Clean Your Room, Harvey Moon* (1991), which is based on memories of her brother's resistance to keeping his childhood bedroom neat and clean, is full of the kind of cheerful exaggerations that appeal to many young readers. His mother insists that he clean his room instead of watching TV, but when he has "finished," it is clear that he has only rearranged the mess, which they will tackle after lunch. *Angel Baby* (2000), in which an older sister helps to take care of her frisky younger brother, whom their mother sees as ever so angelic, has similar elements of humor. These two books have rhyming texts, which adds to their sense of fun. Set at summer camp, *Petey Moroni's Camp Runamok Diary* (1992) is a humorous "mystery" in which a raccoon causes all sorts of trouble while the campers try to figure out the cause of the mischief. The pictures are full of clues for the observant reader. Both the setting and the format make this book one of a kind among African American picture books.

Dolores Johnson is one of the few African American authors of picture books to use school as a setting. In *The Best Bug to Be* (1992), a young girl takes her parents' advice to make the most of being cast in what she considers an undesirable role in the school play. *My Mom Is My Show and Tell* (1999) recalls the much earlier *What Mary Jo Shared* (Udry 1966), in which Mary Jo's father was her "show and tell." Given the importance of school in children's lives, it is somewhat surprising that so few African American writers choose school as a setting for their picture books. Nevertheless, contemporary African American children from working class and middle class families can discover reflections of their life experiences in these books, which as a group de-emphasize the focus on urban living and low-income families that was prevalent in the 1970s.

In contrast to the slice-of-life picture books that de-emphasize African American cultural distinctiveness, some such stories are set in identifiably African American cultural contexts, such as Black churches, beauty shops and barbershops. *Sunday Week* (Dinah Johnson, 1999), for example, lyrically celebrates a week of activities in a southern African American community, from Blue Monday to Sunday, the day "when church bells make it sound like heaven is right here." The family has been anticipating Sunday all week. Church service is the focus of the day, but Sunday dinner and the Sunday family ride are also very important. Full of familiar experiences and familiar songs and sayings, Johnson's book highlights the importance of religion, faith, and spirituality to many Black Americans.

Beauty shops and barbershops can be much more than simply places of business in African American neighborhoods; they are sometimes community gathering places, filled with talk. In Michael Strickland's *Haircuts at Sleepy Sam's* (1998) for example, the men "cut hair and talk, cut hair and joke, cut hair and argue, cut hair and laugh, cut hair and boogie to the oldies on the radio" while the narrator and his brothers wait for their haircuts. *Saturday at the New You* (Barber 1994) follows Shauna through her Saturday as she helps her mother in the beauty shop. While the book focuses on a close mother-daughter experience, it also provides a glimpse of the African American beauty shop as a social setting.

These and other slice-of-life books are evidence that, while many African American writers are staying "close to home" in that their stories continue the thematic traditions that characterized earlier African American picture books, they are also finding new stories to tell about growing up African American in this society. These books help to fulfill Lucille Clifton's mandate to "authenticate the lives" of contemporary African American children by celebrating their everyday realities.

ENCOURAGING BLACK CHILDREN TO LOVE THEMSELVES

The desire to use literature to affirm Black children, to authenticate their lives, and to encourage them to see themselves in a positive light has persisted through to the end of the twentieth century and beyond. One example of that theme in a late-century book is found in Sharon Dennis Wyeth's *Something Beautiful* (1998) in which a young girl searches for beauty in her urban neighborhood and learns not only to see beauty in everyday things and in herself but also that she can empower herself to help create beauty around her. *To Be a Drum* (Coleman 1998) echoes the focus on pride in an African heritage that was so important in the 1970s. Through a story in which drums represent the spirit, resiliency and determination of African America, Daddy Wes tells his two children the story of how Africans were brought to America and enslaved and of African Americans' triumph over oppression. He then calls on the children to follow the example of those who have gone before and made significant contributions in various fields—to "become a drum." Both these books seem to be intent not only on helping children see themselves in a positive light but also on inspiring them to take effective action for the greater good.

A few 1990s picture books directly confront some factors that have kept some Black children from feeling positive about themselves and their appearance. Part of the rationale for slavery was the assertion that physical differences between Africans and Europeans, such as skin color and hair texture, were evidence of Africans' inferiority. Thus, dark skin, broad noses, full lips, and hair that was not straight were stigmatized and through the years ridiculed in books, films, cartoons, and popular novelty items, such as salt and pepper shakers and ashtrays. During the era of slavery, lighter-skinned Blacks with straight hair and small features—ironically, often the offspring of White plantation owners and their kin, who frequently sexually abused or exploited Black women—often received better treatment than their darker-skinned counterparts.

One insidious feature of this appearance-based hierarchy was that Black people themselves began to absorb those attitudes, which for some have carried over even to the present. Thus, aspects of African Americans' appearance have been doubly stigmatized—from both within and outside African American communities. For many African Americans, at least up until the middle of the twentieth century, to be called "black" was to be insulted. And straight hair was considered "good hair," while tightly curled, kinky, or "nappy" hair was considered "bad hair." The 1960s saw a surge of "Black is beautiful" pride and a celebration of Black hair in its natural state (big afros), but negative attitudes toward dark skin and kinky hair persist. In light of that historical context and the social significance that still attaches to Black people's appearance, African American writers are producing—well into the 1990s and beyond—children's books aimed at countering negative attitudes toward skin color, facial features, and hair and encouraging Black children to love their physical selves.

Bright Eyes, Brown Skin (Hudson and Ford 1990), for example, celebrates young African American children, their capabilities, and their physical features. The art shows children confidently and happily engaged in preschool activities, while the rhyming text emphasizes their physical features. In addition to the bright eyes and brown skin of the title, for example, the text sings of "a playful grin, a perfect nose" and "very special hair and clothes." Thus, both the text and the art offer Black children positive images of themselves.

A decade later, Sandra and Myles Pinkney (2000), in *Shades of Black*, celebrated the great variety in skin color and hair texture, as well as eye color, to be found among African Americans. Illustrated with color photographs of children, the text carries the refrain "I am Black. I am unique." It compares physical features to positive or pleasant images. Skin is the color of vanilla, chocolate, licorice, or ginger; hair is like puffy cotton balls, the straight edge of a blade of grass, or in the case of dreadlocks, like stiff ringlets in lambs' wool—and all of it is "good." This book emphasizes not only the physical diversity to be found among African Americans but a sense of group identity as well.

Entire books have been written about the social, psychological, and political significance of hair textures and hairstyles among African Americans, particularly women. Although a relatively few children's picture books have focused specifically on the topic, at least one, Carolivia Herron's *Nappy Hair* (1997), gave rise to a national conversation about the choice of the topic, the use of the word *nappy*, and the use of the book in the classroom. Earlier, *Cornrows* had been well received, as had the less well known *Enchanted Hair Tale* by Alexis DeVeaux. But, a firestorm erupted when a young White teacher in New York read *Nappy Hair* aloud and sent home a black-and-white photocopy of an illustration from the book. A number of parents and community people became upset, and before it was over, the teacher had been so intimidated that she transferred out of the district.

Herron based her story on her own family experience and presented the text in a call-and-response pattern. Backed by a chorus of family commentary, an uncle declares that Brenda's hair is the nappiest hair in the world ("Ain't going to be nothing they come up with going to straighten this chile's hair" (n.p.) and "one nap of her hair is the only perfect circle in nature"). The uproar was in part over Joe Cepeda's illustrations, especially the cover, which called up for some viewers stereotyped comical images of the past. A second concern was the appropriateness of the word *nappy*. It is a term that has been used pejoratively among Black people for years, although it was generally taboo to use it in the presence of Whites, and many protesters feared that publicizing it in a children's book would provide one more epithet that budding White racists could use to embarrass and degrade Black children. The situation was complicated by the fact that the young teacher who presented the book was White. That such a tempest should arise over a picture book written by an African American woman, and based on her own experience, is a testament to the depth and complexity of the issues that continue to swirl around racial matters in children's books. Interestingly, the publicity over the New York case caused sales of the book to skyrocket.

Two years later (1999), bell hooks published *Happy to Be Nappy*, another celebration of nappy hair, this time causing no great stir. Perhaps the *Nappy Hair* controversy had made it safer to use the term. The different response among Black critics may also be related to the fact that there is no ambiguity in the hooks text about the positive, celebratory stance the author/narrator takes toward nappy hair. In this book, there is no teasing about its intransigence in the face of attempts to straighten it. In fact, the very idea of straightening nappy hair would be antithetical to the theme of this book, which touts the positive qualities and versatility of such hair in its natural state. It may also be that Chris Raschka's stylized illustrations were so close to abstract that they avoided the concerns that Cepeda's art for *Nappy Hair* had raised for some parents and critics.

One of the childhood experiences that most African American women with nappy hair have in common is sitting on the floor between our mothers' knees to have our hair combed. It was both a bonding experience and, for those who are "tender headed," one to be dreaded since pulling the comb through the hair can hurt when the hair is tangled. Natasha Anastasia Tarpley's (1998) *I Love My Hair* and Rita Williams-Garcia's (2000) *Catching the Wild Waiyuuzee* both recall that experience. Like *Happy to Be Nappy*, Tarpley's book celebrates the versatility of the child's hair and all the different ways she can wear it. So, even though it sometimes hurts to have her mother pull the comb through the tangles, in the end she decides that she loves her hair. In Williams-Garcia's imaginative *Wild Waiyuuzee*, a little girl tries to hide from "Shemama the Catcher" when it is time to get her hair combed by fantasizing that she runs away to a mango grove (her bedroom). But, Shemama catches the Wild Waiyuuzee, rubs "nut-nut oil" on her head, and combs and braids her hair (plait-a-plait and string-a-bead). When the Wild Waiyuuzee sees herself in the mirror, she becomes a little girl again and thinks the result is beautiful. The publication of these books about Black hair at the end of the twentieth century speaks to the need that many African American writers and artists feel to continue to use children's books as vehicles of affirmation.

KEEPING THE PAST ALIVE: THE WAY IT USED TO BE

For all the focus on contemporary lives in African American children's books, there is also a strong focus on the past woven through the literature. This attention to times gone by comes in part from the perceived need to keep alive for younger generations the unsung stories of African Americans' history and struggle, both at the level of individuals and families and on the larger stage of American society. It is part of the expressed desire of writers like Eloise Greenfield to pass on knowledge of Black history and heritage as a means both to set the record straight and to inspire young people to prepare themselves for a productive future.

One author who has specialized in telling stories based on her own family history is Elizabeth Fitzgerald Howard, a history major and retired professor of library science. Through telling her personal family stories, Howard also illuminates something of African American history from Reconstruction through the early part of the twentieth century. In one of the best known of the 1990s picture books, Howard's *Aunt Flossie's Hats (and Crab Cakes Later)* (1991a), Sarah and Susan visit their Great-great Aunt Flossie on Sunday afternoons. One of the reasons the girls enjoy their time with Aunt Flossie is that she has "boxes and boxes and boxes of HATS!" Every hat has a story and trying on any one elicits a telling from Aunt Flossie. Her stories combine family history with larger historical events, such as a great fire in Baltimore and the parade welcoming the African American 92nd Division back from World War I. As witness to these events, Aunt Flossie helps the girls understand the emotional impact they had on her as a child and thereby makes the history come alive. Howard has noted, "But this story of mine is not unique. Being African American means having stories. We all have our Aunt Flossies and our Cousin Chitas and our Great Aunt Lulus, who have given so much and who have made us what we are" (1991b, 98). In particular, because of her specific family history, Howard offers glimpses of the lives of African Americans who, though not necessarily famous, were achievers—doctors, lawyers, teachers, business people—at a time when limited educational opportunities and oppressive social conditions meant that such Black professionals represented only a small percentage of the African American population.

One of her relatives, for instance, was Chita McCard, Howard's father's cousin, and the daughter of one of the first Black doctors in Baltimore, which placed Chita's family high on the African American social ladder. In David Levering Lewis's (2000) biography of W.E.B. Du Bois, Chita McCard is listed as one of the bridesmaids at the wedding of Du Bois's daughter Yolanda to poet Countee Cullen, which was the major African American high society event of that year. Howard has retold stories about Chita in two of her picture books, both set in the early twentieth century. In *Chita's Christmas Tree* (1989), Papa and Chita go off on an excursion to the deep, deep woods to find the perfect Christmas tree, on which Papa carves Chita's name so Santa will know which tree to bring on Christmas Eve. There is a sumptuous Christmas Eve family dinner to which all the aunts and uncles and cousins are invited. On Christmas morning, Chita rushes downstairs to find her tree, beautifully decorated and lighting up the living room.

The actual Dr. McCard had served in the Spanish-American War to earn money for his medical education, and in *Papa Tells Chita a Story* (Howard 1995), Papa relates a story about his adventures as a soldier. Although his exact exploits are not known, this story is based on Chita's recollections of a story her father had often told her about his adventures as a brave soldier carrying a message to the far side of Cuba. His adventures have been exaggerated for the story, but it is true that African Americans served in the military during the Spanish-American War (as in every one of America's wars), and Howard's picture book is a reminder of that little-known history.

Another of Howard's stories, *Virgie Goes to School with Us Boys* (2000), is set in the nineteenth century and concerns her grandfather's generation. His parents had been enslaved, but by the time of the story they were free and living on a farm in Tennessee with their family of six boys and one girl. The children walked to a school established by the Quakers to educate newly freed African Americans. They spent the week at school and returned home on weekends. The book celebrates Virgie's determination to get an education along with the boys and the importance the family placed on education as the road to true freedom.

Howard's books are her attempt to help fill in gaps in history. She asserts that these stories are part of the American story. The people in her stories "worked hard. . . . They led active community lives, they supported their church, saved their money, aspired for higher education for their children, and believed in this country, all the while living within the segregated system. All Americans need to know that the history of these people is part of the history of all of us" (1991b, 95).

Howard's stories present just some of the rich and diverse history of ordinary, but exceptional, African Americans in this country.

Part of that history reveals how African Americans have had to overcome racial discrimination, including restricted job opportunities, in order to achieve success or just to survive. Sandra Belton's *From Miss Ida's Porch* (1993), for instance, recounts, through stories told on a front porch by those who had been witnesses, some of the encounters with racial discrimination that musicians Duke Ellington and Marian Anderson had to face in order to establish and advance their careers. It also recalls the tradition of gathering on the front porch to listen to and tell stories.

An outstanding example of a book that highlights both struggle and triumph— and honors an elder—is *Uncle Jed's Barbershop* (Mitchell 1993). Set in the segregated South of the 1920s, it describes how Sarah Jean's great-uncle inspired her to dare to dream. As he traveled around the county cutting Black people's hair in their homes, he saved money so that one day he could open his own modern barbershop. When five-year-old Sarah Jean became ill and her family found itself at the mercy of White doctors who demanded payment before they would perform life-saving surgery, Uncle Jed's nest egg saved the day. He was forced to start over, only to lose his savings again when his bank failed during the Great Depression. Undaunted, he started over once again and finally opened his dream barbershop on his seventy-ninth birthday. The story portrays not only the sense of love and responsibility within that extended family (Sarah Jean was Uncle Jed's brother's grandchild) but also the social context in which Uncle Jed's dream was hatched. Against the dual challenges of poverty (most of his customers were poor sharecroppers) and racism (White doctors would not even examine Sarah Jean until they had served all their White patients), it was extraordinary that Uncle Jed could dare to nurture the dream of owning his own business. That he did so and then accomplished his goal against all odds is the core of the story. James Ransome's richly colored oil paintings bring both the social and the geographic settings of *Uncle Jed's Barbershop* to life. Especially poignant is the painting of the Black patients huddled in the segregated doctor's office with a sign pointing to the "white only" and "colored only" waiting rooms, separated by a white wall. It is through the illustrations that the details of daily living in a bygone era are revealed to young readers.

Other stories of struggle focus on the kind of hard work in which many African Americans, now and in the past, must engage in order to survive. Set early in the twentieth century, Patricia McKissack's *Ma Dear's Aprons* (1997) recalls the way many Black women made a living doing domestic work—washing and ironing, cleaning homes, cooking—without benefit of modern appliances and for very little pay. This story highlights the relationship between Ma Dear and her son, who can tell what day it is and what the day's work will be by the apron Ma Dear wears. In spite of the exhausting demands on her time and energy, she always managed to find time for her son, telling him stories, teaching him games, instilling pride, giving him a special treat. At the center of the story is the love between mother and son and the dignity with which Ma Dear approached life.

A more contemporary story of struggle and oppressive labor is the Caldecott Honor book *Working Cotton* (Williams 1992). Narrated by a young girl, it is the story of a day when a migrant worker family picks cotton. Although Shelan's narrative is straightforward and matter of fact, there is no doubt that this family's life is very difficult, and that the hardship is shared among all its members, including the children. Carole Byard's award-winning paintings capture both the natural beauty of the fields and sky and the backbreaking nature of the work. They also capture the strength of the family unit and the spirit of hope, as symbolized by a late-blooming cotton blossom. Both *Working Cotton* and McKissack's *Ma Dear's Aprons* express the resiliency of spirit that refused to be defeated by difficult circumstances.

A number of African American writers dipped into their own pasts to create fictionalized accounts of experiences remembered from their childhoods. One outstanding "childhood remembrance" story that weaves together struggle and triumph is Patricia McKissack's *Going Someplace Special* (2001). Unlike *Uncle Jed* (Mitchell 1993), which features an older adult, McKissack's story centers on a young girl. 'Tricia Ann's grandmother permits her to make the trip downtown on her own. Along the way, 'Tricia Ann, who is living in a Southern city, experiences hurtful and potentially demoralizing episodes of segregation and discrimination. But, remembering her grandmother's teachings about her self-worth and the admonition to hold her head up, and with the help of knowledgeable and supportive African American adults, she navigates her way safely to the special place, the public library, which is open to all. The story celebrates both 'Tricia Ann's refusal to be dehumanized and the Nashville Public Library's refusal to conform to the racist customs of the day.

Other stories based on childhood experiences recall the pleasures of visiting family or simply the pleasures of being children. Donald Crews's first-person narratives in *Bigmama's* (1991) and *Shortcut* (1992) recount the story of his family's annual trip when he was a child to Cottondale, Florida, to spend the summer with his grandmother, whom the children called Bigmama. The same theme is echoed in Gloria Jean Pinkney's *Back Home* (1992), in which Ernestine rides the train from Philadelphia to Lumberton, North Carolina, where she had been born. Once there, she experiences life on a farm and gets to know members of her family, including Cousin Jack, who is a tease, but who in the end shows his affection for his "citified" cousin. The experience of traveling South, of going "back home" is a familiar story in the African American community and is a motif that appears frequently in African American literature. Other childhood remembrance stories, such as Gloria Jean Pinkney's *The Sunday Outing* (1994), Francine Haskins' *I Remember 121* (1991), and Irene Smalls' *Irene and the Big Fine Nickel* (1991) center on everyday living in urban settings. Unlike the 1970s focus on contemporary, "relevant" urban stories, these books recall the small pleasures of an earlier, gentler time as the authors relate something of their childhood experiences with friends and family.

The emphasis on the past in such a large portion of late twentieth century African American picture books is an indication of the extent to which African American writers continue to believe that arming children with knowledge of their personal, social, and cultural history will inspire and empower them. On the assumption that "knowledge is power," these books are apparently intended to foster appreciation of the past achievements of countless ordinary African Americans and to encourage youngsters to believe that the same strength, determination, and resilience lives in them.

ENCOURAGING CHILDREN TO FOLLOW THEIR DREAMS: THE UNIQUE BOOKS OF FAITH RINGGOLD

Faith Ringgold has brought a unique vision to a set of picture books that highlight African American history and seek to inspire children to follow their dreams and make a difference. Ringgold was already a well-known and internationally acclaimed artist long before the 1990s when she entered the field of children's books. Her first picture book, *Tar Beach* (1991), was an immediate success, winning twenty awards, including the 1992 Coretta Scott King Illustrator Award and a Caldecott Honor Book citation. *Tar Beach*, with its striking illustrations, was based on a story quilt, owned by the Solomon R. Guggenheim Museum, that is part of a series of five quilts called "Woman on a Bridge." The original narrative was not created as a children's story, but Andrea Cascardi, an editor at Crown, a division of Random House, saw a poster of the story quilt and realized it would make a good picture book for young children. Thus, Ringgold's entry into the world of children's picture books was not something she had actively sought. Once in the field, however, Ringgold embraced the form and made it a platform for presenting some African American history, celebrating African American women, and affirming and empowering her readers. She has this to say about her work: "These children's books seek to explain to children some of the hard facts of slavery and racial prejudice, issues that are difficult but crucial to their education. But my books are even more about children having dreams and instilling in them a belief that they can change things" (1995, 261).

Although Ringgold's distinctive art for *Tar Beach* is based on the quilt, the book illustrations were new creations. The extraordinary art combines acrylic paintings and a quilt border. The book is its own hybrid genre—part autobiography, part history, and part fantasy. The book text has also been adapted from the text of the story quilt. It relates the story of Cassie, a young girl whose family uses their New York City rooftop as a gathering place for a picnic. Lying on the roof, Cassie imagines that she is flying over her neighborhood, looking down, and taking ownership of all that she can see, including the George Washington Bridge. She intends to fly over the union building and strike a blow against the job discrimination that has prevented her father from making a decent living in a job for which he is well qualified. Ringgold notes that the "message" of Tar Beach (1991) is that "anyone can fly, anyone can achieve anything they truly want to achieve. All they have to do is try"[1] It is, like so much of African American children's literature, a message of empowerment. Although Ringgold aims this message at all her readers, the book has roots in African American history and culture. The flying motif is one that is fairly common in African American literary traditions, and Cassie's concern about her father's inability to find a job that utilizes his skills recalls the history of racist practices in labor unions, in this case the use of a "grandfather clause" to exclude African Americans and Native Americans. The use of quilting as a medium recalls the history of quilt making as an art form by numerous unsung African American women across generations.

Following *Tar Beach* (1991), Ringgold produced several other books, all of which incorporate some aspect of African American history or biography, along with elements of fantasy, such as time travel, a talking bus, and talking portraits. Ringgold has also been an advocate for women's rights, and almost all of her books involve women or girls as active, empowered protagonists or as subjects. In *Dinner at Aunt Connie's House* (1993), for example, Melody discovers the talking portraits of twelve African American women, including Rosa Parks, Fannie Lou Hamer, Dorothy Dandridge, Madame C. J. Walker and Augusta Savage. The women in the portraits represent diverse fields from civil rights activists to artists, to educators, to businesswomen. Each one tells the children something of her life story. Ringgold has also written books about Harriet Tubman (*Aunt Harriet's Underground Railroad in the Sky*, 1992) and Rosa Parks (*If a Bus Could Talk*, 1999a). Ringgold has always been an activist against discrimination and racism, so it is not surprising that one of her books centers on the life of Martin Luther King Jr.

Ringgold also wrote and illustrated *The Invisible Princess* (1999b), an original fairy tale with a number of Biblical echoes. Set in the time of slavery, it involves a beautiful haloed princess, who is born in a cotton field and protected from slavery by being made invisible under the cloak of the Prince of Night. Visible only to the blind daughter of the slaveholder and hunted in a Herod-like search, the Invisible Princess, with the help of the Great Powers of Nature, eventually brings freedom to the enslaved plantation workers. A combination of history and myth, it fits well into the tradition of African American children's literature intended to affirm and empower its readers. It also projects a utopian wish for a world where peace and harmony abound. The book, with its dramatic illustrations, responds to the query of Ringgold's granddaughters, likely echoed by many other young Black girls: "Where are the African American princesses?" Ringgold's children's books, for all their creative uniqueness, are purposeful, celebrating African American heroes, especially women, relating something of the history of African Americans as it affected ordinary people and affirming the strength and beauty of African American children.

FOLKLORE AND FANTASY IN AFRICAN AMERICAN PICTURE BOOKS

Just as Ringgold drew on history to create her literary fairy tale, most African American writers have borrowed freely from African and African American folk traditions and other aspects of African American culture to create a number of literary folktales. That is, their stories read like folktales but are actually, like Ringgold's *Invisible Princess* (1999b), original stories. Their roots in African American folk traditions are reflected in elements such as the story types, the characters, the style of the narration, and the discourse of the characters.

Patricia McKissack, for example, an accomplished oral storyteller as well as writer, has recalled and adapted for children one African American storytelling tradition in a tale set in southern Louisiana. According to Zora Neal Hurston, Arna Bontemps, and others, the tellers called these exaggerated tales "lies." In McKissack's story *A Million Fish, More or Less* (1992), Papa-Daddy and Elder Abbajon initiate Hugh Thomas into the storytelling tradition by telling him some whopping lies about their exploits with a 500-pound turkey. Hugh Thomas catches on, and when he returns from his fishing trip, relates to the two older men his own tale that explains what happened to the million fish—more or less—that he had caught in the bayou. Although the story has a contemporary setting, it evokes the tradition of storytelling as entertainment and is a reminder of the high value African Americans have historically placed on speaking as performance and on the ability to improvise.

McKissack continued the tradition of creating original folk-like stories in *Precious and the Boo Hag*, co-authored with Onawumi Jean Moss (McKissack and Moss 2005). In her cleverness and her spunk, Precious bears some resemblance to Flossie of McKissack's earlier book, *Flossie and the Fox* (1986). Precious, however, is her own unique self. Left at home with a stomachache while the rest of the family works, Precious is instructed not to let anybody in the house, and her brother warns her to be particularly careful not to let in the shape-changing and scary Pruella the boo hag. Precious, of course, repeatedly outwits Pruella, each time singing a little victory refrain, but in the end it appears that Pruella may not yet be defeated. *Precious and the Boo Hag* is a somewhat scary, but funny and satisfying version of a cautionary tale.

In 1996, Walter Dean Myers followed *Mr. Monkey and the Gotcha Bird* (1984) with *How Mr. Monkey Saw the Whole World* (1996). In this one, Mr. Monkey outwits Mr. Buzzard, who has been extorting food from fellow animals by inviting them on a flight to "see the whole world" and then turning them upside down until they give in to his demands. When it is Mr. Monkey's turn to see the whole world, he turns the tables on Mr. Buzzard and forces him to return the food to its rightful owners. Not only does this story recall animal stories from Africa and America, but also it brings to mind the Nat King Cole hit song "Straighten Up and Fly Right," which begins as follows:

The buzzard took the monkey for a ride in the air
The monkey thought that everything was on the square
The buzzard tried to throw the monkey off his back
The monkey grabbed his neck and said "Now listen, Jack."
"Straighten up and fly right."

Thus, Myers weaves a new story out of elements of folklore and popular music, which in this case is also rooted in the "signifying monkey" repertoire, an example of the kind of intertextuality that accounts in part for a certain coherence in African American literature.

Walter Dean Myers's more recent tale *The Blues of Flats Brown* (2000) is the story of a blues-playing dog, his dog buddy Caleb, and his mean junkyard-keeping human owner, A. J. Grubbs. After they run away, Flats and Caleb begin to earn a living playing and singing the blues, but Grubbs pursues them from Mississippi to Memphis to New York. It is one of Flats's improvised blues that finally touches Grubbs's heart. Again, Myers has turned to African American folk culture and rooted his story in an important African American musical form.

Linda Goss, author of *The Frog Who Wanted to Be a Singer* (1996), the story of how rhythm and blues was born, explains the importance of the blues in her "Backstage Notes" or afterword:

The blues itself is rooted in Africa and is the foundation of American popular music. It was created by African Americans from the cotton fields, farm areas, cypress swamps, and backwoods of the South, especially along the Mississippi Delta. . . . The Blues tells a story and expresses feelings of pain and joy. It allows one to improvise, to be spontaneous. The blues awakens the creativity in our souls. (Unpaged)

The title frog in Goss's 1996 story actually invents boogie-woogie, and "*that* is how Rhythm and Blues was born." He wanted to be a singer, but of course frogs do not sing. This frog, however, is very determined, and when he finally does sing at the Big Time Weekly Concert, he is a big hit with his boogie-woogie, "Dooba Dooba" tune. Frog becomes a regular at the Big Time Weekly Concert, and the rest, as the cliché goes, is history.

Goss's *The Frog Who Wanted to Be a Singer* (1996) represents another story type found in African American folk traditions, the "why" or "pourquoi" story, an often-exaggerated and humorous tale that imagines how some phenomenon originated. Another such story, Julius Lester's irreverent *What a Truly Cool World* (1999), is an original tale built on a folk story that appears in Zora Neale Hurston's famous folklore collection, *Mules and Men* (1935/1978). Lester's story, which explains how butterflies came to be, features a contemporary humanized heaven presided over by a very human-like God. Like Myers's *The Dragon Takes a Wife,* it features contemporary Black vernacular in the dialog and a sassy, hands-on-hips Black woman who is instrumental in moving the story forward. This time it is Shaniqua, the angel "in charge of everybody's business" who inspires God to beautify his newly created earth. Stories about a humanized heaven were an important component of African American folklore.

Hurston (1958) also wrote lovingly of High John the Conquer, a folk hero who was the principle character in numerous African American folktales from the days of plantation slavery. Jerdine Nolen's (2000) picture book *Big Jabe* recalls the spirit of High John, whom Hurston characterized as "a hopebringer," one who could "beat the unbeatable." High John stories usually entertained and inspired people enslaved on plantations by relating how John was able to repeatedly outsmart old Master and get himself out of trouble and out of hard work. On the other hand, when it suited his purposes, he could do the work of four or five men. Big Jabe is in the latter vein, a gentle giant who kept hope alive on Plenty Plantation. In Nolen's original tale, the magical Big Jabe is discovered, like the Biblical Moses, as a baby floating on the river in a basket. Within a very short time, Jabe acquires extraordinary size and strength and begins to take on all the hard work on Plenty Plantation, resulting in the resentful overseer becoming more abusive to the others. When mistreated slaves begin to disappear, the rumor in the quarters is that Jabe has spirited them off to freedom. When his work on Plenty Plantation is done, Jabe moves on, like High John, to pass the spirit of hope on to others in need. *Big Jabe* is a story within a story, the outer frame being a conversation between a young boy and Momma Mary, who relates the legend to him. Momma Mary is a reminder of the tradition of older members of the family passing on the history of the group or the family to the young, a kind of African American family griot.

ORIGINAL FANTASIES

A few African American picture books with elements of fantasy seem unrelated to, or at least farther removed from, African American folk traditions than the ones discussed. Humor is an important element in most of these books, and the topics and themes vary. For the most part the books seem intended mainly to entertain. In *The Adventures of Sparrow Boy* (1997), Brian Pinkney uses a comic book format to create a lively story about a paperboy who is transformed into a superhero. Angela Johnson's *Julius* (1993b) features an Alaskan pig that was sent by Maya's granddaddy to teach her "fun and sharing." Of course, Julius causes havoc in the house, but Maya and Julius do learn to share and have fun. These stories add a welcome thread of playfulness to the fabric of African American picture books.

If there is one African American picture book author who seems to be specializing in fanciful stories, it is Jerdine Nolen. Her first two books, *Harvey Potter's Balloon Farm* (1994) and *Raising Dragons* (1998), were humorous creations featuring female protagonists. The narrator in Harvey Potter learns the secret of farming balloons, and when she becomes an adult, she becomes a balloon farmer herself, with her own secret methods. The girl in *Raising Dragons* finds a dragon egg, raises dragon baby Hank to adulthood, and discovers that she has found her calling. Both these stories appear to be set in the rural South, and both narrators use an informal vernacular that seems more regional than identifiably Black vernacular. Her other books, such as the aforementioned *Big Jabe* (2000), appear to be rooted in folk traditions.

One exception to the trend toward fanciful stories as strictly entertainment is Christopher Myers's *Wings* (2000), which is a recasting of the Icarus legend to make a point about celebrating differences and being true to oneself. Although the flying motif appears frequently in African American literature, Myers chose to connect his book to Greek myth by naming his character Ikarus. "I wanted to create a book that tells kids never to abandon the things that make them different, to be proud of what makes them unique. . . . Ikarus Jackson can fly through the air; I want kids to find their own set of wings and soar with him" (quoted on book jacket). Myers, the son of Walter Dean Myers, is one of the second-generation author-artists whose work has received well-deserved critical attention.

In African American picture books, as in African American children's literature in general, fantasy seems to take a back seat to realism. Nevertheless, both fantasy and humor have been important elements in African American folk traditions. Recently, African American writers and artists have begun to tap those traditions and their own imaginations and experiences to produce fanciful and often funny picture books. With so much of the focus of African American picture books on authenticating the real worlds of African American children, these books remind us that imagination can be liberating, and laughter can be healing.

ABOUT AFRICAN AMERICAN PICTURE BOOKS

As they have developed since the 1960s, African American picture books have come to reflect a wide range of African American experience, echoing the diversity within the national Black community. Although African Americans share much common ground with the rest of America, most African Americans also share with each other a collective cultural experience or worldview shaped and informed in part by our responses to the racism to which we have all been subjected and in part by the cultural traditions and values transmitted through generations by a people who know themselves to be both a part of and apart from the larger nation. This common cultural ground is reflected in a set of thematic and stylistic concerns and features that recur across the body of twentieth century African American picture books. This is not to imply that African American authors of picture books are monolithic in their thinking or in their expressed goals for their literary creations. Nevertheless, an overview of twentieth century African American picture books reveals a recurring set of overlapping, interrelated themes, emphases, values, and stylistic devices that can be said to characterize, at least in part, the body of African American picture book texts.

African American picture books tend to emphasize three main themes: love in the family; pride in Black heritage, history, and heroes; and fostering self-love and self-esteem. One distinctive aspect of the focus on family in African American picture books is the strong emphasis on elders and intergenerational relationships, on extended family, and on family as the primary support system. The focus on roots and heritage means that preserving the past is very important in the body of African American picture storybooks. More prevalent than books about the distant past are books that relate recent history and highlight the everyday African American heroes—and some famous ones—who overcame obstacles to accomplish their dreams, take care of their families, and contribute to society. Elders are often cast as the keepers and transmitters of this knowledge. This focus on the past also relates a sense of continuity, affirming the importance of roots, of connecting with the generations that have gone before, with a view to empowering young people to move forward.

From *The Brownies' Book*'s expressed intention to impress "colored" children with their own beauty, to Langston Hughes's call for literature to give "Negro" children back their own souls, to Greenfield's expressed desire to encourage children to love themselves, African American writers have seen literature as one vehicle for bolstering self-esteem in Black children. This is an attempt in part to contradict the caricatured images of Black children popular in books and media for years and in part to counter the message that the scarcity of their images in children's literature and in school texts means that they are not highly valued. It is also a recognition that race continues to matter in our society, and that many Black children, even today, are forced to confront insults and other psychological assaults based on their racial identity. Although strands of this focus appear as a subtext in many books with a variety of central themes, it is confronted directly in a number of books that celebrate African American children's physical features and affirm their beauty and normalcy. These books also function to resist the notion that European standards of beauty (e.g., ivory skin, straight blond hair, blue eyes) are the only ones that are valid and worthy.

African American picture books, both in dialogue and in narrative, reflect the language variation to be found among Black Americans. Many African Americans are speakers of Mainstream American English (MAE), and many African American writers choose to reflect only that dialect in their books for children, both in narration and dialogue. In some other texts, such as McKissack's *Goin' Someplace Special* (2001), the narration is in MAE, but the dialogue reflects the informal speech that would be typical of African Americans in the setting, in this case Southern urban African Americans (e.g., "I reckon. . . . But you best hurry 'fore I change my mind"). Such texts recognize that many African Americans, across socioeconomic lines and levels of formal education, including speakers of MAE, use features of Black vernacular English in a variety of social situations. A number of African American picture book texts, however, are distinguished by their celebration of an African American oral voice in both narration and dialogue. In many texts, the narrative voices reflect not only the syntax of Black vernacular English, but also traditional oral discourse modes, such as call and response in *Nappy Hair* (Herron 1997). African American discourse styles are also apparent in the use of such stylistic elements as inventive metaphors, creative imagery, proverbial statements, and naming and in the recurrence of familiar phrases, such as "getting on my nerves." This reflection of African American oral traditions is a part of what Clifton referred to as authenticating the world of Black children.

One frequently occurring feature of these picture books is the device of including stories within stories. In these picture books, this usually takes the form of an elder, or less frequently a parent, telling a story to a child, usually to make a point. The prominence of elders as transmitters of family and group history means that a number of picture book texts have a contemporary outer frame that has the elder relating a story about the past to a child. This recalls not only the tradition of elder functioning as storyteller, but also, since the stories often make a point, it recalls the tradition of using story as a vehicle of instruction to provide information, to transmit some moral value, or both.

Sprinkled throughout individual picture books, as well as sets of two or three, are references to various aspects of African American cultural values, customs, beliefs, attitudes, and manners or to aspects of traditional oral culture. Flying (e.g., symbolizing freedom) appears in a few books across the decades, such as Walter Dean Myers's early book *Fly, Jimmy, Fly* and Ringgold's *Tar Beach* (1991), recalling the often-retold tale of the enslaved Africans who freed themselves by flying back to Africa. Literary folktales incorporate motifs from traditional African American folk stories, such as the trickster character or the clever John from slave tales. The journey "down home" from the North to the South occurs in a handful of picture books, reflecting the importance of maintaining family connections between those who migrated to the North and the family "back home." Spiritual beliefs appear in a few books. Quilts and quilting are important to a few stories.

In short, in the process of creating stories that reflect an African American cultural milieu, African American writers of picture books weave throughout their stories the specific details that make that cultural milieu distinctive. In so doing, they have been a part of creating an African American tradition in children's literature.

NOTE

1. Scholastic, Inc. (n.d.) Authors and Books Page. Faith Ringgold's Interview Transcript. Interview by Scholastic students. http://books.scholastic.com/teachers/authorsandbooks/authorstudies.jsp.

BIBLIOGRAPHY OF BOOKS FOR CHILDREN AND YOUNG ADULTS

Sources other than books for children and young adults are documented in a reference list at the end of the book.

Barber, Barbara. 1994. *Saturday at the New You*. Illus. by Anna Rich. New York: Lee and Low.

Belton, Sandra. 1993. *From Miss Ida's Porch*. Illus. by Floyd Cooper. New York: Four Winds Press.

———. 1994. *May'naise Sandwiches and Sunshine Tea*. Illus. by Gail Gordon Carter. New York: Four Winds Press.

Caines, Jeannette. 1982. *Just Us Women*. Illus. by Pat Cummings. New York: Harper and Row.

Coleman, Evelyn. 1995. *The Glass Bottle Tree*. Illus. by Gail Gordon Carter. New York: Orchard.

———. 1998. *To Be a Drum*. Illus. by Aminah Brenda Lynn Robinson. New York: Albert Whitman.

Crews, Donald. 1991. *Bigmama's*. New York: Greenwillow.

———. 1992. *Shortcut*. New York: Greenwillow.

Cummings, Pat. 1991. *Clean Your Room, Harvey Moon*. New York: Bradbury.

———. 1992. *Petey Moroni's Camp Runamok Diary*. New York: Bradbury.

———. 2000. *Angel Baby*. New York: Lothrop, Lee and Shepard.

DeVeaux, Alexis. 1987. *Enchanted Hair Tale*. Illus. by Cheryl Hanna. New York: HarperCollins.

English, Karen. 1998. *Just Right Stew*. Illus. by Anna Rich. Honesdale, PA: Boyds Mills Press.

Flournoy, Valerie. 1985. *The Patchwork Quilt*. Illus. by Jerry Pinkney. New York: Dial.

Goss, Linda. 1996. *The Frog Who Wanted to Be a Singer*. Illus. by Cynthia Jabar. New York: Orchard.

Greenfield, Eloise. 1993. *William and the Good Old Days*. Illus. by Jan Spivey Gilchrist. New York: HarperCollins.

Haskins, Francine. 1991. *I Remember 121*. San Francisco: Children's Book Press.

———. 1992. *Things I Like about Grandma*. San Francisco: Children's Book Press.

Herron, Carolivia. 1997. *Nappy Hair*. Illus. by Joe Cepeda. New York: Knopf.

hooks, bell. 1999. *Happy to Be Nappy*. Illus. by Chris Raschka. New York: Hyperion.

Howard, Elizabeth Fitzgerald. 1991a. *Aunt Flossie's Hats (and Crab Cakes Later)*. Illus. by James Ransome. New York: Clarion.

———. 1989. *Chita's Christmas Tree*. Illus. by Floyd Cooper. New York: Bradbury.

———. 1995. *Papa Tells Chita a Story*. Illus. by Floyd Cooper. New York: Simon and Schuster.

———. 2000. *Virgie Goes to School with Us Boys*. Illus. by E. B. Lewis. New York: Simon and Schuster.

Hudson, Cheryl and Bernette Ford. 1990. *Bright Eyes, Brown Skin*. Illus. by George Ford. Orange, NJ: Just Us Books.

Johnson, Angela. 1989. *Tell Me A Story, Mama*. Illus. by David Soman. New York: Orchard.

———. 1990a. *Do Like Kyla*. Illus. by James Ransome. New York: Orchard.

———. 1990b. *When I Am Old with You*. Illus. by David Soman. New York: Orchard.

———. 1991. *One of Three*. Illus. by David Soman. New York: Orchard.

———. 1992. *The Leaving Morning*. Illus. by David Soman. New York: Orchard.

———. 1993a. *The Girl Who Wore Snakes*. Illus. by James Ransome. New York: Orchard.

———. 1993b. *Julius*. Illus. by Dav Pilkey. New York: Orchard.

———. 1996. *The Aunt in Our House*. Illus. by David Soman. New York: Orchard.

———. 1997. *The Rolling Store*. Illus. by Peter Catalanotto. New York: Orchard.

———. 1999. *The Wedding*. Illus. by David Soman. New York: Orchard.

———. 2000. *Down the Winding Road*. Illus by. Shane W. Evans. New York: DK Children's.

Johnson, Dinah. 1999. *Sunday Week*. Illus. by Tyrone Geter. New York: Holt.

Johnson, Dolores. 1992. *The Best Bug to Be*. New York: Macmillan.

———. 1993. *Your Dad Was Just Like You*. New York: Macmillan.

———. 1999. *My Mom Is My Show and Tell*. New York: Marshall Cavendish.

Lester, Julius. 1999. *What a Truly Cool World*. Illus. by Joe Cepeda. New York: Scholastic.

McKisssack, Patricia. 1986. *Flossie and the Fox*. Illus. by Rachel Isadora. New York: Dial.

———. 1992. *A Million Fish, More or Less*. Illus. by Dena Schutzer. New York: Knopf.

———. 1997. *Ma Dear's Aprons*. Illus. by Floyd Cooper. New York: Atheneum.

———. 2001. *Going Someplace Special*. Illus. by Jerry Pinkney. New York: Atheneum.

——— and Onawumi Jean Moss. 2005. *Precious and the Boo Hag*. Illus. by Krysten Brooker. New York: Atheneum.

Mitchell, Margaree. 1993. *Uncle Jed's Barbershop*. Illus. by James Ransome. New York: Simon and Schuster.

Myers, Christopher. 2000. *Wings*. New York: Scholastic.

Myers, Walter Dean. 1972. *The Dragon Takes a Wife*. Illus. by Ann Grifalconi. New York: Bobbs Merrill.

———. 1974. *Fly, Jimmy, Fly*. Illus. by Moneta Barnett. New York: Putnam.

———. 1984. *Mr. Monkey and the Gotcha Bird*. Illus. by Leslie Morrill. New York: Delacorte.

———. 1996. *How Mr. Monkey Saw the Whole World*. Illus. by Synthia Saint James. New York: Doubleday.

———. 2000. *The Blues of Flats Brown*. Illus. by Nina Laden. New York: Holiday House.

Nolen, Jerdine. 1994. *Harvey Potter's Balloon Farm*. Illus. by Mark Buehner. New York: Lothrop, Lee and Shepard.

———. 1998. *Raising Dragons*. Illus. by Elise Primavera. San Diego, CA: Silver Whistle/Harcourt.

———. 2000. *Big Jabe*. Illus. by Kadir Nelson. New York: Lothrop, Lee and Shepard.

Pinkney, Brian. 1994. *Max Found Two Sticks*. New York: Simon and Schuster.

————. 1995. *JoJo's Flying Side Kick*. New York: Simon and Schuster.

————. 1997. *The Adventures of Sparrow Boy*. New York: Simon and Schuster.

Pinkney, Gloria Jean. 1992. *Back Home*. Illus. by Jerry Pinkney. New York: Dial.

————. 1994. *The Sunday Outing*. Illus. by Jerry Pinkney. New York: Dial.

Pinkney, Sandra. 2000. *Shades of Black*. Photos by Myles Pinkney. New York: Scholastic.

Ringgold, Faith. 1991. *Tar Beach*. New York: Crown

————. 1992. *Aunt Harriet's Underground Railroad in the Sky*. New York: Crown.

————. 1993. *Dinner at Aunt Connie's House*. New York: Hyperion.

————. 1999a. *If a Bus Could Talk*. New York: Simon and Schuster.

————. 1999b. *The Invisible Princess*. New York: Crown.

Rochelle, Brenda. 1994. *When Jo Louis Won the Title*. Illus. by Larry Johnson. Boston: Houghton Mifflin.

Smalls, Irene. 1991. *Irene and the Big Fine Nickel*. Illus. by Tyrone Geter. New York: Little, Brown.

————. 1996. *Louise's Gift*. Illus. by Colin Bootman. New York: Little, Brown.

Strickland, Michael. 1998. *Haircuts at Sleepy Sam's*. Illus. by Keaf Holliday. Honesdale, PA: Boyds Mills Press.

Tarpley, Natasha Anastasia. 1998. *I Love My Hair*. Illus. by E. B. Lewis. New York: Little, Brown.

Udry, Janice May. 1966. *What Mary Jo Shared*. Illus. by Eleanor Mills. Morton Grove, IL: Albert Whitman.

Williams, Sherley Anne. 1992. *Working Cotton*. Illus. by Carole Byard. San Diego, CA: Harcourt, Brace Jovanovich.

Williams-Garcia, Rita. 2000. *Catching the Wild Waiyuuzee*. Illus. by Mike Reed. New York: Simon and Schuster.

Woodson, Jacqueline. 1997. *We Had a Picnic This Sunday Past*. Illus. by Diane Greenseid. New York: Hyperion.

Wyeth, Sharon Dennis. 1998. *Something Beautiful*. Illus. by Chris Soentpiet. New York: Doubleday.

Yarbrough, Camille. 1979. *Cornrows*. Illus. by Carole Byard. New York: Coward, McCann & Geoghegan.

CHAPTER 8

African American Illustrators of Children's Books: Nine Pacesetters

With the rise of picture books about African Americans in the 1970s came increased opportunities for African American artists to develop careers as children's book illustrators. Although a few such artists had begun illustrating African American picture books in the 1960s, they did not all achieve the immediate recognition that *Stevie* (1969) brought to John Steptoe. In fact, even by the end of the twentieth century fewer than two dozen African American artists had achieved prominence in the field. Nine of these artists—John Steptoe, Tom Feelings, Ashley Bryan, Jerry Pinkney, Carol Byard, Pat Cummings, Leo and Diane Dillon, and Donald Crews—started illustrating children's books in the late 1960s and 1970s and, with the exception of Steptoe, who died in 1989, continued through the end of the twentieth century and into the twenty-first, their careers overlapping those of the artists who entered the field in later decades. These nine illustrators emerged as the premier African American picture book artists, the first African Americans to attract major critical attention and to win recognition by the children's literature establishment in the form of prestigious awards.

Beginning with a discussion of the work of George Ford and Moneta Barnett, pioneering illustrators whose work has significance in the development of African American children's literature, this chapter goes on to survey the work of this premier group of African American illustrators of children's picture books, with a view to identifying common threads across artists, such as what sort of books they choose to illustrate in terms of topics or themes, the choices they make regarding which scenes to illustrate and which details to include, and which images they emphasize in their work. It also discusses briefly some of the artistic choices they make, such as the media in which they work and to some extent their stylistic choices, which help to determine the images they present of Black people. The chapter also includes some attention to comments that the artists have made about their work and what they hope it will accomplish.

UNSUNG BEGINNINGS: MONETA BARNETT AND GEORGE FORD

Although *Stevie* (Steptoe 1969) is rightly considered the breakthrough contemporary African American picture book, John Steptoe was not the only African

American artist illustrating children's books in the late 1960s and early 1970s. For example, Leo Carty, who is currently best known for his paintings depicting historical scenes of St. Croix in the Virgin Islands, illustrated Walter Dean Myers's first book and several other picture books in the late 1960s and 1970s. Among the most notable pioneering illustrators in post-1965 African American picture books were Moneta Barnett and George Ford, who both began illustrating children's books prior to the publication of Steptoe's *Stevie*. Those two artists were important contributors to the move from caricatured images of African Americans to realistic ones. Across a variety of genres, they built a body of work that helped to advance the development of African American children's literature.

Moneta Barnett (1922–1976) started illustrating children's books in the 1950s. Her first illustrated book, *Ready-made Family* (Murphy 1953), was a children's novel, with a few black-and-white drawings scattered throughout, about White siblings who find love and happiness in a foster family. Between 1953 and 1967, she illustrated two or three other books, but her first picture storybook was *Timothy's Flower* (Van Leeuwen 1967), which was illustrated in color and included a multicultural cast of characters, a forerunner of the late-century focus on multiculturalism. It featured an urban African American boy who becomes fascinated with a yellow flower he finds in the park. Barnett illustrated books in a number of genres, including poetry and biography, and beginning in 1966 and continuing until her death, she illustrated at least one book a year, including a few that were not focused on African Americans.

In terms of African American picture books, her most significant illustrations were for texts written by three of the most prominent African American authors— Lucille Clifton (*My Brother Fine with Me*, 1975b), Eloise Greenfield (*Me and Neesie*, 1975a; *First Pink Light*, 1976), and Walter Dean Myers (*Fly, Jimmy, Fly*, 1974). While the children in these books all bear a resemblance to each other, as if Barnett used the same models for every book, they are attractive and appealing. Her soft pencil drawings portray pretty, long-legged little girls with neat plaits or cornrows, bright eyes, and expressive faces, and there are equally expressive, bright-eyed boys. Her adults sport neat Afro hairdos, and her illustrations reveal details of daily living in working-class and middle-class African American homes. Although that seems unremarkable three decades later, at the time her work was an important contribution to the campaign to diversify the "all-white world of children's books" that Nancy Larrick criticized in her 1965 article.

George Ford also started illustrating children's books before *Stevie* (Steptoe 1969). He is noteworthy as the recipient of the first Coretta Scott King Illustrator Award, in 1974, for *Ray Charles* (Mathis 1973), for having illustrated at least thirty children's books and for his significant contributions to the body of work published by Just Us Books. Ford illustrated his first children's book, *African Beginnings* (Vlahos) in 1967. His early work spanned the range from nonfiction to the Crowell picture book biography series, to Nikki Giovanni's 1973 collection of poems, *Ego-tripping*. The illustrations for these works were mainly black-and-white drawings that both extend and reflect the spirit of the texts. He also illustrated two of Eloise Greenfield's picture books, *Darlene* (1980) and *Alesia* (1981).

Ford's early picture books were part of the late 1960s and early 1970s focus on urban life. His first picture storybook for young children was *Freddie Found a Frog* (Napjius 1969), which was also his first book in color and was published the same year as *Stevie* (Steptoe 1969). Similar in theme to *Timothy's Flower* (Van Leeuwen 1967) and also set in the city, *Freddie Found a Frog* has an all–African American cast of characters. In 1972, Ford and Mel Williamson published *Walk On!* a picture book that bears some thematic similarity to Steptoe's *Uptown.* A young boy, accompanied by two girls, takes a walk through their neighborhood and comments—in informal urban Black vernacular—on the people and sights they see. Ford's black-and-white drawings carry most of the story and bring the city scenes to life.

If the early work of Ford and Barnett did not dazzle the children's literature critics, it is nonetheless significant in that it was part of the 1960s' efforts to add a new perspective to American picture books. They pioneered in the endeavor to infuse books about African Americans with realistic, positive images that would boost the self-images of African American children and invite others to see such children in a new light. Ford's later work continues to strengthen that perspective. As noted, he has illustrated many books for Just Us Books, such as *Bright Eyes, Brown Skin* (Hudson and Ford 1990), which celebrates, in text and in the full-color pictures, the beauty of Black children. In *Jamal's Busy Day* (Hudson 1991), Ford's paintings add important details to the story of a young boy who compares his day with those of his accountant mother and architect father. Just Us Books is committed to presenting positive images of African American children and their families, and Ford's contributions to that effort have been a mainstay of their output.

PACESETTING AFRICAN AMERICAN ILLUSTRATORS

Judging from the longevity of their careers and the recognition they have received, the nine artists named as the premier African American children's book illustrators—John Steptoe, Tom Feelings, Ashley Bryan, Jerry Pinkney, Carol Byard, Pat Cummings, Leo and Diane Dillon, and Donald Crews—set the standard for illustration in African American children's books. Only one of them, Leo Dillon (in collaboration with his wife Diane), has been awarded the prestigious Randolph Caldecott Medal, given to the "artist of the most distinguished American picture book for children" published in a given year. All of them, however, have been recipients of one or more prestigious national awards—Caldecott Honor Book citations, Coretta Scott King Awards or Honor Citations, or Boston Globe-Horn Book Awards or Honor Books. In fact, as a group they have received eighteen of the twenty-six Coretta Scott King Illustrator Awards given between 1974 and 2000. These artists began a tradition, although it would be difficult to argue that this tradition is marked by some standardized African American or ethnic stylistic conventions. What ties them and their work together for the most part is their sense of responsibility and commitment to filling what they recognized as a void in children's literature: the missing faces of Black children and the lack of attention to them, their history, and their lives. Almost all of them, at one time or another, asserted that they did not find people who looked like themselves in the books they read as children and expressed a desire to correct that situation for contemporary youngsters.

Nevertheless, based on their expressed goals, purposes, and ideological views, these nine artists could also be placed on a continuum from those with strongly held and overtly expressed sense of responsibility as Black artists to Black children and the Black cultural community to those whose main expressed concern is with the integrity of their own artistry. At one end of the continuum are John Steptoe, Tom Feelings, and Carole Byard, all of whom expressed strongly held beliefs about the ways art should function in the African American cultural community and in children's books specifically. In particular, they expressed the desire to infuse children's books with realistic depictions of African Americans, to increase the visibility of Black children and families in children's books, and to affirm the beauty, humanity, and cultural identity of Black children. At the other end is Donald Crews, who has illustrated only two books about African Americans but whose main publicly expressed concern is with the quality of his work as a graphic artist.

JOHN STEPTOE: GROUNDBREAKING AFRICAN AMERICAN AUTHOR-ARTIST

John Steptoe (1950–1989) was the first post-1965 African American to both write and illustrate a fictional picture storybook for children and to have it published by a "mainstream" publisher. Inspired by his own response to babysitting his younger brother, he took an ordinary experience and set it in the specific context of a Black urban family and neighborhood, brilliantly confirming that portraying the particulars of a cultural setting can capture something of the universality of human emotion. Steptoe grew up in Bedford-Stuyvesant, apparently marching to his own drumbeat even as a child, when he mixed time for active play with time for art, an uncommon interest for boys in his neighborhood. He attended New York's High School of Art and Design but dropped out three months before graduating. "Art and Design was strictly commercial," he noted. "It wasn't my thing. I was getting sick on the train fighting all those people when it wasn't that important for me to get where I was going" ("I Am a Painter," 1969, 59). Nevertheless, he followed the suggestion of one of his high school teachers, who had urged him to submit his portfolio to a publisher. Fortunately, a staff member at Harper brought his work to the attention of Ursula Nordstrom, then the highly respected director of their children's book department and editor for acclaimed artists and writers such as Maurice Sendak, Margaret Wise Brown, and E. B. White. Although Steptoe was just sixteen, Nordstrom recognized his talent and his potential. She invited him to make a dummy book and, as his editor, served as midwife to the birth of *Stevie* (1969). *Stevie* was an immediate success; it was named an American Library Association Notable Book of 1969 and received a number of other significant honors as well. It launched Steptoe on an exceptional career during which he received, among numerous other awards and honors, two Coretta Scott King Awards, two Caldecott Medal Honor citations, and a Boston Globe-Horn Book Award.

Steptoe not only held independent ideas about his art but also expressed a strong commitment to pursuing his own identity, a concern reflected in the themes and topics he explored in both art and text in his picture books. Steptoe's intention to make visible the world of Black children is realized in his illustrations as well as the verbal text. It is the paintings that make evident the physical details of the environment and provide the warmth that suggests Steptoe's affection and respect for his characters and the communities he portrays. Thematically, his picture books focus on the experiences of urban Black boys, Black family life, Black/African identity, and folktales. He also worked in a variety of styles, moving from his early Rouault-like expressionistic art to his realistic later books. For his early books, he noted that he began his paintings with a background of burnt umber, after which he added color to "turn on the lights." The colors are vibrant and intense, and as in *Stevie* (1969), the figures are outlined in black. In these works, he does not so much provide lifelike portraits of African American children and families as he evokes an emotional intensity and expresses the feelings and the spirit of his characters. As his art evolved, he experimented with color and with various media and techniques, including painting, crayon, pencils, and silkscreen.

No matter which style and media he chose, however, he focused on the faces of his characters, making available to his intended readers the kind of images he missed seeing in books when he was a child. In the paintings for his last major picture book, *Mufaro's Beautiful Daughters* (1987), Steptoe had moved to naturalistic portrayals, in full color, of his characters and their landscapes. The story was the result of his search for an African "Cinderella" story, and once he found that story, a great deal of research into the architecture, clothing, flora, and fauna of ancient Zimbabwe. His daughter Bweela was the model for both sisters, and other family members modeled for some of the other characters. *Mufaro*, with its lush colors and striking detail, is considered by some to be his greatest achievement. It may be the book for which he will be best remembered, and the loving portraits of his daughter and the care with which he executed the paintings make *Mufaro* a fitting legacy.

Even his last book, *Baby Says* (Steptoe 1988), was forward-looking. It was part of the trend that extended the targeted picture book audience to preschoolers and babies. Like *Stevie*, it features two boys, this time a baby and his older brother. In contrast to *Stevie's* vivid colors and expressionistic style, the paintings are realistic portraits of the two children, rendered in soft colors. The text in *Baby Says* is limited to a few words familiar to very young children (e.g., here, uh-oh, baby), so in true picture book form, the story is carried mainly by the visual images. In this, as in all of his books, particularly the ones for which he created the text, Steptoe proved himself to be an expert picture book artist, not merely mirroring the text, but marrying the dual narratives of text and visuals.

As the premier African American picture book author-artist, Steptoe was clearly a pacesetter. Early on, he expressed, both in his verbal comments and in his work, a Black nationalist political stance. As was noted in Chapter 6, he made clear his commitment to Black children as the primary audience for his work and his intention to fill a void, to make visible in children's books the faces and the lives of Black urban children. Steptoe was coming of age during a time when civil rights struggles were quite visible, and the Black Arts Movement was flourishing.

Steptoe's perspective, and perhaps his artistic style, may have been influenced in part by one of his mentors, Norman Lewis, an activist artist and the first major African American abstract expressionist. In 1963, along with artists Romare Bearden and Hale Woodruff, Lewis had founded Spiral, an artists' workshop established to foster discussions of artistic, political, and racial issues. Lewis taught art in a Harlem program, HarYou Act, which provided grants for research on poverty and for projects that promoted culture and education. Steptoe participated in the program and attended Lewis's classes. In its introduction to *Stevie*, *Life* had noted that the book, with its urban setting, its all-Black cast of characters, and its use of Black vernacular English "ushers in a new era of realism in children's books" ("I Am a Painter," 54). Steptoe was daring in his choices of media and style and thereby opened the way for others to be innovative as well.

After the success of *Stevie*, Steptoe was sought after by many publishers but maintained a commitment to his ideals and values, refusing to accept just any and every manuscript that came his way. He once mentioned to Ursula Nordstrom that he had turned down a particular manuscript, and when she asked what he did not like about it, Steptoe replied, "Well, it was just untouched by human love" (Nordstrom 1998, 303). Steptoe's books were, of course, just the opposite, steeped in human love. His untimely death just before his thirty-ninth birthday, twenty years—almost to the day—after the publication of *Stevie* in *Life* was a tragic loss to the field of African American children's literature.

TOM FEELINGS (1933–2003): IMPROVISING WITHIN A RESTRICTED FORM

Brooklyn-born artist Tom Feelings was the "dean" of contemporary African American illustrators of children's books. Three years after Steptoe's *Stevie* ushered in the contemporary African American picture book, Feelings became the first African American artist to receive a Caldecott Honor Book citation, in 1972, for *Moja Means One: Swahili Counting Book* (1971), with text by Feelings's first wife, Muriel Feelings. Three years later, another of their collaborations, *Jambo Means Hello: Swahili Alphabet Book* (1974), was cited as a 1975 Caldecott Honor Book as well as the recipient of the 1974 Boston Globe-Horn Book Award for a picture book. *Moja* and *Jambo* were part of a cluster of picture books concerned with engendering pride in an African heritage, a sense of kinship between Africa and African Americans, and an understanding of how African Americans have contributed to the richness of American culture and American prosperity. In the introduction to *Moja*, Muriel Feelings expressed her intentions: "As our people in the Western Hemisphere learn more and more about our African heritage, we become increasingly proud. . . . I have written this book in the hope that young boys and girls of African origin enjoy learning to count in Swahili, together with gaining more knowledge of their African heritage" (n.p.).

Focused on village life in East Africa, *Moja* and *Jambo* paint a visual and verbal portrait of rural Africans as ordinary people going about their everyday lives—growing food, going to market, making music, worshipping, playing games, creating articles that are both useful and beautiful, and so on. These portraits are in direct opposition to popular concepts of Africa as promulgated by Tarzan films and other media. The luminous illustrations respectfully portray the details—and normality—of life in a geographical climate very different from that of the North American children to whom the books are explicitly addressed.

Earlier, Feelings had illustrated Julius Lester's *To Be a Slave* (1968), which was only the second book by an African American to be cited as a Newbery Honor Book. Although the Newbery citation for *To Be a Slave* was for the author rather than the artist, Feelings's powerful paintings contributed a great deal to the impact of the book, which became a landmark in African American children's literature. His last book published before his death, *The Middle Passage: White Ships Black Cargo* (1995), a pictorial narrative of the voyage of a slave ship, was the culmination of twenty years of research and personal reliving of that painful experience as he transformed it into a singular artistic achievement.

Feelings's art was a reflection of his personal philosophy and sense of himself as an "African born in America." He freely admitted to being influenced by the Black power/Black Arts Movement of the 1960s. He described his work as that of a "storyteller in picture form, who tries to reflect and interpret life" as he sees it (1985, 685). Deeply affected by his experiences living in Ghana and in Guyana in the 1960s and 1970s, Feelings was a Pan Africanist in that he perceived Black people throughout the African diaspora as Africans, with shared kinship and shared cultural roots. At the same time, he recognized that those cultural roots have been "expanded by the experiences of being Black in America" (685) or wherever African peoples have been transplanted. Across the decades, Feelings's illustrations reflected this sense of a dual heritage—African roots, American experience—and all of his books have dealt with those themes in one way or another.

As a self-identified African, and in keeping with the ideas of the Black Arts Movement, Feelings rejected the idea of "art for art's sake." He likened himself to the African griot, whose stories not only entertain but also inform or instruct. Not surprisingly then, his first published work, a comic strip, served an educational purpose; it was intended to acquaint readers with Black heroes, to transmit what Feelings considered to be vital knowledge to as wide an audience as he could reach. *Tommy Traveler in the World of Negro History* originally ran in *The New York Age*, a Harlem newspaper, in 1958 and 1959. (In 1991, Black Butterfly Press reissued the strips as a full-color book, *Tommy Traveler in the World of Black History*.) In this innovative work, Tommy Traveler, Feelings's alter ego, imagined himself participating in events in the lives of several Black historical figures, such as Frederick Douglass, Crispus Attucks, and Joe Louis. Thus, like Du Bois and Carter before him, Feelings took on the task of empowering Black youngsters with knowledge about the contributions of Black men and women.

It was almost a decade after *Tommy Traveler* before Feelings began to illustrate children's books. Disillusioned by his forays into formal art training, where he had encountered an arrogant lack of recognition and respect for African and African American art, Feelings honed his skills drawing from life in Brooklyn and in the American South, where he traveled on assignment for *Look* magazine. Although he sketched the people and places he saw around him, he was particularly drawn to children as subjects because he believed they were not yet jaded by life, as Black adults often were, and less likely or able to mask their emotions. Sadly, he discovered over time that many of the children had learned to think of themselves as ugly, a lesson that motivated Feelings to want to create books that would reflect back to such children the beauty he saw in each of them.

During his time in Africa and in Guyana, Feelings continued his habit of drawing the children and adults he saw around him. The contrast between the happiness he found on the faces of African and Guyanese children and the sadness behind the eyes of the American children confirmed his sense that Black American children needed books that would mirror their beauty. Many of his drawings from those years became the basis for picture books that combined his illustrations with poems by African American poets. His time in Africa also provided the background for his award-wining early picture books. And, it was an African friend's inquiry about the fate of the captives who had long ago been taken away from the African continent and enslaved in the Americas that prompted Feelings to spend twenty years creating his magnum opus, *The Middle Passage* (1995).

Altogether, Feelings illustrated about twenty children's books, the majority of which focus on three themes or topics—African life and history, celebrating and affirming Black children, and African American history. Fortunately for posterity, Feelings also published his views about his art and his philosophy in several articles over the years and in a memoir, *Black Pilgrimage* (1972), which is both an autobiography of his early years and a remarkable portfolio of his art up to that time. Threaded through his essays and reflected in his art are four recurring themes: the importance of emotional expression, the infusion of warmth and light into dark faces, a certain "dance consciousness" and rhythm, and the interaction between the opposing forces of joy and pain.

Most of his early books were set in Africa, including *Moja* (1971) and *Jambo* (1974), the two award winners written by his first wife, Muriel. They exemplify his concern with warmth and light and with rhythm and dance consciousness. Working primarily in black and white, Feelings softens the dark tones, and the contrast, by adding subtle coloring, either with paint or in the printing process. The result is a certain luminosity that recalls the light and warmth of the African sun on dark faces. The effect of rhythm and a dance consciousness comes from the use of many curves and diagonal lines as well as the repetition of lines and forms, all of which impart a sense of movement. Most important in these illustrations—as in the text—is the dignity with which the people of East Africa and the details of their daily living are represented. One is also left with a sense of harmony and of a strong communal spirit.

Feelings's basic media were pen and ink, wet tissue paper, and tempera. The wet tissue paper provided an element of unpredictability and the excitement of balancing between exercising some control over the process and allowing effects simply to happen. He started using it when, as a young aspiring artist, he did not have the funds to buy more expensive materials. Later, he characterized it as an instance of "improvising within a restricted form," a phrase that appears frequently in his essays. He related the concept to the ways in which Black people in America have often used the limited resources available to them to create within and often to transcend traditional or non-African forms in their environment, such as music, dance, visual art, quilts, and even basketball moves. He compared his technique to the ways jazz musicians often improvise on rather simple melodies and thereby transcend the original form to create something new (Feelings 1985b). The concept of improvising within a restricted form functioned for him not only as a description of his own technique but also as another metaphor for the Black experience in America.

His two best-known historical works are Julius Lester's award-winning *To Be a Slave* (1968) and his own wordless narrative, *The Middle Passage* (1995). *To Be a Slave*, for which Feelings created fourteen paintings, presents excerpts from the Works Progress Administration interviews with former slaves, along with Lester's own eloquent and impassioned commentary. The written text, along with Feelings's muted and powerful black-and-white drawings, put a human face on the terrible experience of slavery in America. *The Middle Passage* consists of a series of more than 50 dramatic paintings that relate the story of the dreadful voyage from Africa to the Americas on a slave ship. Using only black and white, Feelings draws the reader/viewer onto the ship and into the experience. In an effort to reverse the popular connotations of black and white, he makes his White figures eerily ghost-like, reserving the human warmth for his dark figures. The drawings for this book, some of which combine realism and symbolism, exemplify Feelings's concern with emotional expression, which he has noted is more important to him than accuracy. It is impossible to come away from the book unmoved by the suffering of the captives and their ultimate triumph in having survived the journey, the interaction of joy and pain that Feelings perceived as an elemental aspect of Black American culture.

In the two decades between *Jambo* (1974) and *The Middle Passage* (1995), Feelings produced a handful of books, more accurately labeled collaborations. Each book consists of poems composed or selected to accompany and interpret a series of Feelings's drawings. In a sense, then, the poems "illustrate" the art and not the other way round (see Chapter 5). Using the life drawings he created over a number of years, Feelings in effect created albums of loving portraits of Black women and children in America, Africa, and South America. These are the books that he thought were needed when he first left the United States, books in which

Black children—and in one case, Black women—could see reflections of the beauty that he saw in them. Each portrait highlights the individuality and the dignity of its subject. Many of the portraits are of American children, and in many of those one can see, behind the smiles or the occasional scowls, the sadness Feelings wrote about in *Black Pilgrimage* (1972). Although he experimented with techniques to add texture, warmth, and color tones, such as sepia, to his illustrations, he chose to produce only one of his children's books, *Soul Looks Back in Wonder* (1993), in full color, preferring to try to draw viewers inside the work with his hushed tones.

Taken as a whole, Feelings's work is an answer to Langston Hughes's (1932a) call for literature that would "give them [Black children] back their souls." His portraits of people of African descent, both in Africa and in the African diaspora, reflect the dignity and the beauty that he saw in ordinary Black people. In his historical work, he made visible both the suffering and the triumph—the joy and the pain—that he saw as characteristic of Black experience in America. In articulating his purposes and motivations, Feelings also identified some of the elements that may in part characterize the art of African American picture book illustrators. This is particularly true in terms of the focus on the faces of his subjects, the importance of emotional expression, the infusion of movement or dance consciousness into the art, and the connection he made between the visual art and Black music.

CAROLE BYARD: CULTURAL ACTIVIST

Carole Byard's ideas about art and illustration are similar to those of Steptoe and Feelings. According to an oral history interview, Byard was influenced both by Malcolm X and by Amiri Baraka, playwright and poet of the Black Arts Movement (Raymond 1997). She believes that art should serve the community, and she has long been an activist, having been a founding member of an artists' collective and having lent her skills to various community projects, such as wall murals. In addition to being an illustrator of children's books, she is a prize-winning sculptor, painter, and art teacher. In relation to children's books, Byard sees African American artists and writers as having an important responsibility: "History relies on whoever is telling the story to tell the story well. We must be responsible for our stories, our telling, our history, our words, and our imagery" (Wesley 2000, 27).

In terms of African American children's books, her output has been relatively small—I am aware of fewer than twenty books—but her work has won enough critical attention and praise to place her in the company of the other pacesetting artists who also started publishing in the late 1960s and early 1970s. One of her books, *Working Cotton* (Williams 1992), was cited as a Caldecott Honor Book, making her one of only two African American women to have a book in that category. (The other is Faith Ringgold.) *Working Cotton* was also a Coretta Scott King Illustrator Honor Book, as was *Grandmama's Joy* (Greenfield 1980). Byard won the 1980 Coretta Scott King Illustrator Award for *Cornrows* (Yarbrough 1979).

Byard's first children's book was published in 1971, but it was not until near the end of that decade that she began to publish her best-known and most well received books. In 1972, she received a Ford Foundation grant that allowed her to travel to Africa, and at a later time she attended an international Black arts conference in Nigeria. Her experiences on the African continent, like those of Tom Feelings, had an important influence on her subsequent work in children's books, some of which reflect her study of African art and culture. *Africa Dream* (Greenfield 1977), *Cornrows* (Yarbrough 1979), and *The Black Snowman* (Mendez 1989) all contain images of Africa and Africans, although none of the three is actually set in Africa. The Africa of each of these stories is an imagined place, illustrated with realistic pictures of African peoples in traditional cultural or historical settings. In *Africa Dream*, the fantasy element is played up by Byard's use of swirling lines and circular shapes, repeatedly placing the dreaming main character within the circle of her African ancestors. These lines also convey a sense of movement, similar to what Feelings calls in his own work a dance consciousness. In *Cornrows*, similar lines and shapes indicate the movement between past and present as the adults relate to the children the origins and significance of cornrows, the hairstyle. Byard's work, then, contributed to the effort to engender in African American children pride in their African ancestry.

A number of Byard's books have been illustrated in black and white, using charcoal and graphite. An interesting feature of these books, as noted by Feelings (1991), is that the characters are shown with very dark skins, and yet "there's a glow to the faces." Regarding Byard's striking portrait of Rhondy in Greenfield's *Grandmama's Joy* (1980), he stated, "When you first look at it, you see beautiful form and design—but then she pulls you into the center of it by creating a mood for the audience to complete" (52). His point is that Byard's drawings resist the traditional association of the color black with things negative by making her characters warm, attractive, and appealing, a goal he also set for himself. And, he saw both himself and Byard trying, through the technique of infusing light and warmth into dark faces, to draw readers into the paintings and compel them to *look* closely at the people being portrayed.

While Byard shares some philosophical ideas and ideals with Feelings, her work stands out on its own. Thanks to the Caldecott Honor citation, she may be best known in children's literature circles for her acrylic paintings for *Working Cotton* (Williams 1992). In these evocative illustrations, Byard very effectively portrays the tension between the backbreaking work in the fields and the lush beauty of the landscape as the family works from sunup to sundown, perhaps another example of Feelings's concept of the interaction of joy and pain in African American life. With individual portraits and impressive double-page spreads, she emphasizes the emotions as well as the strength, dignity, and endurance of the family as they labor all together, each at his or her given task. Particularly powerful are the two dramatic close-ups of the father, one showing how skilled he is at picking cotton and how strong he is, the other showing him gently holding a late-blooming cotton blossom, a symbol of hope. In the context of African American children's literature, this is one of the few picture books set in contemporary times that features a rural family at the very bottom of the socioeconomic ladder and celebrates their dignity and their resilience.

Byard started illustrating children's books when Black artists were just beginning to win recognition as children's book illustrators. That she was the first woman to win the Coretta Scott King Illustrator Award also confirms her status as a pacesetter. Her illustrations for popular and critically praised African American picture books such as *Cornrows* (Yarbrough 1979), *The Black Snowman* (Mendez 1989), and *Working Cotton* (Williams 1992) have made Byard an important contributor to the development of African American imagery in children's books. Among the threads that connect Byard, Steptoe, and Feelings is their attention to African cultures and African American ties to Africa. This concern is also shared by Ashley Bryan, another of the "elders" in African American picture book illustration.

ASHLEY BRYAN: CONNECTING CHILDREN TO THEIR ROOTS

Ashley Bryan is a storyteller, musician, poet, performer, painter, and illustrator. He began illustrating children's books in 1967, with *Moon, for What Do You Wait?* (1967), a selection of short poems by poet Rabindranath Tagore. Since then, he has illustrated more than thirty children's books, almost all of which focus on African and African American culture. Bryan's commitment has been to share the poetry and stories of Africa and African America, particularly with the children who are rooted in those cultures, but also with those who are not. Accordingly, the main emphases in the books and stories he has written, compiled, edited, and adapted have been African and Afro-Caribbean folktales, African American spirituals, and African American poetry. Like many African American authors and artists of his day, he noted the absence of people like himself in the books he read as a child, and as an adult he has tried to help fill the void.

It is difficult to separate Bryan's roles as storyteller, poet, musician, and artist from his illustrating since they all work together to create his unique style. His prose relies heavily on the musical components of poetry—rhythm, rhyme, ono-matopoeia, repetition, alliteration. The rhythm of the prose in Bryan's African stories is often reflected in the rhythms in the paintings, which are influenced by his study of African art. In fact, Bryan identifies strongly with his African ancestry: "As a Black American I have African roots. Retelling and illustrating African tales has kept me close to African sources" (1988, 175).

The illustrations in his collections of African tales—*The Ox of the Wonderful Horns* (1971), *The Adventures of Aku* (1976), *Beat the Story Drum, Pum Pum* (1980), and *Lion and the Ostrich Chicks* (1986)—reflect Bryan's extensive study of African art, sculpture, masks, and rock painting, which he absorbed into his own style (1988, 175). In illustrating these stories, he does not attempt to emulate the style of any one African group but to capture something of the spirit of African art. Although the bold lines and strong contrasts in the artwork give the appearance of block prints, the striking illustrations in these African collections are actually paintings. Mostly rendered in black and white, each of the collections also contains a number of full-page illustrations in earthy tones of black and red ochre, accented with white. The richly detailed paintings often incorporate into the overall design patterns that are similar to those in African textiles. Bryan also sometimes includes words from the story, especially onomatopoetic ones, as part of the compositions.

Three of his picture books, *The Cat's Purr* (1985), *The Dancing Granny* (1977), and *Turtle Knows Your Name* (1989), are adaptations of Caribbean folktales. *The Dancing Granny* in particular has been lauded for the illustrations, which are influenced by Bryan's study of Japanese brush painting, particularly those of Hokusai, a wood engraver and painter who lived in the eighteenth and nineteenth centuries (1988, 176). Bryan's brush paintings capture perfectly the dancing movement and the dancing spirit of the granny, who is based on his own grandmother. In making these stories from Africa and the African diaspora available and accessible to children, Bryan is attempting in part to acquaint African American children with their cultural heritage.

In Bryan's view, one of the most important gifts African Americans have bestowed on the world is the African American spirituals, religious songs that emanated from enslaved Africans in the United States. They were created anonymously by those whom poet James Weldon Johnson referred to as "Black and unknown bards." They fused stories from the Bible with aspects of African musical culture (e.g., call and response) to create a new form of music. When Bryan discovered that there were no collections of those songs available to children, he made it his mission to create such collections, intending to select 100 spirituals in four volumes. As it turns out, he illustrated five such volumes, two of which were selected by his friend John Langstaff.

The second cultural gift that is close to Bryan's heart is African American poetry. Part of his mission has been to bring this poetry to the attention of a wide audience, as well as to help African American children become more strongly rooted in who they are. He has also produced a picture book volume of his own poetry, *Sing to the Sun* (1992), accompanied by his own illustrations. In addition, he has illustrated collections of poems by Nikki Giovanni, Langston Hughes, and Paul Laurence Dunbar, as well as an ABC of African American poetry, and he has edited a selection of Dunbar poems illustrated by several different African American artists, including himself.

Bryan has developed a recognizable style even though he uses different media. The first two collections of spirituals, *Walk Together Children* (1974) and *I'm Going to Sing* (1982), are illustrated in black and white with block prints, a technique chosen to evoke early religious block-printed books. He returned to this medium again when he illustrated new editions of Charlemae Hill Rollins's anthology *Christmas Gif'* (1993) and Lorenz Graham's Liberian-flavored Bible stories, *How God Fix Jonah* (2000). For the two black-and-white collections of spirituals, Bryan not only made blocks for the pictures but also cut the titles and the musical notes by hand, a true labor of love. He often chose scenes from everyday life to illustrate the songs, making a connection between past and present. He also added an element of multiculturalism, showing, for example, people from diverse cultures in the double-page spread illustration for "The Gospel Train" (Get on board, little children). Other illustrations, such as the one accompanying "Steal Away," clearly connect the spirituals to their slave era roots.

The illustrations for the later collections of spirituals and for most of his other books have been rendered in jewel-like colors with tempera or with tempera and gouache. Evidence of his study of African art appears in some of this later work as it did in the folktale collections. Although many of his paintings are straightforward scenes or portraits, they often incorporate abstract or near-abstract elements, such as geometric designs, quilt-like borders, or stylized waves to represent flowing water. Bryan's very effective use of color and design is sometimes described as being kaleidoscopic in that his paintings seem to embody movement; others perceive them as resembling stained glass. Bryan's style often recalls naïve or folk art, although in reality it is very sophisticated. His vibrant illustrations often incorporate humor and are full of details that invite inspection and reward repeated examinations with new discoveries.

One striking feature of the illustrations for all his Christian-oriented works—the spirituals, the Bible stories in *How God Fix Jonah* (Graham 2000), and the references to the Nativity in *Christmas Gift* (Rollins 1993)—is that they represent all Biblical figures as Black. In the television film *Looking for a Face Like Mine* (WBGU-TV, 2004), Bryan relates a story told to him by a librarian in which a Black child noted, "That baby Jesus looks like me. I could be the baby Jesus!" For non-Black readers, this is a thought-provoking proposition; for Black children, it is a very powerful affirmation.

In a marked departure from his signature style, Bryan illustrated *Beautiful Blackbird* (2003) with cut-paper collages. In a touching tribute, Bryan includes in the endpaper collages photographs of the actual scissors that his mother had used in her sewing and embroidery, and that he used to make the collages for the book. The story, a retelling of a tale from Zambia, is a celebration of "Black is beautiful." The illustrations are full of brightly colored cut-paper birds, all vying for a touch of black from Blackbird, who they agree is the most beautiful bird of all. Blackbird provides a touch of his black color for all the birds, but with the caution that "Color on the outside is not what's on the inside," and later, "Just remember, whatever I do, I'll be me and you'll be you." With those comments, Bryan extends the meaning of the story to include the idea of taking pride in one's own heritage, whatever it may be. *Beautiful Blackbird* won the 2004 Coretta Scott King Illustrator Award.

As one of the pacesetting contemporary African American illustrators of children's books, Ashley Bryan expanded the breadth of African American children's literature. While his work is focused on affirming the cultural roots of Black children, he is also committed to sharing the cultural, aesthetic, and literary heritage of Africans and African Americans with as wide an audience as he is able to reach. He sees himself as fulfilling dual roles as both Black artist and one who can relate to people across diverse cultures.

JERRY PINKNEY: PORTRAYING AFRICAN AMERICANS WITH DIGNITY

Although Jerry Pinkney's statements about his goals and purposes tend to be less overtly political than those made by Feelings, Steptoe, or Byard, his expressed intention to create dignified portrayals of African Americans and African American life and history is in harmony with theirs. In recent years, Pinkney, like Bryan, has spoken of his commitment to communicating across cultures, placing him on the continuum at a place that both overlaps and moves away from the aforementioned pacesetters.

Jerry Pinkney is certainly one of the most prominent African American children's book illustrators in terms of the number of books he has illustrated and the public recognition he has received. As of 2000, he had illustrated more than 100 books and won more awards from the children's book establishment than had any other Black artist. He has dominated the Coretta Scott King Illustrator Awards by winning five times as of this writing, more than any other artist. Five of his books have been cited as Caldecott Honor Books, although the Caldecott Medal itself has inexplicably eluded him. To date, he is the proverbial bridesmaid of the Caldecott, the only artist in the history of the award to have received so many Honor citations but not the Caldecott Medal itself. He also received the Boston Globe-Horn Book Award in 1995 for *John Henry* (Lester 1994), and he was the 1997 U.S. nominee for the Hans Christian Andersen Illustrator Award, the most prestigious international prize for children's book artists.

Perhaps more than any other African American illustrator of children's books, Pinkney has also been recognized beyond the circle of librarians, teachers, and other children's literature professionals. In 1978, he created the Harriet Tubman Commemorative Stamp, the first of a series of African American commemorative stamps produced by the U.S. Postal Service and the first of eleven he created for the series. He has also done work for the National Park Service and created the illustrations for Seagram's Black History Calendars. In 1984, Pinkney produced a cover painting for a *National Geographic* issue that featured a story on the Underground Railroad. More recently, he was the subject of a story on the front page of the August 21, 2001, Living Arts section of the *New York Times*. That same year, he was commissioned by First Lady Laura Bush to create the 2001 Christmas brochure for the White House and as a result was featured on *CBS Sunday Morning* on December 17, 2001. In a career that has extended more than forty years, Pinkney has achieved a "mainstream" success unprecedented in African American children's literature.

After he graduated from art school in Philadelphia, Pinkney moved to Boston, where he worked for a greeting card company and came to the attention of children's book publishers. Pinkney has noted that the timing was significant; he benefited from the 1960s' activism and the economic incentives that drove publishers to seek out African American writers and artists. His first children's book was *The Adventures of Spider* (Arkhurst 1964), a collection of West African folktales. Between 1964 and 1985, Pinkney illustrated about two dozen children's books: folktales and folktale collections from various cultures, nonfiction and biography, a few fiction books, and *Yagua Days* (Martel 1976), a realistic picture book about a New York boy's first visit to his family's home in Puerto Rico. Many of these books were illustrated with Pinkney's black-and-white pencil drawings, although often the covers were produced in full color.

In 1985, Pinkney illustrated what can be considered his breakthrough picture storybook, Valerie Flournoy's *The Patchwork Quilt*, the book that introduced what would become his signature style. For the 1984 *National Geographic* cover, he had, for the first time, hired models and used a professional photographer, and he had found himself working both in front of the camera as a model and behind it as a director. He even took a trip with the writer of the story to follow a portion of the route of the Underground Railroad. He notes, "My total participation in all aspects of the project is what pulled my style together. Upon completion of the assignment, I realized I had an approach that was quite my own" (Pinkney 1998, 31).

The Patchwork Quilt is the first Pinkney-illustrated picture storybook to take full advantage of this approach. The book is significant in part because it celebrates the themes of family and intergenerational relationships that are so important in African American children's literature. But, Pinkney's illustrations extend the text by celebrating the individuality of the family members, highlighting the family ties, and portraying the specifics of living in a particular African American middle-class cultural setting.

Pinkney's approach involves searching out, often with the aid of his wife, Gloria Jean, models who seem to exhibit something of what Jerry sees as the spirit or the personality of the character he is portraying. He shares the text with the models and invites them to respond both to his direction and to their own interpretation of the character. In that way, he notes, the models actually help him to create the characters he portrays. In part, he sees himself as staging scenes for theatre, and he tries to create a "space that the reader feels compelled to enter" (Pinkney 1997, 26) as well as a sense of the drama of the moment being depicted. "When I sit down to draw, I'm not actually working from a photograph, I'm drawing on the experience I had with the model" (27). Pinkney's signature media are pencil and watercolors. He usually draws in pencil first and then paints watercolor washes over the drawings, often allowing the pencil lines to remain and show through the watercolors. This transparency or gem-like quality is one marker of his personal style, as is his color palette. Although in books set in particular historical times the colors may be dictated by a desire for historical accuracy, Pinkney usually uses soft, muted tones, but at times his colors are bright and lively.

A substantial portion of Pinkney's illustrations in African American picture books are for works set in past historical periods—from nineteenth century America up through the 1930s and 1940s. His historical work ranges from realistic biographical pieces such as *Minty* (Schroeder 1996b), a book about Harriet Tubman, and *Black Cowboy, Wild Horses* (Lester 1998), the story of Bob Lemmons, to legendary figures like John Henry, to stories of ordinary people such as those in *Mirandy and Brother Wind* (McKissack 1988). Like *Mirandy*, a number of the books set in the past incorporate fanciful characters or events. Pinkney has also illustrated some African American folktales. These works, and others as well, require Pinkney to conduct research into the details of living in the times and the places depicted in the books. Such research results in detailed and accurate depictions of landscapes, clothing, homes, furnishings, toys, flora, and fauna—any and all aspects of living in the given context. Often, a close viewing of Pinkney's illustrations reveals nearly hidden details, such as a mouse peeping out of a hole in a barrel or a rabbit hopping off the page.

Pinkney has a playful side and enjoys working with fantasy. Patricia McKissack's *Mirandy and Brother Wind* (1988) is one of the books for which he is best known and most highly acclaimed. Pinkney posed himself for the character of Brother Wind, depicted as a huge, translucent blue man with puffy cheeks and wearing a top hat and trailing a long silver cape, a unique cultural interpretation. Pinkney also posed for the animal characters in the four collections of the Brer Rabbit stories as told by Julius Lester. Although one of Pinkney's strengths is his realistic depiction of animals, he was dissatisfied with the drawings he made based on pictures of real animals, so he decided to pose himself to better capture the anthropomorphic qualities of Brer Rabbit and his associates. Close readings of his picture books reveal that Pinkney often shows up in the illustrations in one guise or another.

Pinkney and Lester have collaborated on several books, including *Black Cowboy, Wild Horses* (1998) and the award-winning *John Henry* (1994). Their most controversial collaborative effort was *Sam and the Tigers* (1996c), a retelling of *The Story of Little Black Sambo* (Bannerman 1899). Although it is not a story with African American roots, both Pinkney and Lester saw in Sambo a Black child hero whose heroic qualities were undermined by the stereotyped pictures and derogatory names given the characters in the original. Their interpretation was an attempt to rescue this story, which they believe transcends its stereotypes, for new generations. Certainly, Pinkney's illustrations of the doings of Sam and all the other Sams in Sam-sam-sa-mara, and especially of the tigers, are outstanding examples of his art.

Throughout his career as an illustrator of children's books, Pinkney has committed himself to telling the stories of African Americans and to portraying Black people realistically as individual personalities who possess dignity and command respect. Much of his work—both in and out of books—has focused on African American history and African American heroic figures, including child heroes. Three of his collaborations with Julius Lester have been on books about the three characters Pinkney (1996) identifies as his childhood book heroes: Little Black Sambo, John Henry, and Brer Rabbit. One of Pinkney's goals, shared with other African American artists, is to see that today's readers can meet in their books a much wider range of African American characters, famous and unknown, real and fictional, than was available in the past. And, through his extensive research,

Pinkney has been able to bring to life these characters and specific details of their historical, social, and cultural contexts. When asked about the concept of "Black imagery," Pinkney notes that such imagery is "shaped by the lifestyles one sees as he grows up—the rhythm of people's voices, music and culture influence the mental pictures one draws of the black experience" (Pinkney 1998, 26). In the same interview, Pinkney speaks of trying to "convey the emotional, flowing quality of jazz in my work. I would like for my work to look like the music sounds" (27). This idea of movement and flow is echoed by a number of African American artists, such as Tom Feelings. Barry Gaither, curator of an exhibit of Pinkney's paintings, places Pinkney within a tradition of African American artists such as Charles White and John Biggers, who were "great figurative artists committed to narrative painting and fascinated with historical themes" (Gaither 1998, 14).

Although the main body of his work focuses on African American African life, culture, and history, Pinkney has, almost from the beginning of his career in children's books, illustrated some works that are not set in an African or African American cultural context (e.g., *Babushka and the Pig* [Trofimuk 1969]). Pinkney sees himself in some sense as a multiculturalist, linking people together (1997, 29) as he works with material from diverse cultural settings. In recent years, he has focused on illustrating books that are often referred to as classics in children's literature. He has also retold or adapted the texts for these stories, making them the first books for which he is both writer and illustrator. Two are Hans Christian Andersen tales, *The Little Match Girl* (1999a) and *The Ugly Duckling* (1999b). The other two are *Aesop's Fables* (2000) and *Noah's Ark* (2002). *The Ugly Duckling* and *Noah's Ark* have both been cited as Caldecott Honor Books. Thus, even after more than forty years as a children's book illustrator, he continues to expand the range and scope of his work. That he has the opportunity to do so is testament to his stature in the field of children's books.

Parenthetically, it should be noted that Pinkney is not only prominent in his own right, but also is the head of a creative family of "children's book people." His wife, Gloria Jean, has written books that Jerry illustrated. His son Brian is a highly respected, award-winning illustrator of children's books, a number of which were written by his wife, Andrea, an editor at a major children's book publisher. Another son, Myles, is a photographer who has also illustrated children's books, some in collaboration with his wife, Sandra. And, their daughter Troy Pinkney-Ragsdale has also recently entered the field. Although several two-generation author-artist families exist in American children's literature, the Pinkneys are probably unique in terms of the sheer number of family members engaged in the enterprise and are certainly unique in that regard among African American families. That there are so many members of two generations—three if one counts the grandchildren who appear as models in some recent works—of one family engaged in producing African American children's literature is evidence of the great distance African American children's literature has traveled since 1965.

PAT CUMMINGS: HUMAN KIDS WHO JUST HAPPEN TO BE BLACK

Pat Cummings's perspective on her work places her at a philosophical distance from those artists who are concerned with passing on and celebrating African American history and culture and the African roots of Black people in the United States. Although Black children and families are at the center of all, or nearly all, of Cummings's books, in statements about her work she rejects the idea of race or culture as the salient aspect of her stories. Rather, she proclaims the universality of her stories and argues that the appeal of the storyline, rather than the ethnic/racial identity of its characters, is primary in children's responses to her books. "I've never had a child come to me and say, 'This is a black story, isn't it?' No, it's a story about coping with sibling rivalry, or surviving the first day of school, or finding a new lunch box, and it just happens that the kids and their families are black" (1997b, 34).

Although her stories do not highlight African American ethnicity or identity, they nevertheless come out of her own experiences growing up as a Black American woman. Unlike the foregoing artists, Cummings's worldview was not shaped by a childhood in a Black cultural community in the United States. She grew up in a military family and spent her childhood among diverse groups of people on army bases around the world. "I want to do books with black characters from my own experience. . . . I want to bring what I know to the stories" (Cummings 1993, 56). Cummings has chosen to cast her stories in the larger mold of middle-class America, making a case for diversity by including African American children and families as a part of that reality.

Cummings was born in the same year as John Steptoe, but her first published book came eight years after *Stevie* (1969). In that regard, she began her work later than the others in the pacesetter group, but her debut in the 1970s separates her from the group who did not begin publishing until the latter part of the 1980s. Since her 1984 Coretta Scott King Illustrator Award for *My Mama Needs Me* (Walter 1983), she has had three other books cited as Coretta Scott King Illustrator Honor Books, and *Talking with Artists* (1992b), her collective biography of children's book illustrators, was cited as an Orbis Pictus Honor Book. This award, sponsored by the National Council of Teachers of English, honors outstanding nonfiction. Its two sequels have also been critically acclaimed for their liveliness and appeal to young readers.

Cummings has illustrated a variety of types of books. Whether her own or others' texts, however, most of the picture books she has illustrated have been about family relationships, such as *Just Us Women* (Caines 1982), *Storm in the Night* (Stolz 1988b), *My Mama Needs Me* (Walter 1983), and *Carousel* (Cummings 1994). She has also created board books for very young readers, for example, *My Aunt Came Back* (1998) and *Purrrrr* (1999), which have lively rhyming texts. She has also illustrated a couple of folktales, one from Spain and one from West Africa. And, in *I Need a Lunch Box* (Caines 1988a) and *C Is for City* (Grimes 1995), she demonstrates her capacity to use colorful visual images to engage early readers in exploring concepts such as color and the alphabet.

In her picture storybooks, Cummings frequently takes a lighthearted approach in both her art and her storytelling. Certainly, other African American picture book illustrators have included humorous touches in their drawings, but none have been so boldly comical as Cummings when she is in a playful mood. Cummings's art, with a few exceptions (e.g., *Storm in the Night* [1988b], *Just Us Women* [1982]), is marked by a profusion of bright color, frequently painted with gouache and watercolors. She often uses family members—and her white cat Cash—as models for her realistic paintings. Typically, her works are also full of eye-catching details and funny touches, especially in books for which she wrote the text herself, such as *Jimmy Lee Did It* (1985), *Clean Your Room, Harvey Moon* (1991), and *Petey Moroni's Camp Runamok Diary* (1992a). *Petey Moroni*, a story with a multiracial cast of campers whose food keeps disappearing, is particularly playful and exuberant.

Cummings uses whatever medium is suggested by the story—gouache, watercolors, acrylics, collage, rubber stamps, oils, and so on. Her usually strong colors are also suggested by her reading of the story. She has commented, for example, that "fantasies always seem to present themselves as heavily blue. Nighttime blue, ocean blue, shadow blue" (Cummings 1997b). Cummings's pictures also usually include an abundance of intriguing details and careful attention to facial expressions. Like Jerry Pinkney, she often uses family members as models for her characters. She has stated that she often (Cummings 1993, 59) dreams about flying and therefore enjoys creating paintings in which the action is seen from above. Showing scenes from various visual perspectives is one of the markers of Cummings's style.

For all her focus on universality and on humor, Cummings is well aware of past omissions and concerned about the need for African American youngsters to find affirmation in the books they read. "Primarily, I do want the black kids who are out there, who have been underrepresented, to feel that they are represented in the books" (1993, 56). Like Jerry Pinkney, she also has an interest in multiculturalism. She assumed a leadership role in establishing a now-defunct Center for Multicultural Children's Literature, sponsored in part by HarperCollins, the goal of which was to help identify and mentor writers and artists from various underrepresented groups.

LEO AND DIANE DILLON AND THE "THIRD ARTIST": FOCUSING ON SHARED HUMANITY

Like Pat Cummings, Leo and Diane Dillon do not, in their public statements about their work, profess a commitment to portraying or affirming specifically African American life and culture. Instead, two themes emerge in their comments: a belief in a shared common humanity in which art is a universal expression of the human spirit and a commitment to the integrity and excellence of their art. Their fortieth illustrated book, *To Everything There Is a Season* (1998), exemplifies the way those themes are manifest in their work. It is a tour de force in which each two-page or double-page spread is rendered, using various media, in the style of a different world culture. The illustrations, which obviously required prodigious amounts of research, display the tremendous versatility and attention to detail that mark the Dillons' work. The endpapers show a procession of humans—man, woman, child—from various cultures, underscoring our common humanity along with our great diversity. In the context of verses from Ecclesiastes—"a time to be born, and a time to die," and the like—the striking illustrations also bear witness to the timelessness of human connections.

Leo and Diane Dillon are unique in African American children's literature and, in one sense, in American children's literature in general. They are, as of this writing, the only artists to have won the Caldecott Medal in two consecutive years—1976 and 1977. Another aspect of their uniqueness is that they credit a "third artist" for the creation of their work. That is, their paintings are the result of a close, holistic collaboration that produces an end product different from what either artist would create individually. The work of the "third artist," which is rendered in various media and often reflects ethnic art styles, is nevertheless, in its characteristic elegance, almost always identifiable as the Dillons' style. As of this writing, this "third artist" has received, among numerous other honors and citations, and in addition to the two Caldecott Medals, four Boston Globe-Horn Book Awards, three *New York Times* Best Illustrated Book Awards, and three Coretta Scott King Awards.

Although the Dillons have illustrated books and book covers representing a variety of genres, much of their work in children's books has been in what is today called *multicultural literature*, that is, having to do with the histories and stories of people of diverse cultures and, in particular, people of color. Their second picture book, *Whirlwind Is a Ghost Dancing* (1974), a collection of tales from North American Indian tribes, was named an American Library Association Notable Book and established them as important picture book artists. Their next six picture books were derived from African or African American sources. Among them were their two Caldecott Medal winners, *Why Mosquitoes Buzz in People's Ears* (Aardema 1975c) and *Ashanti to Zulu* (Musgrove 1976).

Of particular interest here is their portrayal of African Americans and people of African descent. The Dillons have been associated with some of the most popular, best-loved, and significant books in the canon of African American children's literature. For example, they illustrated Eloise Greenfield's classic poetry collection, *Honey I Love and Other Love Poems* (1978), as well as Sharon Bell Mathis's Newbery Honor Book, *The Hundred Penny Box* (1975a). Within the African American children's literature context, some of their best-known illustrations have been those for books written or compiled by Virginia Hamilton, one of the most prominent African American writers of the twentieth century. Theirs are the images in Hamilton's groundbreaking collection of African American folktales, *The People Could Fly* (1985), and in *Many Thousand Gone* (1993), a collection of profiles and accounts of protests and escapes from slavery. The Dillons also illustrated *Her Stories* (1995), Hamilton's collection of African American tales told by and featuring African American women, and Hamilton's picture book retelling of a West Indian variant of the Rumpelstiltskin tale, *The Girl Who Spun Gold* (2000). Recently, they re-illustrated the title story of the *People Could Fly* as a picture book (2004) in full rich color. The final painting is a portrait of Virginia Hamilton, wearing kente cloth and smiling, as she hovers over an African American family. The book itself is a tribute to Hamilton.

As has been pointed out, the Dillons' work is marked by variety in choice of media, their distinctive way with color, and their versatility in re-creating various ethnic art styles. For example, Lorenz Graham's *Song of the Boat* (1975b) was illustrated with woodcuts; their colorful art for Aardema's African tales reflected aspects of some African art styles; and for the monochromatic illustrations in *The Hundred Penny Box* (1975a), they used dark brown watercolors applied with cotton and lightened where needed with bleach. Their choice of medium is dictated by their interpretation of what is appropriate for the particular text. Often contained within borders or frames, each of their illustrations is typically a work of art itself, even within the visual narrative of a picture book. When their art reflects a particular historical or cultural setting, it is informed by research into every necessary detail and driven by a commitment to accuracy and excellence.

One of their recent picture books has some unusual touches. *Rap a Tap Tap, Here's Bojangles—Think of That!* (2002) is a tribute to Bill "Bojangles" Robinson, the famous tap dancer. The Dillons created the rhyming text, which carries the refrain, "Rap a tap tap-think of that!" on each right-hand page, under a portrait of Bojangles dancing. The idea of his dancing is conveyed by shadow legs and feet that give the impression that they are in motion. The gouache paintings on the left-hand pages look something like collages, with a good deal of white space and strong graphic shapes to represent city scenes. Even as this book might be considered "atypical" in terms of the Dillons' usual style, it conveys a typical Dillons' sense of elegance.

Elegance, strength, and dignity are hallmarks of the Dillons' work. Their illustrations of African American children's books also reflect the emphasis on family that is such an important thematic focus in the literature. Examination of the covers of several of their books reveals that they frequently feature a family grouping, radiating both dignity and strength. Because their work is associated with so many significant works of African American children's literature, the Dillons are among the most highly respected and treasured contributors to that canon.

DONALD CREWS: GRAPHIC ARTIST

Both in his published statements about his work and in his chosen topics, Donald Crews is at the opposite end of the philosophical continuum from Steptoe, Feelings, and Byard. He holds a unique place among African American illustrators of children's books in that only two of his many books are specifically *about* African American children or families. In fact, a number of his books do not feature people at all. He is a highly respected, award-winning graphic artist who has produced an impressive array of concept books for young readers.

His first book began as a demonstration piece created for his portfolio. "I decided on the form of a picture book because of my knowledge of people like Paul Rand and Bruno Munari and designers who had worked in picture books as a medium and had all the elements that I needed for my own work needs: design and color and typography and all the things I wanted to demonstrate my abilities in" (Crews 1998, 112). That book, *We Read: A to Z*, was published in 1967, placing Crews chronologically with other African American artists who began publishing around that time. After several more books, he produced *Freight Train* (1978), which was cited as a Caldecott Honor Book, as was his next book, *Truck* (1980).

Crews has gone on from there to a distinguished career as a children's book illustrator. Most of Crews's concept books for young children contain minimal texts; the focus is on those elements that he identified as important in his early portfolio—design, color, and typography. "I wouldn't be in picture books if it weren't for the fact that they are books that are primarily stories that can be told without the words."

In contrast, then, to the motivations expressed by most of the aforementioned African American illustrators, Crews's professed primary concern is to create books that allow him to demonstrate his ability as a graphic artist. Two of Crews's books, however, do reflect the tradition of African American artists portraying African American (and African) life, history, and culture in books for young people, and even though that is a very small number, his stature in the field is such that those two books take on greater significance than would ordinarily be the case. *Bigmama's* (1991) and *Shortcut* (1992) both recall his childhood experiences visiting his grandmother in Cottondale, Florida. Interestingly, both books involve trains. The first shows the train ride from New Jersey to Florida, including the segregation signs on the train cars. *Shortcut* relates what happens when the children decide to take a shortcut home along the railroad tracks and find themselves in trouble when a train approaches. In the previously mentioned interview with George Bodmer (1998), Crews noted that these books arose out of his attempts to explain visually for his nieces and nephews what things looked like at his grandmother's in the 1940s. In terms of the art, he expressed some dissatisfaction with his drawing and noted that he considered *Bigmama's* more personal expression than his usual way of working. *Shortcut* combines this personal style with his more typical graphics in the incorporation of typography into the text and the endpapers to represent the sounds of the approaching train. In that regard, *Shortcut* echoes his early prize-winning book *Freight Train* (1978).

At the end of the Bodmer interview (Crews 1998), Crews expresses some sense of social responsibility:

Partially it's telling the story to family, and partially you're aware of the fact that there aren't very many books about Black families and their lives, and partially you have a responsibility to contribute to some of that. Since there are stories that I have that deal with Black lives and there is an audience out there for them, why not tell those stories as well? (Crews 1998, 117)

His "why not?" point of view toward telling stories that deal with Black lives is in direct contrast to that of some of his contemporaries, for whom telling those stories is paramount. Crews is, to date, the one Black picture book artist whose career has been built primarily, almost entirely, on work that is not centered on Black lives and culture.

These nine artists—Steptoe, Feelings, Byard, Bryan, Pinkney, Cummings, Leo Diane Dillon, and Crews—all began working in children's literature at a time when affirmative African American images were scarce, and these artists continued for the next two or three decades, making theirs the dominant late twentieth century images of and by Black people in children's literature. The discussion of their work was ordered on the basis of their expressed ideological or philosophical stance, ranging roughly from those who view picture book art as having a sociocultural or political function to those who view their art as existing mainly, if not solely, for its own sake. It is difficult to isolate the effect of their views on their finished products since their work is also a reflection of their individual creativity and their craftsmanship.

It appears, however, that their philosophical stance functions in part as a guide to the sort of texts that they accept to illustrate or, in the case of author-artists, which themes and topics they explore in their work. It appears to influence, for instance, the extent to which Africa and things African, or African American history, are important aspects of the body of an artist's work. It may also influence the way artists choose to portray their subjects in terms of such factors as whether there is a strong focus on showing individual and individualized faces of Black people—children in particular—and the extent to which the artist incorporates cultural values, attitudes, or experiences into the illustrations. In a sense, artists at the Steptoe/Feelings end of the continuum, in highlighting their responsibility toward Black children, appear to face inward and to address their work primarily, but not necessarily exclusively, to Black children in an effort to affirm what Langston Hughes referred to as "the beauty they possess." The closer one comes to the Crews end of the continuum, the more likely the artists are to highlight the cross-cultural appeal or the universality of their work, to envision a diverse audience for their work, and to illustrate texts that are not set in a Black cultural milieu.

Nevertheless, these artists set the pace for African American illustration in children's books by portraying Black lives and Black people with dignity and respect and with the kind of specificity that results in art that is, in effect, universal. They created a body of work that was strong enough for younger or newer artists to build and expand on.

BIBLIOGRAPHY OF BOOKS FOR CHILDREN
AND YOUNG ADULTS

Sources other than books for children and young adults are documented in a references list at the end of the book.

The following list is arranged alphabetically by illustrator.

Barnett, Moneta, illus. 1953. *Ready-made Family*. By Frances Salomon Murphy. New York: Thomas Y. Crowell.

———, illus. 1967. *Timothy's Flower*. By Jean Van Leeuwen. New York: Random House.

———, illus. 1974. *Fly Jimmy Fly*. By Walter Dean Myers. New York: Putnam.

———, illus. 1975a. *Me and Neesie*. By Eloise Greenfield. New York: Harper.

———, illus. 1975b. *My Brother Fine with Me*. By Lucille Clifton. New York: Holt.

———, illus. 1976. *First Pink Light*. By Eloise Greenfield. New York: Harper.

Bryan, Ashley, illus. 1967. *Moon, for What Do You Wait?* By Rabindranath Tagore. Poems ed. by Richard Lewis. New York: Atheneum.

———. 1971. *The Ox of the Wonderful Horns and Other African Tales*. New York: Atheneum.

———. 1974. *Walk Together Children: Black American Spirituals*. New York: Atheneum.

———. 1976. *The Adventures of Aku*. New York: Atheneum.

———. 1977. *The Dancing Granny*. New York: Atheneum.

———. 1980. *Beat the Story Drum, Pum Pum*. New York: Atheneum.

———. 1982. *I'm Going to Sing: Black American Spirituals*. Vol. 2. New York: Macmillan.

———. 1985. *The Cat's Purr*. New York: Atheneum.

———. 1986. *Lion and the Ostrich Chicks*. New York: Atheneum.

———. 1989. *Turtle Knows Your Name*. New York: Macmillan.

———. 1992. *Sing to the Sun*. New York: HarperCollins.

———, illus. 1993. *Christmas Gif'*. By Charlemae Hill Rollins. New York: Morrow Junior Books.

———. 1997. *Ashley Bryan's ABC of African American Poetry*. New York: Atheneum.

———, illus. 2000. *How God Fix Jonah*. By Lorenz Graham. Honesdale, PA: Boyds Mills Press.

———. 2003. *Beautiful Blackbird*. New York: Simon and Schuster.

Byard, Carole, illus. 1977. *Africa Dream*. By Eloise Greenfield. New York: Harper.

———, illus. 1979. *Cornrows*. By Camille Yarbrough. New York: Coward, McCann and Geoghegan.

———, illus. 1980. *Grandmama's Joy*. By Eloise Greenfield. New York: Philomel.

———, illus. 1989. *The Black Snowman*. By Phil Mendez. New York: Scholastic.

———, illus. 1992. *Working Cotton*. By Sherley Anne Williams. San Diego, CA: Harcourt, Brace.

Crews, Donald. 1967. *We Read: A to Z*. New York: Harper.

———. 1978. *Freight Train*. New York: Greenwillow.

———. 1980. *Truck*. New York: Greenwillow.

———. 1991. *Bigmama's*. New York: Greenwillow.

———. 1992. *Shortcut*. New York: Greenwillow.

Cummings, Pat, illus. 1977. *Good News*. By Eloise Greenfield. New York: Putnam.

———, illus. 1982. *Just Us Women*. By Jeanette Caines. New York: Harper and Row.

———, illus. 1983. *My Mama Needs Me*. By Mildred Pitts Walter. New York: William Morrow.

———. 1985. *Jimmie Lee Did It*. New York: Lothrop, Lee and Shepard.

———, illus. 1988a. *I Need a Lunch Box*. By Jeanette Caines. New York: Harper.

———, illus. 1988b. *Storm in the Night*. By Mary Stolz. New York: Harper and Row.

———. 1991. *Clean Your Room, Harvey Moon*. New York: Bradbury.

————. 1992a. *Petey Moroni's Camp Runamok Diary*. New York: Bradbury.

————. 1992b. *Talking with Artists*. New York: Bradbury.

————. 1994. *Carousel*. New York: Bradbury.

————, illus. 1995. *C Is for City*. By Nikki Grimes. Honesdale, PA: Boyds Mills Press.

————. 1998. *My Aunt Came Back*. New York: Harper Festival.

————. 1998. *Purrrrr*. New York: Harper Festival.

Dillon, Leo and Diane Dillon. 1974. *Whirlwind Is a Ghost Dancing*. New York: Dutton.

————, illus. 1975a. *The Hundred Penny Box*. By Sharon Bell Mathis. New York: Viking.

————, illus. 1975b. *Song of the Boat*. By Lorenz Graham. New York: Thomas Y. Crowell.

————, illus. 1975c. *Why Mosquitos Buzz in People's Ears*. By Verna Aardema. New York: Dial.

————, illus. 1976. *Ashanti to Zulu*. By Margaret Musgrove. New York: Dial.

————. Illus. 1978. *Honey I Love and Other Love Poems*. By Eloise Greenfield. New York: Harper and Row.

————, illus. 1985. *The People Could Fly*. By Virginia Hamilton. New York: Knopf.

————, illus. 1993. *Many Thousand Gone*. By Virginia Hamilton. New York: Knopf.

————, illus. 1995. *Her Stories*. By Virginia Hamilton. New York: Scholastic.

————. 1998. *To Everything There Is a Season*. New York: Scholastic.

————, illus. 2000. *The Girl Who Spun Gold*. By Virginia Hamilton. New York: Scholastic.

————. 2002. *Rap a Tap Tap, Here's Bojangles—Think of That!* New York: Scholastic.

————, illus. 2004. *The People Could Fly: The Picture Book*. By Virginia Hamilton. New York: Knopf.

Feelings, Tom. 1968. *To Be a Slave*. By Julius Lester. New York: Dial.

————, illus. 1971. *Moja Means One: A Swahili Counting Book*. By Muriel Feelings. New York: Dial.

————. 1972. *Black Pilgrimage*. New York: Lothrop, Lee and Shepard.

————, illus. 1974. *Jambo Means Hello: A Swahili Alphabet Book*. By Muriel Feelings. New York: Dial.

————. 1991a. *Tommy Traveler in the World of Black History*. New York: Black Butterfly Press.

————, illus. and compiler. 1993. *Soul Looks Back in Wonder*. New York: Dial.

————. 1995. *The Middle Passage: White Ships Black Cargo*. New York: Dial.

Ford, George, illus. 1967. *African Beginnings*. By Olivia Vlahos. New York: Viking.

————, illus. 1969. *Freddie Found a Frog*. By Alice Napjius. New York: Van Nostrand Reinhold.

————, illus. 1973a. *Ego-tripping and other poems for young people*. By Nikki Giovanni. New York: Lawrence Hill and Co.

————, illus. 1973b. *Ray Charles*. By Sharon Bell Mathis. New York: Thomas Y. Crowell.

————, illus. 1980. *Darlene*. By Eloise Greenfield. New York: Routledge, Kegan Paul.

————, illus. 1981. *Alesia*. By Eloise Greenfield. New York: Philomel.

————, illus. 1990. *Bright Eyes, Brown Skin*. By Cheryl Hudson and Bernette Ford. Orange, NJ: Just Us Books.

————, illus. 1991. *Jamal's Busy Day*. By Wade Hudson. Orange, NJ: Just Us Books.

Ford, George and Mel Williams. 1972. *Walk On!* New York: Odarkai Books.

Pinkney, Jerry, illus. 1964. *The Adventures of Spider*. By Joyce Arkhurst. New York: Little, Brown.

————, illus. 1969. *Babushka and the Pig*. By Ann Trofimuk. Boston: Houghton Mifflin.

————, illus. 1976. *Yagua Days*. By Cruz Martel. New York: Dial.

————, illus. 1985. *The Patchwork Quilt*. By Valerie Flournoy. New York: Dial.

————, illus. 1988. *Mirandy and Brother Wind*. By Patricia McKissack. New York: Knopf.

————, illus. 1994. *John Henry*. By Julius Lester. New York: Dial.

————, illus. 1996b. *Minty*. By Alan Schroeder. New York: Dial.

————, illus. 1996c. *Sam and the Tigers*. By Julius Lester. New York: Dial.

————, illus. 1998. *Black Cowboy, Wild Horses*. By Julius Lester. New York: Dial.

————, illus. 1999a. *The Little Match Girl*. By Hans Christian Andersen. New York: Penguin.

————, illus. 1999b. *The Ugly Duckling*. By Hans Christian Andersen. New York: Morrow.

————, illus. 2000. *Aesop's Fables*. New York: Sea Star.

————, illus. 2002. *Noah's Ark*. New York: Sea Star.

Steptoe, John. 1969. *Stevie*. New York: Harper and Row.

————. 1987. *Mufaro's Beautiful Daughters*. New York: Lothrop, Lee and Shepard.

————. 1988. *Baby Says*. New York: Lothrop, Lee and Shepard.

John Steptoe from *Stevie*. Copyright © 1969 by John L. Steptoe. Use licensed by the Steptoe Literary Trust and HarperCollins Publishers.

John Steptoe, realistic painting from *Mufaro's Beautiful Daughters*. Copyright © 1987 by John Steptoe. Permission granted by the estate of John Steptoe and the John Steptoe Literary Trust. All Rights Reserved.

Tom Feelings's rhythmic painting showing "dance consciousness" from *Moja Means One*. From *Moja Means One: Swahili Counting Book* by Muriel Feelings, illustrations by Tom Feelings, copyright © 1971 by Tom Feelings, illustrations. Used by permission of Dial Books for Young Readers, A Division of Penguin Young Readers Group, A Member of Penguin Group (USA) Inc., 345 Hudson Street, New York, NY 10014.

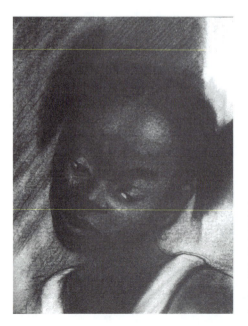

Rhondy's face from *Grandmama's Joy* by Carole Byard. Light in a dark face. From *Grandmama's Joy* by Eloise Greenfield, illustrated by Carole Byard, copyright © 1980 by Carole Byrd, illustrations. Used by permission of Phiomel Books, A Division of Penguin Young Readers Group, A Member of Penguin Group (USA) Inc., 345 Hudson Street, New York, NY 10014.

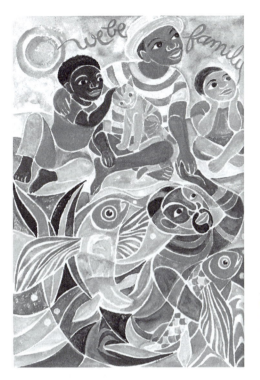

Ashley Bryan's kaleidoscopic art from *Jim Flying High*.
Illustration by Ashley Bryan, from *Jim Flying High* by
Mari Evans and Ashley Bryan, Illustrator, copyright ©
1979 by Mari Evans. Illustrations copyright © 1979 by
Ashley Bryan. Used by permission of Doubleday, a divi-
sion of Random House, Inc.

Donald Crews, train segregation, from *Bigmama's*. Copyright © 1991 by
Donald Crews.

Jan Spivey Gilchrist's portrait of Daniel in the snow. Used with permission courtesy of Jan Spivey Gilchirst.

Leo and Diane Dillon's dignified family, from *The People Could Fly*. Illustrations by Leo and Diane Dillon, copyright © 1985 by Leo and Diane Dillon, from *The People Could Fly: American Black Folktales* by Virginia Hamilton, illustrated by Leo and Diane Dillon. Used by permission of Alfred A. Knopf, and imprint of Random House Children's Books, a division of Random House, Inc.

Jerry Pinkney's grandmother hugging child, from *The Patchwork Quilt*. From *The Patchwork Quilt* by Valerie Flournoy, pictures by Jerry Pinkney, copyright © 1985 by Jerry Pinkney, illustrations. Used by permission of Dial Books for Young Readers, A Division of Penguin Young Readers Group, A Member of Penguin Group (USA) Inc., 345 Hudson Street, New York, NY 10014. All rights reserved.

Floyd Cooper's grandmother hugging child, from *Imani's Gift at Kwanzaa*. Used by permission of Floyd Cooper.

Nina Crews's collage from *One Hot Summer Day*. Copyright © 1995 by Nina Crews. Used by permission of HarperCollins Publishers.

Javaka Steptoe's collage from *Do You Know What I'll Do?* Illustrations copyright © 2000 by Javaka Steptoe.

Christopher Myers's collage, girl having hair combed, from *Harlem*. Illustration by Christopher Myers from *Harlem: A Poem* by Walter Dean Myers. Published by Scholastic Inc./Scholastic Press. Illustration copyright © 1997 by Christopher Myers. Used by permission.

Moneta Barnett, girl having hair combed, from *Me and Neesie*. Illustrations copyright © 1975 by Moneta Barnett.

Illustration by Pat Cummings from *My Aunt Came Back*. Exuberant art for young readers. Courtesy of Pat Cummings.

CHAPTER 9

Newer African American Illustrators: Expanding Possibilities, Maintaining Traditions

Following in the footsteps of the pacesetters, two clusters of newer African American children's book illustrators entered the field in the 1980s and 1990s. The 1980s saw an overall decline in the number of new African American books, reflected in the paucity of new African American artists getting into publication. At the end of the decade, however, four noteworthy African American illustrators—Jan Spivey Gilchrist, Brian Pinkney, James Ransome, and Floyd Cooper—published their first picture books with major publishers and launched careers that have continued for about two decades.

Fortunately, during the 1990s there was a noticeable increase in the number of new African American artists entering the field of children's book illustration. Among those who started illustrating children's books during the decade were three women who were already well-known, established artists—Aminah Brenda Lynn Robinson, Synthia Saint James, and Faith Ringgold. A third group of mostly younger artists, including "second-generation" artists Javaka Steptoe, Christopher Myers, and Nina Crews, are garnering critical praise and showing great promise for long and productive careers.

By the end of the century, newer artists were able to take as a given the existence of realistic visual images of Black people in children's books. In general, therefore, they chose to illustrate books that covered a wider range of topics and to explore different media and styles. At the same time, however, they continued to choose to illustrate books dealing with themes that are characteristic of African American children's literature, such as family relationships and African American history and culture.

THE 1980s: FOUR NEW ARTISTS BEGIN THEIR CAREERS

JAN SPIVEY GILCHRIST: THE ART OF AFFIRMATION

In her comments about her work, Jan Spivey Gilchrist echoes the stance of Eloise Greenfield, whose expressed goals are reflected thematically in much of African American children's literature. This is not surprising since, as an illustrator, Gilchrist is most closely associated with the books of Greenfield and members of her family.

Her first illustrated children's book was *Children of Long Ago* (1988), a collection of poems written by Greenfield's mother, Lessie Jones Little, and she has illustrated books by Greenfield's daughter Monica.

Although Gilchrist has also illustrated some books by other authors, as well as two of her own texts, her collaborations with Eloise Greenfield have largely defined the content and the style of her book illustrations. *Nathaniel Talking* (1989) was the first of Eloise Greenfield's books that Gilchrist illustrated, and she has gone on to illustrate every book Greenfield has produced since, including poetry collections, picture storybooks, and several board books for young children. She won the 1990 Coretta Scott King (CSK) Illustrator Award for *Nathaniel Talking* and a CSK Illustrator Honor Citation for another collection of Greenfield poems, *Night on Neighborhood Street* (1991).

Gilchrist and Greenfield are a particularly well-matched author-artist pairing. Their compatibility is enhanced by their shared views on the functions they want their work to serve. In her 1975 "manifesto" article, Greenfield wrote that she wanted to reinforce the positive aspects of children's lives and to encourage them to develop positive self-concepts. For her part, Gilchrist had this to say about her goals in illustrating children's books, "I want my readers to feel that they are important. I want them to see that the work is honest, that it's very positive, and that they—when they put the book down—feel that there is hope" (Gilchrist 2002, 65). Gilchrist also echoes Du Bois in identifying her primary target audience, noting that she wants to offer positive images for all children, but especially for African American children. When asked what there is about Gilchrist's work that resonates with her, Greenfield spoke of the way Gilchrist captures emotional expressions in the eyes of her characters and noted that her paintings are "always respectful of African American people" (Bishop 1997, 632–633). Gilchrist is a professional portraitist, and her ability to capture emotional expression is a reflection of that talent. Since much of Greenfield's writing emphasizes emotions, this skill further enhances their compatibility.

Gilchrist works in a variety of media, including pencil, pen and ink, watercolors, gouache, and oils. Some of her most striking work can be found in two poetry collections, Greenfield's *Nathaniel Talking* (1988) and *Angels* (1998). In the latter, Greenfield's poems were written to accompany Gilchrist's drawings. The black-and-white illustrations for both books were done in pencil and feature close-ups of African American children and adults, all with very expressive faces and eyes. Gilchrist's skill as a portrait artist can also be seen in *For the Love of the Game: Michael Jordan and Me* (1997b), which includes a number of realistic drawings of the basketball star.

Most of her books have been done in color, and although they generally focus on realistic drawings of the people being portrayed, they also tend to be somewhat expressionistic, using swirling lines, color, and symbolic elements to reinforce some of the thematic, emotional, or imaginative elements of the text. This is particularly true in *Indigo and Moonlight Gold* (Gilchrist 1993), *Lift Every Voice and Sing* (Johnson 1995), and to a lesser extent *Madelia* (Gilchrist 1997a). Gilchrist's interpretation of *Lift Every Voice and Sing*, the hymn that is considered the national African American anthem, invokes both African Americans' cultural roots in Africa and the importance of empowering children to move forward. Her note at the end of the book provides some insight into her expressionism: "I wanted to paint the music I heard in sunsets, in the faces of loved ones and friends, and especially, in the faces of children. I wanted to paint not just what was easy to see, but what existed beneath the surface; to paint not just the eyes, but the sparkle in them. I wanted to paint the power, the strength, and the beauty of life."

The two books that she both wrote and illustrated, *Madelia* (1997a) and *Indigo and Moonlight Gold* (1993), keep with tradition in African American children's literature by focusing on family relationships—*Indigo and Moonlight Gold* on a mother-daughter interaction and *Madelia* on a father-daughter story. *Indigo* is illustrated with oil paintings full of rich colors—mahogany hues for Autrie and her mother and nighttime blues, browns, and whites. Gilchrist also shows Autrie from some unusual perspectives and uses multiple images to show movement across time and space. In these evocative paintings, Gilchrist also makes very effective use of light and shadow. The art is both expressive and eloquent. *Madelia* is unusual in that its main setting is a Sunday church service. The gouache-and-pastel paintings reflect the visual images created by Madelia's father in his sermon, which inspire Madelia to go home and paint the visions he inspired her to see. Both books also reflect Gilchrist's craft as portrait artist, seen especially in the lovely painting of Autrie on the cover of *Indigo*.

One of Greenfield and Gilchrist's more recent books, *I Can Draw a Weeposaur and Other Dinosaurs* (2001) shows the lighter side of their imaginations. Gilchrist's dinosaurs are light, colorful, and humorous, created with watercolors, markers, and black pen. Another departure from her usual style and media can be seen in her illustrations for Greenfield's *In the Land of Words* (2004), the originals of which are sewn fabric collages. Most of her work in African American children's literature, however, tends to be realistic and serious, although not necessarily without humor. In her books that feature African American children, Gilchrist endeavors to hold up a mirror that shows Black children a reflection of their strengths, their beauty, and their dignity. In that regard, she carries on the tradition begun in the late 1960s by artists like Carole Byard and the other pacesetters.

BRIAN PINKNEY: NEW GENERATION, NEW DIRECTION

In one sense, Brian Pinkney carries on the tradition begun by one particular pacesetter. The son of premier artist Jerry Pinkney, Brian's choice of career was a natural outcome of his childhood wish to emulate his father. In fact, his first picture book, *The Boy and the Ghost* by Robert San Souci (1989), was rendered in watercolors, the same medium his father usually uses. Soon afterward, however, Brian discovered the satisfactions of working with scratchboard, and that became his signature medium. Since *The Boy and the Ghost*, Brian has published about three books a year and has become a prize-winning pacesetter in his own right.

Brian's distinctive pictures have illustrated a wide variety of books, including story and poetry collections, nonfiction, single folktales in picture book format, biographies in picture book format, self-authored storybooks, and board books for very young children. While most of his work has centered on African American life, history, and culture, he has also illustrated books that have other cultural settings.

Among his best-known and most highly praised illustrations are those for the picture book biographies written by his wife, Andrea Davis Pinkney. The subjects of the biographies are African American achievers, including Alvin Ailey (1993), Benjamin Banneker (1994), Duke Ellington (1998), and Ella Fitzgerald (2002). Brian's art for the Duke Ellington biography earned citations as both a Caldecott Honor Book and a CSK Honor Book. In a telephone interview (Pinkney and Pinkney 1995), Brian and Andrea noted that they chose as biographical subjects

African Americans whose lives excite them. It is important to them, they noted, to write about these Black heroic figures because many people are not aware of them and their contributions. They refer to their biographies as "nonfiction with a twist" because they look for some intriguing tidbit around which to build a story. These books are painstakingly researched, resulting in text and illustrations full of engaging details. For example, they took dancing lessons to better understand the world of Alvin Ailey and to better portray the way dancers move. This focus on African American heroes and "sheroes" echoes and extends the emphasis on Black history and Black achievement that is central to much of twentieth century African American children's literature. Together, Andrea and Brian have also produced a picture book about Kwanzaa, a Christmas book with a historical setting, and perhaps spurred by their own parenthood, a number of board books for very young readers.

Brian has also won critical praise for his illustrations of traditional tales derived from African American and Afro-Caribbean sources. He received CSK Illustrator Honor citations for Robert San Souci's retellings of *Sukey and the Mermaid* (1992) and *The Faithful Friend* (1995), both of which were also cited as Caldecott Honor Books. He won the CSK Illustrator Award for Kim Siegelson's *In the Time of the Drums* (1999), the legend of the Africans who landed on one of the Sea Islands and, refusing to be enslaved, chose to try to make their way back to Africa by walking through the water. While these tales may require extensive research into the chronological and geographical settings, they also allow for imaginative interpretations of the characters and of the fantasy elements they contain. Brian's scratchboard technique, with its lines that can seem to be in motion, seems well suited to these stories.

Brian also belongs on the list of African American author-artists, along with John Steptoe and Pat Cummings, having produced a number of picture books that he both wrote and illustrated. These stories appear to be rooted in his childhood experiences, his childhood fantasies, and his personal interests, such as drumming and Tae Kwan Do. The main character in each of these stories is an African American child who achieves something extraordinary, whether realistic or fantastic. One of these stories, *The Adventures of Sparrow Boy* (1997), won the prestigious Boston Globe-Horn Book Illustrator Award in 1997. Set in middle-class African American cultural environments, these books help to expand the thematic range of African American stories.

Brian became enamored of scratchboard when he tried it at the suggestion of an art instructor at the School of Visual Arts in New York. He found that working with scratchboard, in which pictures are produced by using a sharp instrument to scratch the lines of a drawing into a black surface, is similar to etching and resembles sculpting. The initial image is in black and white, which he often paints over with oil paint and oil pastels to add color. Using this technique, Pinkney has developed a recognizable style characterized by its fluidity. In the aforementioned interview (Pinkney and Pinkney 1995), he spoke of the importance of rhythm in his work, attributing his concern with rhythm in part to his avocation as a drummer. He describes scratchboard as being "very percussive." He also describes himself as "using a lot of lines to do a book" (1997b, 51). These lines not only impart a sense of movement by producing a rhythmic, flowing quality to his work, but also provide texture and depth to the pictures, confirming his sense of scratchboard as "sculptural." His paintings also include a surprising amount of detail in both the physical setting and the facial expressions of his characters. Brian's choice of medium, his characteristic style, and to some degree his choice of imaginative topics in his self-authored books make him unique among contemporary African American author-illustrators of children's books. As a second-generation children's book artist, he is part of a group that is extending the artistic boundaries of African American children's books.

JAMES RANSOME: "MUSEUM ART" IN AFRICAN AMERICAN CHILDREN'S BOOKS

Like Brian Pinkney, James Ransome was also influenced by the work of Jerry Pinkney, although he did not become aware of that work until he was already starting his career as an artist. After art school, while Ransome was pursuing his dream of becoming a professional artist, he saw a copy of Flournoy's *The Patchwork Quilt* (1985), which had been illustrated by Jerry Pinkney, the first living African American illustrator whose work Ransome had encountered. Ransome was inspired to add some paintings of a child to his portfolio, and when he received a contract to illustrate his first picture book, Angela Johnson's *Do Like Kyla* (1990), it was Jerry Pinkney to whom he turned for advice. Since then, Jerry Pinkney has become friend, mentor, and sometime model for Ransome's illustrations. Ransome identifies two other influences on his work: his early experiences with film making and the painters he studied in art classes, such as Mary Cassatt, John Singer Sargent, Winslow Homer, and Edgar Degas. Ransome's usual medium has been oil paintings, and he has noted that he has an interest in introducing "museum-type" paintings to young children (Ransome 1997, 95–96).

Ransome has illustrated books and book jackets on a wide range of topics. Among African American children's picture books, he has illustrated a number of significant works that reflect familiar themes and topics—family history in *Aunt Flossie's Hats (and Crab Cakes Later)* (Howard 1991b) and *Uncle Jed's Barbershop* (Mitchell 1993b); contemporary family stories, such as *Do Like Kyla* (Johnson 1990) and *Visiting Day* (Woodson 2002b); and historically based stories such as *Freedom's Fruit* (Hooks 1996) and *Sweet Clara and the Freedom Quilt* (Hopkinson 1993b). He has also illustrated nonfiction and biography. In creating these illustrations, he has sometimes called on his own Southern background and family history to help him include authentic details. His interpretation of James Weldon Johnson's *The Creation* (1994), in which he has a Black man telling the story/poem to a group of Black children, reflects an understanding of the importance of the oral tradition out of which Johnson's poem emanated. Ransome has thus played a role in advancing and increasing the quantity of finely crafted African American picture books that portray Black people, Black culture, and Black history realistically and accurately. He won the CSK Illustrator Award for *The Creation* and a CSK Illustrator Honor Citation for *Uncle Jed's Barbershop*.

Ransome's remarkable and sometimes dramatic oil paintings are evidence of his affinity for strong design and strong colors. He often includes outdoor scenes or landscapes in his picture books, perhaps reflecting the influence of John Singer Sargent. His paintings also sometimes reflect his experiences as a filmmaker, with changing perspectives, close-ups, and "snapshot images" that cut off part of a figure in the way an amateur photographer might. Ransome has also embraced the art of the picture book with some striking endpapers in a number of his books. And, Clinton, his Dalmatian, has become something of a trademark, appearing in many of his books. Like Jerry Pinkney, Ransome almost always uses models for his paintings in an effort to invite readers to see the characters as real people. "By conveying to young readers the individual traits of characters I only hope that I am instilling an appreciation for the wonderfully unique qualities and cultural and racial differences we all possess" (1997, 103) Thus, characters such as Aunt Flossie, Uncle Jed, and Sweet Clara seem as familiar as one's own relatives and neighbors.

Recently, Ransome has illustrated some books using watercolors instead of his usual oils, most notably for Virginia Hamilton's posthumously published *Bruh Rabbit and the Tar Baby Girl* (2003). He has also illustrated two well-received concept books with texts by his wife, Lesa Cline Ransome. Although most of the books Ransome has chosen to illustrate have been about African American life and history, he maintains that he does not wish to be typecast; he has interests other than African American stories. In that regard, he has illustrated books such as *All the Lights in the Night* (Levine 1991a) that do not focus on African American life and culture. In his wife Lesa's book *Quilt Counting* (2002a), the characters appear to be Euro-American. *Quilt Alphabet* (2001) and *Quilt Counting* offer Ransome the opportunity to demonstrate his versatility and craft as a "museum artist," creating striking paintings that could easily stand alone as framed pieces and that reflect his commitment to drawing, design, and color.

FLOYD COOPER: EMBRACING MULTICULTURALISM

Like Ransome, Floyd Cooper sees no reason to confine himself to books about African Americans. Although most of his books *are* about African Americans, Cooper's work has been featured in a wide range of picture books representing various cultural groups. The contract for his first picture book, Eloise Greenfield's *Grandpa's Face* (1988), came to him through an agent at a time when Cooper was hardly even conscious of children's book illustration as a possible career. He had worked for Hallmark cards and in advertising, but once he discovered children's book illustrating, he had found his niche.

Known for his appealing and realistic portrayals of diverse people, Cooper has been remarkably productive, having illustrated more than fifty children's books since he entered the field in 1988. The books he has illustrated cover a wide variety of topics and genres, including family stories, folktales, biography, history, and poetry. He has developed a signature style using his favorite medium, an oil wash on top of which he draws with a kneaded eraser, "pulling" the picture out of the background. When the oil wash is dry, he adds color with acrylic watercolor washes.

Within the context of African American children's literature, Cooper has illustrated almost all of the picture book poetry collections of fellow Oklahoman Joyce Carol Thomas. He won a CSK Honor citation for Thomas's collection *Brown Honey in Broomwheat Tea* (1993), as he did for *I Have Heard of a Land* (Thomas 1998b). He also received a CSK Honor citation for his illustrations for Nikki Grimes's *Meet Danitra Brown* (1994b), another picture book poetry collection. Cooper's sensitive and often light-filled portraits have made his work especially appealing to those seeking positive images of Black children and adults. He has illustrated work by many other well-known African American authors, among them Eloise Greenfield, Pat McKissack, Elizabeth Fitzgerald Howard, James Haskins, and Virginia Hamilton. In addition, Cooper has written and illustrated two picture book biographies, one on Langston Hughes (*Coming Home* 1994a) and one on Nelson Mandela (*Mandela* 1996), as well as *Cumbayah* (1998a), his own interpretation of the well-known song of that name.

Most of his written commentary on his work focuses on his technique and his goals for his art: "I want to take the reader on a journey into the story, to get a sense of the smells, the atmosphere, and the emotions conveyed by the characters" (H. Smith 1999, 85). Cooper also sees himself as using his art to explore cultures and to build bridges between cultures. He also professes some sense of social responsibility along with his goals as an artist: "I feel children are in the front line of improving society. I feel children's books play a role in counteracting all the violence and other negative images conveyed in the media" (85). In this era of multicultural children's literature, Cooper is an artist for his time.

ESTABLISHED WOMEN ARTISTS ENTER THE FIELD

During the 1990s, three notable African America female artists started illustrating children's books. This is significant not only because they are among the few African American women in the field, but also because they were already highly regarded outside the field of children's books and so brought the attention of a wider audience to the art of African American picture books. In each case, they added a unique touch to that body of work. Synthia Saint James, a self-taught artist whose signature style features bold shapes, minimal details, and vibrant primary colors, illustrated about a dozen children's books during the 1990s. Saint James's work is popular and familiar; she created the Kwanzaa stamp for the U.S. Postal Service and has created cover illustrations for numerous books for children and adults. For children, Saint James has illustrated a variety of picture books, including folktales, holiday stories, and stories for young children. Her pictures tend to resemble cut-paper collages, but they are acrylic paintings, using blocks of bold color and relying heavily on design. The faces of her people are without drawn features, a departure from the concern of earlier artists with portraying realistic-looking Black people and capturing their emotional expressions. The reader/viewer is left to infer expressions from the characters' movements, their stances, and their placement in relation to each other. Nevertheless, in books such as *Sunday* (1996b), for which Saint James also wrote the text, she is able through her paintings to express the spirit of the text. *Sunday* follows an African American family as they spend the day together in worship and in fellowship. Saint James was awarded a CSK Illustrator Honor citation for the illustrations for *Neeny Coming, Neeny Going* (1996a), a story about friendship and change and set on Daufuskie Island.

Another established African American woman artist who became involved in children's book illustration during the 1990s is Aminah Brenda Lynn Robinson, who is an internationally known recipient of a MacArthur Fellowship, a so-called genius grant. In the main, Robinson's art celebrates her African and African American cultural heritage as well as the history of the community in which she grew up. Robinson often uses mixed media, combining diverse materials, such as paint, fabric, clay, shells, and buttons, to create various kinds of art, including unusual fabric books, quilts, and sculptures. Her style often looks like folk art, but she is in reality a trained artist, and her work is quite sophisticated. Her paintings are usually expressionistic, often with oversize hands to emphasize the work those hands are doing.

Robinson's first children's book was *Elijah's Angel* (1992), written by Michael J. Rosen. It features Robinson's friend and mentor, the late Elijah Pierce, a beloved and well-known barber, Christian minister, and woodcarver who lived in Columbus, Ohio. It tells the story of Pierce's friendship with a young Jewish boy to whom he gave a carved angel one Christmas. The paintings are based on Robinson's memories of the times she spent with Pierce in his barbershop. A goodly portion of her work is based on such memories. One of her more spectacular published works for children, for example, is an accordion book called *A Street Called Home* (1997), which portrays people and their activities in the Columbus neighborhood in which she grew up in the 1940s and early 1950s. The opened book stretches out for a few feet, each page depicting a typical 1940s scene on Mt. Vernon, the main street in her childhood community. It features various vendors, such as the chicken foot woman, who cooks and sells chicken feet on the street, and the sock man, who mends and washes socks. Lifting a flap reveals the vendor's wares. With the original art made from many different kinds of materials, the book is an uncommon delight for children and adults, full of color and fascinating detail. Robinson has a particular passion for preserving and passing on African American history and was therefore especially suited to illustrate Rosen's tale of an ex-slave, *A School for Pompey Walker* (1995), and Evelyn Coleman's *To Be a Drum* (1998), which celebrates African American history and achievements and urges children to become like African drums. Although her output of children's books has been relatively small (about a half dozen books), Robinson's stature in the art community adds even more significance to her unique contributions.

Like Robinson, Faith Ringgold is also internationally known and acclaimed. She burst onto the children's picture book scene with the 1991 publication of *Tar Beach*, which garnered numerous awards, including the second and most recent Caldecott Honor citation honoring the work of an African American woman. In *Talking to Faith Ringgold* (Ringgold, Freeman, and Rocher 1996), an autobiographical work for young readers, she discusses briefly the evolution of her personal style, which she sees as a composite of American-European and classical African art. In addition to her formal training in classical Western art, she taught herself about African art by copying it on her own.

I learned a lot about African design—symmetry, repetition, pattern, texture, and so on—and then I incorporated these elements into my art, which became not African art, but African-American art. And I used it to express not the African experience, which I didn't have, but the African-American experience—and that's what my art really is. It's the expression of the African-American-female experience. (10)

Her inclusion of "female" as an important dimension of her work stems in part from her personal experiences fighting discrimination based on both race and gender. She was, for example, denied membership in Spiral, the organization founded by John Steptoe's mentor, Norman Lewis, and other Black male artists. Such experiences turned her toward activism and are reflected in some of the protest art for which she is well known. Ringgold has created the text for all of her own books, adding her name to the short list of African American author-artists. Her distinctive and eye-catching art, as well as her tendency to cross genre boundaries, make her books unique contributions to the canon of African American children's literature.

As an artist, Ringgold works in a variety of media, including painting, soft sculptures, and quilting. She is best known for her story quilts, which are combinations of paintings on canvas, quilting, and fictional narratives. Her story quilts are both vehicles for expressing "the African-American-female experience" and a solution to a practical problem. Ringgold credits African American women with initiating the quilt-making tradition in America as part of their duties under slavery. Quilting had been a tradition in her own family, going back to her enslaved great-great-grand-mother. When Ringgold needed a way to transport her art to show it and to ship her paintings at less expense than it cost to crate large wood-framed pieces, she naturally turned to quilting. Remembering some Tibetan tankas she had seen on display, she borrowed from them the idea of framing with cloth and started using quilted cloth frames for her own paintings. Later, she began incorporating written stories into the paintings. The uniqueness of the story quilt is in part what garnered such acclaim for *Tar Beach* (1991). Although *Tar Beach* is the only one of her children's books that incorporates quilting directly into the illustrations, there are close ties between Ringgold's quilting and some of her other picture books as well. Both *Tar Beach* and *Dinner at Aunt Connie's* (1993) are derived directly from story quilts. In an interesting reversal, her original fairy tale, *The Invisible Princess* (1999), became the basis for a later story quilt, "Born in a Cotton Field."

In describing her children's book illustrations, Ringgold notes:

They look like Egyptian paintings. Well, the colors are flat. They are the way to paint pictures for children because children have such a great sense of color. You paint flat, you can get more contrast in your colors, and you can use purer coloring. . . . I paint differently when I'm not painting for children's books. But I know that children like bright colors, and I like them too.[1]

This flatness imparts something of a naïve quality to the illustrations and, along with the vivid colors, accounts in large part for their distinctiveness.

Aside from expanding the range of illustrative styles in African American picture books, Ringgold's major contribution as a visual artist is her ability to help her readers visualize and personalize African American history. In having her child characters interact with the historical figures who populate her books, Ringgold brings her subjects to life for young readers. With her art and the dialogue, she invites the readers to participate in the events in the book, often in such a way as to exemplify her conviction that, just as the subjects persevered and overcame obstacles, they also can do anything to which they set their minds.

THE NEXT GENERATION

In the mid- to late 1990s, the daughter of Donald Crews and the sons of Walter Dean Myers and John Steptoe, along with Brian Pinkney, became the first group of African American children's book artists who had grown up in households in which at least one parent made a living in children's books. Given the dearth of African American illustrators when their fathers were first published, their entry into the field is significant as an indication of progress and change as well as a promise of continuity. These "second-generation" artists made auspicious beginnings. Javaka Steptoe won the CSK Illustrator Award for his first book, *In Daddy's Arms I Am Tall* (1997), a collection of poems about fathers. Christopher Myers won both a CSK Illustrator Honor citation and a Caldecott Honor citation for his first picture book, *Harlem* (W. D. Myers 1997a), a poetic celebration of the African American "cultural capital," which was written by his father. He later received a Boston Globe-Horn Book Honor citation for *Blues Journey* (2003), which was also written by his father. Although Nina Crews has not yet received one of those awards, her work invariably garners critical praise, including starred reviews in prestigious journals and inclusion on "best of" lists.

Nina Crews, who is both author and artist for her books, calls on her love of the city and adds elements of fantasy to her portrayals of young children playing imaginatively in urban environments. Her first book, *One Hot Summer Day* (1995), shows a young African American girl experiencing the joys of a summer day in the city. Crews is primarily a photographer, and her illustrations are collages created from color photographs. *I'll Catch the Moon* (1996) and *Snowball* (1997) also feature young children enjoying their urban environment and using their imagination. Although her story lines tend to be simple, as is appropriate for her audience, her vision is fresh. She has recently created a modern urban version of Mother Goose, *The Neighborhood Mother Goose* (2003), for which she manipulated the photographs with a computer to illustrate both the nonsensical and the real. In all her books, Crews puts her photo collages together in a way that shows both realistic images and images that represent thoughts, dreams, or imaginings, sometimes with very clever and often-surprising results.

Like Crews, Javaka Steptoe's preferred medium to date has been collages, which he creates from paper, paint, and a variety of found objects. His illustrations for *In Daddy's Arms I Am Tall* (1997), for example, incorporate, among other things, shells, coins, burlap, and insects. Thematically, he has tended to illustrate books having to do with family relationships, reflecting one of the traditional emphases in African American children's books. His second book, *Do You Know What I'll Do?* (2000), is a revised version of a Charlotte Zolotow story in which a big sister makes clear her love for her little brother. *The Jones Family Express* (2003), which is, as of this writing, the only one of Steptoe's books for which he created the text, focuses on the relationship between a young boy and his aunt, who sends him postcards from her travels. It celebrates not only family, but also the boy's creativity as he devises a special gift for his aunt.

In his imagery, which often focuses on faces, Steptoe sometimes challenges traditional views about what has been considered "acceptable" imagery in African American literature by highlighting certain physical features associated with African Americans. In *Do You Know What I'll Do?* (Zolotow 2000), *Hot Day on Abbot Avenue* (English 2004), and *Pocket Full of Poems* (Grimes 2001), for example, he shows positive images of Black faces that emphasize the full lips, broad noses, and very dark skin that were often caricatured when African Americans images were included in books as comic relief. In contrast to those early caricatures, however, Steptoe's inventive compositions clearly show the respect and affection he has for his subjects.

Christopher Myers has also embraced collage as a medium, although he uses a variety of media in his art, including paint, photographs, cut paper, brown paper bags, and ink. He has both written his own texts and illustrated texts written by his father. His bold collages for his father's *Harlem* (W. D. Myers 1997a) and for his own poetic text, *Black Cat* (1999), capture the spirit of the city as the place to call home. In *Wings* (2000), in which he re-interprets the Icarus myth, Myers uses cut-paper collage to illustrate a purposeful story that celebrates difference and individuality. His father's poetic text for *Blues Journey* (W. D. Myers 2003), which both celebrates and explicates the blues, is very effectively illustrated with blue ink, white paint, and brown paper bag. Aside from the picture books, Myers has also illustrated three longer books with texts by his father, including two novels and a collection of re-envisioned Old Testament stories. Myers's work tends to be bold in color, layered in meaning, very powerful, and quite sophisticated.

Although the style of each of these second-generation artists—Crews, Steptoe, and Myers—is distinctive, in their first five or six books they have all embraced collage in some form. Although reference sources generally indicate that collage as an art form was popularized through the work of Cubists like Picasso, both Christopher Myers and Javaka Steptoe perceive in the medium a metaphor for the African American experience. The connection should not be surprising given the influence of African art on the Cubists. When Christopher Myers was asked in a telephone interview (1997b) to speculate on what might account for collage being the medium of choice for all three of these-second generation artists—himself, Javaka Steptoe, and Nina Crews—he replied:

I think that collage is one of those central metaphors of the African Diaspora. A lot of art work, be it jazz, be it blues, be it musical forms, be it artistic forms, be it dance forms, are oftentimes collages of other forms. It's about making do, it's about economic factors that we had in our past. . . . I think it's something that we've both had the necessity to do and we've had the facility to do. This is part of what quilt making is for me right now. It's about taking those little pieces of something and putting them together. It's the same with jazz. Hip hop even is very much a collage form in that its main instrument is the DJ table and the DJ table is into taking little pieces of other records and putting those together. I think that's why we have such giants of collage, people like Romare Bearden and Jacob Lawrence, because I feel like as Black people we have a special relationship to it.

In that statement are echoes of Tom Feelings's emphasis on "improvising within a restricted form" as a metaphor for African American experience and his own art. All three of these young artists pay homage to Romare Bearden (1911–1988), an acclaimed African American artist who found that collage was the medium that best allowed him to express his vision of the African American experience. Like others before him, Myers also makes explicit a connection between African American music—jazz and blues—and other art forms, such as quilting and visual art, a thread that surfaces in many discussions of African American art. Thus, even though these young artists create work that looks different from that of most of the pacesetter artists who started illustrating children's books decades before they did, they acknowledge a common thread that in some sense ties their work together.

In addition to Crews, Steptoe, and Myers, several other illustrators who might also be considered second generation in relation to the pacesetters are also in the vanguard of early twenty-first century African American picture book artists. Among them are E. B. Lewis, Bryan Collier, R. Gregory Christie, and Kadir Nelson, all of whom have received important awards for their books. These artists started illustrating children's books near the end of the 1990s, and it is clear at this writing that they will be the pacesetters of the twenty-first century. As such, their work is worth noting here, if only briefly.

E. B. Lewis started illustrating children's books in the mid-1990s and before the decade was over had illustrated at least a dozen books. He has continued to be very productive and has received a good deal of critical attention and praise. Known for his mastery of watercolor technique, his outstanding realistic illustrations have garnered at least three CSK citations, including the CSK Illustrator Award for Nikki Grimes's *Talkin' about Bessie* (2002). Jacqueline Woodson's *Coming on Home Soon* (2004) was cited as a 2005 Caldecott Honor Book. Bryan Collier's first illustrated children's book, *These Hands*, was published in 1999. Since then, a number of his books have been critically acclaimed. Collier's work features stunning collages, which incorporate cut paper, painted images, and photographs. He was awarded a CSK Illustrator Award for *Uptown* (2000), a picture book about Harlem, which he wrote himself, and another for his illustrations for Nikki Giovanni's *Rosa* (2005), a picture book biography of Rosa Parks. He has received three other CSK Honor Awards, as well as a Caldecott Honor citation for *Martin's Big Words* (2001), a biographical work about Martin Luther King Jr.

Kadir Nelson entered the field at the end of the 1990s and, like Lewis and Collier, has received high praise for his rich and often-striking paintings. He won the 2005 CSK Illustrator Award for Ntozake Shange's *Ellington Was Not a Street* and a 2004 CSK Illustrator Honor citation for Jerdine Nolen's *Thunder Rose* (2003). On his Web site, Nelson writes of wanting "to show the strength and integrity of the human being and the human spirit."[2] This sentiment seems apt in that he has chosen to illustrate books about some heroic, bigger-than-life figures, such as Nolen's *Big Jabe* (2000), as well as the real-life notables he portrays in Shange's book. It is also interesting to note that Nelson has illustrated a number of books written by celebrity authors, such as Debbie Allen, Will Smith, and Spike Lee.

R. Gregory Christie also has won several awards in a relatively short time for his outstanding expressionistic illustrations. The first book he illustrated, *The Palm of My Heart* (1996), a collection of poems by young people, was cited as a CSK Honor Book, as was *Only Passing Through* (2000), a biographical piece about Sojourner Truth. To date, he has illustrated more than a dozen books, including stories, poems, biography, and other African American nonfiction. His art is distinctive, acrylic pieces in which the figures are often elongated or distorted, a combination of realism and abstraction. On his Web page, Christie makes a statement about his art:

In children's books my focus is to depict strong images of brown people and to give the characters a sense of dignity. I choose to illustrate manuscripts that come from the world's history and vast cultures. The disproportional figures bathed in planes of color are meant to be a directional device and to serve as visual rhythm contained within the restrictions of a book's pages.[3]

His commentary about visual rhythm and the restrictions of a book's pages echoes Tom Feelings's comments about his work. The focus on strong images of brown people also echoes the goals of African American artists who started illustrating children's books about three decades earlier is a testament to a sense of purpose that is shared by African American children's book writers and artists across time and across at least two generations.

A PERSPECTIVE ON AFRICAN AMERICAN ILLUSTRATORS

Although other artists have contributed to the growth and development of African American children's literature, judging from their productivity and the recognition they have received, the artists discussed in this chapter and Chapter 8 constitute the core group of African American children's book illustrators of the last third of the twentieth century. It is quite clear, however, that these artists do not hold a monolithic point of view about either the purposes of their work or its function in relation to the African American cultural community and society in general. Nevertheless, almost all of them have committed themselves to increasing the visibility of Black people in children's books and to portraying Black people realistically and respectfully in their work. In fulfilling this commitment, these award-winning artists of course have developed unique individual styles and have chosen to work with a variety of media, thus resisting attempts to find common ground in their art beyond its focus on African Americans. Nevertheless, it is useful to consider some aspects of their illustrations that are shared across a number of artists.

An exhaustive comparative examination of all the images in picture books illustrated by various African American artists might reveal several recurring images, but in my reading two such images stand out: the image of a grandmother embracing her grandchild and that of a mother (or female elder) combing and braiding a girl's hair. To note a few examples, the grandmother/grandchild dyad appears in Jerry Pinkney's illustrations for *The Patchwork Quilt* (Flournoy 1985), Floyd Cooper's illustrations for *Imani's Gift at Kwanzaa* (1992), Carole Byard's illustrations for *Grandmama's Joy* and for *Cornrows* (1969), Francine Haskins's illustrations for *Things I Like About Grandma* (1992), and Anna Rich's illustrations for *Just Right Stew* (English 1998). In these full-page iconic illustrations, the grandmother is usually holding the child close to her heart, both arms around the child—comforting, reassuring, or just sharing love. Given the emphasis on intergenerational relationships and on African American elders in picture books, the recurrence of a grandmother/grandchild image may not be surprising. Even so, an artist is free to select which scene or which moment of the story to illustrate. That several artists chose to depict that particular scene emphasizes its significance as an important theme in the literature and as a cultural value.

The other image, that of a mother (or grandmother) combing a girl's hair, is to be expected in books such as *Cornrows*, in which hair is the focus. But, it also appears in books such as *Imani's Gift at Kwanzaa* (illustrated by Floyd Cooper), *Me and Neesie* (illustrated by Moneta Barnett, 1975), *Harlem* (illustrated by Christopher Myers, 1997a), and *Quinnie Blue* (illustrated by James Ransome, 2000). Usually, the girl is shown seated on the floor between her mother's or grandmother's knees and having her hair combed, brushed, or braided while the two are engaged in conversation. This image of female bonding is very familiar to most African American girls and women, and since the activity is not always mentioned in the text that is being illustrated, it is one of the ways in which the illustrators situate the story in a specific African American context.

In spite of the great diversity to be found in styles and media among African American illustrators, at least three thematic threads run through their work and their commentary about their work: an emphasis on rhythm, fluidity, or movement; a focus on conveying emotion; and the improvisational nature of many African American art forms. These common threads appear frequently enough that they at least hint at shared cultural sensibilities. For example, Tom Feelings, Brian Pinkney, and Jerry Pinkney all make references to movement and music in speaking about their art. Feelings's concept is that of a "dance consciousness"; Jerry Pinkney spoke of wanting to "convey the emotional, flowing quality of jazz"; and Brian Pinkney speaks of the "percussive" quality of scratchboard. Ashley Bryan also speaks of the importance of rhythm in his art. This concern with rhythm, a sense of movement and a "flowing quality" or fluidity, is reflected in the paintings and drawings of these and other artists through various stylistic devices such as repetition of lines and forms and the use of many curves and diagonals. The references to music, particularly jazz, connect their visual art to other African American art forms and recall Feelings's assertion that the visual arts "must be fused with the rest of our art forms—poetry, drama, dance, and music—in order to give direction and life-giving force to Black people" (Feelings 1972, 67).

The importance of conveying emotion is reflected in what I perceive to be a strong emphasis on portraying faces in the work of these artists. Eloise Greenfield, for example, cited Jan Spivey Gilchrist's ability to capture the "emotional expressions in the eyes of her characters" as one of the reasons Gilchrist's art resonates for her. Tom Feelings (1972, 1985) stressed the importance of the emotional content in his work. In Feelings's 1985 article, he cited Aaron Douglas, a famous Harlem Renaissance "New Negro" artist, who noted that, for an artist, developing the power to convey emotion was more important than technique. The similarity between the two artists' views suggests some continuity in the thinking of African American artists.

The third theme, the improvisational nature of African American art forms, was expressed by Tom Feelings as "improvising within a restricted form" and was echoed by second-generation artists Christopher Myers and Javaka Steptoe, who referred to "taking the scraps of life and transforming them into art." In Feelings's case, he was referring to his use of tissue paper and tempera; the younger artists were referring to their use of collage as a medium. Aminah Robinson, with her use of fabric, buttons, clay, and other such material, also exemplifies this improvisational process, as does Faith Ringgold in her quilt stories. It is significant that, thirty years apart, both Tom Feelings and Christopher Myers link their art to what they consider "one of the central metaphors of the African diaspora."

Over the last third of the twentieth century, African American artists have taken it on themselves to dignify the image of African Americans in picture books. For the most part, the work of these illustrators exemplifies the effort of the African American cultural community to influence, if not control, the ways Black people are portrayed visually in children's books. Their illustrations have challenged old stereotypes and replaced them with authentic depictions of African Americans and African American life in all their diversity. Although their illustrations are necessarily tied to the book texts, as creators of complementary visual narratives they go beyond the text to provide specific details and interpretations that place their books solidly in African American cultural contexts. Their art answers Langston Hughes's 1932 call for "books that will give them [Negro children] back their own souls" and show to them and to others "the beauty they possess" (Hughes 1932, 110).

It should be noted that the majority of these artists are men, a fact that is easily observed but not easily explained. One could speculate that this imbalance reflects the art world in general since most of the acclaimed artists with whom we are most familiar are men. For now, it is sufficient to note that, in the field of African American children's literature, the overwhelming majority of the writers are women, while a substantial majority of the artist-illustrators are men. The next three chapters, on African American children's fiction, are focused, with a few notable exceptions, on the work of Black women writers.

NOTES

1. "Faith Ringgold's Intereview Transcript." n.d. Interviewed by Scholastic students. Scholastic, Inc. http://books.scholastic.com/teachers/authorsandbooks/authorstudies/authorstudies.jsp.

2. "The Art of Kadir Nelson." About the Artist. http://www.kadirnelson.com/ArtistBiography.html.

3. "Gregarious Art Statements: The Art of R. Gregory Christie." http://www.gasart.com/books.html.

BIBLIOGRAPHY OF BOOKS FOR CHILDREN AND YOUNG ADULTS

Sources other than books for children and young adults are documented in a reference list at the end of the book.

This list is arranged alphabetically by illustrator.

Barnett, Moneta, illus. 1975. *Me and Nessie*. By Eloise Greenfield. New York: Harper.

Byard, Carole, illus. 1979. *Cornrows*. By Camille Yarbrough. New York: Coward, McCann and Geoghegan.

———, illus. 1980. *Grandmama's Joy*. By Eloise Greenfield. New York: Philomel.

Christie, R. Gregory, illus. 1996. *The Palm of My Heart*. By Davida Adedjouma. New York: Lee and Low.

———, illus. 2000. *Only Passing Through*. By Anne Rockwell. New York: Knopf.

Clay, Will, illus. 1992. *Little Eight John*. By Jan Wahl. New York: Lodestar.

Collier, Bryan, illus. 1999. *These Hands*. By Hope Lynn Price. New York: Jump at the Sun/Hyperion.

———. 2000. *Uptown*. New York: Henry Holt.

———, illus. 2001. *Martin's Big Words*. By Doreen Rappaport. New York: Jump at the Sun/Hyperion.

———, illus. 2005. *Rosa*. By Nikki Giovanni. New York: Henry Holt.

Cooper, Floyd, illus. 1988. *Grandpa's Face*. By Eloise Greenfield. New York: Philomel.

———, illus. 1992. *Imani's Gift at Kwanzaa*. By Denise Burden-Patmon. Boston: Children's Museum.

———, illus. 1993. *Brown Honey in Broomwheat Tea*. By Joyce Carol Thomas. New York: HarperCollins.

———. 1994a. *Coming Home: From the Life of Langston Hughes*. New York: Philomel.

———, illus. 1994b. *Meet Danitra Brown*. By Nikki Grimes. New York: Lothrop, Lee and Shepard.

———, illus. 1995. *Gingerbread Days*. By Joyce Carol Thomas. New York: HarperCollins.

———, 1996. *Mandela: From the Life of the South African Statesman*. New York: Philomel.

———. 1998a. *Cumbayah*. New York: Morrow Junior Books.

———, illus. 1998b. *I Have Heard of a Land*. By Joyce Carol Thomas. New York: Joanna Cotler/HarperCollins.

Crews, Nina. 1995. *One Hot Summer Day*. New York: Greenwillow.

———. 1996. *I'll Catch the Moon*. New York: Greenwillow.

———. 1997. *Snowball*. New York: Greenwillow.

———. 2003. *The Neighborhood Mother Goose*. New York: Amistad/HarperCollins.

Gilchrist, Jan Spivey, illus. 1988. *Children of Long Ago*. By Lessie Jones Little. New York: Philomel.

———, illus. 1989. *Nathaniel Talking*. By Eloise Greenfield. New York: Black Butterfly Press.

———, illus. 1991. *Night on Neighborhood Street*. By Eloise Greenfield. New York: Dial.

———. 1993. *Indigo and Moonlight Gold*. New York: Black Butterfly Press.

———. 1995. *Lift Every Voice and Sing*. By James Weldon Johnson. New York: Scholastic.

———. 1997a. *Madelia*. New York: Dial.

———, illus. 1997b. *For the Love of the Game: Michael Jordan and Me*. By Eloise Greenfield. New York: HarperCollins.

———, illus. 1998. *Angels*. Eloise Greenfield. New York: Hyperion.

———, illus. 2001. *I Can Draw a Weeposaur and Other Dinosaurs*. By Eloise Greenfield. New York: Greenwillow.

———, illus. 2004. *In the Land of Words*. By Eloise Greenfield. New York: Amistad/HarperCollins.

Haskins, Francine. 1992. *Things I Like About Grandma*. San Francisco: Children's Book Press.

Lewis, E. B., illus. 2002. *Talkin' about Bessie*. By Nikki Grimes. New York: Orchard.

———, illus. 2004. *Coming on Home Soon*. By Jacqueline Woodson. New York: Putnam.

Myers, Christopher, illus. 1997a. *Harlem*. By Walter Dean Myers. New York: Scholastic.

———. 1997b. Telephone interview by Rudine Sims Bishop. November 26.

———. 1999. *Black Cat*. New York: Scholastic.

———. 2000. *Wings*. New York: Scholastic.

———, illus. 2003. *Blues Journey*. By Walter Dean Myers. New York: Holiday House.

Nelson, Kadir, illus. 2000. *Big Jabe*. By Jerdine Nolen. New York: HarperCollins.

———, illus. 2003. *Thunder Rose*. By Jerdine Nolen. New York: Silver Whistle.

———, illus. 2004. *Ellington Was Not a Street*. By Ntazoke Shange. New York: Simon and Schuster.

Pinkney, Brian, illus. 1989. *The Boy and the Ghost*. By Robert San Souci. New York: Simon and Schuster.

———, illus. 1992. *Sukey and the Mermaid*. By Robert San Souci. New York: Four Winds Press.

———, illus. 1993. *Alvin Ailey*. By Andrea Davis Pinkney. New York: Hyperion.

———, illus. 1994. *Dear Benjamin Banneker*. By Andrea Davis Pinkney. San Diego: Harcourt Brace.

———, illus. 1995. *The Faithful Friend*. By Robert San Souci. New York: Simon and Schuster.

———, 1997a. *The Adventures of Sparrow Boy*. New York: Simon and Schuster.

Pinkney, Brian. 1998. *Duke Ellington: The Piano Prince and His Orchestra*. By Andrea Davis Pinkney. New York: Hyperion.

———, illus. 1999. *In the Time of the Drums*. By Kim Siegelson. New York: Jump at the Sun/Hyperion.

———, illus. 2002. *Ella Fitzgerald: The Tale of a Vocal Virtuoso*. By Andrea Davis Pinkney. New York: Jump at the Sun/Hyperion.

Pinkney, Jerry, illus. 1985. *The Patchwork Quilt*. By Valerie Flournoy. New York: Dial.

Ransome, James, illus. 1990. *Do Like Kyla*. By Angela Johnson. New York: Orchard.

———, illus. 1991a. *All the Lights in the Night*. By Arthur Levine. New York: William Morrow.

———, illus. 1991b. *Aunt Flossie's Hats (and Crab Cakes Later)*. By Elizabeth Fitzgerald Howard. New York: Clarion.

———, illus. 1993a. *Sweet Clara and the Freedom Quilt*. By Deborah Hopkinson. New York: Knopf.

———, illus. 1993b. *Uncle Jed's Barbershop*. By Margaree Mitchell. New York: Simon and Schuster.

———, illus. 1994. *The Creation*. By James Weldon Johnson. New York: Holiday House.

———, illus. 1996. *Freedom's Fruit*. By William Hooks.

———, illus. 2000. *Quinnie Blue*. By Dinah Johnson. New York: Henry Holt.

———, illus. 2001. *Quilt Alphabet*. By Lesa Cline Ransome. New York: Holiday House.

———, illus. 2002a. *Quilt Counting*. By Lesa Cline Ransome. New York: Sea Star.

———, illus. 2002b. *Visiting Day*. By Jacqueline Woodson. New York: Scholastic.

———, illus. 2003. *Bruh Rabbit and the Tar Baby Girl*. By Virginia Hamilton. New York: Blue Sky/Scholastic.

Rich, Anna, illus. 1998. *Just Right Stew*. By Karen English. Honesdale, PA: Boyd's Mills Press.

Ringgold, Faith. 1991. *Tar Beach*. New York: Crown.

———. 1992. *Aunt Harriet's Underground Railroad in the Sky*. New York: Crown.

———. 1993. *Dinner at Aunt Connie's House*. New York: Hyperion.

———. 1999. *The Invisible Princess*. New York: Crown.

Ringgold, Faith, Linda Freeman, and Nancy Rocher. 1996. *Talking to Faith Ringgold*. New York: Crown.

Robinson, Aminah Brenda Lynn, illus. 1992. *Elijah's Angel*. By Michael J. Rosen. San Diego, CA: Harcourt.

———. illus, 1995. *A School for Pompey Walker*. By Michael J. Rosen. San Diego, CA: Harcourt.

———. 1997. *A Street Called Home*. San Diego, CA: Harcourt Brace.

———, illus. 1998. *To Be a Drum*. By Evelyn Coleman. New York: Albert Whitman.

Saint James, Synthia, illus. 1996a. *Neeny Coming, Neeny Going*. By Karen English. New York: BridgeWater Books.

———, illus. 1996b. *Sunday*. New York: Albert Whitman.

Steptoe, Javaka, illus. and compiler. 1997. *In Daddy's Arms I Am Tall*. New York: Lee and Low.

———, illus. 2000. *Do You Know What I'll Do?* By Charlotte Zolotow. New York: HarperCollins.

———, illus. 2001. *Pocket Full of Poems*. By Nikki Grimes. New York: Clarion.

———. 2003. *The Jones Family Express*. New York: Lee and Low.

———, illus. 2004. *Hot Day on Abbott Avenue*. By Karen English. Clarion.

CHAPTER 10

African American Children's Fiction: Illuminating the Life of the People

Given the sociocultural context of the late 1960s and early 1970s, when contemporary African American authors and artists began to be published in fairly substantial numbers, it is not surprising that realistic fiction would become an important mode of expression, a purposeful response to the near exclusion of Black people, Black history, and Black cultural traditions from the existing body of American children's literature. Although our common humanity makes it both possible and desirable for readers to engage with literature across cultural divides, good literature connects with readers through particulars: credible characters, the dilemmas they face and resolve, and the specifics of the sociocultural context and the time and place evoked in the story. What had been missing from the canon of children's literature prior to the late 1960s was attention to the particularity, the distinctiveness, and the multifaceted nature of the experience of growing up Black in America. Acclaimed author Virginia Hamilton (1981) characterized this distinctiveness:

I am convinced that it is important to reveal that the life of the people is and always has been different in a significant respect from the life of the majority. It has been made eccentric by slavery, escape, fear of capture; by discrimination, and constant despair. But it has held tight within it happiness, and subtle humor, a fierce pride in leadership and progress, love of life and family, and a longing for peace and freedom. Nevertheless, there is an uneasy, ideological difference with the American majority basic to black thought. (57)

It is the intention to illuminate the eccentric "life of the people" and to pass on the cultural values and ideals derived from that distinctive experience that has spurred the creation of most African American children's literature.

Much of that literature is in the form of realistic fiction, that is, fiction that reflects "the life of the people" in the real world as we know it. Everything that happens in the imagined story could conceivably happen or could have happened in the past. In children's and young adult literature, realistic fiction is generally sorted into two categories: contemporary and historical. The term *contemporary realistic fiction* generally refers to stories that deal with problems of today, in contrast to *historical fiction*, which places the characters in a past time and re-creates that era in accordance with what is known about the social environment and historical events of that time. One problem in applying these categories in children's books is that what feels contemporary to an adult may seem like ancient history to a young reader, and there is no firm definition of how far back a novel for young people must be set to be called historical.

As with other genres, the development of African American realistic fiction for children began with developments that took place or began in the late 1960s—the work of two authors who became giants in the field and the publication of the milestone African American novel of what was then called the "new realism." Virginia Hamilton and Walter Dean Myers, both of whom published their first books in the late 1960s, went on to become the premier African American authors of children's books, with careers that spanned the rest of the century and beyond. Hamilton's first book marks the beginning of the modern era of African American children's literature, and the rest of her work is highly significant to that canon. A number of her important contributions are unique, and some cross into other genres, such as fantasy and folklore. An appraisal of her significance in the field therefore requires a temporary digression from the focus on realistic fiction to a brief consideration of her work in those genres. Myers has been for three decades the major Black male voice in African American fiction and the premier African American creator of contemporary young adult literature. Although Kristin Hunter did not become a giant in the field of children's literature, her 1968 book *The Soul Brothers and Sister Lou* was a landmark. It made a splash as the first African American exemplar of the new realism in children's books.

As was true with picture books, in the 1970s the major focus of African American fiction for children and young adults was "urban literature," in which the city setting is crucial to the story. A few important young adult novels of the decade were written by authors who were already known in adult literary circles. There were also a few novels in which the urban setting is not highly significant; the focus is on relationships between family members or friends. For all the emphasis on living in Northern cities, however, there was also a singular Southern voice, that of Brenda Wilkinson.

TWO GIANTS AND A MILESTONE

VIRGINIA HAMILTON (1936–2002): CHRONICLING THE LIFE OF THE PEOPLE

When Zeely Tayber, night traveler, assistant pig keeper, and imaginary Watutsi queen, glided serenely through the pages of Virginia Hamilton's first book, she both launched Hamilton's remarkable career and ushered in contemporary African American realistic fiction for children. *Zeely* (1967) tells the story of Elizabeth Perry, a young African American girl who, along with her younger brother John, spends the summer on their uncle's farm. At the beginning of the summer, she renames herself Geeder and her brother Toeboy. Zeely is a very tall, very dark, very calm, and very quiet woman who helps her father with his prize hogs. When Geeder chances on a picture of a Watutsi queen in a magazine, she assumes that Zeely, who bears a striking resemblance to the woman in the picture, must also be a Watutsi queen. Eventually, Geeder's made-up story reaches Zeely's ears, and Zeely takes Geeder aside for a talk. Using a couple of stories of her own, Zeely helps Geeder separate her fantasies from reality while simultaneously holding on to her gift of imagination. Once Geeder understands that an individual, even a queen, is defined by "what's inside" her, she is ready to see Zeely as who she really is and is also ready once again to be her own real self, Elizabeth.

Zeely's significance lies not simply in the timing of its publication but in its focus on an ordinary African American child living happily in the bosom of her extended family somewhere in the Midwest. Much of the literature featuring African Americans published in the 1960s and into the early 1970s focused on topics and themes reflecting social issues of national concern at the time, such as housing and school desegregation, interracial friendships or conflicts, or coping with racist or discriminatory practices. As part of the emergence of tell-it-like-it-is new realism in children's books, a number of realistic books about African Americans also focused on problems popularly associated with Black people in inner cities, such as poverty, drugs, and violent gangs. In contrast, *Zeely* does not concern itself with such problems or with race relations or problems stemming from racism and discrimination. It simply takes its Black sociocultural setting as a given and proceeds to relate a tale about a young African American girl with a vivid imagination, much like Hamilton herself.

From *Zeely* (1967), Hamilton went on to become one of the world's premier writers of literature for young people, and her prominence called worldwide attention to African American children's literature. By the time of her death in 2002, Hamilton had published 38 books; at least two more have been published posthumously. In 1975, she became the first African American writer to win the John Newbery Medal, for *M.C. Higgins, the Great* (1974). The medal is given to the "author of the most distinguished contribution to American literature for children" in a given year. *M.C. Higgins* also won the Boston Globe-Horn Book Award and the American Book Award, an achievement unmatched, as of this writing, by any other children's book.

During her career, Hamilton also received two more Boston Globe-Horn Book Awards and three Coretta Scott King Awards. In addition, three of her books were named Newbery Honor Books. In 1992, Hamilton was awarded, for the body of her work, the Hans Christian Andersen Medal, the most prestigious international award for children's books. She was only the fourth U.S. author to receive the Hans Christian Andersen Medal since it was first given in 1956. Also for the body of her work, the American Library Association presented Hamilton with the Laura Ingalls Wilder Award in 1995. In that same year, Hamilton became the first children's literature author to win a MacArthur Fellowship, commonly known as a "genius award." In short, she won every major award for which her work was eligible, a testament to her eminence in the world of children's literature. No examination or discussion of twentieth century American or African American children's literature would be complete without some attention to her work.

Hamilton wrote in a number of other genres in addition to realistic fiction; she adapted and retold folktales and wrote picture books, biography, fantasy, science fiction and nonfiction. Nevertheless, she saw her work as a holistic endeavor:

My work, as a novelist, a biographer, and a creator and compiler of stories, has been to portray the essence of a people who are a parallel culture community in America. Through my writing I have meant to portray the traditions, the history of African Americans, this parallel culture people, as I see them, while attempting to give readers strong stories and memorable characters. (1995, 440)

In the course of creating her verbal portrait of African America, Hamilton had an impact that extended well beyond the artistic achievements of her individual books. Across several genres and across three-and-a-half decades, she injected the field with new vocabulary or reinterpretations of some concepts, invented new African American mythical tales and characters, revived interest in African American folk-tales retold for young people, produced some of the very few African American science fiction books for children, and lifted African American and American children's literature to greater artistic heights.

Invented Terms and Concepts

Many of Hamilton's speeches and essays were published in professional journals and through those media, Hamilton was able to inject at least two conceptual phrases into the lexicon of current scholarship on African American children's literature: *parallel culture* and *liberation literature*. Her first published use of both terms was in her 1989 acceptance speech for the Boston Globe-Horn Book Award given to *Anthony Burns: The Defeat and Triumph of a Fugitive Slave* (1988). Hamilton referred to this book as a historical reconstruction; it is a hybrid of factual information and narrative "backfill"—invented episodes, thoughts, and dialogue based on the few known facts about Burns's early life. Burns had escaped from slavery and made his way to Boston, where he was caught and imprisoned under the provisions of the Fugitive Slave Law. His case became a cause célèbre, involving prominent abolitionists and attorneys and igniting riots in the streets of Boston. Burns lost his court case and was sent back into slavery. Eventually, he was freed, after which he made his way to Canada, where he died at the age of 28.

The introduction of the term *parallel culture* has relevance both to African American children's literature and to multicultural literature in general. Hamilton simply dropped the term into the text of her speech (1989): "If this were the life of any ordinary individual not of a parallel culture who had become enormously famous toward the end of his life, the factual chronicle of his whole life would have been sifted through and the empty places investigated, filled where possible, and duly recorded" (183). In a later essay, after some scholars in the field had begun to use the term and others to question its use, she provided an explanation:

I use the term parallel culture to describe groups formerly called minority, to suggest to you that so-called minorities—those blacks, browns, and yellows—make up a vast contingent in the world view. It seems fitting to acknowledge that all peoples stand as equals side by side. Thus parallel culture is a more apt term than minority, which imposes a barrier and a might majority behind it. (1993a, 372)

Parallel culture, then, has become, for a number of scholars of children's literature, a useful phrase that resists the connotation of "inferior" or "lesser than" that sometimes attaches to the term *minority* as it refers to people of color and their literature.

Early in the *Anthony Burns* acceptance speech (1989), Hamilton described the book as a study in liberation literature. Later in the same speech, she elaborated:

I bear witness, by documenting the evidence of another's suffering and growing awareness of self in the pursuit of freedom.

Liberation literature not only frees the subject of record and evidence but the witness as well, who is also the reader, who then becomes part of the struggle. We take our position then rightly as participants alongside the victim. We become emotionally involved in his problem; we suffer, and we triumph, as the victim triumphs, in the solution of liberation. (185)

Liberation literature, then, became a subgenre of Hamilton's canon and thereby of African American children's literature. History—family history and African American history more generally—was a central concern for her, and historical references appeared in various forms in her books. Since African American history carries within it documentation of oppression, and since her historical work focuses on the ways people triumphed over that oppression, in my view both her biographical works and all of her books related to the slave experience fit into the category. Hamilton explicitly identified *Anthony Burns* (1988) and her story collections, *Many Thousand Gone* (1993b), *The People Could Fly* (1985b), and *Her Stories* (1995a), as examples of liberation literature. *Many Thousand Gone* is a collection of narratives that trace the history of slavery in the United States up to the Emancipation Proclamation. The stories in *The People Could Fly* are folktales out of the African American oral tradition. *Her Stories* is a collection of folktales traditionally told by African American women. While the folk collections do not relate history in a factual sense, they were often expressions of Black people's attitudes toward their oppression and sometimes a means of personal and group resistance, placing them in the category of liberation literature as Hamilton defines it.

Among Hamilton's first books were young people's biographies of two Black men her father had admired: W.E.B. Du Bois and Paul Robeson. Du Bois was the scholar, writer, and social activist who published *The Brownies' Book*. Robeson was a scholar, an outstanding athlete, a lawyer, and an extraordinary, internationally acclaimed singer and actor. Both Robeson and Du Bois had been ostracized and persecuted by the U.S. government because of their social activism and their flirtation with and advocacy of communism. And both had been pretty much barred from the history texts used in American classrooms. Like Anthony Burns, Du Bois and Robeson experienced both defeat and triumph, and their stories in Hamilton's hands became instances of liberation literature, even though she did not identify them as such. Although the term *liberation literature* may also be used in other contexts, nevertheless it was Hamilton's specific application of it that injected the term into the national conversation about African American and multicultural literature for children.

Modern Myth Making

Hamilton also created the modern myth that captures many of the most important elements of the story of African Americans' journey to and across what she called the American hopescape. *The Magical Adventures of Pretty Pearl* (1983a) is a unique work that combines African American history, fantasy, and Black folklore (e.g., music, story, folk medicine, folk heroes) into a cultural myth. It recasts folk hero High John the Conquer, the "hope-bringer" of the plantation era, and John Henry, the legendary "steel-driving man," as gods whose home is Mount Kenya in Africa. They are the older brothers of Pretty Pearl, a "god-child" whose mission is to alleviate the sufferings of the humans she sees captured and taken away from Africa. High John and Pearl cross the ocean flying as albatrosses above a slave ship, ending up in Georgia, where they lie in wait in the blood red soil. When it is time, Pearl, accompanied by four spirits, leaves to test her courage and her power to help the "Inside People," former slaves living in their well-organized community deep in the forest, in alliance with a community of fugitive Cherokees. Eventually, she and the Inside People cross the Jordan (Ohio) River into Ohio, where Pearl, who has been transformed into the human Pretty Pearl Perry, has become, like Hamilton, the chronicler of the people's story, in essence a modern griot.

Early on, Pearl's voicing of her calling—"I got de most strong desire to know what happen to de ones that got grabbed and taken up" (Hamilton 1983a, 10)—is strikingly similar to the question from a Ghanaian friend of Tom Feelings that eventually led to *The Middle Passage* (Ingalls 1996): "What happened to all of you when you were taken away from here?" The parallel between the two, a kind of intertextuality, exemplifies one of the deeper connections that exist within and across African American children's literature. Both *Pretty Pearl* and *The Middle Passage* respond to what may be the central question that African American history seeks to answer for child readers. Feelings's response was a powerful and realistic visual portrayal of the awful journey across the Atlantic, ending with the captives' arrival in the Americas. Hamilton's response is no less powerful in its imaginative chronicling of the search for true freedom, the survival of hope, and the need to preserve and pass on the story of the people's journey across the Black American hopescape.

In addition to Pretty Pearl, Hamilton also invented at least two other mythical creatures: Jahdu and Drylongso. Jahdu, a two-foot-tall trickster, was born in a Harlem oven beside two loaves of bread. With his magic dust and his wits, he is able to get into and out of all kinds of mischief. He is also a shape shifter, able to transform himself into whatever and whoever he wants to be. Although Jahdu is an African American character, he is not tied specifically to traditional African American folklore; he is an original invention. He appears in four books, the last of which, *The All Jahdu Storybook* (1991), incorporates all the stories from the earlier ones and adds four new tales. As an invented character with a cycle of stories that are in essence original literary folktales, Jahdu is unique in African American children's literature.

"Drylongso" is a Gullah expression used to describe long-lasting drought (dry-so-long). Over time, it came to mean "ordinary." In Hamilton's book by that title (1992), Drylongso, a contemporary mythical figure, arrives at Lindy's family farm during a Midwestern drought in 1975. He blows in at the front of a dust storm, a tall skinny boy. He leaves after a brief stay as Lindy's "play brother," having taught the family some lessons on agriculture and having used a dowsing rod to find water on the farm. Like High John the Conquer, Drylongso is an African American hope-bringer—"where he goes, life will grow better"—this time invented by Hamilton. In this text, Hamilton also focuses on environmental/ecological issues, a concern she touches on in a number of her works.

Reviving Interest in African American Folklore

Although Hamilton was certainly not the first African American writer to publish a collection of African American folktales for young readers (e.g., Julius Lester published *Black Folk Tales* in 1969), her 1985 collection *The People Could Fly* (1985b) took on milestone status. Winner of the 1986 Coretta Scott King Award, it has become a children's literature classic, although it is suitable for all ages. Presented in four sections, the collection is representative of four major types of African American folktales: the familiar animal tales, fanciful tales, supernatural tales, and freedom tales. Illustrated by the acclaimed artists Leo and Diane Dillon, it was also named a *New York Times* Best Illustrated Book. With its accompanying recording of Hamilton and actor James Earl Jones reading the stories, this was the book that revived interest in African American folktales as children's literature, over and above the numerous African folktales that have been published as picture books and in compilations.

Tales from Africa continue to be popular in American children's literature, but since *The People Could Fly*, they have been joined by more stories derived from the experiences of Africans in the Americas. Given Hamilton's role in the revival of interest in these tales, it is fitting that among her last books was a delightful picture book version of the Tar Baby story, *Bruh Rabbit and the Tar Baby Girl* (2003), illustrated in watercolor by James Ransome and published posthumously.

Inventing African American Science Fiction for Children and Young Adults

Science fiction is a rare commodity in African American children's books; Hamilton, Walter Dean Myers, Joyce Carol Thomas, and perhaps one or two others who are less well known are the only African American writers of children's books to venture into the genre. Hamilton's Justice trilogy—*Justice and Her Brothers* (1978), *Dustland* (1980), and *The Gathering* (1981)—was groundbreaking in that regard. It features an eleven-year old African American female protagonist, her twin brothers, and a neighbor boy, who together form an entity called The Unit. Gifted with telepathy, The Unit engages in time and space travel, visiting the future and discovering what could happen to Earth if humans fail to take care of the environment. Each member of The Unit also possesses an individual power that complements that of the others and enables them to work effectively together. Feminists will note the empowered females, most especially Justice, who is the leader of the four children. Freedom, survival, oppression, sibling rivalry, and the possible uses of power are among the themes Hamilton touches on in these three books, which exemplify her ability to create layered literature that is true to her cultural and historic interests, her concern about social issues, and the requirements of the genre in which she is writing.

Hamilton's Realistic Fiction: Home, History, and Heritage

The majority of Hamilton's books were realistic novels for children and young adults. Her realistic fiction is tied together by a strong focus on a few recurring themes, which can be characterized as home, history and heritage—with home representing both place and family, history including both African American and family history, and heritage meaning both cultural/racial heritage and individual identity. This complex of thematic threads, as well as other characteristics of her writing, was evident even in *Zeely* (1967), Hamilton's first book and one of her most easily accessible novels.

Set near a small Midwestern village much like Hamilton's own Ohio hometown, *Zeely* (1967) both evokes a strong sense of place and celebrates the ties among extended family as the children spend a summer with their uncle. Issues of identity can be discerned in Elizabeth/Geeder's renaming and reinventing herself and her brother and in Zeely's two stories, one of which is a creation myth. The story within story is a device Hamilton used frequently and a reminder of how important storytelling has been to her and her family. She calls attention to ancestry and heritage by creating a Black character who came from Canada, where self-emancipated slaves often fled, and is closely tied visually to her African ancestors. The history of slavery and the will to freedom is invoked in Geeder's evocation of "night travellers" [*sic*] and Uncle Ross's verification of a night traveler as "somebody who wants to walk tall. And to walk tall, you most certainly have to run free" (83). The night traveler story also provides an opportunity for Hamilton to introduce some music, which is a secondary theme in many of her books. Uncle Ross sings for Toeboy a few of the songs that slaves had used to signal each other about running away.

Often, Hamilton's books incorporate some element of mystery, as in this description of Geeder's first glimpse of the night traveler: "Something tall and white was moving down the road. It didn't quite touch the ground. Geeder could hear no sound of footsteps. She couldn't see its head or arms. Beside it and moving with it was something that squeaked ominously" (29). All of her work has a touch of something "different," and this trait also was evident from the beginning. In *Zeely* (1967), the difference is related to Zeely's social isolation and her physical appearance:

Zeely Tayber was more than six and a half feet tall, thin and deeply dark as a pole of Ceylon ebony. She wore a long smock that reached to her ankles. Her arms, hands and feet were bare, and her thin, oblong head didn't seem to fit quite right on her shoulders. She had very high cheekbones and her eyes seemed to turn inward on themselves. Geeder couldn't say what expression she saw on Zeely's face. She knew only that it was calm, that it had pride in it, and that the face was the most beautiful she had ever seen. (31)

Zeely was published at a time when pride in African heritage and "Black is beautiful" were important ideas embraced by many African Americans, and Geeder's awe for Zeely's decidedly non-European beauty was a subtle confirmation of that pride. These themes and characteristics would be repeated and reinvented within and across the body of Hamilton's work.

It is beyond the scope and purpose of this chapter to describe or review in depth each of Hamilton's books, even though most of them have deservedly garnered awards and critical acclaim. However, a brief overview of the range of her fiction will serve to illustrate the breadth and variety of her contributions to the canon of African American children's literature. The body of Hamilton's work includes about a score of novels, including the Justice cycle and *Pretty Pearl* (1983a). *Sweet Whispers, Brother Rush* (1982) is also classified as a fantasy novel because the title character, Brother Rush, is actually a ghost. Mostly, however, the book is realistic; the book is in part about the importance of family roots, and the function of the ghost is to connect Tree, the protagonist, with her family's past, which has been hidden from her.

Among Hamilton's works were also two mysteries, *The House of Dies Drear* (1968) and a sequel, *The Mystery of Drear House* (1987a), which were centered on the secrets and arcane happenings within and around an old house in southern Ohio that had been a station on the Underground Railroad. Although the Dies Drear books incorporate much history, their setting is contemporary. Hamilton also wrote a work of historical fiction, *The Bells of Christmas* (1989), which is not a novel, but an illustrated long story set in southern Ohio in December 1890, recalling what the Christmas holiday might have been like at the turn of the century.

Although reviewers have labeled many of her books as suitable for readers aged 12 and up, which means they might potentially be considered either for children or young adults, at least three appear to have been written specifically with teenagers in mind: *A Little Love* (1984), *Junius over Far* (1985a), and *A White Romance* (1987b). Nina Mikkelsen (1994), author of the Twayne Young Adult Authors series book on Hamilton, identifies the issues in those books as "those with which teens are often faced: parental desertion or death, female role choices, interracial dating, the drug scene, depression and potential suicide, nuclear disaster and other hemispheric dangers, familial displacement, and the search for a lost home or heritage" (69). Reviewers also routinely categorize *Pretty Pearl* (1983a), *Brother Rush* (1982), and *Arilla Sun Down* (1976) as young adult books, although in the case of *Pretty Pearl* the designation has more to do with the length and complexity of the book than with the issues Mikkelsen identified in the "teen books." *Arilla Sun Down* is one of the first and one of the few African American children's novels to explore notions of identity and heritage within an interracial family in which the mix is African American and Native American, or Amerind, as Hamilton preferred. Both Arilla and Sweet Tree, the protagonist of *Sweet Whispers, Brother Rush,* are dealing with two or three of the issues Mikkelsen identifies: a parent who is frequently absent, making choices about their own roles, and at the same time seeking to connect with their heritage.

Only two of Hamilton's novels are set in a large city—specifically New York. One of her two "urban" novels, *The Planet of Junior Brown* (1971a), raises the issue of homelessness among children. Although it is a realistic novel, its elements "of difference"—a nearly 300-pound title character, an insane piano teacher, an over-protective mother who has silenced the keys on Junior's piano, an ex-teacher janitor who hangs out in the school basement with truants constructing a movable solar system, a teenager who takes care of groups of homeless children in abandoned houses called planets—place it on the outer edges of realism. *Bluish* (1999), the last novel published before Hamilton's death, is her second big city novel, although the focus here is not on place but rather on the relationships that develop among three girls from differing backgrounds, one of whom is in a wheelchair as a result of chemotherapy.

Bluish is geared to an upper elementary or middle school audience, as are several of Hamilton's novels that dwell in the arenas of family and home, themes that were never far from Hamilton's heart. *Willie Bea and the Time the Martians Landed* (1983b) is set at the time of the Orson Welles Halloween broadcast of a Martian invasion and involves the often-humorous responses and reactions of Willie Bea and her large extended family. *Cousins* (1990), *Second Cousins* (1998), and *Plain City* (1993c) explore family relationships from the perspective of spirited young African American girls. Fictionalized recollections of actual events and family members abound in these books.

M.C. Higgins, the Great (1974) was a landmark, the first book by an Africa American writer to win the John Newbery Medal. In this novel, Mayo Cornelius Higgins's father Jones has given him a forty-foot steel pole as a reward for swimming the Ohio River. From the top of that pole, which he has rigged with a bicycle seat and pedals, M.C. can survey his surroundings, reigning above the earth as M.C. Higgins, the Great. He lives at the foot of Sarah's Mountain, named after his great-grandmother, who is buried on the mountain, having arrived long ago carrying her infant son, with whom she had escaped from slavery. At the top of the mountain is a spoil heap, left over from strip-mining operations, that threatens to crash down on the Higgins home and family. Determined to save his home, M.C. naively puts his hope in his mother's becoming a singing star once her voice is discovered by a dude who is known to be traveling in the mountains taping old songs. Her stardom would enable them to move away from the mountain and the spoil heap. In the end, M.C. realizes that the mountain is home, and if there is any chance to save it and his family, he must take action himself. With the help of his father and his six-fingered friend Ben Kilburn, he begins to build a wall.

M.C. Higgins explores many of the themes that interested Hamilton most deeply. It is about roots, about the importance of home, family, and heritage and on one level about taking care of the environment. The story of Sarah is based on Hamilton's own ancestry, the great-grandmother who walked to Ohio with the young son who grew up to become Hamilton's grandfather. It is also about M.C.'s relationships with his parents and siblings, particularly that between M.C. and his father. Even critic David Rees (1984, 175–176), in a piece that mostly flogged Hamilton for not writing up to her potential as he saw it, conceded that "the relationship between M.C. and Jones is one of the most impressive father-son relationships in contemporary children's literature." The book is also about growing up, coming of age, as thirteen-year-old M.C.'s move into adolescence is played out in part through his encounter with the independent older girl Lorhetta, the stranger who stayed on the mountain long enough to alter his outlook and then moved on without saying good-bye. M.C. is learning to be his own person, in the end standing up to his father in choosing to be friends with Ben Kilburn in spite of Jones's superstitious objections. Concern about the environment is present in the crisis of the spoil heap and its danger to the mountain and the Higgins family. With its fully drawn characters, lyrical descriptions, vivid details, hints of the bizarre, and powerful themes, this book is indeed a distinguished contribution to American children's literature.

Hamilton's final novel, *Time Pieces: The Book of Times* (2002) was published posthumously a few months after her death. It seems somehow fitting that it is semiautobiographical since it finally spins out in some fictional detail what appears to have been one of the central stories in Hamilton's life, the story of her great-grandmother Mary Cloud's escape from slavery and her journey to Ohio with her son Levi. Moving back and forth between present and past, *Time Pieces* also celebrates the importance of keeping and passing on a people's stories. The fictionalized version of Levi's story is told, in bits and pieces, to the protagonist Valena McGill by her mother. Harriet McGill's narrative includes the tale of Tunny Maud, a diminutive African captive who eventually helps to found a free settlement for escaped slaves, called Maud Free. It is to Maud Free that young Luke and his mother, Proud Mary, escape. Luke grows up to be Graw Luke, Valena's grandfather, who passed the story of his escape on to his children. Proud Mary, like Hamilton's great-grandmother Mary Cloud, disappeared after ensuring the child's safety, presumably to work on the Underground Railroad.

Although the story of Graw Luke is central, *Time Pieces* is set in the present and relates events of the summer between Valena's fifth- and sixth-grade years, among which are a memorable trip to the circus to view a horribly disfigured gorilla, a frightening and dangerous tornado, and the accidental death of the family dog. In the stories of both the present and past can be found threads that are drawn out in some of Hamilton's other books, such as *Pretty Pearl, Cousins, Arilla Sun Down* and *M.C. Higgins, the Great*. In that regard, *Time Pieces* seems to be the closing of a circle.

It was Hamilton's craft that captured the admiration of her fans, the acclaim of the critics, and the literary prizes. Hamilton enjoyed experimenting with genre, structure, and language. Her fiction was marked by strong characterizations. She had a sharp ear for dialogue but often used a stylized colloquial language to represent certain dialects. Her descriptions could be lyrical and vivid, full of apt metaphors, and her detailed evocations of place could transport a reader directly into the setting. Symbolic elements, such as the tunnels in *Zeely, M.C. Higgins*, and *Plain City* (1993c), were abundant in her fictions, adding to their complexity and depth. Her fertile imagination almost always led her to include a touch of something strange, unusual, or even bizarre in her books, from M.C.'s 40-foot pole and the "witchy" Kilburn compound, to Mr. Pluto and his underground cave in *Dies Drear* (1968), to the Tunny Maud character in *Time Pieces* (2002). Hamilton took risks, and some of her books were less well received than others, but for the most part her work was extraordinary. In her first article in a professional educational journal, Hamilton expressed what may have been an impossible dream: "Perhaps some day when I've written my last book, there will stand the whole of the Black experience in White America as I see it" (Hamilton 1971b, 240). Sadly, that last book has now been written. If she did not capture the whole of the Black experience in America, Virginia Hamilton never veered from her determination to depict African Americans' journey across what she called the American hopescape. Using what she referred to as "the known, the remembered and the imagined," she turned the story of that journey, as she saw it, into remarkable literary art.

WALTER DEAN MYERS: WEAVING THE RECOGNIZABLE FABRIC OF BLACK LIFE

I had learned from Langston Hughes that being a Black writer meant more than simply having one's characters brown-skinned, or having them live in what publishers insist on describing on book jackets as a ghetto. It meant understanding the nuances of value, of religion, of dreams. It meant capturing the subtle rhythms of language and movement and weaving it all, the sound and the gesture, the sweat and the prayers, into the recognizable fabric of black life. (1986, 50)

Walter Dean Myers entered the field of children's books through the door opened by the "minority writers" contest sponsored by the Council on Interracial Books for Children (CIBC). His prize-winning entry was *Where Does the Day Go?* (1969), a picture book with a multiethnic cast of child characters. From that modest beginning, Myers has gone on to become one of the foremost authors of American/African American children's literature. He has garnered much critical acclaim and received numerous well-deserved awards, including five Coretta Scott King Author Awards and two Newbery Honor citations. Two particular awards affirm his status as one of the premier authors of American literature for young adults. In 1994, Myers received the Margaret Edwards Award, given for works that "over a period of time, have been accepted by young adults as an authentic voice that continues to illuminate their experiences and emotions, giving insight into their lives." Although the Edwards award is often referred to as a lifetime achievement award, the selection committee usually singles out particular books by the winning author, and in Myers's case, they cited four novels: *Hoops* (1981a), *Motown and Didi* (1984a), *Fallen Angels* (1988a), and *Scorpions* (1988b). In 2000, *Monster* (1999), the innovative story of a sixteen-year-old boy on trial for murder, was awarded the very first Michael Printz Award for excellence in young adult literature, a historic event.

While he may be best known as a writer of young adult literature, Myers's work covers a broad span. He is a very disciplined writer, demanding of himself ten pages a day. Over the years, those pages have turned into dozens of wide-ranging books. Since 1969, Myers has published over seventy books for children and young adults, an average of two a year, and still counting. Myers seems willing to tackle any genre or any topic that attracts his interest and is seemingly undaunted by any of them. Thus, he has produced—in addition to his contemporary realistic novels—historical fiction, poetry, science fiction, fantasy, literary folktales, nonfiction history, biography, retold Bible stories, picture books, short stories, and a memoir. In addition to his beloved New York City, he has set books in the American South, the American West, Spain, Egypt, Peru, England, and North Africa. He has written detective stories, adventure stories, and fictional journals. His target audiences include everyone from preschoolers to adults. Clearly, it is beyond the scope of this chapter to examine the full body of Myers's writings. The focus here is on his urban fiction, but it should be noted that, with this copious output, he has expanded the range and increased the breadth of the body of African American children's literature. He has also added to it a distinctive voice.

Myers's voice and his perspective were and are particularly welcome additions to the canon since he is one of the few African American male writers in the field. As has been noted, African American writers and illustrators of children's books for the most part separate along gender lines; that is, the majority of African American children's book *writers* are women, and the majority of African American children's book *illustrators* are men. One of Myers's major accomplishments, therefore, has been that he made visible and became the literary voice of urban Black teenage boys. In more than a dozen realistic novels, he illuminated the experiences of young Black males coming of age, learning to accept responsibility, discovering how difficult it is to do the right thing. He did include strong female characters as well—*Crystal* (1987) has a female protagonist—but his focus in these novels, not surprisingly, has been on Black male young adults, not unlike his own teenage self, growing up in New York City. His novels range in tone from near farcical to tragic and, taken together, offer a sense of the diversity within what he calls vertical living. Others have written about Black city teenagers, but in the field of African American young people's literature, Myers owns the territory.

Focus on Humor and Friendship

One set of Myers's urban novels features the lighter side of vertical living. Through these books, Myers injected a welcome touch of humor into the body of African American children's literature. In the early 1970s, when African American children's literature was establishing itself, the focus in realistic fiction tended to be on serious themes, although this is not to imply that the literature was totally humorless. Myers, on the other hand, began his novel writing in a humorous vein, even as he simultaneously dealt with some serious topics.

His first novel was not published until 1975, six years after *Where Does the Day Go?* and following three other picture books. That novel, *Fast Sam, Cool Clyde, and Stuff* relates the adventures of a group of young people growing up in Harlem. The narrator is Francis, facetiously nicknamed Stuff because when he was twelve-and-a-half and new to the neighborhood, he claimed to be able to dunk a basketball, even though he was too short to come anywhere close to the basket. The challenge to stuff the basket had come from Fast Sam, Cool Clyde, and Gloria, who would become Stuff's best friends, along with other members of the group calling themselves the 116th Street Good People. The thirteen loosely connected chapters of this episodic novel recount events in the lives of these young people as remembered by Stuff a few years later. For all its humor, the book also makes some thematic points about the importance of friendship and the need to be able to rely on each other for support in difficult times.

Fast Sam (1975) was the first of a group of humorous novels—*Mojo and the Russians* (1977), *The Young Landlords* (1979), *Won't Know Till I Get There* (1982), *The Mouse Rap* (1990)—set in Harlem and based in part on Myers's own experiences and memories of growing up there. Myers had been born Walter Milton Myers in West Virginia but had been informally adopted by Herbert and Florence Dean, whose name he adopted after his first book. The Deans brought him up in the Harlem of the 1940s and 1950s, which was apparently a gentler environment than it would later become. Although the Harlem of his teenage years was also challenged by some of the ills often associated with so-called inner cities, Myers chose in these novels to focus on the everyday lives of ordinary teenagers mainly from stable, two-parent families in which at least one parent holds a decent job. When they get together, the young people manage to become embroiled in several neighborhood escapades, some of which were downright hilarious.

It is Myers's Black male voice that provides a good deal of the humor in these novels, and that is one of the distinguishing features of his work in this lighter mood. In part, the humor comes from his skillful use of Black vernacular English, through which he celebrates the verbal dexterity of Black urban teenage males. Myers's ear for this language is unerring, and he uses it to full advantage. His male first-person narrators and their friends display their linguistic prowess throughout their dialogue, which is replete with features that linguists describe as characteristic of certain Black vernacular oral discourse modes. Their oral exchanges are, for example, full of exaggeration, boasting, word play, outlandish images, and creative metaphors. Further, the narrators also use this same mode to address the reader, to relate the events of the story.

For example, here is Fred (Mouse) from *The Mouse Rap* (1990), as narrator, describing his friend Styx: "Check out Styx. He is six foot three inches tall. Did you hear that? Six foot three inches tall. He's so big that when we walk down the street I got to decide if I want to walk on his sunny side and cop some Vitamin D or his shady side to relax my tan" (7). Two paragraphs later. Fred describes, again as narrator, his own basketball skills: "Me I can hoop. I can definitely hoop. I ain't jamming but I'm scamming. You may look great but you will look late. You got the ball against me and you blink and all you got left is the stink because I got the ball and gone. I played one on one with my shadow and my shadow couldn't keep up" (7). In part, this language reflects the high value that is placed on oral performance within Black social environments, particularly among Black teenage males.

Myers's characters make use of other features of Black vernacular English as well, including "signifying," which is a specialized use of language closely associated with the Black community. One example of signifying comes in the first episode of *Fast Sam, Cool Clyde and Stuff* (1975), when Gloria tries to goad Robin and Binky into a fight: "You know, Binky, I think you were wrong. . . . Robin looks like a nice cat. I don't believe half those things you said about his mama" (37). Binky responds by identifying Gloria's comment as a rhetorical strategy, an indirect way to convey a nonliteral, partly hidden meaning, or an insult, and not a statement of fact: "I didn't say anything about your mama, Robin. She's just signifying, that's all." A second example reflects a more popular definition of signifying as a kind of ritual insult or round of insults, such as "playing the dozens," in which people say ugly things about each other's mothers or close female relatives—all untrue and mainly outrageous. Earl, in *Won't Know Till I Get There* (1982), has been lecturing his friends on what it is like to be old, when one of them challenges him:

"Well *how* you know, turkey? Hi-Note stepped right in front of Earl. "How long you been old?"

"Since I been running around with your mama!" Earl said in a mean voice. (57)

Given the identification of language features such as signifying and oral performances as characteristic of urban Black vernacular English, Myers's very effective use of those features, both in dialogue and narration, places these texts firmly in a Black cultural and literary tradition. His texts are related to, if not examples of, what renowned professor and critic Henry Louis Gates (1988) calls a "speakerly text," a text that seems determined to sound like an oral narration. They are also related to what Julius Lester calls, a "Black storytelling voice." Not since Arna Bontemps had an African American novelist made such effective use of Black vernacular in realistic novels for young people, and no one is better than Myers when it comes to reflecting the rhetorical styles of contemporary urban Black male teenagers.

The humor in these novels also comes in part from the escapades and situations in which the characters find themselves embroiled—Fast Sam and Clyde entering a dance contest with Clyde in drag; Paul and Gloria, as landlords, accidentally locked in a bathroom together as they try to fix a door; and the groups' attempts to "unmojo" Dean, who has accidentally crashed into the local "mojo woman" on his bicycle. Myers has shown himself to be a master at writing these kinds of scenes. Between the funny episodes, however, Myers's characters sometimes face serious issues, such as parental divorce, the drug-related death of an acquaintance, and concerns about being able to go to college. In these novels, Myers also introduces some of the themes that he would revisit through much of his realistic work. He explores relationships between fathers and sons, promotes the value of friendship, emphasizes the importance of Black people helping each other, and deals with—albeit humorously—the effect of race on encounters with police and other social institutions.

Focus on Hope

With his early lighthearted novels, Myers established himself as someone who could write authoritatively and skillfully about urban life from the perspective of one for whom the place others called the ghetto was simply home. Such a life is not always full of laughter, and Myers also wrote young adult novels about some of the serious issues faced by some Black urban teenagers. Books such as *It Ain't All for Nothin'* (1978), *Hoops* (1981a), *Motown and Didi* (1984a), *The Outside Shot* (1984b), *Crystal* (1987), and *Slam!* (1996) featured young adults searching for the strength to survive and make right choices in the face of situations or circumstances that often threatened to overwhelm them. Tippy, in *It Ain't All for Nothin'* is only 12, but when his grandmother dies, he finds himself living with his father, a virtual stranger who is a petty criminal. Motown and Didi discover that love can help them find the resolve to overcome their life circumstances, which include his homelessness and their attempts to save her brother from drugs. Lonnie, in *Hoops* and *The Outside Shot*, must find the strength to take advantage of the "outside shot" at making a good life that basketball affords him. In *Slam!* Myers returns to basketball as a metaphor for the game of life, which Greg must learn to play as well off the court as on. Crystal must decide whether to embrace the corrupt world of modeling or remain true to her own values.

In these books, Myers succeeds in making the city itself an integral part of the stories of his protagonists. Within that environment, however, he suggests that young people, who are portrayed with great sympathy and great compassion, always have the ability to make choices, to do "the right thing." Myers emphasizes, across the range of this urban fiction, not only the necessity for young people to take responsibility for their own choices, but also the necessity for the adults in the community to provide guidance and support for youth. In the same sense that Virginia Hamilton's liberation literature bore witness to the suffering of enslaved and oppressed Black people, Myers bears witness in these serious urban novels to the oppressive conditions that affect young people growing up in disenfranchised urban environments. As in the liberation literature, generally both the protagonists and the reader are left with a sense of hope.

Scorpions (1988b), one of Myers's Newbery Honor Books, has an ambiguous ending; if it is hopeful, that hope is tempered by a sense of loss. It is a story about choice and courage and the consequences of unwise decisions. It is also about how difficult it is to be a child in oppressive social circumstances. Twelve-year-old Jamal, as ostensible leader of his imprisoned brother's gang, is given a gun. Even though he is aware of the danger of keeping it, Jamal is unable to resist the sense of power the gun provides, particularly in light of the situations he faces and the pressures he feels. His brother needs money for his legal fees, his mother is struggling alone to support him and his sister, he is bullied at school, and the behavior of school authorities is reprehensible. The gang's plan to obtain drug money seems to offer a way out. At the same time, Jamal is still a child, daydreaming about the future with his best friend Tito. Inevitably, the gun leads to tragedy, and in the end, although both boys have survived, their innocence has not, and their friendship has likely become a casualty as well. Although there is room for hope as Jamal is left turning up his collar against the wind, the reader is also left with a sense of apprehension because the social environment in which Jamal is growing up, with its loss of so many traditional values, is antithetical to the survival of his spirit.

As Myers turned more serious in his novels and his books became more complex and layered, he received greater critical acclaim for his craft. One of his most highly praised books, the young adult novel *Somewhere in the Darkness* (1992), his second Newbery Honor Book, takes up one of the strongest thematic threads woven through Myers's work: father-son relationships. Even his first book had featured a Black father explaining night and day to his son and the son's friends. He also touched on that theme in the humorous novels as the boys complained about their father's lectures or had to resolve some minor conflicts on their way to gaining some insight into their father's perspectives. Tippy, Motown, and Lonnie all found surrogate fathers who provided much needed support in place of their own missing or ineffectual ones. (Incidentally, one of the strongest and warmest relationships in *Crystal* [1987] is between father and daughter.) Finally, in *Somewhere in the Darkness* (1992), Myers makes a father-son relationship the central focus. Jimmy Little receives a surprise visit from his terminally ill father, Crab, a prison escapee who wants to prove his innocence to his son before he dies. They take a trip together and their odyssey is for Jimmy a journey of self-discovery as well as a search for insight into his father, who is a stranger to him. For Crab, it is too late to change, but Jimmy is left with a legacy of hope and a sense of how, when the time comes, he can be the kind of father he would have wanted Crab to be for him.

Raising Moral Questions

Monster (1999), Myers's award-winning turn-of-the-century novel, was praised both for its innovative format and the complex moral questions it raises about guilt and innocence. Steve Harmon is sixteen and on trial for the murder of a drugstore owner who was killed in a robbery attempt. Steve is accused of being the lookout for the robbers and is facing a sentence of 25 years to life if he is convicted. An amateur filmmaker, Steve narrates his story through a combination of a script for a screenplay and his journal, which is presented in a typeface that looks handwritten. Through the film script and the journal entries, we witness the trial proceedings and obtain a sense of the stultifying and frightening nature of the jail environment. Throughout the dramatic trial, Steve is in part searching for himself beneath the label "monster" that the prosecutor has attached to him and trying to understand the steps that led him to this place. Even if he is judged "not guilty," he is not really totally innocent either, and the reader is left to ponder the extent of his guilt and the ways in which his life has been forever changed as a result of the choices he has made.

Monster (1999) raises moral questions through the choices and actions of one teenage individual, but *Fallen Angels* (1988a), a novel, and *Patrol* (2002), a picture book illustrated by Ann Grifalconi, both raise questions about the morality of war in general and the Vietnam War in particular. *Fallen Angels* is a coming-of-age story in which a young man from Harlem joins the military and ends up in Vietnam experiencing the horrors of war, finding the courage to survive the battlefield, and trying to figure out why he (and the nation) were there in the first place. In his acceptance speech for the 2003 Jane Addams Award, given to *Patrol*, Myers (2003) expressed his concerns:

How do we bring ourselves as caring human beings to accept the casual terror of war? How do we embrace the inevitable litany of injury and death? How do our hearts tolerate the images of young bodies being torn apart? How do we sleep when homes are being destroyed, when lives are being cheapened to faceless numbers?

In *Patrol* (2002), Myers raises these questions through the experience of a young soldier in Vietnam, encountering the "enemy" and recognizing that beneath that label are often merely frightened, war-weary humans. Face to face with another very young soldier, the protagonist sees only a reflection of himself and makes a split-second choice that validates the humanity of both of them.

There is a strong moral thread throughout Myers's urban fiction. His work is not preachy, however; his books can entertain and amuse, but at their core is a set of ideals, a deep love and compassion for children and youth, and his conviction that adults have a responsibility to instill in children the ideals and values by which we think we should live. He is particularly committed to make visible those children and youth whom he believes society tries to keep out of our consciousness:

It is this language of values which I hope to bring to my books. I would be the voice of those young adults who come from the same shadows of the past that I knew, . . . I want to bring values to those who have not been valued, and I want to etch those values in terms of the ideal.

Young people need ideals which identify them, and their lives, as central to the ideals. They need guideposts that tell them what they can be, should be, and indeed are. (1995, 132)

In this regard, Myers continues a tradition prevalent in African American children's literature and, to some extent, in much of children's literature in general. Literature for children and youth is often looked on as a vehicle for acculturating and socializing youth and helping them gain insight into what it means to be a decent human being in their society. One of the things Myers does is to illuminate and celebrate the culturally distinctive aspects of growing up Black in an American urban environment and in so doing captures something of the universality of that experience.

As one of the most prolific, versatile, and most talented authors in the field of children's literature, Walter Dean Myers has contributed immeasurably to the canon of African American and American children's literature. Across the body of his work, he has explored themes or topics that are central to African American children's literature: history, heritage, heroes, home, family, and community. His realistic novels convey his deep affection for Harlem and urban living; his deep concern for the welfare of young people, particularly African American teenage males; and his desire to provide for them a moral compass and a sense of hope. They also can remind adults of their responsibilities to these young people and to all our children.

THE SOUL BROTHERS AND SISTER LOU: "NEW REALISM" LANDMARK

I have tried to show some of the positive values existing in the so-called ghetto—the close-ness and warmth of family life, the willingness to extend help to strangers in trouble, . . . the natural acceptance of life's problems and joys—and there is a great deal of joy in the ghetto—and the strong tradition of religious faith. All of these attitudes have combined to create the quality called "soul." (Hunter 1968a)

Like Myers's first book, the manuscript for Kristin Hunter's *The Soul Brothers and Sister Lou* (1968b) had been one of the winners of the first writer's contest of the CIBC. Unlike Myers's and Hamilton's first books, however, *Soul Brothers* did not launch Hunter into a long career as a major writer for children or young adults. She did write a few other books for young people, but she is also a respected creator of works for adult audiences. *Soul Brothers*, which had been selected in the CIBC contest "ages 12 to 16" category, was the first widely popular, realistic, contemporary African American middle school/young adult novel. It is also noteworthy in that it featured a female protagonist since many of the "nitty-gritty" novels at the time were about urban males.

A forerunner to *Soul Brothers*, Mary Elizabeth Vroman's novel *Harlem Summer* (1967) had been published the year before. It is the story of 16-year-old John Brown Jr., who comes up to New York from Alabama to spend the summer with his aunt and uncle and earn some money. It touches on a number of themes and issues that were affecting the lives of Black adolescents at the time, both in the South and in Harlem: racist practices and their sometimes-tragic consequences, street crime and violence, conflicting views on how best to fight racism and its effects, and a sense of identity. Even though *Harlem Summer* was well written and provided a frank, realistic picture of life for a teenager in the Harlem of the 1960s, it did not capture the same kind of critical attention and popularity as other novels of the time that were exemplars of the tell-it-like-it-is new realism. In particular, it was overshadowed by the publication of *The Soul Brothers and Sister Lou* (1968b).

In *Soul Brothers*, Hunter (1968b) dealt with the lives of economically poor Black teenagers in "a Northern ghetto." Louretta Hawkins, the protagonist of *The Soul Brothers and Sister Lou*, at 14, is two years younger than John Brown of *Harlem Summer* (Vroman 1967), a significant difference in teenage years. Unlike John, Lou has lived under harsh conditions in a Northern city all her life, at the time of the novel in a five-room house along with her mother, seven siblings, and a niece. Her father had left the family a few years earlier after he lost his job and the Welfare Department refused to help the family as long as there was a husband in the home. Her older brother William is now the main breadwinner. Fearful of losing William's financial support, their mother discourages him from pursuing his dream of owning his own printing shop. Her sister Arneatha, a single mother, is self-centered and indulged by their sympathetic mother.

Lou's friends are a group of boys who are a part of a gang, although she opposes their gang activity and is not a gang member. The boys are also talented singers in need of a way to redirect their energies. Lou persuades her reluctant brother to rent a vacant storefront church for his print shop and to set aside part of the place, which has a piano, for a "clubhouse," where the young people can gather, meet, and sing. Lou can also sing and play, and with the help of Blind Eddie Bell, an old Black blues musician, she is introduced to the concept of "soul music." The young people have been continually harassed by some of the local police, and at a dance intended to raise funds to buy musical instruments, one of the boys is fatally shot by a policeman. At the funeral, the group sings a song with lyrics composed by one of the boys and set to music by Blind Eddie Bell. Their performance leads to a recording contract for the group, who call themselves the Soul Brothers and Sister Lou. This results in fame and wealth for the group members and causes profound changes in their lives. A sequel, *Lou in the Limelight* (Hunter 1981), describes what happens after their career takes off and they have to cope with people and forces that would divide and exploit them and their inexperience.

Given the portrait of Louretta's life and that of her family and community, the book fit well within the scope of what was called at the time the new realism—literature that broke away from traditional ideas of what was suitable content to present to young people in books. Traditionally, in literature for young people, for example, parents were idealized, endings were generally happy, and certain topics, such as divorce, drugs, and violence, were avoided. In contrast, *Soul Brothers* included teenage violence, police brutality, an unwed mother, an absent father, a fearful and ineffective mother, and some of the harsh details of living in urban poverty, almost none of which would likely have been addressed in a book for young people published a few years earlier. This is especially true since, with a fourteen-year-old protagonist, *Soul Brothers* would likely appeal to a middle school audience.

In addition to its focus on issues faced by teenagers across cultural groups, such as self-identity, *Soul Brothers* also placed itself firmly in a Black cultural milieu, focusing on themes and issues that derive from living in a race-conscious society, such as the role of racism in police interactions with Black citizens, differences among Black people regarding the best ways to fight against racism and discrimination, how to relate to White people of goodwill, and young people's search for validation in a world that devalues their humanity. It also focused on aspects of Black culture, such as relationships between Black sacred and secular music, Black religious practices, and the meaning of the concept of soul.

More than thirty years after its publication, *The Soul Brothers and Sister Lou* is still available for purchase. Although it is a bit dated, apparently it still resonates with readers who connect with its insider's view of life in an inner city neighborhood and with the plucky character of Lou, the dilemmas she faces, and the solutions she works out. Critics have found the ending to be too rosy and unrealistic, but for many readers it is likely very satisfying. In any case, this was the novel that launched African American literature for young people into the realm of contemporary, realistic, tell-it-like-it-is young adult books.

AFRICAN AMERICAN REALISTIC FICTION IN THE 1970s: FOCUS ON CITY LIFE

As was true of African American picture books, one of the strongest features of the 1970s contemporary realistic African American fiction was a focus on urban living, exemplified by Hunter's novel and by all of Walter Dean Myers's 1970s novels.

Virginia Hamilton's major urban novel, *The Planet of Junior Brown* (1971a), was also published in this decade. The emphasis on depicting life in inner city Black communities grew out of the convergence of several factors, among which were the urban upheavals of the late 1960s, the influence of the Black Arts Movement, and the emergence of the new realism in children's and young adult literature. The urban uprisings spurred the production of literature about Black urban children, especially males, while the new realism encouraged explorations of topics such as violence, drugs, and dysfunctional families. Black authors approached their urban novels from differing angles, some rejecting the new realism and emphasizing humor and the ordinariness of the lives of Black city children, others focusing on the challenges inherent in living in economically poor, underserved city neighborhoods. In any case, it appears that the major underlying thematic thrust was what Lucille Clifton had called "authenticating the world" of urban Black children by reflecting the realities of their lives.

One surprising effort in that direction was *Little Man, Little Man* (1976), James Baldwin's only children's book. Set in Harlem, it features four-year-old TJ describing his day, his observations, and the neighborhood ambience. Although the book is in picture book format and is illustrated with watercolors, at ninety-five pages it is too long for the usual picture book audience and not likely to hold the attention of those who could sit through it. Its significance lies mainly in its having been produced by one of America's foremost authors.

Other writers known for their works for adults also tried their hand at writing children's books in the 1970s, most with better success than Baldwin. Kristin Hunter, for example, produced at least two books in addition to *Soul Brothers* (1968b) and its sequel (Hunter 1981). *Boss Cat* (1971) was a humorous story about what happens when a father brings a black cat, which he names Pharaoh, to live with his family on the fourth floor of the Benign Neglect Apartments. *Guests in the Promised Land* (1973) is a collection of hard-hitting short stories, appropriate for young adults, that illuminate what it is like to be a "guest" in the Promised Land of America but never allowed to be a member. The stories relate how a variety of Black guests deal with that situation. The rest of Hunter's work is aimed at an adult audience.

Three of the most highly praised urban novels of the 1970s were young adult novels produced by Black women known for their writing for adults: June Jordan, Alice Childress, and Rosa Guy. The first, *His Own Where* (1971), by the late activist poet and essayist June Jordan, was named an American Library Association Best Book for Young Adults and a *New York Times Book Review* Outstanding Book of 1971. It was also nominated for a National Book Award. Aimed at the upper end of the young adult age group, it is the story of a teenage couple who make a place for themselves—ironically in a cemetery—where love can survive and even thrive in spite of the cruel circumstances that could easily overwhelm them. One of the most notable features of this brief novel is its language. Reflecting the Black Arts Movement emphasis on oral language, it was written entirely in a lyrical, stylized rendition of what Jordan called Black English: "His own where, own place for loving made for making love, the cemetery where nobody guard the dead" (7). Although it does not appear on many current lists of recommended young adult books, it is significant as one of the first modern African American young adult novels to receive such high critical acclaim.

Two important African American young adult novels appeared in 1973. Rosa Guy's highly acclaimed novel *The Friends* was the first book in a trilogy that featured three teenage girls, two of whom were members of a family of West Indian immigrants. The friends of the title are fourteen-year-old Phyllisia Cathy, whose family has recently moved to New York from the Caribbean, and Edith Jackson, a classmate struggling to care for her siblings with few financial resources and no adult support. When other classmates insult and bully Phyllisia because they resent her superior knowledge and see her as foreign and strange, Edith steps in to befriend and protect her. These two young women live very different lives, however, and their friendship is sorely tested when Phyllisia's father, Calvin, forbids his daughter to associate with Edith, whom he calls a "ragamuffin." In the face of their mother's death and their father's prideful and stubborn verbal and physical maltreatment, Phyllisia and her sister struggle to define themselves and their place in the family and in the cultural communities of which they are a part. *Ruby* (1976), the second book in the trilogy, focuses on Phyllisia's older sister. It is historically significant as the first young adult book to deal with lesbianism. *Edith Jackson* (1978), the final book, follows Phyllisia's friend as she struggles toward adulthood.

Part of the significance of Guy's trilogy, especially the first two books, is that they reflect something of the life experiences of Black West Indian immigrants in the United States. She explores some of the tensions that often exist between those immigrants and many Black people born in the United States. Calvin Cathy places himself above his Black American counterparts—"I ain't like these damn fool black people!" (Guy 1973, 28)—and tries to protect his daughters by keeping them close to home and limiting their social contacts. Phyllisia, on the other hand, is subjected to the scorn of her Black American classmates, in part because their teacher uses her scholastic achievement to belittle them. In a sense, Phyllisia's dilemma is the classic literary one of the immigrant child trying to find her way between two differing cultural points of view. Guy's books play that dilemma out in the context of clash between the life experiences of Black people from different parts of the African diaspora and thereby call attention to some of the cultural diversity that exists *within* Black America.

Rosa Guy followed her trilogy with at least six other books for children and young adults, including the Imamu Jones trilogy of mystery stories involving a teenage street kid from Harlem who finds himself suspected of crimes he did not commit and is forced to solve the crimes to clear himself. Guy is one of the very few African American writers who produce mysteries for young readers. She has continued to write for adults even as she has maintained a reputation as a highly respected author of children's and young adult books.

The other important African American young adult novel of 1973 was Alice Childress's *A Hero Ain't Nothin' But a Sandwich,* which became the basis of a film starring Cicely Tyson and Paul Winfield. Childress, a well-known writer, actress, playwright, and director, wrote the novel in response to an editor's request to produce a fictional book about drug addiction. The protagonist of *Hero* is Benjie Johnson, who is thirteen and hooked on heroin. In twenty-three chapters, Childress used ten different first-person narrators to tell the story, including Benjie's mother, his stepfather, his grandmother, a friend, the pusher, various school personnel, and Benjie himself. In addition to producing an honest, if disheartening, portrait of a thirteen-year-old drug addict who is in denial and spiraling downward, Childress broke new literary ground in African American young adult novels. Her use of multiple narrators, essentially a series of monologues rendered in an informal Black vernacular, was at the time uncommon, if not unique, in children's/young adult books of the time. *Hero* is compelling in its exploration of the complexities involved in the efforts to save Benjie, while the characters are at the same time endeavoring to solve their own problems.

While *Hero* was very widely read, it was not without its detractors. In keeping with the new realism of the time, Childress did not shy away from language that some adults considered offensive, including one or two obscenities and a racial epithet. Also consistent with the realistic fiction of the time, Childress provided an ambiguous ending, leaving Benjie's stepfather, who is the real hero in the story, desperately holding on to hope as he waits for Benjie to take a necessary step toward his own salvation. When authors of African American children's and young adult literature embraced the new realism, they opened themselves to the criticism that by appearing to highlight the sensational and the dysfunctional, they reinforced existing negative stereotypes of Black urban residents. On the other hand, their books also reflected the realities of some urban lives and for the most part stressed the strength of character that enabled the protagonists to prevail over their circumstances.

Sharon Bell Mathis also emphasized the strengths of African American children and teenagers. Like Walter Dean Myers and Kristin Hunter, Mathis launched her career through the CIBC Minority Writers Contest. Her winning entry, *Sidewalk Story*, was published in 1971, and during the 1970s Mathis became one of the most productive and well-received African American children's book authors of the decade, producing six other books, winning a Coretta Scott King Award for her picture book biography of Ray Charles, and receiving a Newbery Honor citation for *The Hundred Penny Box* (1975). She wrote for both primary and middle-grade readers (around eight to ten years old) and young adults. Three of her four best-known and best-received fictional books are set in economically poor and troubled urban neighborhoods, and her attention to the harsh living conditions place these books with the so-called new realism of the decade. Mathis's writing is also closely tied ideologically to her perspective on Black children and Black culture. In the author's note for her biography of Ray Charles, she asserts, "The triumphs of Charles are the triumphs of all Black people—a story of great will, of great strength, and a profound sense of survival." About her young adult novels, she declared, "Say the same thing about all my books—say that I write to salute Black kids."

Sidewalk Story (Mathis 1971), a book for younger readers, salutes the will and strength and determination of Lilly Etta Allen, a nine-year-old who is outraged when her friend Tanya's large family is evicted and their belongings placed on the sidewalk. When rain threatens to ruin the furniture, Lilly Etta gets up in the middle of the night and tries to protect it with her mother's sheets and blankets. A newspaper reporter, whose help she had unsuccessfully solicited earlier, discovers Lilly Etta asleep on top of the pile of belongings, and the resulting publicity brings the desired help. It is a story not only of the friendship between two girls, but also of the forces that affect the lives of poor urban residents. Evictions are not uncommon in the neighborhood. Tanya's mother is a single mother of seven unable to pay the rent because of the unavailability of affordable child care, making it necessary for her to stay home from work when the children are sick. Lilly Etta's mother feels helpless in the face of her friend's situation because she does not have the resources to help and cannot even store the furniture temporarily without defying the rules of the housing authority and risking eviction herself. Meanwhile, as the embarrassed adults concede defeat, Lilly Etta takes action, demonstrating that a determined individual can make a difference.

Mathis's two young adult novels focused on teenagers desperately trying to hold together a family. In *Teacup Full of Roses* (1972), Joe is coping with a drug-addicted older brother, a disabled and weak father, and a mother who is in denial about her favorite son's addiction and emotionally unable to show any concern or affection for any other members of her family. Joe's attempts to protect and provide for his gifted younger brother lead to tragedy, and Joe is left on his own to find the strength to survive and fulfill his dreams.

In *Listen for the Fig Tree* (Mathis 1974), Muffin's father, a taxi driver, had been killed in a robbery attempt. A year later, Muffin, who is blind but remarkably self-sufficient, is coping with a mother trying to drown her grief in alcohol. Muffin is also trying to be a normal teenager, planning to attend a Kwanzaa program with her friend Ernie. Just before the program, she is attacked on the stairway of her building, but her neighbor friends rescue her before her attacker can carry out his intended sexual assault. She attends the ceremony and comes away with a stronger sense of who she is and of her own strength, ready to move forward toward being a responsible adult and to meet the challenge of pulling her mother back from the edge of total despair.

In these two novels, as in *Sidewalk Story*, Mathis emphasizes the resilience of individual children and young adults faced with extremely difficult situations. She does not shy away from writing about the kinds of tough problems many urban young-sters were and are coping with (e.g., drugs, violence, ineffectual parents, dysfunctional families), but she suggests thematically that the youth are strong enough to overcome those problems and implies that they can find strength within themselves and within the Black community and its values. At the Kwanzaa ceremony, Mathis's narrator expresses, through Muffin's epiphany, a perspective on the significance of cultural Blackness:

To be Black was to be strong, to have courage, to survive. And it wasn't an alone thing. It was family. It was her father automatically trusting two Black men. It was a crumbling old man coming out of his safe place into a danger place. It was a man who knew everything and had everything, giving it to her, letting her butt into his life whenever she wanted. It was a preacher saying God was Black and you are God. It was a lady finding her life in other families, helping them. It was a boy being a man all the time. It was her mother. It was as precious as that. (1974, 170)

The concept of equating being Black with possessing the strength and courage to survive in spite of circumstances is the value that is presumably at the root of Mathis's writing for young people.

EMPHASIS ON FAMILY AND FRIENDS

In Mathis's *The Hundred Penny Box* (1975) the challenges of city living are not central to the story. The focus is on family and a determined nine-year-old boy's close and loving relationship with his 100-year-old great-great aunt. Aunt Dew had raised Michael's father after his parents died, and she is now living with their family since she can no longer live alone. One of Michael's joys is to count out the pennies in Aunt Dew's 100-penny box while she relates a story from each year of her life. Michael's mother wants to throw out the old box and replace it, but Aunt Dew insists, "When I lose my hundred penny box, I lose me." Michael makes it his mission to save Aunt Dew's box from his exasperated mother, who finds it difficult to please Aunt Dew and does not seem to understand the old woman's need to hold onto her own possessions. Even Michael is sometimes frustrated when Aunt Dew calls him by his father's name and insists on singing, and sometimes moving to, her long-favorite hymn. In the end, Michael can only assure Aunt Dew that he loves her. For the time being, their closeness and love for each other is enough.

Mathis's focus on family and specifically on the special relationship between a young child and a very elderly family member echoes one of the prominent themes of African American children's literature. Aunt Dew's role as family historian/storyteller is also characteristic, as is Mathis's attention to aspects of African American culture such as the well-known and well-loved hymn, "Take My Hand, Precious Lord." The book stands out for its honest handling of the tensions in the family around caring for a 100-year-old, particularly those between Aunt Dew and Michael's mother, and for Mathis's obvious respect and affection for her characters. The Dillons' outstanding watercolor paintings in shades of brown enrich the book and add to its distinctiveness.

Eloise Greenfield also published two children's novels focusing on relationships within families. *Sister* (1974), which was named an Outstanding Book of the Year by the *New York Times*, relates episodes in the life of Doretha/Sister from the time she was nine to her current age, thirteen. Through rereading her memory book, Doretha recollects, among other events, her father's sudden death and her sister's acting out and emotional withdrawal from the family. Doretha also remembers some of the good times and gains some understanding of how her life experiences have helped to shape the person she has become. Greenfield's other 1970s novel, *Talk about a Family* (1978), deals directly with divorce. Genny pins her hopes on her brother, who is returning home from the military, to put her parents' broken marriage back together. She eventually learns to accept the inevitable separation and to recognize that, although the configuration of her family has changed, the family has not been destroyed, and she still has a place in it.

Nikki Grimes also published her first novel in the 1970s. *Growin'* (1977) tells the story of Yolanda/Pumpkin, who writes poetry. It seems that only her father understands and appreciates her love of poetry, and when he dies, she is devastated. At a new school, she finds a friend in Jim Jim, a sensitive kindred spirit who loves to draw. Both Greenfield and Grimes would later become best known as accomplished children's poets, and it is in that genre that they maintained and extended their thematic focus on friends and family.

Another poet, Lucille Clifton, also produced two brief books during the 1970s that focused on friends and family and were as well precursors to the strong emphasis on recalling the past in the picture books of the 1990s. In *The Times They Used to Be* (1974), a mother, who had been called Sooky as a child, recalls events of her twelfth year, 1948, and time spent with her best friend, Tassie. The book is full of the vivid details of daily living at that time in the "colored" community of Cold Spring. It was an eventful year. Uncle Sunny, a veteran of the 92nd Division, chased a ghost nun off a bridge, television came to the hardware store, and Tassie "comes into her nature." It is a warm, humorous, and affectionate evocation of that time, framed as the memory of the now-grown-up Sooky.

Tee, the narrator of *The Lucky Stone* (Clifton 1979), relates stories told to her in childhood by her great-grandmother. The lucky stone was a shiny black one that had brought good luck to three generations of Black women. It seems the stone had helped save an escaped slave named Mandy, then had saved Mandy's daughter Vashti from a lightning strike, and had helped the great-grandmother meet her future husband. Tee relates how the stone had been passed on to her and the good luck it brought. This book also is full of warmth and humor, but one of its main features is the close and loving relationship between Tee and her great-grandmother, anticipating by a couple of decades an important thematic thread in African American picture books.

A SOUTHERN VOICE

As has been pointed out, almost all of the African American contemporary realistic fiction of the 1970s was set in Northern cities; even the few books that did not have an urban setting were set north of the Mason-Dixon line. One exception was *Ludell* (1975), Brenda Wilkinson's story of growing up in Waycross, Georgia, in the 1950s. It covers the years between fifth grade and seventh grade, when Ludell, who is being raised by her grandmother, experiences her first romance and learns to appreciate the joys and challenges of living in a close-knit community. The book paints a vivid picture of small town Black Southern life in that era—Ludell's strict, church-going grandmother (Mama) doing White people's laundry, a segregated school with some good and some not-so-good teachers, the large family next door struggling to make ends meet, the local store where people can run up charges, the caring neighborliness, the gossip, the small pleasures, and the disappointments.

One of the major strengths of the book is its voice. Although the third-person narration is rendered mainly in an informal standard English voice, both the dialogue and the inner thoughts of the characters reflect informal southern Black speech:

So she wouldn't spoil her appetite by watching Mis Rivers, who looked right doggish, Ludell turned sideways in her seat, only to discover Ruthie Mae, her next door neighbor and best friend, staring at her. Just as she was about to say something to her, she dropped a cookie. "Dog!" Ludell said to herself as she reached down to pick it up. "That Ruthie Mae done stared my food clean out of my hand!"

"You didn't have no money to buy nothing today, Ruthie Mae?" she asked, knowing obviously that she hadn't.

"I aine hungry," Ruthie Mae replied. (Wilkinson 1975, 6)

Many African Americans have Southern roots, and in *Ludell* (1975) Wilkinson captured, through her skilled rendering of Southern speech and a Southern Black community, a sense of the familiar. Wilkinson published two sequels, *Ludell and Willie* (1977) and *Ludell's New York Time* (1980). Although the third book ends up in a Northern city, Wilkinson's injection of a small town Southern setting was at the forefront of the expansion of the scope of African American children's literature that became a marker of the 1980s.

BIBLIOGRAPHY OF BOOKS FOR CHILDREN AND YOUNG ADULTS

Baldwin, James. 1976. *Little Man, Little Man*. Illus. by Yoran Cazac. New York: Dial.
Childress, Alice. 1973. *A Hero Ain't Nothin' But a Sandwich*. New York: Coward, McCann.
Clifton, Lucille. 1974. *The Times They Used to Be*. New York: Holt, Rinehart and Winston.
———. 1979. *The Lucky Stone*. New York: Delacorte.
Feelings, Tom. 1972. *Black Pilgrimage*. New York: Lothrop, Lee and Shepard.
———. 1995. *The Middle Passage: White Ships Black Cargo*. New York: Dial.

Greenfield, Eloise. 1974. *Sister.* New York: Lippincott.

———. 1978. *Talk about a Family.* New York: HarperCollins.

Grimes, Nikki. 1977. *Growin'.* New York: Dial.

Guy, Rosa. 1973. *The Friends.* New York: Holt, Rinehart and Winston.

———. 1976. *Ruby.* New York: Viking.

———. 1978. *Edith Jackson.* New York: Viking.

Hamilton, Virginia. 1967. *Zeely.* New York: Macmillan.

———. 1968. *The House of Dies Drear.* New York: Macmillan.

———. 1971. *The Planet of Junior Brown.* New York: Macmillan.

———. 1974. *M.C. Higgins, the Great.* New York: Macmillan.

———. 1976. *Arilla Sun Down.* New York: Greenwillow.

———. 1978. *Justice and Her Brothers.* New York: Greenwillow.

———. 1980. *Dustland.* New York: Greenwillow.

———. 1981. *The Gathering.* New York: Greenwillow.

———. 1982. *Sweet Whispers, Brother Rush.* New York: Philomel.

———. 1983a. *The Magical Adventures of Pretty Pearl.* New York: Harper and Row.

———. 1983b. *Willie Bea and the Time the Martians Landed.* New York: Greenwillow.

———. 1984. *A Little Love.* New York: Philomel.

———. 1985a. *Junius over Far.* New York: Harper and Row.

———. 1985b. *The People Could Fly.* Illus. by Leo and Diane Dillon. New York: Knopf.

———. 1987a. *The Mystery of Drear House.* New York: Greenwillow.

———. 1987b. *A White Romance.* New York: Philomel.

———. 1988. *Anthony Burns: The Defeat and Triumph of a Fugitive Slave.* New York: Knopf.

———. 1989. *The Bells of Christmas.* San Diego, CA: Harcourt Brace.

———. 1990. *Cousins.* New York: Philomel.

———. 1991. *The All Jahdu Storybook.* San Diego, CA: Harcourt Brace.

———. 1992. *Drylongso.* San Diego, CA: Harcourt Brace.

———. 1993a. *Many Thousand Gone.* New York: Knopf.

———. 1993b. *Plain City.* New York: Blue Sky/Scholastic.

———. 1995. *Her Stories.* New York: Scholastic.

———. 1998. *Second Cousins.* New York: Blue Sky/Scholastic.

———. 1999. *Bluish.* New York: Blue Sky/Scholastic.

———. 2002. *Time Pieces.* New York: Scholastic.

———. 2003. *Bruh Rabbit and the Tar Baby Girl.* Illus. by James Ransome. New York: Scholastic.

Hunter, Kristen. 1968. *The Soul Brothers and Sister Lou.* New York: Scribners.

———. 1971. *Boss Cat.* New York: Scribners.

———. 1973. *Guests in the Promised Land.* New York: Scribners.

———. 1981. *Lou in the Limelight.* New York: Scribners.

Jordan, June. 1971. *His Own Where.* New York: Thomas Y. Crowell.

Lester, Julius. 1969. *Black Folk Tales.* New York: Richard Baron.

Mathis, Sharon Bell. 1971. *Sidewalk Story.* New York: Viking.

———. 1972. *Teacup Full of Roses.* New York: Viking.

———. 1974. *Listen for the Fig Tree.* New York: Viking.

———. 1975. *The Hundred Penny Box.* New York: Viking.

Myers, Walter Dean. 1969. *Where Does the Day Go?* Illus. by Leo Carty. New York: Bobbs-Merrill.

———. 1975. *Fast Sam, Cool Clyde, and Stuff.* New York: Viking.

———. 1977. *Mojo and the Russians.* New York: Viking.

———. 1978. *It Ain't All for Nothin.* New York: Viking.

———. 1979. *The Young Landlords.* New York: Viking.

———. 1981. *Hoops.* New York: Delacorte.

———. 1982. *Won't Know Till I Get There.* New York: Viking.

———. 1984a. *Motown and Didi.* New York: Viking.

———. 1984b. *The Outside Shot*. New York: Delacorte.

———. 1987. *Crystal*. New York: Viking.

———. 1988a. *Fallen Angels*. New York: Scholastic.

———. 1988b. *Scorpions*. New York: Harper and Row.

———. 1990. *The Mouse Rap*. New York: Harper and Row.

———. 1992. *Somewhere in the Darkness*. New York: Scholastic.

———. 1996. *Slam!* New York: Scholastic.

———. 1999. *Monster*. New York: HarperCollins.

———. 2002. *Patrol*. Illus. by Ann Grifalconi. New York: HarperCollins.

Vroman, Elizabeth. 1967. *Harlem Summer*. New York: Putnam.

Wilkinson, Brenda. 1975. *Ludell*. New York: Harper and Row.

———. 1977. *Ludell and Willie*. New York: Harper and Row.

———. 1980. *Ludell's New York Time*. New York: Harper and Row.

CHAPTER 11

African American Contemporary Realistic Fiction: Focus on Teens and Preteens

Only a few new African American writers entered the field in the 1980s. In a sense, the decade in African American fiction was carried by Walter Dean Myers and Virginia Hamilton, who published at least sixteen novels between them in that period. But, five other writers also emerged as important voices in African American children's and young adult literature: Joyce Hansen, Candy Dawson Boyd, Eleanora Tate, Mildred Pitts Walter, and Joyce Carol Thomas. Thomas's fiction is mainly for young adults, but the other four took the lead in producing novels that shone a spotlight on the lives of African American children in late elementary and middle school. Their books are especially appealing to readers in about fourth through eighth grades, when children typically begin to establish their independence from parents and the peer group becomes increasingly important. Walter, Boyd, and Hansen all taught school at some point in their lives, and in a number of their books, school is an important aspect of the social setting. These writers also move away from the harsh urban realities depicted in many of the 1970s novels and expand the settings of African American children's novels beyond the East Coast and Ohio to Chicago, California, South Carolina, and Missouri. Oklahoma is the setting for much of the work of Joyce Carol Thomas, whose fiction demands recognition both for its prize-winning quality and for its distinctiveness.

During the 1990s, there was a notable increase in the sheer number of new children's books published annually—between 4500 and 5500, compared to 2500 to 4000 in the latter half of the 1980s—and a concomitant increase in the quantity of new children's books by African Americans, even though the percentage of such books remained at its usual low. With many more new books being published and greater attention to diversity in children's books, the field opened to several new African American authors who published realistic fiction for elementary and middle school readers in that decade. Among these were Jacqueline Turner Banks, Joyce Annette Barnes, Sandra Belton, Veronica Chambers, Debbie Chocolate, Joanne Hyppolite, Vaunda Micheaux Nelson, Andrea Davis Pinkney, and Sharon Dennis Wyeth. For the most part, their first novels did not launch these authors into literary stardom, but their books are solid contributions to the body of African American literature for an age group that is frequently neglected in favor of picture books for younger children and young adult novels for older ones.

The 1990s also saw the emergence of a new group of stars and rising stars—award-winning, critically acclaimed novelists who herald the future of African American children's and young adult literature. Among the authors in this group are Angela Johnson, Jacqueline Woodson, Rita Williams-Garcia, Sharon Flake, and Sharon Draper. Much of their work is aimed at young adults, although some is appropriate for children across several age ranges. Although most of them started publishing only in the late 1980s or early 1990s, already they are among the best-known contemporary African American writers of fiction for young people.

HIGHLIGHTING THE PRETEEN YEARS

JOYCE HANSEN: REFLECTING THE LIFE OF CITY SCHOOL KIDS

Joyce Hansen's urban novels continue the focus on urban living that was so popular in the 1970s. Her first published books were fictional stories set in contemporary New York City, where she taught school for twenty-two years. Like many African American writers, Hansen was interested in making visible children who had been neglected or omitted from mainstream American children's literature.

My aim in my first three novels . . . was to give those young people who rarely see themselves reflected in the literature they read, characters, settings and themes that they could relate to. I wanted to write about preteens and teens who are like themselves—having the same dreams, hopes, fears, pain and joy. And in *The Gift Giver* and *Yellow Bird*, I also wanted to show another perspective of a black, inner city urban community—a non-sensational, non-dysfunctional view. (1999, 62)

Her first novel, *Home Boy* (1982), is a young adult book featuring a teenager from the Caribbean who runs into difficulty while trying to adjust to life in the Bronx. It was based in part on the true story of a Jamaican immigrant who had stabbed another boy for teasing him about his clothes and accent. It was also inspired by some of the students Hansen had known and by stories her father had told about his life in the Virgin Islands. Like Rosa Guy's earlier novels, it called attention to the challenges and intragroup prejudices faced by many Black people who immigrate from the West Indies to Black urban communities.

Hansen's other two contemporary novels, *The Gift Giver* (1980) and *Yellow Bird and Me* (1986), which focus on the friendships between a young Bronx girl and some of her classmates, were aimed at younger readers. Although Doris is the first-person narrator of *The Gift Giver*, at its center is also Amir, a particularly sensitive and sensible foster child who is her fifth-grade classmate. His sound advice and quiet self-assurance help Doris gain self-confidence and deepen her understanding of her friends and family. By the end of the school year, Amir has become Doris's best friend, but his placement in a foster home upstate means he will be leaving the neighborhood. *Yellow Bird and Me* focuses on the following school year, during which Doris and Amir exchange letters, and Doris tries to resist Yellow Bird's persistent pleas for help with his schoolwork. Bird has a learning disability, and with Amir's urging, Doris becomes involved with helping him in spite of herself. When an actor-in-residence comes to school, Bird and Doris overcome their shyness and fear of failure to participate in the school play. By that time, Bird and Doris have become friends.

In these two novels, Hansen succeeds in representing realistically the everyday world of children similar to those she taught. In some respects—the circle of friends, the urban Black vernacular, the focus on the ordinary, the references to Black cultural experiences—these books are reminiscent of Walter Dean Myers's early novels, although Hansen's protagonists tend to be a bit younger. As Myers did in those books, Hansen chose to highlight the commonplace experiences of school, friendships, and family rather than the attention-grabbing issues that had played prominently in some of the urban novels of the 1970s. It should also be pointed out that although Hansen was among the first African American authors to create urban novels for upper elementary and middle school readers, she may be best known for her nonfiction histories and her historical fiction, which are discussed in Chapter 12.

MIDDLE GRADES, MIDDLE SCHOOL, MIDDLE CLASS: THE NOVELS OF CANDY DAWSON BOYD

During the 1980s Candy Dawson Boyd was the African American writer most consistently portraying middle-grade/middle school, middle-class African American children and their friends and families. With one exception, her main characters are girls, growing up, working out problems at home and school, with family and friends. Thus, she carved a writing niche that has served her well through the end of the twentieth century and beyond. Her first two novels are set in Chicago and revolve around two friends, fifth graders Mattie and Toni. In the first, *Circle of Gold* (1984), Mattie, who believes that her twin brother is their widowed mother's favorite, strives to win her own place in her mother's heart. She enters an essay contest to try to win the money for a special Mother's Day gift but, lacking confidence, persuades Toni to write an essay for her. Predictably, Mattie makes the right ethical decision on the essay, but more important, she develops a stronger sense of her own self-worth and an acceptance of her place within her family circle. Boyd has described the book as "a story about love, it is a story about love yearned for, love needed, love wanted" (1990, n.p.). It is also a story about friendship and growing up. *Circle of Gold* was chosen as a Coretta Scott King Honor Book.

Boyd's second novel *Breadsticks and Blessing Places* (1985), reissued as *Forever Friends* (1986), involves Toni's relationships with friends and family and her efforts to improve her math scores, but mainly it centers on her learning to cope with grief. Toni and Mattie are still best friends, but Toni also adores a new friend, Susan. When Susan is killed by a drunk driver, Toni is devastated, but with the help of Mattie and Mrs. Stamps, a family friend, she finds a way to say good-bye and move on. The novel grew out of Boyd's desire to recognize the depth of grief that children can experience:

When I wrote *Breadsticks and Blessing Places* I was angry because I did not find children's books that honored the fact that they grieve so deeply when they lose, and because I needed to write about love lost, because I had lost a child. And when I wrote that book, what I wanted to do was to honor children's right to grieve and their need to grieve and to also honor the voices of elders. I believe so strongly that we must act as elders for our children. (1990, n.p.)

In *Breadsticks* (1985), Mrs. Stamps fulfills the role of wise elder, an adult who is not the parent of the protagonist but who listens and gives good advice. Such characters appear frequently in Boyd's fiction, a manifestation of her professed belief in the importance of supportive, mentoring adults.

With *Charlie Pippin* (1987), Boyd shifted her settings to California but continued her focus on Black middle-class family life. Charlie (Chartreuse) is a strong-willed eleven-year-old who is prone to clash with authority, particularly with her father, a Vietnam veteran embittered by his war experience. As part of her research for a school report on the war, Charlie maneuvers her way to the Vietnam War Memorial. She returns with a gift that is the catalyst for a heart-to-heart talk with her father, during which each gains a deeper understanding of the other. *Charlie Pippin* not only deals effectively with family relationships, but also explores the larger social issues surrounding the Vietnam War, its justification, and its aftereffect on individual soldiers.

Boyd's writing career and her focus on Black middle-class life have continued well beyond the 1980s. In *Chevrolet Saturdays* (1993), Joey, her sole male protagonist, is dealing with the aftermath of his parents' divorce, including a new stepfather. As he reluctantly comes to appreciate his stepfather, he also benefits from the wisdom of another older male mentor, the owner of a pharmacy where Joey helps out from time to time. In part, this book is about learning what it takes to become a good man: working hard, standing up for oneself, making responsible choices, making up for mistakes, being honest. *Fall Secrets* (1994) and *A Different Beat* (1996) follow Jessie Williams as she experiences sixth grade at Oakland Performing Arts Middle School. She has a particularly close relationship with her grandmother, who is head of a repertory theater group. Jessie's main problem, in addition to keeping her grades high enough for her father to permit her to continue at Oakland Performing Arts, is restoring her self-esteem. Her sense of self-worth had been severely damaged by a cruel comment she overheard a teacher make comparing her unfavorably to her sister, whose lighter skin and straighter hair make her prettier and smarter in that teacher's eyes. With the aid of her supportive family, including her grandmother and her sister, she is able to face and overcome that hurdle and move forward.

Boyd's novels explore some of the common themes found in African American children's literature, such as the importance of family relationships and of elders. She also calls attention to the effect of color prejudice on the self-esteem of darker-skinned children. As do many African American writers, she injects some Black history and black cultural knowledge and attitudes into her fiction, especially in *Fall Secrets* (1994) and *A Different Beat* (1996). For example, Jessie's stage rival and friend, Addie Mae Cooper, whose idol is the famous dancer Judith Jamison, struggles to accept her family connection to Addie Mae Collins, one of the Sunday School children killed in the Birmingham Church bombing in 1963. Through her characterizations, Boyd also helps to expand the literary image of African Americans and African American families in children's fiction. The parents of her protagonists tend to be professionals, businesspeople, or white-collar workers. The grandmothers of her California girls are extraordinary, creative, and independent women. Charlie Pippin's grandparents are divorced but still good friends; he owns a store; she sells painted bottles at craft shows. Jessie's grandmother is head of a repertory theater group. Both artistic occupations are uncommon in African American children's fiction, and these modern grandmothers contrast to the more traditional portrayals found in most African American picture books. Boyd's books, like Hansen's, also have school as one of the important contexts, a step away from the home, which tends to be at the center of African American picture books, but not as far as the wider context found in many young adult novels.

SMALL TOWN GIRLS: THE NOVELS OF ELEANORA TATE

Eleanora Tate's children's novels also helped to enlarge the landscape of African American children's fiction. She set her stories in small towns in Missouri and coastal South Carolina, reflecting something of her own growing up years and her more recent place of residence. Although she published her first novels in the 1980s, she also has continued her career into the twenty-first century. As past president of the National Association of Black Storytellers, Tate has a particular interest in Black oral and folk traditions, which are reflected in her two story collections. In addition to her fiction, Tate has published nonfiction, a collective biography of Black musicians, and an American Girl "history mystery." Tate's writing tends to be purposeful; that is, in addition to its literary qualities, it is often a vehicle for passing on some African American history or cultural values or encouraging self-pride.

Two of Tate's children's novels evoke African American life in a small Missouri town. Her first children's novel was *Just an Overnight Guest* (1980), in which a young girl learns to accept a new child in the family. Four-year-old Ethel is half-White, neglected, abused, and undisciplined; she and her mother were social outcasts in both the Black and White communities. Margie is less than eager to have this interloper in her home and in her life, stealing the affections of her parents and embarrassing the family, but as the "overnight" stay looks more and more like a permanent one, Margie changes her attitude. Set in a small town in Missouri, this family story also explores various forms of bigotry and exposes some of the warts on the noses of small towns where everybody knows everybody else's business. The novel was well received and in 1983 was made into an award-winning film, which was shown on PBS's *Wonderworks* and *Nickelodeon*.

The companion book to *Overnight Guest* (1980) was *Front Porch Stories at the One-Room School* (1992). The setting recalls the one-room school in Canton, Missouri, that Tate attended before the local schools were racially integrated. The stories are loosely based on memories and experiences from her growing-up years. On a summer night when Margie is feeling terribly bored, her father sits on the schoolhouse steps telling stories to Margie and Ethel, who are now 12 and 7, respectively. Mr. Carson's stories are recollections of his childhood years at the one-room school. Some are funny, some are scary, some involve historical figures, such as Eleanor Roosevelt, but all are entertaining. The stories and the informal language bring to life a small Black community and its residents while offering some insight into Black history. The book also affirms the importance of the tradition of oral storytelling as entertainment and as a means to preserve and transmit history and cultural values.

Tate is probably best known for her South Carolina trilogy, which portrays life in a small southern Black community. The first book of the three, *The Secret of Gumbo Grove* (1987), does so with warmth, honesty, and affectionate humor. Gumbo Grove is a resort town in South Carolina with much of its history buried in old records and an old neglected cemetery. Raisin Stackhouse, a curious and spirited eleven-year-old who enjoys learning about history and heroes, helps to uncover some of the town's historical secrets, working closely with Miss Effie, the elderly church secretary who knows all about the town's early Black residents. Many adults in the community, including Raisin's parents, would rather keep the past buried in the old cemetery so as not to resurrect racial tensions, but in the end both Black and White citizens of Gumbo Grove come together to commemorate their shared history. The novel affirms the importance of history and the elders who preserve the stories of the past and pass them on.

In the second Gumbo Grove novel, *Thank You, Dr. Martin Luther King, Jr.* (1990), Mary Elouise Avery, best friend of Raisin's younger sister Mattie, struggles with issues of self-esteem. She longs to be friends with Brandy, whose long blond hair, blue eyes, and skin color Mary Elouise admires, in contrast to her own dark skin and larger lips and nose, which she has been taught are ugly. She is also embarrassed by the version of Black history transmitted by her teacher. With the help of her grandmother and two Black storytellers who visit their school, Mary Elouise learns to appreciate both her physical self and a more accurate version of Black history. As in the first book of the trilogy, one of the themes in this book was Black children's—indeed all children's—right to an accurate history and an acquaintance with Black heroes, an echo of Eloise Greenfield's "manifesto" (1975) on the functions of African American children's literature.

Tate's third South Carolina novel, *A Blessing in Disguise* (1995), features twelve-year-old Zambia Brown, who desperately wants to be loved by her father, "Snake," a club owner and drug dealer. Because her mother is hospitalized, Zambia has been living with straitlaced Uncle Lamar and Aunt Limousine and their daughter Aretha. Dazzled by the seeming glamour of Snake's life, Zambia wants to live with him and her twin half-sisters. Predictably, Snake hurts and disappoints her, but in her reckless zeal, Zambia also manages to hurt those who love her most. She almost gets herself killed before she and Aunt Limo, who is Snake's sister, realize that even though they may love Snake, he must not be allowed to destroy their family and their community. Tate's sympathetic portrayal of Zambia and the hard lesson she learns about life, love, and family is realistic, as is the picture of the community as a place where the good, the bad, and the ugly coexist, but where the good prevails.

In her Carolina trilogy, Tate provides an image of African American life in a small Southern coastal town. Raisin, Mary Elouise, and Zambia are all strong characters, and their communities are painted in vivid detail and with honesty. Tate clearly has a strong interest in African American history and culture and manages to weave aspects of both, especially local history, into the novels. She also has an obvious interest in nurturing the self-esteem and pride of identity in Black children, in part by helping them overcome color prejudice—the valuing of light skin and straight hair over dark skin and facial features and hair textures associated with African Americans. This issue is at the core of *Thank You, Dr. Martin Luther King, Jr.* (1990). A third thematic thread in Tate's work is the importance of community, which is particularly significant in the first and last books of the set. Tate's work confirms yet again the important thematic emphases that underlie much of African American children's literature.

MILDRED PITTS WALTER: THE DYNAMICS OF CHOICE, COURAGE, AND CHANGE

The fourth African American female writer whose voice helped to define African American children's literature in the 1980s was Mildred Pitts Walter, who actually published her first children's book in 1969. *Lillie of Watts: A Birthday Discovery* and a sequel, *Lillie of Watts Takes a Giant Step* (1971), grew out of Walter's response to a challenge thrown back to her when she complained to a book salesman about the lack of children's books by and about Black people. Set in Los Angeles, *Lillie* is centered on an eleven-year-old learning about the strength of family love and acquiring some pride in her identity. These two books were part of the emphasis on life in poor Black urban communities that was prominent in 1970s fiction.

From *Lillie*, Walter went on to create books in a number of genres, including picture books, young adult novels, and nonfiction. Her active commitment to and participation in the African American civil rights movement is reflected in two of her works, *Mississippi Challenge* (1992) and *The Girl on the Outside* (1982). *Mississippi Challenge*, a nonfiction book, describes the long struggle for human and civic rights in Mississippi from slavery to the mid-1960s. *The Girl on the Outside* focuses on the courage displayed by two high school students, one Black, one White. It is a fictionalized account of the dramatic confrontation that occurred when nine Black students desegregated Central High School in Little Rock, Arkansas, in 1957. Both girls find the courage to face an ugly, spitting mob, with the Black girl being assaulted for trying to enter the school, the White girl for coming to her aid. Two of her other young adult novels, *Because We Are* (1983) and *Trouble's Child* (1985), feature young women on the edge of adulthood who make choices about their future and take a courageous stand in the face of opposition from friends, family, or community. These two young women also learn to value their connection to the Black communities of which they are a part. *Trouble's Child* is particularly interesting in that regard because it is set on an isolated island off the Louisiana coast, and its inhabitants retain old knowledge, old beliefs, old superstitions, old language, and a resistance to change. Martha comes to understand that she can respect the traditional even as she widens her horizons. Both books were cited as Coretta Scott King Honor Books. Walter characterizes the main theme that runs through her books as "the dynamics of choice, courage, and change" (1992, 31), all three of which are readily apparent in these works.

In the same vein as Candy Dawson Boyd, Walter also has written for and about preteen girls. *Mariah Loves Rock* (1988) and *Mariah Keeps Cool* (1990) focus on an eleven-year-old coping with the challenges of growing up, including the introduction of a half-sister into the family. Walter's best-known, and in my view her best, novel for middle graders is *Justin and the Best Biscuits in the World* (1986), the 1987 winner of the Coretta Scott King Author Award. Ten-year-old Justin, the only male in the family since his father's death, cannot seem to do anything right in the eyes of his two sisters. As a result, he decides that housework is "women's work." His grandfather takes Justin to his ranch for a visit and teaches him that self-reliant men do perform household tasks. More important, Grandpa shows Justin how to do them well. Grandpa also teaches Justin how to make his prize-winning "best biscuits in the world," enabling Justin to impress his mother and his sisters with his new-found competence and confidence when he returns home.

The setting, a Missouri ranch, provides Walter (1986) with an opportunity to weave in some lesser-known aspects of African American history. Through conversations with Grandpa and their reading of a journal written by Justin's Great-Grandpa, Justin learns about the history of African Americans in the West—Black cowboys and homesteaders who moved West after slavery, sometimes in the face of resistance from Southern night riders. Walter has Grandpa tell Justin, "You must know where you've come from in order to find the way to where you want to go" (p. 84). This is a familiar sentiment in African American children's literature, expressed in various ways by authors and the narrators of their books and listed among the goals and purposes expressed by pioneers such as W.E.B. Du Bois and Eloise Greenfield.

JOYCE CAROL THOMAS: AFRICAN AMERICANS IN THE SOUTHWEST

Although most of her novels are appropriate for young adults, Joyce Carol Thomas also added a distinctive voice to African American youth literature in the 1980s.

In the previous decade, Thomas had published poetry and plays for adult audiences, but her first novel, *Marked by Fire* (1982), won the 1983 National Book Award. It tells the story of Abyssinia Jackson, who was branded by a stray ember from a brush fire, when she was born, surrounded by Black women, in an Oklahoma cotton field. Having been "marked by fire," Abby is destined to suffer both "unbearable pain and unspeakable joy," according to Mother Barker, the local healer. This reference to joy and pain echoes Tom Feelings's assertion that the interaction of those two opposites is a fundamental aspect of Black American culture. In part, Abby's pain comes by way of a sexual assault and the attempts of a crazed old woman to destroy her. But, she grows up surrounded by the love and support of a circle of women who help her to grow and to heal. The novel has allegorical elements—Abyssinia is the ancient name for Ethiopia; she was born to Patience and Strong Jackson, the daughter of patience and strength, descended from an ancient Black culture, surviving the storms of life. It is an extraordinary work, poetically celebrating African American sisterhood, the strength of community, the importance of tradition. Abyssinia's story continues in *Bright Shadow* (1983), which follows Abby to college, and in *Water Girl* (1986b), the story of Amber, who discovers her connection to Abby when she is a teenager.

Thomas grew up in Ponca City, Oklahoma, and much of her work, like that of Virginia Hamilton, is firmly anchored in her home place. This southwestern setting, with its fields and ranches, is uncommon in African American children's literature. It provides an opportunity for Thomas to depict lesser-known aspects of African American history and culture, such as Black cowboys and rodeo riders. One of her novels that brings that setting to life for a somewhat younger audience is *The Golden Pasture* (1986a), a coming-of-age story about Carl Lee Jefferson, the man Abyssinia falls in love with in *Bright Shadow* (1983). In *The Golden Pasture*, Carl Lee is twelve years old. He is the son of Rose Branch, a Cherokee woman whom he has never known, and Samuel, a Black man who is angry at life. Carl Lee spends summers with his beloved paternal grandfather, Grayson, who lives on a ranch and is full of stories and wisdom. Samuel has erected a wall of anger to keep him emotionally distant from both his father and his son. When Carl Lee rides a wild appaloosa in the rodeo, his performance becomes the catalyst for the reconciliation of the three generations of Jefferson males. Thomas's lyrical voice and her strong characterizations, along with the book's "cowboy" setting, make this a distinctive and appealing novel.

Since the 1980s, Thomas has explored other genres in children's literature, most notably poetry. She has also lent her poetic voice to board books for young children, and her love of Black gospel music has inspired her to write two versions of a gospel Cinderella: *When the Nightingale Sings* (1992), a young adult novel, and *The Gospel Cinderella* (2004), a picture book. She has even produced one of the few African American horror stories for young adults, *Journey* (1988), in which fifteen-year-old Meggie and her friends solve the mystery surrounding the disappearances and murders of teenagers. Meggie had been blessed in her cradle by a tarantula, and spiders play a role in helping her triumph over the villains. Although *Journey* is likely to appeal to a smaller audience than many of Thomas's books, its strength lies in Thomas's lyrical language and in the evident care and concern for Black youth that comes through the unusual plot. This lyrical style, which is part of Thomas's "Black storytelling voice" and her celebration of Black youth and Black culture, are markers of her work.

ENDING THE DECADE WITH *SHIMMERSHINE*

One other book, published at the end of the decade, bears mentioning. At the end of the 1970s, Camille Yarbrough captured in *Cornrows* (1979) the concern about African heritage, pride in identity, and self-esteem that was an important theme of that decade. At the end of the 1980s, Yarborough once again published a book that explores some of the same themes and values and offers what can be interpreted as a cultural perspective on the importance of literature as a way to illuminate the life of the people. *The Shimmershine Queens* (1989) is the story of Angie, a fifth-grade dreamer who, with the help of an elderly cousin and a drama and dance teacher, develops a healthy self-respect.

Like Zambia in Tate's *Thank You, Dr. Martin Luther King, Jr.* (1990), Angie is convinced—in part by the teasing of school bullies—that her dark skin and tightly curled hair are ugly. Also like Zambia, as well as Bird in Hansen's *Yellow Bird and Me* (1986) and Jessie in Boyd's *Fall Secrets* (1994), Angie finds strength and empowerment through the arts, recalling Greenfield's (1975) desire to "give children a love for the arts." Angie has other problems as well, including her father's desertion of the family and her mother's depression. It is ninety-year-old Cousin Seatta who offers the wisdom and perspective that enables Angie to overcome. Understanding that the negative attitudes toward dark skin and kinky hair, as well as an active rejection of school learning, are motivated by ignorance of "our story," Aunt Seatta tells Angie, "A people's story is the anchor dat keeps um from driftin, it's the compass to show the way to go and it's a sail dat holds the power dat takes um forward" (21). She then proceeds to give Angie a lecture on Black history, including the historical importance of education and the "get-up" gift that enabled enslaved and oppressed Black people to overcome. The feeling of empowerment that comes with knowledge and achievement or doing one's best is what she calls "shimmershine." In spite of its "blackboard jungle" depiction of the classroom and the distracting dialect spellings representing Aunt Seatta's speech, *The Shimmershine Queens* is significant for its explicit expression of the ideological stance that "a people's story" is a means to guide, direct, and empower the group, particularly the young.

THE BURGEONING OF AFRICAN AMERICAN FICTION

The last decade of the twentieth century was a period of expansion for African American children's fiction. At least nine "new" authors—Jacqueline Turner Banks, Joyce Annette Barnes, Sandra Belton, Veronica Chambers, Debbie Chocolate, Joanne Hyppolite, Vaunda Micheaux Nelson, Andrea Davis Pinkney, and Sharon Dennis Wyeth—published novels during the decade, most of which continued the emphasis on preteens. There were also a few young adult novels among their output. A number of the books of these authors appear to reflect something of the authors' childhood experiences and were set as far back as the 1950s and 1960s. They might be considered historical fiction, but their focus seems not so much on recreating a past era as on the characters finding ways to resolve the issues they face and remain whole in the process.

Because there is quite a bit of overlap in the themes and subthemes in their books, it is convenient to organize a discussion around those themes rather than individual authors. Four topics or themes seem to be of most interest to these writers: the consequences of racial integration or desegregation, self-esteem issues relating to class and color, the importance of friendship/peer relationships, and family relationships, including those within Black immigrant families.

STORIES OF DESEGREGATION/INTEGRATION

No Black child grows up in this society without encountering racism's harmful effects, in one form or another. Learning to confront and cope with hurtful comments or overt racist behaviors becomes one of the developmental tasks of growing up as a Black child. From the time of *Call Me Charley* (Jackson 1945), African American authors have written stories that call attention to the challenges Black families and children face when they pioneer in desegregating a school or a community and, more important, the means by which the children become empowered to cope successfully. Although one might wish that novels dealing with desegregating schools and neighborhoods might all be historical fiction rather than contemporary, that is not necessarily the case, and those stories set in earlier times are still relevant.

In the 1990s, Andrea Davis Pinkney, Vaunda Micheaux Nelson, and Joanne Hyppolite produced novels that involved Black children and families moving into schools or neighborhoods that were formally all White. Nelson's companion books, *Mayfield Crossing* (1993) and *Beyond Mayfield* (1999), involve a racially mixed group of children who are bused to a larger formerly all-White school when their own small village school in Pennsylvania is closed. All the Mayfield children experience bigotry at Parkview, but the Black children are marked for particular scorn and ugly name-calling. A baseball game becomes the means to settle a feud, and the book ends on a hopeful note. *Mayfield Crossing* is set in 1960, when Meg, the narrator, is in fourth grade. In the sequel, set a few years later, Meg encounters problems with a racist substitute teacher, and she and her friends continue to deal with bigotry, particularly from one fellow student. But events in the larger world also intrude on Mayfield Crossing. The older brother of one of Meg's White Mayfield friends is killed when he joins the Freedom Riders trying to register Black voters in the South. Thus, the book makes the case that the fight for equality is a national issue as well as the local one, and that all people of goodwill can join in the struggle.

Andrea Davis Pinkney's first novel, *Hold Fast to Dreams* (1995), is a more contemporary story that illuminates the ongoing nature of the struggle for respect, dignity, and social justice. Deidre's father's promotion requires the family to move from Baltimore to a Connecticut suburb, where twelve-year-old Dee and her sister are the only Black children in their classes. When Dee discovers that her classmates have not even heard of Langston Hughes, she knows it may be a long year. Her sister Lindsay tries to fit in by "acting White" and playing lacrosse but predictably that does not save her from racist cruelty. Dee eventually uses photography to establish herself in the new school environment. Their father, who is a vice president of his company, also encounters racism in the form of a hateful guard who harasses him until Mr. Willis makes it clear he will no longer tolerate the disrespect. With their father's example and the support of both parents, the girls find the strength to stand proud and refuse to be demoralized by other people's behaviors and attitudes.

Joanne Hyppolite's *Ola Shakes It Up* (1998) is set in suburban Boston. Like the Willis family, Ola's family has moved to a community in which they are the only Black residents. Not surprisingly, at school Ola and her older siblings encounter prejudice and fear, based on people's perceptions of Roxbury, their former home, as a poor and dangerous neighborhood. But, this fairly lighthearted book focuses mainly on nine-year-old Ola's efforts to "loosen up" the community rules. With the help of a few fellow "rebels," a rather precocious Ola succeeds in transforming the neighborhood into a warmer and more child-friendly place.

The parents in these novels play a major role in helping their children learn to cope. Living in different times and different situations, they offer somewhat different perspectives on how to respond to the racism their children encounter. Meg's parents in *Mayfield Crossing* (1993) believed that "prejudice" (they do not speak of racism) came from ignorance and admonished the children to avoid fights and not let others turn them into haters. Dee's parents encouraged their children to take a stand and refuse to tolerate disrespect. Hyppolite's lighter novel plays down the racism and emphasizes Ola's spunk as well as the interactions among family members. Clearly, helping children learn to confront racism has been a long-lasting concern of Black children's authors. One of Du Bois's goals for *The Brownies' Book* in the early 1920s had to do with teaching Black children "a code of honor and action in their relations with white children" (1919, 286). That Black authors late in the twentieth century were still treating the issue testifies to the extent to which racism endures as part of the very fabric of our society. As Du Bois had accurately asserted in 1903 in his book of essays, *The Souls of Black Folk* (1903/1969), "the problem of the twentieth century is the problem of the color line."

MATTERS OF COLOR: LEARNING TO LOVE ONESELF

Racism by its very nature is so insidious that some Black people have internalized negative attitudes, left over from the days of slavery, toward themselves and their appearance. Thus, lighter skin color and straight hair have often been more highly valued even among Black people than darker skin and kinky hair. The tradition of using literature to counteract such negative self-images and promote self-esteem among Black children has continued through the end of the twentieth century, as exemplified in books such Sandra Pinkney's *Shades of Black* (2000), and Eleanora Tate's *Thank You, Dr. Martin Luther King, Jr.* (1990). Like Tate's novel, Sandra Belton's *McKendree* (2000), which aims at an older audience, depicts a young woman overcoming negative attitudes toward her own dark skin. Fourteen-year-old Tilara is convinced that her dark brown skin precludes her ever being considered beautiful since her father has assured her that her cream-colored mother, who died when Tilara was two, was "the loveliest woman that ever lived." When Tilara spends the summer of 1948 in her father's small West Virginia hometown with her father's sister, she joins a group of teens volunteering at McKendree, the "colored" old folks' home. Aunt Clo, the old folks, and the teenagers all help Tilara gain insight into various attitudes toward skin color, its relationship to perceptions of beauty, and its irrelevance to goodness. Belton develops her themes of self-love and inner beauty through strong characterizations and the specifics of life in that small town in that time.

A related intragroup issue among African Americans involves attitudes toward people of mixed racial heritage. Historically, people with one Black and one White parent have been considered Black in this country and have identified themselves in that way, no matter what their coloring. An example appears in Joyce Barnes' novel, *The Baby Grand, the Moon in July, and Me* (1994), although it is not central to the plot. Because of his skin color, the child characters assume that one of the adult characters is White until they notice a photograph that shows his late wife as a "deep chocolate" in color. "But she's black," blurts out one of the children. "So am I," the man replies, much to their surprise, and goes on to explain his mixed heritage. The book is set in 1969; in recent years, however, many people of mixed racial heritage, particularly young people, have begun to resist categorizations that ignore their multiple ethnicities.

In *The World of Daughter McGuire* (1994), for example, Sharon Dennis Wyeth writes about a biracial child trying to define and come to grips with her ethnic identity. Eleven-year-old Daughter is of African American, Irish, Russian Jewish, and Italian descent. Her father is White; her mother is African American. At her new school, she makes friends but she also becomes the target of racial slurs (e.g., she is called a zebra). A school assignment motivates her to learn her families' stories, and her grandparents and parents help her to value her uniqueness and to develop enough confidence to stand up to a bully. As multiculturalism becomes more widely discussed, if not practiced, more literary attention is being paid to the concerns and experiences of mixed-race families.

GOOD FRIENDS AND POSSES: PEER RELATIONSHIPS

Most of the African American middle-grade novels of the 1990s were not centered on problems related to race. They depict the daily worlds of preteens and the problems that matter most to them—family, friends, and school. And yet, the issue of racism often hovers just below the surface. Jacqueline Turner Banks, Sandra Belton, Joanne Hyppolite, and Debbi Chocolate all wrote about the adventures of groups of two or more preteen friends. All except Hyppolite actually produced a series of such books. Hyppolite's lighthearted first novel, *Seth and Samona* (1995), which won the second Marguerite de Angeli Prize for New Children's Fiction, focuses on the friendship between a Haitian American boy and his adventuresome, self-confident fifth-grade girl classmate. Seth often wishes Samona would leave him out of her crazy schemes, but when she enters a beauty pageant and begins to act like a "normal" girl, Seth wishes for the old Samona. The children's antics are played out in the context of two families who are quite different from each other, but both loving and supportive.

Sandra Belton's Ernestine and Amanda series centers on two girls who are not quite friends. Set in the 1950s, the four novels are narrated alternately by the two girls, who never quite see eye to eye and sometimes bring different perspectives to the same event. Further, each one is dealing with her own problems: Ernestine is overweight, and Amanda's parents are headed for a divorce. In the first book, *Ernestine and Amanda* (1996), they are in fifth grade and taking piano lessons from the same teacher, ensuring that they keep running into each other as they prepare for a recital. They also compete to be best friends with the same girl. What they are unable to see is how much they really have in common. The other three books in the series—*Summer Camp, Ready or Not* (1997b), *Mysteries on Monroe Street* (1997a), *Members of the C.L.U.B.* (1998)—continue to explore events and situations that bring the girls together and offer them glimpses of a potential friendship, even as the tensions between them continue. The series follows the girls through to the beginning of seventh grade and chronicles Amanda's family problems, Ernestine's self-esteem issues, and some of the social issues that were part of the early 1950s incipient moves toward racial desegregation of schools and public facilities.

In this series, Belton very successfully goes about "authenticating the world" of middle-class and upper-middle-class Black children of the era. The books are full of the details of that world—college-educated professional parents; a mother involved in a major Black sorority; piano lessons, dance lessons, and summer camp for the girls; family involvement in church; learning about Black history; and so on. At the same time, many of the dilemmas and problems the girls face are familiar to those of girls their age across time and across subcultural divides; Ernestine and Amanda and their friends are recognizable as realistic American fifth and sixth graders. Divorcing parents, worries about physical appearance, relationships with siblings, and getting along with peers are familiar aspects of the lives of many preteens. Belton's characters have dimension, and their world is described in convincing detail, elevating the quality of the books well above that of typical formulaic series.

Jacqueline Turner Banks's series of books, set in a small town in Kentucky, involve an interracial "posse" of sixth graders—Angela Collins and twins Judge and Jury Jenkins, who are African Americans; Tommy Masaki, who is Japanese American; and Faye Bennick, who is Caucasian (Banks 1993, 1994, 1995). Each book in the series is narrated by one of the posse members. The plots involve such events as Angela's fundraising project to help a paralyzed classmate, the twins dealing with their mother's new boyfriend as a new student brings tension to the group, Judge's efforts to bring up his science grade, and Tommy's initiation into the importance of civic action.

Banks's books are light, entertaining, and often humorous, although clearly they also sometimes deal with serious issues. It is interesting to note the similarity between the humorous names Judge and Jury and character names of an earlier time, such as Sears and Roebuck, which have raised a few questioning eyebrows, including mine. Perhaps enough time has passed, in Banks's view, to permit African American authors to engage in the sort of humor that in earlier years was used for ridicule. On the other hand, Banks does not ignore the presence of racism, even as she tends not to make it the central problem of her books.

Similarly, Just Us Books has published a series about a posse of African American preteens who call themselves NEATE. Naimah, Anthony, Elizabeth, Tayesha, and Eddie are the posse members, whose initials form the name of their group. In their first book, written by Debbi Chocolate, *NEATE to the Rescue* (1992), Naimah's mother finds her city council seat in jeopardy, threatened by an unscrupulous political opponent who does not hesitate to use the race card to frighten White suburban voters. Naimah and friends provide just the help that Mrs. Gordon needs to win the election. Shorter and lighter in tone than Belton's series, this one is similar in that it focuses on a diverse group of Black families. Naimah's father is a lawyer, Anthony's single mother works for a newspaper, Tayesha is the daughter of an African American factory foreman and a German-American woman, Liz's father buys her all kinds of material things, and Eddie's family believes strongly that education is the road to success. Other NEATE books focus on other members of the posse. These kinds of books are appealing because they offer a mirror in which African American preteens who are not yet ready to tackle more complex literary works can find reflections of themselves, their friends, and their lives.

PRETEENS AND THEIR FAMILIES

In her three middle-grade novels, Johniece Marshall Wilson also writes about the family lives of contemporary African American preteens. In *Oh, Brother* (1988),

Alex and Andrew have to work out a way to resolve their sibling rivalry. In *Robin on His Own* (1990), a boy has to come to grips with his mother's death, and in a much lighter vein, Miranda in *Rich Girl, Poor Girl* (1992) is determined to earn money to buy contact lenses and get rid of her ugly glasses. Wilson's books received mixed reviews, but at the very least, like the books about peer groups, they helped to enlarge the choices available to middle-grade readers—particularly African American ones—looking for accessible books in which they could recognize something of themselves.

Joyce Annette Barnes wrote two novels about a young African American girl who dreams of becoming an astronaut. *The Baby Grand, the Moon in July, and Me* (1994) opens when Annie is ten and brimming with excitement about NASA's moon mission. She is distracted when her nineteen-year-old brother Matty, a jazz musician, purchases a grand piano without his parents' knowledge, and their furious father throws Matty out of the house. Through her friendship with an elderly neighbor who owns a concert grand piano, Annie arranges a neighborhood concert that brings Matty and their father together.

In the sequel, *Promise Me the Moon* (1997), Annie is thirteen and visiting Matty and his wife in New York City. Her dilemma is how and whether to prepare herself for admission to one of the finest high schools in the state, but she is worried about being called an "egghead" and dealing with typical eighth-grade romance. Annie is a spunky and likeable character; her problems and dilemmas are centered on growing up in a loving and supportive, if strict and imperfect, family. Like many of these middle-grade/middle school books, this one portrays a hard-working, upwardly mobile Black family living in a stable community, with a father working two jobs and a mother working as a secretary. It is basically about holding fast to one's dreams.

Like many similar American middle-grade books, these books about African American posses and family interactions are generally light reading not likely to join the ranks of twentieth century classics. Nevertheless, they perform the important function of expanding the range of African American children's literature by offering accessible reading that reflects the lives and experiences of ordinary African American preteens in a variety of familiar situations.

FAMILIES FROM THE DIASPORA

In the 1980s, Rosa Guy and Joyce Hansen produced novels that focused on the experiences of Black families who had emigrated from the Caribbean. In *Seth and Samona* (1995), Joanne Hyppolite focused on a Haitian American family. The novel is filled with linguistic and cultural references to their Haitian background. The family names and titles, the Haitian Kreyol verbal expressions, the food, and the religious practices all speak to Seth's family's cultural roots.

Veronica Chambers, in *Marisol and Magdalena* (1998) and its sequel *Quinceañera Means Sweet 15* (2001), reflects the worlds of two Brooklyn-born Latinegra (Black and Latina) best friends whose families are from Panama. In the first book, Marisol, who narrates both books, is sent off to Panama to live with her grandmother for a year so that she can get in touch with her roots, and so that her single working mother does not have to worry. In the second, the girls prepare for their traditional fifteenth birthday celebrations. Both books are filled with Spanish words and phrases and numerous cultural details, including food and family values and interactions. Chambers's books call attention to the diversity to be found within the larger

Black community in the United States. As the number of immigrants from Latin America, the West Indies, and the African continent increases and their impact is felt in schools and communities, it is likely that the number of books featuring people from all parts of the African diaspora will also increase, further diversifying the body of Afrocentric literature for children and young adults.

THE "NEW GENERATION": STARS AND RISING STARS

In the 1990s, approximately one generation removed from the birth of modern African American children's literature, a new wave of African American writers emerged and began to garner critical acclaim. Most of them were still children when *Zeely* (Hamilton 1967) was published, and more than a quarter of a century later, it is interesting to note the similarities and differences between their work and that of writers who started writing decades earlier. Although these writers explore some issues that were uncommon a generation before them (e.g., sexuality, sexual orientation), they also focus on family, self-esteem, and peer relationships. Most of these authors write in more than one genre, but for the most part, they have become best known for their young adult books. In that regard, they join Walter Dean Myers as premier African American young adult authors. Among the best known of this new wave of writers are Angela Johnson, Jacqueline Woodson, Rita Williams-Garcia, Sharon Draper, and Sharon Flake.

ANGELA JOHNSON: NOVELS OF LONGING, LOSS, AND HOPE

As has been pointed out, MacArthur Fellow Angela Johnson was, by virtue of the number of picture books she published, the dominant voice in African American picture books in the 1990s. By the end of the decade, she was also well on her way to becoming one of the most noteworthy African American young adult novelists. *Toning the Sweep* (1993), her first novel, won the 1994 Coretta Scott King Author Award. Since then, she has received two other Coretta Scott King author awards, and her lyrical and moving young adult novel, *The First Part Last* (2003), won the 2004 Michael Printz Award. Johnson has been both versatile and productive; her output includes numerous picture books, a few board books for young children, short stories, middle-grade "chapter books," a couple of poetry collections, and several young adult novels.

Like Virginia Hamilton, Johnson has a distinctive voice and an imagination that takes her in unusual directions. Although her work is generally rooted in African American life, Johnson does not echo, in her statements about her writing, Hamilton's desire to "portray the essence" of African Americans as a parallel culture people in America. Johnson most often treats race/culture as a given and reaches from that foundation to explore themes and topics that command her attention and that affect people across cultures. As in her picture books, however, one of Johnson's strongest themes, which is also prevalent in African American children's literature in general, is the importance of family—however defined—as a source of support and love.

Johnson also writes often about loss. In the preface to her collection *The Other Side: Shorter Poems* (1998c), she wrote about the attractions that poetry held for her as a teenager: "Poetry was immediacy and spoke to longing, loss, hope, and absurdity." Some of those themes—longing, loss, hope—seem also to be central to much of Johnson's fiction. *Toning the Sweep* (1993) is set in the California desert, where Emily's grandmother, Ola, lives. Ola has been diagnosed with cancer and is preparing to go to Cleveland to spend her last days with her daughter and grand-daughter. Emily spends her time in California videotaping Ola, her friends, and her desert, saving her grandmother's happy memories to take back East. The novel's title refers to a Southern tradition of tolling a death knell by banging on a kind of plow with a hammer. It relates to events in Alabama, where Ola had lived until her husband's tragic death in 1964. Before they leave the desert, Emily and her mother find their own way to belatedly sound a death knell for their father and grandfather and thereby achieve a certain degree of closure. The story of the grandfather's murder by White racists plants this novel firmly in an African American context. At the same time, it is a powerful three-generation story of life and death, of love and loss, of family and friends.

Johnson published three other novels in the 1990s. *Humming Whispers* (1995) explores the effect of mental illness on the family members of the sufferer. Sophy is fourteen, just the age her sister Nikki was when she started hearing voices and was diagnosed as schizophrenic. Sophy loves her sister but fears that she also may be schizophrenic. Aunt Shirley, who has taken care of the girls since their parents died in an automobile accident, helps Sophy understand that sometimes there is nothing they can do when her sister runs away but wait and hope and continue to love her. Sophy also finds solace in dance and support from an aging neighbor, who is a Holocaust survivor and former dancer. Nikki's devoted boyfriend also offers steadfast hope. Mental illness is an uncommon topic in African American children's fiction, but Johnson's focus is on the importance of hope and the necessity to remain connected to each other.

In *Songs of Faith* (Johnson 1998c), Doreen and her brother are reeling from their parent's divorce and their father's move to Chicago. It is 1975, the year before the American Bicentennial, but the closing of the mill and the lack of jobs make for an atmosphere that is anything but festive. Doreen's mother says that the town of Harvey, Ohio, is becoming a place full of just-divorced women and their children. Doreen, Robert, their friend Jolette, and the grown-ups all find their own ways of coping, while the children learn that love endures and sustains, even in the midst of change and loss.

In *Heaven* (Johnson 1998a), the thematic focus on longing and loss is played out in the context of defining the meaning of *family*. Heaven is the town in Ohio in which Marley, who is fourteen, is living with her Mom, Pops, and little brother. But, Heaven feels like its opposite when Marley learns that her parents are not her biological parents. She also learns about the tragic death of her birth mother and the identity of her biological father. She is then faced with the problem of working through her anger over not being told the truth earlier and figuring out who she is now and what constitutes a family, really.

Johnson has also published a collection of twelve short stories, *Gone from Home: Short Takes* (1998b), featuring teenagers who are, in one sense or another, outsiders, whether literally homeless or simply misfits in their environment. Like her early poetry, these stories speak to "longing, loss, hope, and absurdity" in voices that teenagers will recognize and understand.

The First Part Last (2003) is unusual in that it focuses on a teenage father who has taken responsibility for raising his daughter. His parents, though supportive, have made it clear that they will not raise the child for him. The story is told in alternating "now" and "then" chapters, in which we see Bobby, who is sixteen, coping with the nearly exhausting demands of caring for an infant while attending school, and we learn about the relationship between Bobby and the baby's mother, Nia. Not until late in the novel do we learn that Nia is in an irreversible coma as a result of complications during birth and understand why Bobby chose not to put the baby up for adoption. Possibly the most striking feature of the book is Johnson's writing, which is poetic and beautiful.

One of the most distinctive elements of Johnson's writing, in fact, is her spare lyrical voice. She is a poet at heart, and it is the poetic quality of her work that makes it so vivid and appealing. If she seems preoccupied with longing and loss, she also is convincing in her apparent conviction that human connections—especially family connections and love—are a major source of support, sustenance, and hope for young people. Her books and stories reaffirm for readers the power of love to help us get through pain.

JACQUELINE WOODSON: CONFRONTING SOCIAL ISSUES

Another versatile and prolific new-generation writer who has won widespread and well-deserved critical acclaim is Jacqueline Woodson. Although she is probably best known as a young adult author, Woodson's first published novel was part of a trilogy for upper elementary/middle school readers. She has also published several picture books, one of the most popular of which is *The Other Side* (2001), which features two girls, one Black and one White, defying the unwritten adult social rules to cross over the literal and metaphorical fence that divides them on the basis of race. The interesting angle in this book is that, contrary to the traditional pattern in books of this type, the Black child takes the lead in reaching out.

Race is not the only issue of interest to Woodson; her work speaks to other matters that are of concern to her but were never discussed in the literature she read as a child. Although Woodson writes about social issues, some of which are controversial, hers are not typical "problem novels." She is noted for writing well-crafted, compelling novels with strongly delineated and multidimensional characters. Two of Woodson's novels, *From the Notebooks of Melanin Sun* (1995) and *I Hadn't Meant to Tell You This* (1994), received Coretta Scott King Honor citations. Woodson also received the Coretta Scott King Author Award for *Miracle's Boys* (2000), which has become the basis for a television series.

Woodson's first novel, *Last Summer with Maizon* (1990), engaged the issue of how best to nurture gifted Black girls. Along with *Maizon at Blue Hill* (1992) and *Between Madison and Palmetto* (1993), it formed a trilogy featuring Maizon and Margaret, best friends who live in Brooklyn. In the first book, Margaret grieves the death of her father and dreads facing the new school year without Maizon, who has won a scholarship to an exclusive private school in Connecticut. Although she misses her friend terribly, during Maizon's absence Margaret discovers her own gift as a writer. Maizon meanwhile cuts short her stay at Blue Hill when she finds that, as one of only five Black girls, she is socially isolated, and that both class and race matter much too much. She returns to Brooklyn, where she can count on the support of family and friends.

Maizon at Blue Hill (Woodson 1992) gives Maizon's account of her time away at the private school. Although the academic environment was challenging, it was also rich, and Maizon was not stymied by the work. What was difficult for her was encountering classism and elitism among the few Black students as well as the White ones. Maizon's decision to return home to a nurturing environment is presented as reasonable under the circumstances rather than as a failure.

Besides, both she and Margaret can now attend a public school for gifted children right in the city.

Between Madison and Palmetto (Woodson 1993), which takes place the following year when both girls are at Pace Academy, reaffirms the importance and permanence of their friendship. It is a difficult year, during which the girls cope with changes around them. Their bodies are changing; the neighborhood is becoming somewhat gentrified, they acquire a new White friend, and Maizon's long absent father makes an appearance. Although the issue of cultivating the intellectual and creative gifts of Black children is central to these novels, the importance and value of friendship is the overriding theme, and it is approached with honesty and sensitivity.

Woodson's second novel established her as a talented young adult novelist. In *The Dear One* (1991), Feni, who is twelve, Black, and privileged, must adjust to the presence of the underprivileged and pregnant fifteen-year-old daughter of one of her mother's friends. Her mother, a business executive, has invited Rebecca, a streetwise young woman from Harlem, to spend the last weeks of her pregnancy in their suburban home. Both girls resent the arrangement, but they are surrounded by a group of strong, caring Black women, long-time friends who provide support for each other and the two girls. Woodson highlights several issues in this book. Teenage pregnancy would seem to be at the center, but there is also homophobia (a couple of Feni's mother's friends are lesbians), alcoholism (recovering friends), and a look at class differences. Again, however, the book is much more than an "issues" book; its central focus is how this group of strong Black women and girls sustains their own small community of support.

Attitudes toward homosexuality play a more central role in Woodson's *From the Notebooks of Melanin Sun* (1995). Melanin Sun, named for his dark skin, has a close and loving relationship with his single mother until she informs him that she is in love with a White woman. Melanin is at first outraged since his world seems to have shattered, but in the end his love for his mother and his own strength of character enable him to accept the situation and begin to move forward. In *The House You Pass on the Way* (1997), Staggerlee and her cousin Trout, both of whom are fourteen, spend a summer together and find themselves questioning their identities, wondering if they are gay. Staggerlee, biracial and socially isolated, remembers with pleasure having kissed a girl in sixth grade. She and Trout share their secrets and develop an intimacy of their own. When Trout goes home and writes that she has fallen in love with a boy, Staggerlee is able to acknowledge that she and Trout are probably moving along different life paths, but that both are strong and growing.

One of the issues in *The House You Pass* (1997) is prejudice against interracial marriage. In *If You Come Softly* (1998), an interracial relationship is at the center of the novel. Jeremiah (Miah) and Ellie, both fifteen, meet at an elite New York City prep school. He is Black, the son of famous, well-to-do, but newly separated parents; she is White, Jewish, and struggling with her mother's desertion of the family. They fall in love at first sight and tell their story in alternating voices. The couple appears to be coping successfully with the problems the world throws at them, but tragedy strikes nevertheless, leaving the reader stunned, if not surprised, since the story is told in flashback.

In *I Hadn't Meant to Tell You This* (1994) and *Lena* (1999), Woodson takes on the issue of incest/sexual abuse. Marie and Lena are both living with their fathers—Lena's mother died of breast cancer; Marie's has gone off to "find herself." In a reversal of the usual characterizations, Marie is the privileged, popular daughter of a Black college professor, while Lena is poor and considered in the community to be "White trash." Possibly because of the shared experience of absent mothers and in spite of class and race differences and the bigotry of their fathers and their peers, Marie and Lena become close friends. As their friendship grows, Lena confides the terrible secret that her father is sexually molesting her, but extracts Marie's promise not to tell. When her father starts to abuse her little sister, however, Lena takes her sister and runs away. The companion book follows the journey of the resourceful Lena and her sister, Dion, as they hitchhike their way from Ohio to Kentucky, surviving in part because of the kindness of strangers, and finally find shelter with a caring Black woman who looks after their needs and sees to it that they land back in Ohio in a safe and nurturing environment where all three girls can grow and prosper.

In *Miracle's Boys* (2000), Woodson tells the story of three brothers trying to survive on their own in New York City. Their father died of hypothermia after rescuing a woman and her dog from a pond in Central Park; their mother died of diabetes. Ty'ree, the oldest, gives up his college dreams to keep the family fed, sheltered, and together. Charlie had been in a correctional facility serving time for armed robbery when their mother died. He returns home angry, guilt ridden, and a near stranger to his younger brother, Lafayette, who blames himself for not being able to prevent his mother's death. The odds are against them, and their struggle is difficult, but "brother to brother to brother" they can overcome.

If Woodson's work is issue oriented, it is never superficial. If it is edgy, it is also emotionally honest. Her characters have depth, and the situations they face are complex. She is able to find just the right voice for each of her first-person narrators, and her own voice is sometimes poetic and lyrical. She does not shy away from difficult and complex issues and does not reach for easy solutions. While she writes about friendship and family, she also encourages her readers to examine and reject bigoted assumptions based on differences related to race, class, and sexuality.

RITA WILLIAMS-GARCIA: YOUNG ADULTS TRANSITIONING TO ADULTHOOD

A third powerful voice in newer African American young adult fiction is that of Rita Williams-Garcia. To date, she has published five novels and one picture book. Except for the last one, her novels are unmistakably aimed at young adults. Her first, *Blue Tights* (1988), focused on a fifteen-year-old aspiring dancer whose high school dance teacher informs her that her physique is not suitable for classical ballet. (The original title of the novel was *Blue Tights, Big Butt.*) When Joyce stumbles on a dance troupe specializing in African dance, she has found her home as a performer, and the confidence she gains as a result enables her to take necessary steps toward becoming a responsible and independent adult.

Williams-Garcia's second novel, *Fast Talk on a Slow Track* (1991), features a Black teenage young adult coping with his first experience of academic failure. He has been accepted at Princeton but has done poorly in their summer program for "minority" students. He has returned home to his summer sales job, where he achieves success without half trying, determined not to return to Princeton. It is not an enjoyable summer, but it is a time when he can learn to confront his failures and find a way to move forward. Williams-Garcia is able to capture the language of these urban teenagers as well as their perspective on life.

Williams-Garcia's compelling novel *Like Sisters on the Homefront* (1995) not only confronts the issue of teenage pregnancy but also reflects some of the traditional characteristics of African American children's/young adult literature. At fourteen, Gayle already is the mother of a seven-month-old, and when her mother discovers that Gayle is pregnant again, she marches her off to an abortion clinic and then sends her and her son off to Georgia to live with the mother's family. Gayle's uncle is a pastor, and his daughter Cookie is "country" and innocent, a stark contrast to the feisty, poorly educated, streetwise, sexually experienced Gayle. It takes a while and a number of clashes before Gayle is able to begin to appreciate her cousin and her aunt and uncle, but she gets along well with Great, her great-great-grandmother, who sees in Gayle a kindred spirit. And Great, the family "griot," chooses Gayle to be the next keeper of the family history and link to both the past and the future. *Like Sisters* includes many recognizable elements that appear in African American literature: the journey "down home," the focus on family connections, the emphasis on knowing the past in order to be prepared for the future, the importance of religion and spirituality, the respect for the elderly, and the elder in the role of "culture keeper." In addition, the dialogue feels authentic, and Williams-Garcia has portrayed her characters and their emotions honestly and realistically in this beautifully written work.

SHARON DRAPER: HIGH SCHOOL STUDENTS FACING ISSUES OF TODAY

Sharon Draper became a published author of young adult novels after having spent many years as a high school English teacher. Challenged by one of her students to enter a writing contest, she won first prize, and her entry became the first chapter in her novel, *Forged by Fire* (1997), which won the 1998 Coretta Scott King Author Award. Draper's first novel, *Tears of a Tiger* (1996), had won the first Coretta Scott King Genesis Award for African American authors who have published no more than three books. These two novels became part of a trilogy, the Hazelwood High Trilogy, involving a group of teenagers confronting many of the issues that contemporary teens actually face, such as drunk driving, suicide, child abuse, drug abuse, domestic violence, and eating disorders. The third novel of the trilogy is *Darkness Before Dawn* (2001). Draper also wrote a contemporary novelized version of Romeo and Juliette, *Romiette and Julio* (1999), featuring a romance between an African American girl and a Latino boy. Opposition comes from a Black gang, who disapprove of the interracial relationship, but this version avoids the tragic ending of the original.

Draper's strength is that she knows teenagers and their world and the way they think. She also knows what they want to read. She is an excellent storyteller, and for her teenage readers her books are page-turners. If a proliferation of issues sometimes threatens to overwhelm her books, her characters and their relationships are believable and recognizable and therefore appealing to her readers, who can find themselves in the pages of her books. As a teacher, Draper does not shy away from making clear in her novels the values she espouses; nevertheless, her books are extremely popular with the readers for whom she writes.

SHARON FLAKE: GRITTY URBAN NOVELS

One of the newest critically acclaimed African American young adult authors is Sharon Flake, whose first novel, *The Skin I'm In* (1998), revisits the issue of the color complex within the Black community. The mother of a "beautiful dark-skinned daughter," Flake was aware of the bias against dark skin and wanted to "help people learn to like themselves no matter what people say"[1] Maleeka Madison's journey to self-acceptance is long and painful, and she nearly destroys herself academically before she reaches a point at which she can accept and appreciate herself for who she is. Along the way, she allows herself to be cruelly mistreated by a tough bully of a girl and is subjected to unmerciful teasing by some of her other classmates. Help comes from an English teacher whose face is marked by a white blotch, who has learned to love herself and to achieve success in the business world but is ready to commit herself to teaching children like Maleeka. Flake was able to capture the voices of Black urban middle school youngsters and to convincingly portray both their surface behaviors and the depth of their emotional turmoil.

Flake's second novel, *Money Hungry* (2001), was cited as a Coretta Scott King Author Honor Book. Another gritty urban novel, *Money Hungry* involves a young woman for whom money represents security and the power to provide her and her mother with food, clothing, and shelter. Having tasted homelessness and poverty, she is determined to earn and maintain a bankroll. Eventually, it becomes necessary to examine and reorder her priorities. Given the positive critical reception of Flake's first few works, she promises to be one of the outstanding African American authors of the early twenty-first century.

This handful of prize-winning African American women, most of whom began publishing in the last decade of the twentieth century, are the trailblazers for twenty-first century African American children's literature. Building on the work of writers who began their careers a few decades earlier, they have already enriched and expanded that canon. Writing in the context of increased attention to multiculturalism and children's literature emanating from parallel cultures, they are exploring new themes and topics as well as new ways to work with themes that have become traditional in African American children's literature.

A PERSPECTIVE ON MODERN AFRICAN AMERICAN CHILDREN'S FICTION

Over the last third of the twentieth century, Virginia Hamilton and Walter Dean Myers led the effort to capture in books for young people the eccentricity and distinctiveness of African Americans' journey across what Hamilton called the American hopescape. In the 1970s and over the next two decades, as attention to diversity and multiculturalism increased publishing opportunities for parallel culture writers, several other African American authors entered the field and launched successful careers, even as Hamilton and Myers maintained their positions of prominence. Like the creators of African American picture books texts, these writers were in part filling a void left by the near absence of juvenile books about Black people. They were also in part offering a corrective vision of African American life by presenting the truth about the "life of the people" as they saw it. By the end of the century, a new group of rising stars had appeared, ensuring that stories of "the people" will continue to be written for new generations of young readers.

African American life is marked as much by diversity as it is by a shared cultural sensibility, and that diversity is clearly reflected in the stories for children that emanate from African American cultural contexts. Early on, in the late 1960s and 1970s, much of the focus of African American children's fiction was on urban living, mainly on the East Coast, reflecting in part the location or "hometowns" of its authors and in part the national focus on the social issues revolving around urban centers.

Although some of those issues, such as drug abuse, were central to a number of urban novels for young adults, one strand of urban-focused literature centered on what Joyce Hansen referred to as a "non-sensational, non-dysfunctional view," a counter to the "new realism."

Even in the 1970s, however, there was some diversity in settings; Virginia Hamilton, with two exceptions, set her novels in and around her own home place in historic southern Ohio, and Brenda Wilkinson took her readers to a small southern community. By the end of the century, the geographical settings of African American children's and young adult novels were almost as varied as the places African Americans live in this country. There are also great socioeconomic differences within the African American cultural community, and by the end of the century that diversity also was being reflected in the literature, sometimes simply as different social settings and sometimes as explorations of class tensions within those settings.

In its thematic emphases, African American realistic fiction for children reflects most of the goals and purposes Eloise Greenfield identified as hers in the 1975 article I have called her manifesto: encouraging children to have positive attitudes toward themselves; reflecting the positive aspects of their lives; exploring ways to cope with the negative aspects of their lives; inspiring new ways to solve problems; instilling knowledge of Black history/heritage; reflecting the strength of the Black family; fostering an appreciation of the contributions of elders; inspiring dedication to the cause of freedom. Underlying these goals and purposes is a sense that they are necessary to counteract the existing literary and popular culture images of African American children and families and a conviction that literature/story can influence children's attitudes and their lives. Thus, these realistic novels echo much of the thematic content of the African American picture books.

As creative literary artists, African American writers of realistic fiction for children and young adults do not confine themselves to a restricted set of themes or topics. In a general sense, however, they seem to emphasize four sometimes-overlapping themes: relationships with family and friends; growing up; heritage/identity issues; and developing self-esteem or self-love. Although these themes echo Greenfield's goals, they are not all, in and of themselves, unique to African American children's or young adult literature. Certainly "growing up" and relationships with family and friends, for example, are themes commonly explored in American children's fiction. Many African American authors, however, delve into those themes in the context of examining what it means to grow up both Black and American. In so doing, they tend to weave into their texts historical information, as well as certain cultural values, beliefs, and traditions that reflect the distinctiveness of African American cultural contexts.

Much of the realistic fiction by African Americans aimed at middle grades or middle schools features children and young adults working out relationships within their families and with their friends or members of their peer group. Family relationships in these books for older children are more likely than in picture books to involve problems of one kind or another (e.g., divorce, misunderstandings, conflicts) or to focus on youngsters working out their own place and their own responsibilities within the family. But, they nevertheless tend to emphasize the importance of family as a bedrock source of love and support and strength. Fathers are more visible in these longer works than in picture books, and a few novels, such as *M.C. Higgins the Great* (Hamilton 1974) and *Somewhere in the Darkness* (Myers 1992), highlight fathers and sons working out their relationships as the sons take steps into manhood. As in picture books, elders also play an important role in these novels, although relationships between children and their elders tend to be played out within the larger context of the dynamics of the family unit rather than the one-to-one focus often found in picture books. Extended families are common, and elders—grandparents, uncles, aunts, or nonrelatives—serve as teachers, keepers, and transmitters of family or group history, confidants, counselors, and sources of love and support.

Since the main characters in these books are school-age children or teenagers, many of them focus on friendships or relationships with members of peer groups, reflecting the increased importance of peers as children's social circles expand. Some such books focus on the joys and challenges of maintaining a friendship between two young people. Some of those, such as *Scorpions* (Myers 1988), are quite serious, while others, such as *Seth and Samona* (Hyppolite 1995), are light in tone. Other books feature groups of youngsters sharing activities and adventures, resisting or succumbing to peer pressure, getting into and out of trouble, or just having fun together.

Not surprisingly, like many books for young people, African American fiction often focuses on characters taking steps toward maturity—gaining insight into themselves and others, taking on responsibility, making moral and ethical choices, accepting the consequences of their actions, and becoming contributing members of their families and communities. Because growing up happens gradually over a lifetime, this theme can be and is played out both in relatively uncomplicated and in more difficult and complex fictional circumstances. In the middle-grade novel *Justin and the Best Biscuits in the World* (Walter 1986), for example, Justin comes to understand something about gender roles and a little of what it means to be a man in his world. In *M.C. Higgins, the Great* (Hamilton 1974), however, M.C. grapples with several challenges at once: his relationship with his father, his covert friendship with Ben, his concern about the slag heap and its threat to his home, and his own awakening interest in girls. Walter Dean Myers's young adult characters, even in his humorous books, such as *The Young Landlords* (1979), are often faced with moral decisions, and the reader is led to the insight that one always has a choice. In a few cases, such as Andrea Davis Pinkney's *Hold Fast to Dreams* (1995), the characters' dilemmas, choices, and decisions are also related to issues of race—what it means to be Black in a race-conscious society and how to cope with the negative consequences of that race consciousness without losing some vital aspect of oneself.

In African American children's literature, issues of identity are frequently tied to a focus on cultural/racial heritage, often in the context of African American history. In Virginia Hamilton's work, for example, M.C. Higgins (1974), Arilla in *Arilla Sun Down* (1976), and Theresa in *Sweet Whispers, Brother Rush* (1982), among others, learn something about who they are by learning something about their historical and family roots. Lou and her friends in *The Soul Brothers and Sister Lou* (Hunter 1968) gain strength and confidence through their growing understandings of the concept of soul. And, at the end of Sharon Bell Mathis's *Listen for the Fig Tree* (1974), Muffin gains strength from her insight into what it means to be Black. These novels suggest that, in order to move forward, either as an individual or as part of the parallel culture group, one has to have a sense of one's relationship to the past and that that knowledge is empowering. This theme echoes Greenfield's (1975) stated goal of giving children knowledge of Black heritage so that they can develop a sense of direction for their future.

A relatively small, but significant, number of realistic books by African American writers take up the issue of African American children having negative self-images, particularly in relation to their skin color and hair texture. Generally, their concern is not with non-African American attitudes toward those features, but with intragroup bias, mainly dark-skinned girls feeling that their coloring makes them unattractive. This concern with encouraging African American children to view themselves and their physical features in a positive light, in contradiction to acquired attitudes to the contrary, is testament to African American writers' understandings of one of the important challenges faced by Black children living in a society in which they are undervalued and their beauty unappreciated. Children of other so-called visible minorities may face similar issues, but in some sense this theme is one that is distinctive to African American children's literature.

If the overarching themes identified above are not exclusive to African American children's literature, nevertheless African American realistic fiction does carry some distinguishing features. One obvious but highly significant feature of this literature is that it both reflects and illuminates African American social and cultural contexts. That is, this literature is not generally concerned with intercultural relations, but with what poet Lucille Clifton called "authenticating" the worlds of Black children and families. Thus, almost all the characters, certainly all the main characters, are African Americans living in African American communities, reflecting what the writers see as an accurate sense of the life of the people.

One of the most important ways these books reflect African American life and culture is in their rendering of the vernacular language and the discourse styles of many African Americans. Not every African American writer chooses to employ an identifiably Black voice, either for narration or to represent characters' speech. Aside from author preferences, this also reflects the fact that not all African Americans speak the same variety of English. For those authors, such as Walter Dean Myers and Joyce Hansen, who choose to highlight Black discourse styles in their novels, Black vernacular language is a significant feature of the dialogue of the characters and, in some cases, the voice of the narrator. These works privilege oral communication and reflect Black rhetorical strategies, as in Myers's male teenagers' linguistic performances, which featured elements such as a heavy use of metaphor and other figurative language, word play, hyperbole, and the verbal strategy known as "signifying." Some writers, such as Hamilton, do not attempt an accurate rendition of a Black dialect but create stylized versions that offer a flavor of the vernacular. In any case, one means of creating a sense of the life of the people is to reflect in the texts the ways that the people use language, their ways with words.

Woven throughout African American realistic fiction are also numerous reflections of specific aspects of African American cultural traditions, beliefs, values, and mores. Among those details are references to African American sacred and secular music, which abound in these books, from Geeder's uncle's recollection of spirituals in *Zeely* (Hamilton 1967), to the Soul Brothers and Sister Lou's experiences with the blues (Hunter 1968), to Aunt Dew's preoccupation with "Precious Lord" (Mathis 1975). Aunt Dew's clinging to that song is a reflection of religious/spiritual beliefs and practices, which also are referenced frequently in the literature, usually in relation to the elders, such as Benjie's grandmother in *A Hero Ain't Nothin But a Sandwich* (Childress 1973) and Ludell's grandmother in *Ludell* (Wilkinson 1975).

Another cultural value that is prominent in these books is the importance of forming and maintaining communities of support. *Marked by Fire* (Thomas 1982), *The Dear One* (Woodson 1991), and *Like Sisters on the Home Front* (Williams-Garcia 1995), for example, all feature small communities of Black women or teenagers. Walter Dean Myers's early urban books also stress the value of what he referred to as "Black people helping Black people." This focus on community or communality, as well as the focus on family and on the importance of story as a means to inform and entertain, echoes something of the cultural themes and educational instruments that Webber (1978) identified in his study of education in the slave quarters, suggesting long-lasting cultural values.

Another value that is highlighted is the importance of art, particularly drama, as a vehicle for empowering troubled youngsters, which occurs in books such as *Yellow Bird and Me* (Hansen 1986), *Thank You, Dr. Martin Luther King, Jr.* (Tate 1990), and *The Shimmershine Queens* (Yarbrough 1989). In addition, references to African American history and African American heroes are abundant in these books, emphasizing the value the authors place on informing young people about their heritage.

In short, in creating a body of fiction for children, African American authors delve into African American cultural traditions and cultural history to piece together works that are an accurate representation of "the recognizable fabric of black life" as they know and understand it.

NOTE

1. Flake, Sharon. NYPL Presents Sharon Flake. Author Sharon Flake. July 18, 2002. http://liveworld.com.transcripts/NYPL/7-18-2002.1-1.html.

BIBLIOGRAPHY OF BOOKS FOR CHILDREN AND YOUNG ADULTS

Banks, Jacqueline Turner. 1993. *Project Wheels*. Boston: Houghton Mifflin.
———. 1994. *The New One*. Boston: Houghton Mifflin.
———. 1995. *Egg-Drop Blues*. Boston: Houghton Mifflin.
Barnes, Joyce Annette. 1994. *The Baby Grand, the Moon in July, and Me*. New York: Dial.
———. 1997. *Promise Me the Moon*. New York: Dial.
Belton, Sandra. 1996. *Ernestine and Amanda*. New York: Simon and Schuster.
———. 1997a. *Mysteries on Monroe Street*. New York: Simon and Schuster.
———. 1997b. *Summer Camp, Ready or Not*. New York: Simon and Schuster.
———. 1998. *Members of the C.L.U.B.* New York: Simon and Schuster.
———. 2000. *McKendree*. New York: Greenwillow.
Boyd, Candy Dawson. 1984. *Circle of Gold*. New York: Scholastic.
———. 1985. *Breadsticks and Blessing Places*. New York: Macmillan. Reissued in 1986 as *Forever Friends*. New York: Viking.
———. 1987. *Charlie Pippin*. New York: Macmillan.
———. 1993. *Chevrolet Saturdays*. New York: Macmillan.
———. 1994. *Fall Secrets*. New York: Penguin.
———. 1996. *A Different Beat*. New York: Penguin.
Chambers, Veronica. 1998. *Marisol and Magdalena*. New York: Jump at the Sun/Hyperion.
———. 2001. *Quinceañera Means Sweet 15*. New York: Jump at the Sun/Hyperion.
Childress, Alice. 1973. *A Hero Ain't Nothin' But a Sandwich*. New York: Coward, McCann.
Chocolate, Debbie. 1992. *NEATE to the Rescue*. Orange, NJ: Just Us Books.
Draper, Sharon. 1996. *Tears of a Tiger*. New York: Simon and Schuster.
———. 1997. *Forged by Fire*. New York: Atheneum.
———. 1999. *Romiette and Julio*. New York: Atheneum.
———. 2001. *Darkness Before Dawn*. New York: Atheneum.

Flake, Sharon. 1998. *The Skin I'm In*. New York: Jump at the Sun/Hyperion.

———. 2001. *Money Hungry*. New York: Jump at the Sun/Hyperion.

Hamilton, Virginia. 1967. *Zeely*. New York: Macmillan.

———. 1974. *M.C. Higgins, the Great*. New York: Macmillan.

———. 1976. *Arilla Sun Down*. New York: Greenwillow.

———. 1982. *Sweet Whispers, Brother Rush*. New York: Philomel.

Hansen, Joyce. 1980. *The Gift Giver*. New York: Clarion.

———. 1982. *Home Boy*. New York: Ticknor and Fields.

———. 1986. *Yellow Bird and Me*. New York: Clarion.

Hunter, Kristen. 1968. *The Soul Brothers and Sister Lou*. New York: Scribners.

Hyppolite, Joanne. 1995. *Seth and Samona*. New York: Delacorte.

———. 1998. *Ola Shakes It Up*. New York: Delacorte.

Johnson, Angela. 1993. *Toning the Sweep*. New York: Orchard.

———. 1995. *Humming Whispers*. New York: Orchard.

———. 1998a. *Heaven*. New York: Simon and Schuster.

———. 1998b. *Gone From Home: Short Takes*. New York: DK Publishing.

———. 1998c. *The Other Side: Shorter Poems*. New York: Orchard.

———. 1998c. *Songs of Faith*. New York: Orchard.

———. 2003. *First Part Last*. New York: Simon and Schuster.

Mathis, Sharon Bell. 1974. *Listen for the Fig Tree*. New York: Viking.

Myers, Walter Dean. 1988. *Scorpions*. New York: Harper and Row.

———. 1992. *Somewhere in the Darkness*. New York: Scholastic.

Nelson, Vaunda Micheaux. 1993. *Mayfield Crossing*. New York: Putnam.

———. 1999. *Beyond Mayfield*. New York: Putnam.

Pinkney, Andrea Davis. 1995. *Hold Fast to Dreams*. New York: Morrow.

Pinkney, Sandra. 2000. *Shades of Black: A Celebration of Our Children*. New York: Scholastic.

Tate, Eleanora. 1980. *Just an Overnight Guest*. New York: Dial.

———. 1987. *The Secret of Gumbo Grove*. New York: Franklin Watts.

———. 1990. *Thank You, Dr. Martin Luther King, Jr.* New York: Franklin Watts.

———. 1992. *Front Porch Stories at the One-Room School*. New York: Bantam.

———. 1995. *A Blessing in Disguise*. New York: Delacorte.

Thomas, Joyce Carol. 1982. *Marked by Fire*. New York: Avon.

———. 1983. *Bright Shadow*. New York: Avon.

———. 1986a. *The Golden Pasture*. New York: Scholastic.

———. 1986b. *Water Girl*. New York: Avon.

———. 1988. *Journey*. New York: Scholastic.

———. 1992. *When the Nightingale Sings*. New York: Harper.

———. 2004. *The Gospel Cinderella*. Illus. by David Diaz. New York: HarperCollins.

Walter, Mildred Pitts. 1969. *Lillie of Watts: A Birthday Discovery*. Los Angeles: Ward Ritchie Press.

———. 1971. *Lillie of Watts Takes a Giant Step*. New York: Doubleday.

———. 1982. *The Girl on the Outside*. New York: Lothrop, Lee and Shepard.

———. 1983. *Because We Are*. New York: Lothrop, Lee and Shepard.

———. 1985. *Trouble's Child*. New York: Lothrop, Lee and Shepard.

———. 1986. *Justin and the Best Biscuits in the World*. New York: HarperCollins.

———. 1988. *Mariah Loves Rock*. New York: Bradbury.

———. 1990. *Mariah Keeps Cool*. New York: Bradbury.

———. 1992. *Mississippi Challenge*. New York: HarperCollins.

Wilkinson, Brenda. 1975. *Ludell*. New York: Harper and Row.

Williams-Garcia, Rita. 1988. *Blue Tights*. New York: Lodestar.

———. 1991. *Fast Track on a Slow Track*. New York: Lodestar.

———. 1995. *Like Sisters on the Homefront*. New York: Lodestar.

Wilson, Johniece Marshall. 1988. *Oh, Brother*. New York: Scholastic.

———. 1990. *Robin on His Own*. New York: Scholastic.

———. 1992. *Rich Girl, Poor Girl.* New York: Scholastic.

Woodson, Jacqueline. 1990. *Last Summer with Maizon.* New York: Delacorte.

———. 1991. *The Dear One.* New York: Delacorte.

———. 1992. *Maizon at Blue Hill.* New York: Delacorte.

———. 1993. *Between Madison and Palmetto.* New York: Delacorte.

———. 1994. *I Hadn't Meant to Tell You This.* New York: Delacorte.

———. 1995. *From the Notebooks of Melanin Sun.* New York: Blue Sky/Scholastic.

———. 1997. *The House You Pass on the Way.* New York: Delacorte.

———. 1998. *If You Come Softly.* New York: Putnam.

———. 1999. *Lena.* New York: Delacorte.

———. 2000. *Miracle's Boys.* New York: Putnam.

———. 2001. *The Other Side.* Illus. by E. B. Lewis. New York: Putnam.

Wyeth, Sharon Dennis. 1994. *The World of Daughter McGuire.* New York: Delacorte.

Yarbrough, Camille. 1979. *Cornrows.* Illus. by Carole Byard. New York: Coward, McCann and Geoghegan.

———. 1989. *The Shimmershine Queens.* New York: Knopf.

CHAPTER 12

African American Historical Fiction: Telling a People's Story

A people's story is the anchor dat keeps um from driftin, it's the compass to
show the way to go and it's a sail dat holds the power dat takes um forward.
Aunt Seatta in *The Shimmershine Queens* (Yarbrough 1989, 21)

African American history holds a highly significant place in African American
children's literature. From *The Brownies' Book* and Carter G. Woodson's publications forward, twentieth century African American writers and artists have articulated their desire to make Black children—and all American children—aware of
the achievements of individual African Americans, the contributions of African
Americans to this society, and the enduring struggle against oppression and discrimination. To that end, threads of history and references to historical figures and
events are woven throughout contemporary African American children's literature
in all genres. This strong emphasis on African American history functions both as a
corrective to the historical neglect, distortion, or omission of that history in school
curricula and a manifestation of the belief that knowledge of their history will function as anchor, compass, and sail for African American children as they undertake
their life journeys.

Not surprisingly, much of this history is conveyed as straightforward nonfiction,
some of which has become classic or near classic in the canon of African American/
American children's literature. In fact, the first two African American-authored
books cited as Newbery Honor Books by the American Library Association were
Arna Bontemps's *The Story of the Negro* (1948) and Julius Lester's *To Be a Slave*
(1968), both of which are nonfiction. More recently, well-known African American
authors have also produced important, acclaimed nonfiction books, such as Walter
Dean Myers's historical survey *Now Is Your Time* (1991), Patricia and Fredrick
McKissack's comparative chronicle *Christmas in the Big House, Christmas in the
Quarters* (1994), and Tom Feelings's masterwork, *The Middle Passage: White Ships,
Black Cargo* (1995), a visual interpretation of the horrific journey of Black cap-
tives from Africa to the Americas. Since the 1960s, a handful of African American
authors, most notably James Haskins, Patricia and Fredrick McKissack, and Joyce
Hansen, have produced a substantial body of nonfiction Black history.

African American history for children has also been conveyed in the form of scores
of biographies and works of biographical fiction. Recently, the scope of African

American biographies for children has expanded to include a wider range of African American men and women than in previous times. Too, in recent years, many biographies—both fictionalized and authentic—have appeared in picture book format and have therefore been accessible and appealing to a wide audience. In placing their subjects in the context of their times, biographers—and illustrators—often provide vivid and detailed depictions of the era in which the subject lived, thus making both the biographical subjects and history come alive for young readers.

The focus of this chapter, however, is historical fiction, the genre in which authors set about to re-create a past era, often by placing fictional characters in the midst of some major historical event, such as a war, but sometimes just portraying what life would have been like for an ordinary person living in that past time and place. Generally, this fiction is realistic, but in rare cases authors create their own hybrid genre by combining history with fantasy, as in Hamilton's *The Magical Adventures of Pretty Pearl* (1983), or combining biography with elements of fiction, as Hamilton did in *Anthony Burns* (1988).

Because a significant aspect of African American history involves the era of slavery, under which literacy was forbidden fruit, some history is also embedded in stories that have been passed down through the oral tradition. Recall, for example, Virginia Hamilton's designation of her collections of Black tales as "liberation literature," which bears witness to the oppression of individuals as well as their pursuit of freedom. *The People Could Fly* (1985), for instance, contains examples of the kinds of tales enslaved people told to each other and passed on. Many of these tales were realistic, relating how slaves managed to obtain their freedom, often by outsmarting the slaveholder or by running away. Also included are tales with an element of magic, such as the title story of the collection, in which enslaved workers magically regained their ancient ability to fly and simply rose above the fields and flew back to Africa. These stories, which have been handed down orally over generations, offer an accurate sense of the values shared among enslaved Black people and passed down to their descendents, most particularly the desire and the right to be free. They also offer glimpses of the physical and psychological conditions under which enslaved people lived on Southern plantations.

Liberation literature, as Hamilton defines it, is closely tied to the history of slavery and the pursuit of freedom. No part of the African American or American past has been of greater social significance than the institution of slavery; consequently, a substantial portion of African American historical fiction for children is set in the era when slavery flourished in America. Julius Lester was among the first post-1965 African American writers for young people to focus on creating fiction based on the stories of slaves and former slaves. In addition to the highly praised nonfiction *To Be a Slave* (1968), he produced two volumes of short stories, both of which were also hailed by critics. Recently, he has returned to the theme with two prize-winning books. In the 1980s, Joyce Hansen shifted from writing realistic novels centered on contemporary urban middle school/junior high school youngsters to historical fiction depicting the lives of enslaved Black people. In the decade from 1991 to 2001, Harriet Gillem Robinet published eight books of historical fiction featuring feisty young Black protagonists, with half of these books related to the slave era.

In the process of humanizing enslaved people of African descent, this fiction also highlights the importance of family, however families were formed and defined under the conditions of slavery, when slaveholders felt no obligation to keep together traditional family units. Echoing one of Webber's (1978) major cultural themes, this focus on family is also a second important strand of African American historical fiction for young people. Most famously represented by the work of Mildred D. Taylor, this strand depicts African American families and their progress across the Black American hopescape over generations and across time. As in the books set during slavery, these books emphasize the resilience of spirit that enabled the families, and by extension African Americans in general, to survive.

The third African American to win a Newbery Medal, Christopher Paul Curtis, has also published two novels of historical interest. His first book, a Newbery Honor Book, was set in 1963 during the civil rights movement. His second book, set during the Great Depression, won the 2000 Newbery Medal. Although the five authors mentioned above—Lester, Robinet, Hansen, Taylor, and Curtis—are highlighted in this chapter, it also discusses the work of a number of other African American writers who have produced important historical fiction for young people. The chapter is organized generally under the main topics addressed by African American children's books: slavery, struggle, and family.

SLAVERY AND ITS AFTERMATH

> To be a slave was to be a human being under conditions in which that humanity was denied. They were not slaves. They were people. Their condition was slavery.
>
> Julius Lester, *To Be a Slave* (1968, 28)

African American writers have made it a point to depict life under slavery from the perspective of the enslaved—to represent the view from the slave quarters rather than the view from the "Big House." In part, this perspective has been presented in opposition to some earlier fiction that portrayed slavery as slaveholders saw it or wished it to be—slaves as carefree and content with their lives, not nearly as high on the scale of humanity as the slaveholders, and slavery as an institution sanctioned by the gods of economic prosperity, as well as the God of Abraham, Isaac, and Jacob. In direct contrast to this viewpoint, African American writers tend to represent enslaved Africans as complex human beings experiencing the full range of human emotions (including love and joy); responding to slavery in whatever ways they think will enable them to survive, including siding with the slaveholders; or wearing "the mask that grins and lies," pretending to be and do what the slaveholder expects.

Thus, African American authors attempt to humanize Black slaves by inviting their readers to live through the experiences of characters who seem much like themselves or people they know and love. Although the inhumane conditions of slavery are generally realistically depicted in these novels, enslaved people are not depicted merely as passive victims. There is much stress on their desire for and the pursuit of freedom. The writers also attempt to destigmatize slave ancestry by laying responsibility on the shoulders of slaveholders and their supporters. Slave ancestry in these novels becomes a source of pride—in an African heritage, in a history of subversion and resistance, in the preservation of human dignity, and in the miracle of survival in the face of potentially crushing cruelty.

To those ends, three thematic threads predominate in African American writings for children about slavery. One is the desire for freedom, the impulse to escape from slavery, always at great personal risk. Another is the anguish caused by the callous buying and selling of spouses, siblings, parents, and children, forcibly separating loved ones from each other—sometimes permanently. A third theme is the importance of literacy as a liberating power and as a threat to the institution of slavery. Most of this fiction is in the form of novels, but some writers have chosen to aim their fiction at a younger audience.

PICTURE BOOKS ON SLAVERY

Only a few African American writers have taken on the task of creating picture storybooks depicting for young children what life might have been like for Black people enslaved in the United States at a time that, for today's youngsters, seems like ancient history. For the most part, the picture books they have produced on the topic tend to deal with enslaved African Americans' quest for freedom and their active, though necessarily covert, resistance to slavery.

One exception was Courtni Wright's *Jumping the Broom* (1994b), the story of the wedding of a couple enslaved on a plantation. Because enslaved people were not permitted legal marriages, the ceremony consisted of jumping over a broom to symbolize jumping into a new life together. Lettie, younger sister of the bride, describes the wedding preparations, the ceremony, and the celebration on the wedding day. The atmosphere is festive; women sew quilts and men make furniture, baskets, and utensils. Food comes from their gardens or is purchased. Although there are references to some of the hardships of slavery, for the most part Wright and, especially, the illustrator Gershom Griffith paint a fairly rosy picture of the lives of the Black people on this plantation, an image that is contradicted by most other accounts. On the other hand, the jumping-the-broom ceremony is another illustration of Tom Feelings's concept of "improvising within a restricted form" (1985); Wright's book does place the wedding in the context of the restrictions imposed on the enslaved people planning and participating in it.

Another picture book that focuses on a celebration is Irene Smalls's *Irene Jennie and the Christmas Masquerade: The Johnkanus* (1996). It is a Christmas story that features the tradition of the masked revelers known as the Johnkanus. Although Irene Jenny looks forward to the Johnkanus, she is also saddened by the absence of her parents, who have been loaned out to another plantation. Her parents' early return enables her to share in the joy of the celebration. Like Wright's book, this one also has the merit of showing enslaved Blacks as a community of humans trying to live their lives as best they can under the circumstances, experiencing joy as well as pain.

Most picture books about slavery, however, equate joy with freedom. *Sweet Clara and the Freedom Quilt* (Hopkinson 1993), possibly the best-known picture storybook about slavery and the quest for freedom, was not written by an African American. It was illustrated, however, with vibrant oil paintings by African American artist James Ransome. The author, Deborah Hopkinson, was inspired by a National Public Radio report about quilts that served as maps of escape routes. In Hopkins's story, an enslaved girl named Clara creates a quilt that is also a map, using information gathered in bits and pieces by enslaved men and women in the course of their work and passed to her surreptitiously. The book celebrates not only the quest for freedom, but also the ingenuity and creativity of countless enslaved women like Clara.

Dolores Johnson, author-artist, published two picture books that focus on various strategies enslaved Africans used to gain their freedom. *Now Let Me Fly: The Story of a Slave Family* (1993) is, in essence, a fictional slave narrative in miniature, a first-person account that follows Minna from life in Africa through her capture and her life enslaved on a Southern plantation. The fictional Minna and her children exemplify some of the heartbreak that enslaved families had to endure—being sold away from each other, seeing family members whipped, the bittersweet separation when loved ones run away. It also illustrates some of the possible paths to freedom: escaping to the North through the Underground Railroad, linking up with Native Americans, buying their freedom with money they were permitted to keep when their labor was rented out, and for the majority, enduring until emancipation.

Johnson's second picture book about slavery, *Seminole Diary* (1994), provides a more detailed picture of the alliances between escaped slaves and Native Americans. Structured as the diary of an ancestor being read to a contemporary child, the story follows Libbie and her family as they run away from a plantation and are taken in by a band of Seminoles. Interestingly, the Black people were nominally the slaves of the Seminoles, but that status served to protect them—as legal "property" of the Seminoles, they could not legitimately be taken away by plantation owners. When the Seminoles were ordered by the U.S. government to give up their lands and walk to Oklahoma, they and the Black people who had joined them were forced to choose between obeying the orders and becoming fugitives from the government.

The best-known escape route was the Underground Railroad, and the most famous "conductor" on that railroad was the legendary Harriet Tubman, who escaped slavery and then returned to the South numerous times to lead others to safety. *Journey to Freedom: A Story of the Underground Railroad* (Wright 1994a) is a fictional account of a family's flight from Kentucky to Canada, led by Tubman. It follows the family on the last few days of their journey, showing the kinds of dangers they faced, the courage and kindness of "station masters" along the way, and the joy of finding themselves in Canada, free at last. Harriet Tubman—brave, Black, female—caught the imagination of numerous writers; this book is but one example of the body of writing for children that casts Tubman as a heroine, a Moses leading her people to the promised land of freedom.

Another fictionalized picture book based on an actual incident and actual people is *Amistad Rising* (Chambers 1998), which relates the story of the group of African captives who, led by a courageous Mende named Cinque, revolted on board the slave ship *Amistad*. Deceitful crew members sailed to Connecticut rather than back to Africa as ordered by the rebels, and the Africans were detained, tried, and eventually defended in federal court by John Quincy Adams. The Supreme Court declared the Africans free, and abolitionists raised enough money to enable them to return to West Africa. The *Amistad* episode became the basis for a major motion picture, which generated renewed interest in the case and spawned a few children's books. The dramatic story highlights the fact that, more frequently than is generally mentioned, Africans revolted or attempted to revolt against their captors.

Not many books about slavery are written for the youngest readers, presumably in part because of the complexity and cruelty of the circumstances. One outstanding picture book, however, tells the story of slavery with a simple but eloquent text and striking, bold, child-like illustrations. *Jalani and the Lock* (Pace 2001), follows a little boy from the African forest where he loved to play, to his kidnapping by strangers, to the Middle Passage, to America, where he was enslaved—"he had to work and was never allowed to play again" (n.p.). Jalani kept the lock that had held him in chains and eventually passed it to his oldest son, to be handed down to the generations so they would not forget where they came from. The lock of the story is based on the actual lock that had confined the great-great-grandfather of Lorenzo Pace, the artist who wrote and illustrated the book. When Pace was commissioned to create a sculpture for the recently discovered African Burial

Ground in New York City, he placed a bronze replica of the lock, which he has inherited, inside his sculpture. A note at the back of the book gives information about the lock and the burial ground. In addition to its eye-catching illustrations, the book is significant because it successfully tells the story of slavery in a way that young children can understand.

As in Pace's book, one of the factors that makes some books about slavery by African American writers and artists especially affecting is that the authors or artists have personal connections with the material. They have been able to trace their own ancestry at least as far back as slavery, and their family stories inspire and enrich their works. James Ransome, for example, in conducting research before illustrating *Sweet Clara* (Hopkinson 1993), discovered that his ancestors had been enslaved on the Verona plantation in North Carolina, which became the model for the illustrations in the book. For another example, Virginia Hamilton's family story of her great-grandmother's escape from slavery in Virginia to Ohio with her young son became an important motif in several of her works. The emotional connection these authors or artists have with the material is a reminder that liberation literature absorbs not only the reader as witness but the writer or artists as well, and that those witnesses are also freed through the reliving of the stories and the liberation of their characters.

BOOKS FOR OLDER READERS ON SLAVERY

The first modern landmark African American historical novel for upper elementary/ middle school readers was Ann Petry's *Tituba of Salem Village* (1964). Based on an actual person, the novel tells the story of a woman who was enslaved in Barbados, then sold to a minister, and taken eventually to the village of Salem. In seventeenth century Puritan Massachusetts, many people believed in witchcraft, and since Tituba engaged in activities, such as reading fortunes, that left her vulnerable to gossip and mischief, she was suspected of being a witch. The suspicions were fed by the minister's clever and spiteful niece and her friends. Tituba was prosecuted at the famous Salem witch trials, as were two others she identified as fellow witches. Since Tituba, after being beaten by the minister, had confessed to being a witch, she was not hanged but was held in jail until a weaver for whom she had worked paid her fees.

By the time *Tituba* was published, Petry was already an experienced and respected author of adult fiction, so it is not surprising that the novel was well crafted and favorably reviewed. In fact, the book has become something of a staple for upper elementary and middle school students studying American colonial history and is still readily available forty years after its publication. Petry was clear about her intentions; in an autobiographical piece, she noted:

I write about relationships between black people and white people in the United States: novels, short stories, poetry, books for children and young people. When I write for children I write about survivors: Tituba of Salem Village, indicted for witchcraft in the seventeenth century; Harriet Tubman who helped runaway slaves escape from the South before the Civil War. (1988, 253)

Recent scholarship asserts that Tituba was not Black, but Arawak Indian; nevertheless, Petry's fictional account paints a vivid picture of the life of an enslaved woman of color in seventeenth century Massachusetts. Petry clearly considered Tituba Black, but whether she was Black or Indian, for purposes of the novel what matters is that she was oppressed, regarded as property, and that she survived. John Indian, Tituba's husband, had told her as they were leaving Barbados, "Remember, always remember, the slave must survive. No matter what happens to the master, the slave must survive" (12). Although the eventual fate of the real Tituba is unknown (she was pardoned along with all other surviving defendants), Petry ends her novel with these words: "Tituba lived on, leading a full and useful life in Boston with her husband, John Indian." She and her husband had survived and that is the thought that Petry sought to leave with young readers.

Julius Lester: Putting a Human Face on Slavery

One of the most powerful voices on the topic of slavery is that of Julius Lester, who has produced several books—fiction and nonfiction—on the topic for children or young adults. Lester was among the first contemporary American writers to attempt to put a human face on slavery for youthful readers. He explicitly expressed his viewpoint in the epigraph above (Lester 1968), from the introduction to the thirtieth anniversary edition of *To Be a Slave* (1997), and in an undated essay about his work circulated by his publisher:

Some of my work is concerned with telling the stories of those who were once slaves—To Be a Slave, Long Journey Home, This Strange New Feeling. I feel the spirits of hundreds of slaves waiting for me to put their stories on paper. They want others to know them as men, women, and children who were forced to live under the condition of slavery, an extraordinary condition under which to try to be human. Yet they tried, and more often than not, were more successful than those who held them as slaves. (15)

The stories in Lester's two collections, *Long Journey Home: Stories from Black History* (1972) and *This Strange New Feeling* (1982), though fictionalized, are all based on real people and events. *Long Journey Home*, a National Book Award Finalist, is a collection of six stories for older readers about former slaves and their journeys to home, or freedom. The stories also raise the question of what it means to be free. The ex-slaves include Rambler, a blues player who believes that the only way to be free is to keep moving; Louis, a runaway who is forced to go all the way to Canada to evade the slaveholder who pursues him; and Ben, a slave who actually runs the plantation until a new overseer tries to break Ben's spirit, prompting him to run away. In another story, Jake's wife and children are sold away from him; when he finally locates them after the war, their reunion is heartbreaking. Bob Lemmons was the Black cowboy with a special affinity for horses who is featured again in Lester and Pinkney's picture book, *Black Cowboy, Wild Horses* (1998). The title story recounts the legend of the captives who walked into the water off Ibo's Landing on one of the Sea Islands off the coast of Georgia. These dramatic stories not only humanize enslaved individuals, they illuminate the lasting effects of slavery on the enslaved—and to some extent the slaveholders—and reaffirm the strength of the slave's compulsion to be free. They also demonstrate that the journey to home/freedom was sometimes long indeed.

Lester has reimagined and fleshed out the Ibo Landing story in a recent book illustrated by Jerry Pinkney. *The Old African* (2005b) is a powerful retelling of that legend, centered on an enslaved African who has retained the power to change form and to communicate mentally without words. It begins with the brutal whipping of a young boy who has run away, with the African using his powers to take away the boy's physical pain, and the mental anguish of the slaves who are being forced to watch. When the African learns that the runaway had found the ocean, the events of the legend are set in motion, and he leads a group of slaves through the water and back to Africa and to freedom. Pinkney's dramatic paintings, full of rich color, depict both the horrors of the slave experience and the dignity of the individuals who experienced it. Lester's other recent book about the era of slavery is *Day of Tears* (2005a), a fictionalized depiction of the biggest slave auction in American history. It is a multivoiced novel told completely in dialogue. Based on a true incident, it makes real the inhumanity of slavery and the humanity of those who were forced into it.

Lester's other early collection, *This Strange New Feeling* (1982), relates the love stories of three couples who escaped from slavery. In the title story, Ras escapes, but when he is betrayed and caught, dons the grinning mask that wins his way unharmed back to the plantation, where he continues to wear the mask for the slaveholder while helping slaves escape from the plantation. As he and his love, Sally, attempt to make their own escape, they confront and successfully defend themselves against the plantation owner and experience for the first time the strange new feeling of freedom. In the second story, Maria, who is enslaved, and Forrest, a free blacksmith, fall in love and marry. Eventually, Forrest pays the planter and becomes Maria's nominal owner. When Forrest dies prematurely, Maria's freedom is once more at risk. The final story is the well-known one of the daring escape of William and Ellen Craft, she posing as a White male slave owner, and he as her slave. Disguised in that way, they are able to use public transportation to make their way to Boston, where they become participants in the abolitionist movement and eventually escape to London. In these stories, Lester dramatizes the profound and enduring love these once-enslaved people had for each other, thereby connecting them to all humans who experience this universal emotion. At the same time, he sheds light on the deeply felt need to be free and to have control over one's own life decisions, a need experienced particularly urgently by those to whom such self-determination is denied. In so doing, Lester and other African American authors help young readers understand something of what it was like "to be a human being under conditions in which that humanity was denied" (1968, 28).

Joyce Hansen's Fictional Slave Narrative

Joyce Hansen's *The Captive* (Hansen 1994) is based on *The Life of Alaudah Equiano, or Gustavus Vassa, the African. Written by Himself* (1814/1987), the classic eighteenth century autobiography of an Ibo prince who was captured and enslaved when he was about ten years old. Such autobiographies, known as slave narratives, are extremely significant in African American history and literature and are a uniquely American genre, centered on the themes of liberation and literacy. Thus, it is not surprising that, when contemporary African American authors of literature for children, including Hansen, write about slavery, they place strong thematic emphasis on the need to be free and the desire to be literate.

In reworking Equiano's story for younger readers, Hansen created a new protagonist and a fictional slave narrative. Like his account, Hansen's 1994 novel begins in Africa, where Kofi is the son of an important Ashanti chief. Betrayed by his father's slave, Kofi is sold to various African slave traders, endures the Middle Passage, and ends up in Salem, Massachusetts, enslaved to a pious but mean Puritan. "Master Browne" also holds Joseph, another African captive, and Tim, a White indentured servant. The three boys escape to a Black settlement and eventually are rescued by Paul Cuffe, an ex-slave who has become a well-to-do merchant and shipbuilder. Through the legal system, Cuffe secures freedom for Kofi and Joseph, but the court sentences Tim to serve out his contract. Kofi and Joseph become Cuffe's apprentices, and eventually Kofi marries, settles in Massachusetts, and spends the rest of his life working for the abolitionist cause.

Part of what makes *The Captive* successful is that Hansen was able to weave a great deal of historical and cultural information seamlessly into the novel (1987), providing insight into aspects of life both in Africa and in eighteenth century New England. Paul Cuffe, for instance, was an actual person, a freed slave who became a wealthy maritime merchant, shipbuilder and abolitionist. It is well known that Africans participated in the slave trade, and *The Captive* offers some insight into the circumstances that supported that practice. In Hansen's story, however, Kofi's father's slave was about to marry Kofi's sister, something that would have been unthinkable under slavery in the United States. Hansen also emphasizes that Kofi had been acculturated in Ashanti society, so that one of the complicating factors in his enslavement was a clash of cultures. Hansen had this to say about her depiction of Kofi in Africa: "I wanted to expose my young readers to African civilization. The African American experience does not begin with slavery—it begins with the ancestors, the artists, the singers, dancers, musicians, farmers, artisans, holy men, historians and healers, mothers and fathers whose cultures did not die in the holds of slave ships" (Hansen 1999, 62–63).

Like *Tituba* (Petry 1964), Hansen's *The Captive* is somewhat unusual in children's literature on slavery in that its setting is New England rather than the more common Southern farm or plantation. Hansen's story paints a picture of the harsh life led by people enslaved in one Puritan household; Kofi's clergyman master was free with his floggings and at the same time insistent on long, knee-breaking prayer sessions. He also stopped his wife from teaching Kofi to read, a cruel prohibition designed in part to keep Kofi unaware of the joy of freedom and of opportunities to obtain it. Hansen draws parallels between indentured servitude and slavery in the United States but she also brings out one important difference. An escaped White indentured servant could disappear and blend in to a new place. Black slaves were easily identifiable visibly and were vulnerable to capture not only by the slaveholders, but also by their neighbors who supported the system.

Through the Paul Cuffe character, Hansen calls attention to the existence of prosperous free Black people in early America, as well as both Black and White abolitionists. And, of course, she uses both Kofi and Cuffe to make her major point: "Though he [Kofi] is enslaved, he does not think of himself as a slave. In the end, Kofi proves himself to be a great man because he does what all truly great men and women do, he takes on the responsibility . . . of helping others secure their freedom. Kofi realizes in the end, that slavery is wrong no matter who practices it or how benign it seems" (1999, 64). Although her themes are clear, one of Hansen's strengths as a writer of historical fiction is that she is able to tell an absorbing story and put a human face on slavery without being "preachy."

Slavery in the Caribbean: *Ajeemah and His Son*

James Berry's novel, *Ajeemah and His Son* (1992), was the winner of the 1993 Boston Globe-Horn Book Award for fiction. Berry is a Jamaican-born poet who currently lives in England. His moving novel extends the depiction of slavery to include the experience of slavery in the Caribbean. Although it is narrated in the third person, *Ajeemah* is similar to *The Captive* in that it begins with life in Africa and follows its title characters through the Middle Passage to Jamaica, where they are sold and enslaved on two separate plantations, never to meet again. Proud Ajeemah never considers himself a slave and refuses to pay money for the freedom that is inherently and rightfully his. In the meantime, his son Atu has purchased a nearly dead horse and nursed him back to health. When the overseer confiscates the horse, Atu, in despair over the realization that he has no power over his own life, commits suicide. Ajeemah intuitively senses the moment of his son's death and is plunged into deep grief. He lives on, however, to see freedom and to give his daughter, on her wedding day, the dowry originally intended for Atu's bride in Africa. One of the striking features of Berry's spare text is that he is able to convey the inner dignity that Ajeemah and Atu held on to, their determination not to give in to the humiliation and attempted dehumanization by which the slaveholders tried to break their spirits. Part of the significance of the story is that it is a reminder that the European and American slave trade with Africa actually created an African diaspora.

In Pursuit of Literacy

For Black people enslaved in the United States, the urge to be literate was just about on a par with the urge to be free and the desire to be reunited with loved ones. Knowing how to read and write was both empowering, in the sense that knowledge confers power, and liberating, in terms of the practical potential for creating useful documents and protest literature and in the Biblical sense that knowing the truth will make one free. Although few African American children's historical novels have taken literacy as their central topic, it was a subtheme or subplot in most of the historical novels for children about slavery. It was also central in at least one picture book, *More than Anything Else* (Bradby 1995), the fictionalized biography that relates a childhood incident in the life of Booker T. Washington. What the child Booker wanted more than anything else was to learn to read. Bradby makes the case that literacy became a jumping off place for Washington, who became the highly influential educator and founder of Tuskegee Institute.

Andrea Davis Pinkney's novel *Silent Thunder* (1999) also focuses on the two predominant themes of literacy and liberation. The novel is narrated alternately by Summer, who is eleven, and her thirteen-year-old brother, Rosco. Summer wants to learn to read and write; Rosco wants to escape. These longings are aptly described as "silent thunder," driving urges that must be kept secret, but threaten to erupt. Rosco has learned to read by listening in on the lessons of the plantation owner's son, and he is determined to teach his sister. Their mother reacts angrily because she knows that if Summer's secret is discovered, the consequences can be dire. Rosco's reading has made him aware of Lincoln's rumored emancipation plans, but his friend Clem urges him to escape rather than wait. Rosco and Clem escape on the Underground Railroad, which puts them in Boston in time to hear the reading of the Emancipation Proclamation on New Year's Day, 1863. Meantime, Summer and her mother have come to an understanding, and although Summer's narration stops on New Year's Eve, the reader knows that legal freedom comes the next day.

In addition to echoing the themes of freedom and literacy, Pinkney's novel also provides a sense of some of the social and racial complexities of plantation life in the slave era. For instance, she deals with the thorny issue of intimate relationships between enslaved women and plantation owners. Usually, such relationships are characterized as rape, but in this case Kit, the children's mother, divulges her own silent thunder when she explains to Summer that she had fallen in love with Gideon Parnell, the master of the plantation and Summer and Roscoe's biological father, when she and Gideon were both young. Kit further reveals that she under-stands the social pressures that prevent him from acknowledging the children he fathered with her. Through her characterization of Kit, Pinkney illuminates some of the complications and paradoxes peculiar to the entwined lives of the slaveholders and the enslaved.

Dear America

A number of African American writers have produced fictional diaries for Scholastic's *Dear America* historical series. Two are particularly relevant here since they involve enslaved young Black women and their pursuit of both literacy and freedom. The mere fact that the novels are in the form of diaries ostensibly written by slaves puts the spotlight on literacy. Patricia McKissack's *A Picture of Freedom: The Diary of Clotee, a Slave Girl* (1997) is set in 1859, just before the outbreak of the Civil War. Clotee has learned to read and write by listening in on the lessons given to William, the son of the plantation owner, while she fans the air to keep the flies away from William and his mother. She has fashioned a makeshift diary out of papers found in the trash. The novel is full of the details of the daily lives of the enslaved people on this antebellum plantation.

One important thread of the plot involves Clotee's efforts to improve her literacy skills while concealing her ability to read and write. Another is the various characters' responses to the urge to be free. Clotee and William's tutor, a covert abolitionist, share each other's secrets, and when he finds himself in trouble, Clotee concocts a scheme that saves him, but he is forced to leave the plantation. When the tutor returns surreptitiously and offers Clotee an opportunity to escape, she decides to stay on and keep open the Underground Railroad station that the tutor has set up on the plantation, helping other enslaved people to become free. In having Clotee make that decision, McKissack's book calls to mind Du Bois's goal of having *The Brownie's Book* inspire children to a spirit of sacrifice, and Greenfield's reference, in her 1975 manifesto, to wanting children to be dedicated to the cause of freedom. It also echoes Hansen's assertion, regarding Kofi in *The Captive*, that taking on the responsibility to help others secure their freedom was a mark of greatness.

Joyce Hansen's contribution to the *Dear America* series, *I Thought My Soul Would Rise and Fly* (1997), is set in 1865 after the Civil War has ended. Patsy, who pos-sesses both a limp and a stutter, has remained on the Davis Hall plantation, along with many other former slaves, working as a salaried employee. Her diary, along with pen and ink, was given to her as a joke by Mrs. Davis's niece, who assumed Patsy was too stupid to learn to read and write when they played school. Patsy *has* learned, of course, and the diary becomes the friend in whom she confides her thoughts and observations. As one of the few literate Black people on the plantation, Patsy begins to teach others, thus emulating her favorite fictional character, Goody Two Shoes, whom she had met through listening in on the White children's lessons.

Through Patsy's experiences, Hansen provides insight into the challenges facing both Black and White Southerners in the immediate aftermath of the Civil War. In particular, she stresses the options the ex-slaves exercised, the dilemmas they faced, and the priorities they set. Now, they could choose their own names, locate and reunite with loved ones, marry their mates, make demands as a labor force (e.g., get rid of the overseer), insist on schooling, and ultimately leave to start a new life elsewhere. These new liberties coexisted with an abundance of confusion and uncertainty—former slaves' fear of the unknown, violent resistance to schooling by White terrorists, former slaveholders' unwillingness to relinquish control over their former slaves, a lack of opportunities to obtain paid employment, divided loyalties among the former slaves, broken government promises. Thus, through Patsy's observations and interactions, Hansen not only puts more human faces on slavery, she makes readers aware that its effects were profound, widespread, and long lasting.

War and Reconstruction

In addition to *The Captive* and her contribution to the *Dear America* series, Hansen produced a trilogy of novels set during the Civil War and Reconstruction: *Which Way Freedom?* (1986), *Out from This Place* (1988), and *The Heart Calls Home* (1999a). They follow the fortunes and misfortunes of Obi, Easter, and Jason as they participate in the Civil War and make new lives for themselves after the war is over. It is also a love story relating the long and roundabout journey Obi and Easter take to end up where their hearts lead them—home with each other. The books are set in and around South Carolina and the islands off its coast, beginning during the Civil War and ending in 1869. Obi, Easter, and Jason, the only three slaves on the Jennings plantation, have as family only each other and Buka, an elderly ex-slave who still lives near the plantation. In the first book, Obi and Easter, disguised as a boy, escape with Buka's help but are forced to reluctantly leave five-year-old Jason asleep in the big house. They are captured and held in camp by Confederate soldiers until Obi is able to escape and join the Union Army. Easter chooses to make her getaway close to the Jennings plantation so she can find and free Jason.

The second book is Easter's story (Hansen 1988). She and Jason, along with a group of other former slaves, escape to one of the Sea Islands, where they work for wages and are able to buy land. Easter learns to read and eventually accepts an opportunity to study in Philadelphia so that she can further her education and return to teach others. Jason has joined a traveling medicine show.

In the final book (Hansen 1999a), Obi searches until he learns where Easter is. In the army, he had taken the name Obadiah Booker, in memory of Buka, and he had learned to read and write. This final story is told partly through their letters, while Easter is in the North studying and Obi is helping to establish a new community of free Black people. When Easter returns to visit old friends and to see Obi, she intends to return to the North, but she realizes that her heart and home are with Obi and the new community.

As in her other historical novels, Hansen has managed to incorporate a great deal of history into the story while keeping the attention of the reader on the characters and their lives. She paints a detailed picture of Reconstruction from the perspective of former slaves and makes clear the choices and challenges they faced. Her stress is on their determination and ability to take control of their lives. She again portrays some of the hardships that were in evidence in her *Dear America* novel, as well as the challenges, such as disease, death, and severe weather, faced by the group as they attempt to establish and maintain a free settlement. She also depicts some of the racial turmoil that followed the defeat of the South. Most notably, she creates a set of very realistic characters through whose eyes readers can come to understand the impact of slavery on the enslaved—their pursuit of freedom, their strong desire for education, the renewing or forging of strong family ties. As Hansen noted:

African Americans contributed much to their own freedom—this spirit is what I wanted to convey to my young readers—a brave, proud people who did not just sit and wait to be freed.

I have tried to capture that spirit in all of my subsequent historical fiction and non-fiction. I also try to find the human emotions behind the facts and figures gleaned during the research. (1999, 63)

Hansen tells a good story, transports readers to a past time and place, and engages them in the lives of her characters while inviting them to make connections between the past and the present.

Historical Fiction for the Middle Grades/Middle School

One of the most prolific producers of African American historical fiction, Harriet Gillem Robinet has specialized in creating historical novels for readers from nine to twelve years old. In the eight novels she published between 1991 and 2001, she places spunky Black children, all about twelve or thirteen years old, in the midst of exciting historical events, often in circumstances involving famous people. Four of these novels, set in the era of slavery/Reconstruction, feature courageous Black children actively engaged in liberating themselves and others or actively resisting oppression. Her enslaved characters are often situated in uncommon circumstances or in atypical settings. In *If You Please, President Lincoln* (1994), for example, Moses is well educated, having been taught by the Jesuit priest who held him as a slave. Moses runs away to avoid being sold and befriends Goshen, a free Black man who is blind but also well educated. Together, they find themselves shanghaied and transported to an inhospitable island off the coast of Haiti with a few hundred others, caught in a futile scheme to colonize freed slaves. Moses, with Goshen's support, becomes a leader in organizing the Black people on board ship, and on the island he becomes a hero. Back in Washington, D.C., Goshen eventually sets up business, and Moses continues his education. The novel is a survival story as well as a fictional slave narrative written in formal language reminiscent of nineteenth century prose.

In *Washington City Is Burning* (1996), young Virginia/Virgie is transferred from the estate of James and Dolley Madison to the White House, ostensibly to help with the First Lady's many parties. While working as a servant to Dolley Madison, Virgie also becomes involved in helping slaves escape. It is August 1814, and Virgie is witness to and participant in events connected with the War of 1812, including the burning of the White House and the city. Also set during the War of 1812, *The Twins, the Pirates, and the Battle of New Orleans* (1997) is a far-fetched adventure story and mystery novel involving twins Pierre and Andrew, who escape from a slaveholder and live in a tree house their father had built for them in the swamp. They have many narrow escapes as they find themselves entangled with Jean Lafitte's pirates and events of the war, including Andrew Jackson's Battle of New Orleans. Their ultimate goal is to liberate their mother and sister before the slaveholder sells them.

Forty Acres and Maybe a Mule (1998), depicts the period from April to September 1865, just after the Civil War. Twelve-year-old Pascal and his brother Gideon, along with some friends, set off for Georgia to collect title to forty acres—and maybe a mule—that the Freedman's Bureau had promised to former slaves. Acting as a family unit, and with Pascal supplying some of the leadership, they set up a promising farm, but all around them angry and hateful Whites, desperately trying to preserve the old social order, threaten violence. Then, the government reneges on its promise and returns the land to Southern Whites, leaving the family to head for the Sea Islands, where land is available for Black people to buy.

Although Robinet's books are not formulaic, they do share some common elements. She aims for a middle-grade/middle school audience and keeps the attention of the reader with a good deal of action. Like many novels for this age group, Robinet's are in a sense "growing up" stories; her child characters mature over time. Virgie notes, for example, that she entered August of her twelfth year "like a staggering caterpillar, and emerged a winged butterfly" (1996, 1). Robinet keeps her plots moving, but she also conveys a sense of her characters' emotions and their growing self-confidence.

Although she does not hesitate to depict the cruelty and meanness of slaveholders and other antagonists, her characters are often complex, showing both strengths and weaknesses. Enslaved people in Robinet's books are not above jealousy, meanness, and betrayal. Some of them exhibit class consciousness—taking pride in the higher social status of their masters, believing house slaves to be superior to field slaves. Part of the protagonists' maturing is that they eventually see the error of their ways.

The characters are not without laughter; even in the midst of describing hardships, Robinet is likely to inject some humor. Pascal, for instance, is a punster who tells terrible jokes. Robinet never excuses slaveholders for their treatment of fellow human beings, but her White characters are not all evil. Some of them are kind and committed to actively pursuing social justice; others simply are not strong enough to rise above the social mores of their times. Dolley Madison, for example, is a Quaker and declares that slavery is not to her liking, yet she continues to hold, buy, and sell slaves.

Each of the books has an author's note at the end, offering information about the factual history on which the novels are based, and a bibliography suggesting further reading. Like Joyce Hansen, Robinet excels at weaving information into her stories. She provides numerous details that make the setting come alive for young readers and packs in numerous historical facts. And, she tells a good story, even though her characters' ventures sometimes stretch credibility.

BEYOND SLAVERY: THE STRUGGLE CONTINUES

Between 1991 and 2001, Harriet Gillem Robinet produced four other historical novels, situated in various periods of the nineteenth and twentieth centuries. Set during the Great Chicago Fire of 1871, *Children of the Fire* (1991) relates the adventures of Hallelujah, a feisty and strong-minded Black girl who finds herself wandering the streets as the fire rages. *Missing in Haymarket Square* (2001) features Dinah, an African American girl, and two children from an Austrian immigrant family, all of whom are drawn into the labor dispute that led to the Haymarket Riot of 1886. *Mississippi Chariot* (1994) is the story of Abraham Lincoln Jackson, a resourceful young African American boy, and his determination to free his father, who is serving on the Mississippi chain gang for a crime he did not commit. *Walking to the Bus Rider Blues* (2000), which is in part a mystery story, focuses on the experiences of Alfa, a young boy in Montgomery, Alabama, who is trying to help keep a roof over his family's head during the bus boycott of 1956.

As with her novels depicting the era of slavery and Reconstruction, Robinet's protagonists are all spirited, courageous young people struggling against formidable odds. All of them are economically poor, although some are better off in that regard than others, and all of them run up against racist attitudes, behaviors, and inequities. The books are full of details that make the time and place and the historical events come alive for young readers. They provide an understanding of how these important events affected the lives of ordinary families. Although the heroic actions of the protagonists sometimes appear improbable, all of Robinet's young people take action to solve problems, contribute to their families and their communities, and thereby make a difference.

In her author's notes, Robinet sometimes expresses the ideological stance that underlies her work. In *Children of the Fire* (1991), she notes:

Children in all times need to realize how important their lives are. Children piled bricks, hauled ash, and sold souvenirs to help their families and their city. The fire taught them, as it should teach us, that diversity of color, class, and culture should add interest to life but should never be allowed to divide us.
We are all equally children of God and of our universe. (134)

Thus, Robinet's Black protagonists often befriend or are befriended by White characters. Hallelujah befriends a Jewish girl and a rich White girl who are also wandering the streets, separated from their families during the fire. She actually takes the rich girl home, and they express to each other their understanding that they are "equally children of God," even though the adults around them have not yet reached that conclusion. In *Mississippi Chariot* (1994), Abraham (Shortning Bread) saves a White boy from drowning, and in turn the White boy tries to be his friend, and he and his mother surreptitiously help the Black family escape a White lynch mob. In *Haymarket Square*, Dinah's family actually shares living space with an Austrian immigrant family, and desperately poor Black Americans and equally desperate White European immigrants work together to fight for improved working conditions and just to survive. Although sometimes a bit heavy handed, Robinet's focus on positive interactions among Black and White people echoes Lorenz Graham's conviction that "people are people are people" (1973).

In addition to their central problem (e.g., working conditions, poverty, paying the rent), all of the Black protagonists and their families are also fighting racism and social injustice on a personal level (name-calling, insults, humiliations, hateful actions), as well as on an institutional/societal level (segregation, job discrimination). In the author's note for *Washington City* (1996), Robinet writes: "May this story of slavery and injustice of yesteryear challenge us to work for freedom and justice today" (147). Apparently, Robinet shares one of the objectives expressed by Greenfield: that her readers be inspired to commit to the cause of freedom.

In a genre focused on the African American struggle against oppression, it is somewhat surprising that so few fictional books are set in the context of the organized opposition of the 1950s and 1960s. Numerous biographies of civil rights leaders have been written for young people, and a substantial number of nonfiction works chronicle some of the major events of the era. It appears, however, that not much more than a handful of novels for young people by African Americans have placed their protagonists in the midst of civil rights protest activities. In addition to Harriet Gillem Robinet's book set during the Montgomery bus boycott, Mildred Pitts Walter, Brenda Wilkinson, Yvette Moore, and the famous playwright and actor Ossie Davis each produced a young adult novel in which the main character has some involvement with protest or civil disobedience. Walter (*The Girl on the Outside*, 1982) and Wilkinson (*Not Separate, Not Equal*, 1987) deal with school desegregation, while Moore (*Freedom Songs*, 1991) and Davis (*Just Like Martin*, 1992) deal with demonstrations against legal discrimination. Based on or incorporating real events, these novels, all of which are set in the South, depict the daily indignities, humiliations, threats of violence, and discriminatory practices that led Black people to protest and to take a stand. They also provide insight into the determination and courage that it took for Black people in Southern communities to defy the White people in power, on whom they often had to depend in order to make a living. Southern Whites often retaliated for organized protest by withholding credit or goods or by firing people or otherwise cutting off their livelihoods. Many also reacted violently to any threat of change. Against those racist threats and actions, the teenage characters in these books, and often their parents and members of their communities, as well as White people of goodwill, show remarkable courage and, in keeping with the tenets of nonviolence, remarkable restraint. These novels capture a moment in time and show the impact of the movement on families and communities, not only in the South, but also nationally. For young readers for whom the civil rights movement seems like ancient history, they are a reminder of some of the cost of the freedoms they take for granted.

FAMILY STORIES, FAMILY SAGAS

A thematic emphasis on family—family love, family connections, family strength—is central to African American children's literature, and historical fiction is no exception. In fact, some of the most compelling African American historical fiction works for children or young adults are family sagas created by two of the most highly respected African American authors of the twentieth century—Walter Dean Myers and Mildred D. Taylor. Myers's fictional Lewis family is brought to life in a single long novel, while the chronicle of Taylor's Logan family occupies a series of four novels and five novellas.

Myers's family saga, *The Glory Field* (1994) relates the experiences of five succeeding generations of one family, beginning with the capture of Muhammad Bilal in Sierra Leone in 1753 and ending in New York in 1994. At the time of his capture, Muhammad is eleven years old. The brief introductory chapter describes the horrors of his journey through the Middle Passage—the painful shackles, the misery in the hold, the struggle to get enough air. On the ship, Muhammad resolves to survive, and for the last part of the journey, he concentrates on just breathing from one moment to the next. He and the shackles that had bound him end up on Live Oaks Plantation on Curry Island, South Carolina, where Muhammad grows up to become the patriarch of the Lewis family. Each of the five sections that follow focuses on one of Muhammad's descendants—within the context of the family—and provides a picture of what life was like for African Americans in similar situations in a given time period.

In 1864, near the end of the Civil War, the family is on the plantation, being abused by the vicious overseer. Muhammad's great-grandson Joshua and Joshua's nephew Lem try to escape, and when the overseer catches thirteen-year-old Lizzy giving the recaptured Lem some water, her fate becomes tied to theirs. The three fugitives stumble on members of a Black Union Army unit and follow them to freedom. By 1900, the family has acquired the glory field of the title, a parcel of land that had been given to them by the Yankees after the Civil War. Lizzy's fifteen-year-old son, Elijah, and his cousin Abby rescue a young White child who has been kidnapped by a local drunk, but in his dealings with the local White supremacists, he is seen as "uppity." They threaten to "teach him a lesson," prompting his family to put him on the first train north to Chicago. Thirty years later, Elijah's sixteen-year-old daughter Luvenia is working in Chicago as a live-in maid.

Luvenia dreams of going to college, but when the shenanigans of her employer's daughter not only spoil Luvenia's chances of obtaining a required letter from him but also get her fired, she decides to strike out on her own as a businesswoman.

In 1964, Abby's grandson Tommy, in his junior year of high school, is being wooed as a basketball player for State, on the condition that he not disturb the racist status quo. When the sheriff tries to cover up a violent incident in which a White neighbor had been badly beaten for participating in a protest march with Negroes, Tommy chains himself to the sheriff with Muhammad's shackles and lands in jail, where he comes to understand that freedom is worth dying for.

In 1994, the scene shifts to New York City, where two of Elijah's teenaged great-grandsons are living. Malcolm is a musician, seeking to create a new style of music, and Shep is addicted to crack cocaine. Aunt Luvenia, now a very successful business-woman, provides airfare for the boys to attend the Lewis family reunion in Curry, but predictably Shep yields to his addiction, and they end up hitchhiking. Riding in the back of a truck, they experience a modern Middle Passage—imperiled by the overwhelming stench of the truck's cargo of animal hides, Shep's forced drug withdrawal, and the struggle just to find enough air to breathe. Like their ancestor Muhammad, they survive their journey and finally reach Curry Island, where they reaffirm family ties and then return to New York to continue the struggle.

Myers's novel parallels and provides insight into two-and-a-half centuries of American and African American history. Across the generations, the Lewis family's experiences provide glimpses into aspects of the African American struggle—plantation slavery, the economic and race-based hardships at the turn of the century, the aftereffects of the Great Migration, the midcentury civil rights movement, and the contemporary slavery of drug addiction. At the center of this novel is the family land, which, in an agricultural economy not only represented a degree of independence, but also functioned as a gathering place for the family, a place to harvest strength.

Myers marks each of the periods with references to African American music—from spirituals, to ragtime, to protest music, to church music, to a contemporary multiethnic music that he describes as "postmodern funk." His big themes are some of the central ones in African American children's/young adult literature—the importance of family as the source of stability, direction, and strength as well as a safe harbor; and the indomitable spirit that has enabled African Americans to survive. Each of the teenage protagonists reaches a turning point and makes a life-changing move toward liberation.

THE LOGAN FAMILY SAGA: MILDRED D. TAYLOR

> I have tried to distill the essence of Black life, so familiar to most Black families, to make the Logans an embodiment of that spiritual heritage.
>
> Mildred D. Taylor (1977, 403)

The story of Mildred D. Taylor's fictional Logan family seems familiar to every Black American family with roots in the South and recollections that stretch four or five generations into the past. The Logans first appeared in *Song of the Trees* (1975), which won first prize in the 1973 Minority Writers Contest sponsored by the Council on Interracial Books for Children (CIBC). From there, Taylor went on to become only the second African American writer to win the John Newbery Medal, for *Roll of Thunder, Hear My Cry* (1976), and justifiably the most highly acclaimed African American author of historical fiction for children and young adults—another testament to the impact of the CIBC contest. It is interesting that Taylor, in the quotation at the start of this section, echoes Virginia Hamilton's declarations that her work is an attempt to capture, through story, the essence of Black life in America. In Taylor's case, Black life is a matter of surviving and maintaining self-respect and dignity while living in a racist cultural context.

Mildred Taylor was born in Mississippi, although she was taken to Toledo when she was still an infant, and she grew up in Ohio. She spent summers in Mississippi, however, on land owned by her family and thereby gained a sense of the rural landscape where her father grew up. More significantly, she absorbed her father's stories about his family and their neighbors and what it was like to grow up in his time and place. Those stories became the basis for nine books to date—four novels (another novel is promised) and five novellas, almost all set in rural Mississippi, mainly in the 1930s and 1940s. Even *The Gold Cadillac* (1987b), which begins and ends in Toledo, Ohio, involves a journey to Mississippi, sometime around 1950. The most recently published Logan novel, *The Land* (2001), which is a prequel to *Roll of Thunder, Hear My Cry* (1976), is set in the 1880s and tells the story of Cassie's grandfather and how he acquired the Logan land.

The CIBC contest winner became *Song of the Trees* (Taylor 1975), which introduces the family and places them in the context of the racist society of Depression-era Mississippi, in which an unscrupulous White man believes he can, without permission or fair compensation and with impunity, cut down the trees on Logan land and sell the lumber simply because he is White and the Logans are not. Cassie loves the trees, and it is she and the other children who discover that they are being stolen when suddenly the song of the trees goes silent. Mary Logan sends for her husband, who is working in Louisiana. When David Logan appears, he threatens to blow up the forest rather than allow Andersen to take the trees or the lumber: "One thing you don't understand, Andersen," Papa said, "is that a black man's always gotta be ready to die. And it don't make me any difference if I die today or tomorrow. Just as long as I die right" (49). Since his oldest son has helped him set the dynamite, and all the children, against their father's orders, witness the confrontation, the children learn a valuable lesson about their father's courage and strength.

Thus, David Logan is established as a no-nonsense, independent Black man with a great deal of self-respect and the will to do whatever is necessary to protect his family and their land, while maintaining that self-respect. *Song of the Trees*, which is only 52 pages long including illustrations, is set at about the same time as the Newbery-winning *Roll of Thunder, Hear My Cry*, which is probably the best known of Taylor's books. It is in *Roll of Thunder* that we acquire a deeper knowledge of the Logans—spunky Cassie, the narrator of most of the Logan books, who is eight at the time; Stacey, the responsible oldest at eleven; cautious Christopher John, who is seven; and fastidious Little Man, who is six. Their mother, Mary, is a courageous schoolteacher who dares to disturb the established order; their father, David, is the strong and loving guardian of his family; and their paternal grandmother, Big Ma, is the family matriarch. In part because of their land ownership, the Logans can maintain a degree of independence not afforded their Black neighbors, who are dependent on the White landowners and businessmen for their livelihood. Because the Logan children's contact with Whites has been limited, they have been somewhat sheltered from some of the most blatant racist actions of their neighbors; they also have never learned to see themselves as inferior.

Along with the Logans, *Roll of Thunder* introduces some of the White characters who live in the community—the Wallaces, who own the local store; Harlan Granger, who owns much of the land; and the Simms family, who are poor and mostly hateful. We also meet the lawyer, Mr. Jamison, who is sympathetic and helpful to the Logans and other Black people in the community; and Jeremy Simms, who does not share his family's hateful attitudes and wants badly to be friends with the Logan children.

In *Roll of Thunder*, the Logan children gain a deeper understanding of how racism affects their everyday lives. They also learn something about how and when to fight back. One of the first incidents in the book involves the White school bus, which regularly runs the Logan children off the road, endangering them and splashing them with mud when it has rained. One day after a rainy spell has made many potholes in the road, the Logan children secretly spend their lunch recess digging a deep trench in the middle of the road and filling it with water. After school, they hide and watch as the bus hits their hole and breaks an axle, making it necessary for the White children to walk to and from school for a week or so. Revenge is sweet, but the Logan children know that their actions must remain forever secret.

In another potentially far-reaching incident in *Roll of Thunder*, Cassie learns a very hard lesson when she goes to town and accidentally bumps into Jeremy's sister Lillian Jean, who demands an apology and orders Cassie off the sidewalk. When Cassie resists, Lillian Jean's father, the hateful Charlie Simms, knocks Cassie down and demands an apology to "Miz Lillian Jean." Big Ma makes Cassie comply, causing Cassie much confusion, hurt feelings, and anger. Cassie's mother explains the situation to Cassie, but it is her father who helps her understand that she must pick her battles and be fully aware of the potential consequences of her actions.

Cassie learns that lesson well and uses her head to work out a way to settle the score with Lillian Jean so that only she and Lillian Jean will ever know. Patiently ingratiating herself with Lillian Jean, Cassie lures her into the woods, where she thrashes her and threatens to reveal Lillian Jean's most embarrassing secrets if she dares to tell anyone. Stacey's friend T. J., weak and gullible and lacking the strong family upbringing that the Logan children have, sets off a crisis when he allows the Wallace brothers to lead him into participating in a robbery in which a White store owner is killed. Only David Logan's quick and drastic action saves T. J. from a lynch mob.

Roll of Thunder was followed by two sequels, *Let the Circle Be Unbroken* (1981), set in 1935, in which T. J.'s murder trial is held and in which Stacey leaves to find work to help the family hold onto the land. *The Road to Memphis* (1990b) is set in 1941. Cassie, who is now college age, and her brother Stacey become involved in saving a friend who dared to strike White men who were publicly taunting him. The prequel to *Roll of Thunder, The Land* (2001), is narrated by Cassie's paternal grandfather, Paul-Edward, the son of a White slaveholder and a woman who was part Indian and part African and held as a slave to the children's father. As a child, Paul-Edward and his sister had been acknowledged and cared for by their White father along with the children he fathered with his White wife, but even his influence could go only so far in Mississippi in the 1880s. Eventually, Paul-Edward, understanding the restrictions under which any Black man in Mississippi had to live, sets out on his own and with great determination endures many hardships until he is able to purchase his own land, which becomes the Taylor family homestead.

Between novels, Taylor also produced four shorter works, each relating an incident in which the Logans or some other Black person or persons encounter racist practices.

The Well (1995) is set when David Logan was a young boy. A drought has dried up all the wells in the area except the Logans's. They permit any and all of their neighbors—Black and White—to draw water, including the hateful Simms family. When the Simms boys and David's quick-tempered brother Hammond meet, trouble follows, and the animosity between the families continues for at least another generation.

In *The Friendship* (Taylor 1987a), Cassie and her brothers witness a confrontation between the elderly Black man Mr. Tom Bee and John Wallace, owner of the general store. Tom Bee had been a surrogate father to Wallace, who had promised that Bee would never have to call him "mister" even though it is understood that Black people must always use a title for White people. Goaded by his sons and his peers, Wallace cannot bring himself to continue to allow Tom Bee to call him by his first name, but Tom Bee intends to see to it that Wallace keeps that promise. In the inevitable confrontation, bullets fly and Tom Bee is injured as the children watch.

Mississippi Bridge (Taylor 1990a) is narrated by Jeremy Simms, who observes the action from the porch of the Wallace's store, which is also the bus stop. He watches as Black bus passengers are humiliated by the Wallaces and the bus driver, while White ones are treated politely. Among the Black passengers is Big Ma, who is accompanied to the bus by Cassie and her brothers. When a large White family appears at the last minute, the Black passengers are forced to relinquish their seats and wait for the next bus. The dramatic and tragic ending, in which the bus plunges into the raging river, leaves a reader to think about issues of justice, injustice, destiny, and divine retribution.

The Gold Cadillac (1987b) is not explicitly about Cassie and her family, but it is also based on Taylor's family remembrances. It relates the story of what happens when a Black man living in Toledo decides to drive his brand new 1950 gold Cadillac to Mississippi to visit family. On this trip, his two daughters realize that the picnic basket they packed with food is not for fun but is a necessity because restaurants and hotels were not open to Black people, especially in the South. Once the family moves into Mississippi, they are pulled over, and the father is arrested. It was dangerous for a Black man, even in 1950, to be seen in Mississippi driving a brand new luxury car with Northern license plates. The father takes the car back to Memphis, where he borrows a cousin's older car to keep his family safe in Mississippi. The trip is the girls' baptism in the fire of racism.

The Logan family saga is unique in African American and in American children's literature. With the clear delineation of her characters and vivid details, Taylor paints a powerful portrait of the struggles of a close-knit Black family determined to survive in a cultural setting that is intended to crush their spirits and maintain them in a place of inferiority and submission. Were it not for her strong characterization and her gifted storytelling, it would be difficult for today's children and young adults to imagine the circumstances in which the Logans lived—the taken-for-granted assumption of superiority that permitted White people to mistreat, cheat, abuse, humiliate, and insult Black people with impunity. It is hard to imagine daily life with its constant reminders of low-caste status for Black people in 1930s and 1940s Mississippi, such as segregated water fountains, schools, and buses; not being waited on in a store until all White customers have been served; not being allowed to try on clothes before buying; being called "boy," "Auntie," "gal," or the "n" word but never addressed with a title such as Mr. or Mrs. Add to that the knowledge that any behavior considered too "uppity" could result in violence or possible death, and any perceived disrespect or violence toward Whites, even in self-defense, could bring a lynch mob. Under such circumstances, the Logan family seems remarkably courageous and strong, the children's upbringing particularly wise and admirable, and the significance of the Logans' land ownership quite clear. When one understands that the Logans' story is grounded in real-life experiences, the family story becomes even more remarkable.

THE NOVELS OF CHRISTOPHER PAUL CURTIS: RECENT HISTORY LACED WITH HUMOR

Christopher Paul Curtis entered the field of African American children's literature with a big splash. His first novel, *The Watsons Go to Birmingham—1963* (1995), was both a Newbery Honor Book and a Coretta Scott King Honor Book; his second, *Bud, Not Buddy* (1999), won both the Coretta Scott King Author Award and the 2000 Newbery Medal, making Curtis the third African American and the first African American male to be awarded a Newbery Medal. His achievement is even more remarkable considering that, before he turned to writing, he spent thirteen years working on an automobile assembly line at the Fisher Body Plant in Flint, Michigan, his hometown. Almost a decade after he left the automobile factory, and after he had worked at several other jobs while attending college, Curtis's wife suggested that she support the family financially while he take a year to write. The result was *The Watsons*, which Curtis says he did not regard as a children's book; he submitted it to a Delacorte young adult writer's contest just to have it read by a professional editor.

The Watsons was originally based on a family trip, in which Curtis wanted to drive from Flint to Florida in 24 hours nonstop. It was called *The Watsons Go to Florida.* Once he got the fictional family to Florida, the story fizzled out, but when Curtis's son brought home a poem about the Birmingham church bombing, *The Watsons Go to Birmingham* came alive.

The novel is episodic, and until the Sunday morning when little sister Joetta goes to Sunday school in Birmingham, very funny. The narrator is Kenny Watson, who is ten. He relates a number of events that happen to the "Weird Watsons," especially to older brother Byron, who is thirteen and exhibiting unacceptable behaviors that have his parents exasperated. Byron's escapades include having his hair straightened in defiance of his father's prohibition, playing with matches in the house, and kissing his image on a frozen car mirror. A good deal of the humor comes from Kenny's—and his father and brother's—rhetorical styles that, much like the protagonists of Walter Dean Myers's early novels, include a great deal of exaggeration, wordplay, outlandish images, and creative metaphors. When Byron's behavior becomes unbearable, their mother decides it is time to take him home to Alabama so that *her* mother can shape him up. But, while in Birmingham, the story turns serious when Byron saves Kenny from a near drowning, and Joetta goes off with the neighbors to Sunday school on the day when the church is bombed, and four little girls are killed. Once back in Flint, Kenny has a difficult time dealing with the trauma brought on by what he witnessed that Sunday, but Byron is able to help him resolve his concerns.

For all his humor, Curtis was also successful in creating a portrait of a loving family with well-delineated personalities and, in the case of Byron, something of the depth and complexity of a teenager with a hard shell hiding a tender heart. The novel is full of the details of daily living that make this family seem real and likeable—the UltraGlide record player, the car named the Brown Bomber, the music of Dinah

Washington and Nat King Cole, and the affectionate banter between the parents. Curtis also is adept at having the father use stories within the larger story as a means to entertain.

Bud, Not Buddy (1999), Curtis's Newbery Award-winning second novel, is the story of an orphan who sets out to find his father. Set in Michigan during the Great Depression, it follows Bud (not Buddy) from an orphanage to a terrible foster home from which he escapes, to a hobo camp, and eventually to Grand Rapids, the home of Herman Calloway, whom he believes to be his father. In his suitcase, Bud carries all that is left of his mother's possessions—a photograph, a pouch of rocks with writing on them, a blanket, and her highly prized flyers advertising Herman Calloway and the Dusky Devastators of the Depression.

Along the way, Bud is helped by a number of sympathetic strangers, among them a poor family in a food line, a kindhearted librarian, and a fatherly Black union organizer. He is also buoyed by his memories of his mother and her staunch belief that when one door closes, another opens, and by his own "Rules and Things for Having a Funner Life and Making a Better Liar Out of Yourself." The union man sees Bud safely to Grand Rapids, where he discovers that Herman Calloway is too old to be his father and too cantankerous to even talk to. Bud is permitted to stay at Calloway's house, however, where the band members are caring, and eventually they all figure out the real connection between Bud, his mother, and Herman E. Calloway. Bud has at last found a home and a family.

Although Bud's ventures sometimes read a bit like a tall tale, he comes across as both a likeable and believable young boy with an active imagination and an abundance of grit. One of the striking features of this novel is the African American male voice of the narrative, which is full of wordplay, repetitions, figurative language, childlike visual imagery, proverbial sayings, and humor. Along with the humor, however, Curtis also depicts the pain and sorrow that Bud experiences as a ten-year-old out in the world on his own with no resources except himself and the caring adults he meets along the way. One such person is the woman at the library that Bud and his mother used to frequent. Bud went there seeking his favorite librarian, a Miss Hill, who had left to get married and live in Chicago. The Miss Hill character is a tribute to the late Charlemae Hill Rollins, the real-life, well-known, and highly respected African American librarian who edited the bibliography of books about African Americans, *We Build Together* (1941/1948/1967).

Curtis also provides a sense of what it must have been like to live during the Great Depression with its food lines and hobo camps, and he gives glimpses of the racism that was also a social issue; the union organizer picks Bud up as he is walking on the highway in the middle of the night near a town known for its KKK-type attitude toward Black people. And the band also has to find ways to get around racist attitudes and policies applied to entertainers. It is Curtis's crafty combination of humor and sadness, realism and tall tale, along with his depiction of the historical setting and his distinctive voice that make this book a winner.

Whatever the time setting, African American historical fiction for young people is overwhelmingly a celebration of the resilience of spirit that has enabled African Americans to survive in a racially hostile environment. It is about illuminating the African American struggle for social justice and human dignity. Even novels cloaked in humor embrace that struggle. This fiction has the potential, like Hamilton's liberation literature, to empower readers by allowing them to participate in the struggle and triumph with the protagonists. African American history, even that presented and interpreted through fiction, is also American history. As such, it transcends cultural boundaries and invites readers to become a part of the struggle for social justice.

BIBLIOGRAPHY OF BOOKS FOR CHILDREN AND YOUNG ADULTS

Sources other than books for children and young adults are documented in a reference list at the end of the book.

Berry, James. 1992. *Ajeemah and His Son*. New York: Harper.

Bontemps, Arna. 1948. *The Story of the Negro*. New York: Knopf.

Bradby, Marie. 1995. *More than Anything Else*. Illus. by Chris Soentpiet. New York: Orchard.

Chambers, Veronica. 1998. *Amistad Rising*. San Diego, CA: Harcourt.

Curtis, Christopher Paul. 1995. *The Watsons Go to Birmingham—1963*. New York: Delacorte.

———. 1999. *Bud, Not Buddy*. New York: Delacorte.

Davis, Ossie. 1992. *Just Like Martin*. New York: Simon and Schuster.

Feelings, Tom. 1995. *The Middle Passage: White Ships, Black Cargo*. New York: Dial.

Hamilton, Virginia. 1983. *The Magical Adventures of Pretty Pearl*. New York: Harper.

———. 1985. *The People Could Fly*. New York: Knopf.

———. 1988. *Anthony Burns: The Defeat and Triumph of a Fugitive Slave*. New York: Knopf.

Hansen, Joyce. 1994. *The Captive*. New York: Scholastic.

———. 1986. *Which Way Freedom?* New York: Walker.

———. 1988. *Out from This Place*. New York: Walker.

———. 1997. *I Thought My Soul Would Rise and Fly*. New York: Scholastic.

———. 1999. *The Heart Calls Home*. New York: Walker.

Hopkinson, Deborah. 1993. *Sweet Clara and the Freedom Quilt*. Illus. by James Ransome. New York: Knopf.

Johnson, Dolores. 1993. *Now Let Me Fly: The Story of a Slave Family*. New York: Macmillan.

———. 1994. *Seminole Diary*. New York: Macmillan.

Lester, Julius. 1968. *To Be a Slave*. New York: Dial.

———. 1997. *To Be a Slave*. 25th Anniversary Edition. New York: Dial.

———. 1972. *Long Journey Home: Stories from Black History*. New York: Dial.

———. 1982. *This Strange New Feeling*. New York: Dial.

———. 1998. *Black Cowboy, Wild Horses*. Illus. by Jerry Pinkney. New York: Dial.

———. 2005a. *Day of Tears: A Novel in Dialogue*. New York: Jump at the Sun/Hyperion.

———. 2005b. *The Old African*. Illus. by Jerry Pinkney. New York: Dial.

McKissack, Patricia. 1997. *A Picture of Freedom: The Diary of Clotee, a Slave Girl*. New York: Scholastic.

McKissack, Patricia and Fredrick L. McKissack. 1994. *Christmas in the Big House, Christmas in the Quarters*. Illus. by John Thompson. New York: Scholastic.

Moore, Yvette. 1991. *Freedom Songs*. New York: Orchard.

Myers, Walter Dean. 1991. *Now Is Your Time*. New York: Harper.

———. 1994. *The Glory Field*. New York: Scholastic.

Pace, Lorenzo. 2001. *Jalani and the Lock*. New York: Rosen Publishing Group.

Petry, Ann. 1964. *Tituba of Salem Village*. New York: Harper.

Pinkney, Andrea Davis. 1999. *Silent Thunder*. New York: Hyperion.

Robinet, Harriet Gillem. 1991. *Children of the Fire*. New York: Atheneum.

———. 1994a. *If You Please, President Lincoln*. New York: Atheneum.

———. 1994b. *Mississippi Chariot*. New York: Atheneum.

———. 1996. *Washington City Is Burning*. New York: Atheneum.

———. 1997. *The Twins, the Pirates, and the Battle of New Orleans*. New York: Atheneum.

———. 1998. *Forty Acres and Maybe a Mule*. New York: Atheneum.

———. 2000. *Walking the Bus Rider Blues*. New York: Atheneum.

————. 2001. *Missing in Haymarket Square*. New York: Atheneum.

Smalls, Irene. 1996. *Irene Jenny and the Christmas Masquerade: The Johnkanus*. Illus. by Melodye Benson Rosales. New York: Little, Brown.

Taylor, Mildred D. 1975. *Song of the Trees*. New York: Dial.

————. 1976. *Roll of Thunder, Hear My Cry*. New York: Dial.

————. 1981. *Let the Circle Be Unbroken*. New York: Dial.

————. 1987a. *The Friendship*. New York: Dial.

————. 1987b. *The Gold Cadillac*. New York: Dial.

————. 1990a. *Mississippi Bridge*. New York: Dial.

————. 1990b. *The Road to Memphis*. New York: Dial.

————. 1995. *The Well*. New York: Dial.

————. 2001. *The Land*. Dial.

Walter, Mildred Pitts. 1982. *The Girl on the Outside*. New York: Lothrop.

Wilkinson, Brenda. 1987. *Not Separate, Not Equal*. New York: Harper.

Wright, Courni. 1994a. *Journey to Freedom: A Story of the Underground Railroad*. Illus. by Gershom Griffith. New York: Holiday House.

————. 1994b. *Jumping the Broom*. Illus. by Gershom Griffith. New York: Holiday House.

Some Concluding Thoughts

Things don't fall apart. Things hold. Lines connect in thin ways that last and
last and lives become generations made out of pictures and words just kept.
Lucille Clifton (1976, 78–79)

Across a century and a half and across three generations of writers and artists in
the twentieth century, African American children's literature has been characterized by both continuity and change. Because it has been in part a response to the
sociopolitical circumstances in which Black people have found themselves, African
American children's literature has been a purposeful enterprise, seldom if ever art
for art's sake. As the literature has developed, across writers and artists and across
time, it appears to have been shaped—in the main—by a few common "lines that
connect in thin ways and last and last," as Lucille Clifton expresses it. It is these
connecting lines that mark the literature as a distinctive body of work.

Across genres, in poetry, picture books, and contemporary and historical fiction, Black authors and artists have created a body of children's literature that
(1) celebrates the strengths of the Black family as a cultural institution and vehicle for survival; (2) bears witness to Black people's determined struggle for freedom, equality, and dignity; (3) nurtures the souls of Black children by reflecting
back to them, both visually and verbally, the beauty and competencies that we as
adults see in them; (4) situates itself through its language and its content, within
African American literary and cultural contexts; and (5) honors the tradition of
story as a way of teaching and as a way of knowing. Aspiring to be "'teachy' but
not preachy," this body of work constitutes a rich resource, a literary treasure for
families, schools, and libraries.

This treasure becomes even richer if one includes the work that is being done
in African American nonfiction and biography for children, which is beyond the
scope of this book. A brief note here, however, recognizes its importance as a
source of both information and pleasurable reading. Much of the African American
nonfiction for children is historical in nature, but today's authors are exploring
little-known aspects of African American history, such as African Americans' participation in the whaling industry. Authors are also writing about African American
arts such as literature and music. The subjects of biographies range from well-
known figures such as Dr. Martin Luther King Jr. and Mrs. Rosa Parks, to lesser

known pioneers and heroes such as aviator Bessie Coleman. As is true of American children's books in general, many of these books are enriched by exciting visuals, including paintings and drawings, as well as photographs.

The modern phase of the vital and dynamic body of work that is African American children's literature began about forty years ago, with the work of a few outstanding African American writers and artists, many of whom have sustained their careers over three or four decades and are continuing to enrich the field. Having built a solid foundation based on their commitment to making Black children and their lives visible in children's books, many of them are expanding the range of their work, exploring new topics, new media, and new styles. Even as we honor and celebrate their work, we can also celebrate the entry into the field of a new generation of writers, artists, stars, and rising stars, whose work is shaping the African American children's literature of the early twenty-first century. They are also expanding the scope of African American children's literature by addressing topics that had rarely been approached in the literature previously, exploring innovations in format, pushing at genre boundaries, and trying new media and new styles.

As in the past, African American children's literature will likely be influenced by developments in publishing and in the wider field of children's literature. Unfortunately, few African Americans hold influential positions with the major children's book publishers, whose marketing and distribution decisions have a major effect on the availability of the literature. The notable exception is Andrea Davis Pinkney, who is currently a vice president and publisher at Scholastic, and who earlier established Jump at the Sun, an imprint at Hyperion that specializes in children's books about African Americans. Other major publishing houses have also established imprints that publish books of Black interest, such as *Amistad* at HarperCollins. Fortunately, today's publishing world also includes independent publishers such as Just Us Books, which publishes books by and about African Americans; and Lee and Low and Children's Book Press, both of which publish "multicultural" children's books about people of color. These smaller publishers offer opportunities that might not otherwise be available for budding African American authors and artists. The foreseeable future, then, promises a steady stream of African American children's literature.

Some of that literature is likely to follow whatever current trends are fashionable within the larger context of American children's literature. For example, children's books by celebrities, such as actors and singers, are currently in vogue, and a number of African American celebrities have produced children's books, with varying degrees of literary quality. African Americans also appear in books that are tie-ins to commercial entities, such as television shows and feature films. Some popular series, such as *The Cheetah Girls*, also feature African American characters. Recent years have also seen a flurry of board books for infants and toddlers featuring African American children. Although most of these books are not likely to become prize-winning literary "classics," they are another reason for believing optimistically that we are not likely to revert any time soon to the "all-White world of children's books."

Even as the new crop of mostly younger writers and artists are exploring new topics and new ways to tell their stories, however, they also continue to address concerns and themes that have been at the center of much of African American children's literature. The literature they are creating, therefore, is firmly tied to the parallel culture group out of which it emanates, the sociopolitical and cultural context that continues to justify its existence, and the body of African American literature that has come before.

References

Documentation for books for children and young adults can be found at the end of chapters.

Abrahams, Roger D. 1970. *Deep Down in the Jungle: Negro Narrative Folklore from the Streets of Philadelphia*. First Rev. Ed. Chicago: Aldine Publishing Co.

Andrews, Siri. 1946. "Florence Crannell Means." *The Horn Book* 22 (January–February): 15–30.

Aptheker, Herbert, ed. 1973. Introduction to *The Education of Black People: Ten Critiques, 1906–1960*, by W.E.B. Du Bois. Amherst, MA: University of Massachusetts Press.

———. 1980. *Writings in Periodicals Edited by W.E.B. Du Bois: Selections from* The Brownies' Book. Milwood, NY: Kraus-Thomson.

"The Art of Kadir Nelson." About the Artist. http://www.kadirnelson.com/Artist-Biography .html.

Bader, Barbara. 1976. *American Picture Books from Noah's Ark to the Beast Within*. New York: Macmillan.

Baker, Augusta. 1944–45. "Books for Children: The Negro in Literature." *Child Study* 22: 58–83.

———. 1969. "Guidelines for Black Books: An Open Letter to Juvenile Editors." *Publisher's Weekly* 96: 131–33.

Berlin, Ira, Marc Favreau, and Steven F. Miller, eds. 1998. *Remembering Slavery: African Americans Talk about Their Personal Experiences of Slavery*. New York: The New Press in association with the Library of Congress.

Bishop, Rudine Sims. 1992. "Profile: A Conversation with Patricia McKissack." *Language Arts* 69(1): 69–74.

———. 1997. "Profile: Eloise Greenfield." *Language Arts* 74, no. 8 (December): 630–634.

Blassingame, John W. 1979. *The Slave Community: Life in the Antebellum South*. Rev. ed. New York: Oxford University Press.

Bontemps, Arna. 1966. "The Lonesome Boy Theme." *The Horn Book Magazine* 42 (December 1966): 673–680.

———. 1974. Interview by Lee Bennett Hopkins. *More Books by More People* (48–53). New York: Citation Books.

———. 1980. *Arna Bontemps-Langston Hughes Letters, 1925–1967*. Ed. by Charles Nichols. New York: Dodd, Mead.

Bontemps, Arna and Langston Hughes, eds. 1958. *The Book of Negro Folklore*. New York: Dodd, Mead.

Boyd, Candy Dawson. 1990. "Children's Booksellers: Power Brokers for Cultural Diversity." Transcript of speech to the American Booksellers Association Convention and Trade Exhibition. Las Vegas, Nevada, June 1–5, 1990.

Bradley, Darcy. 1991. "John Steptoe: Retrospective of an Imagemaker." *The New Advocate* 4 (1): 11–23.

Breed, Clara. 1945. "Books that Build Better Racial Attitudes." *The Horn Book Magazine* 21 (January/February): 55–61.

Broderick, Dorothy M. 1973. *Image of the Black in Children's Fiction*. New York: R. R. Bowker Co.

Brown, Sterling. 1933. "Negro Characters as Seen by White Authors." *Journal of Negro Education* 2 (2) (April): 179–203.

Bryan, Ashley. 1988. "Interview with Ashley Bryan." By Sylvia Marantz and Kenneth Marantz. *The Horn Book Magazine* 44 (March/April): 173–179.

Bullock, Penelope L. 1981. *The Afro-American Periodical Press, 1838–1909*. Baton Rouge: Louisiana State University Press.

Chambers, Bradford. 1971. "Interracial Books: Background of a Challenge." *Publisher's Weekly* 200 (15) (October 11): 23–29.

Child, Lydia Maria. 1865. *The Freedmen's Book*. Boston: Tickner and Fields.

Clifton, Lucille. 1976. *Generations: A Memoir*. New York: Random House.

———. 1981. "Writing for Black Children." *The Advocate* 1 (1): 32–37.

Cook, Mary V. 1887. "Women's Place in the Work of the Denomination." *Journals and Lectures; American Baptist Convention*, Mobile, AL. Repr. in Logan 1999.

Copeland, Jeffrey S. and Vicky Copeland, eds. 1994. *Speaking of Poets 2*. Urbana, IL: National Council of Teachers of English.

Cornelius, Janet Duitsman. 1991. *When I Can Read My Title Clear: Literacy, Slavery and Religion in the Antebellum South*. Columbia: South Carolina University Press.

Cornish, Samuel. 1833. "A Library for the People of Color." Repr. in *The Negro American: A Documentary History*. Ed. by Leslie H. Fishel Jr. and Benjamin Quarles. New York: William Morrow, 1967.

Crews, Donald. 1998. Interview with George Bodmer. "Donald Crews: The Signs and Times of an American Childhood—Essay and Interview." By George Bodmer. *African American Review* 32 (1): 107–117.

Cummings, Pat. 1993. "Profile: Pat Cummings, Artist." By Rudine Sims Bishop. *Language Arts* 70 (January 1993): 53–59.

———. 1997a. "Global Visuals." In *Art and Story: The Role of Illustration in Multicultural Literature for Youth*. Ed. by Anthony L Manna and Carolyn Brodie. Fort Atkinson, WI: Highsmith Press, 33–43.

———. 1997b. "HarperCollins Listserv subscribers' interview with Pat Cummings." http://www.manhattan.lib.ks.us/Kail/%60cummiin.html.

Degrass, Isaiah. 1828/1967. "Isaiah Degrass' Essay." Repr. in *The Negro American: A Documentary History*. Ed. by Leslie H. Fishel Jr. and Benjamin Quarles. New York: William Morrow.

Douglass, Frederick. 1845/1987. *Narrative of the Life of Frederick Douglass*. Repr. in Henry Louis Gates Jr., ed. *The Classic Slaves Narratives*. New York: Penguin.

———. 1892/1962. *Life and Times of Frederick Douglass*. Repr. New York: Bonanza Books.

Du Bois, W.E.B. 1903/1969. *The Souls of Black Folk*. Repr. New York: New American Library.

———. 1919. "The True Brownies." *The Crisis* 18, no. 6 (October): 285.

———. 1968. *The Autobiography of W.E.B. Du Bois: A Soliloquy on Viewing My Life from the Last Decade of Its First Century*. New York: International Publishers.

———. 1995. "Criteria of Negro Art." *W.E.B. Du Bois: A Reader*. Ed. by David Leavering Lewis. New York: Henry Holt.

Ellison, Ralph. 1972. "Twentieth-Century Fiction and the Black Mask of Humanity." In *Shadow and Act*. New York: Random House/Vintage Books.

———. 1985b. "Illustration Is My Form, the Black Experience Mystery and My Content." *The Advocate* 4 (2): 73–82.

EMIERT. 2005. "Coretta Scott King Book Awards." http://www.ala.org/ala/emiert/corettascottkingbookaward/corettascott.htm.

Equiano, Olaudah. 1814/1987. "The Interesting Narrative of the Life of Olaudah Equiano, or Gustavus Vassa, The African. Written By Himself." Repr. in *The Classic Slave Narratives*. Ed. by Henry Louis Gates Jr. New York: Mentor/Penguin.

Evans, Eva Knox. 1941. "The Negro in Children's Fiction." *Publisher's Weekly* 140 (August 30): 650–653.

"Faith Ringgold's Interview Transcript." n.d. Interviewed by Scholastic Students. Scholastic Inc. http://books.scholastic.com/teachers/authorsandbooks/authorstudies/authorstudies.jsp.

Feelings, Tom. 1972. *Black Pilgrimage*. New York: Lothrop, Lee and Shepard.

———. 1985. "The Artist at Work: Technique and the Artist's Vision." *The Horn Book* 41 (December 1985): 685–695.

———. 1985b. "Illustration Is My Form, the Black Experience, My Story and My Content." *The Advocate* 4 (2): 73–82.

———. 1991. Transcending the Form. In *The Multicolored Mirror: Cultural Substance in Literature for Children and Young Adults*. Ed. by Merri Lindgren. Atkinson, WI: Highsmith Press, 45–57.

Fishel, Leslie H., Jr. and Benjamin Quarles. 1967. *The Negro American: A Documentary History*. New York: William Morrow.

Flake, Sharon. NYPL Presents Sharon Flake. Author Sharon Flake, July 18, 2002. http://www.hveworld.com/transcripts/NYPL/7-18-2002.1-1.html.

Franklin, John Hope. 1967. *From Slavery to Freedom: A History of Negro Americans*. 3rd ed. New York: Knopf.

Franklin, John Hope and Alfred A. Moss Jr. 1994. *From Slavery to Freedom: A History of African Americans*. 7th ed. New York: Knopf.

Gaither, Edmund P., ed. 1998. *Historical Themes, Tales, and Legends: The Art of Jerry Pinkney*. California African American Museum. Exhibition Catalogue, December 19, 1998–April 11, 1999.

Gates, Henry Louis, Jr. 1988. *The Signifying Monkey: A Theory of Afro-American Literary Criticism*. New York: Oxford University Press.

Gayle, Addison. 1971/1997. Introduction to *The Black Aesthetic*. Repr. in *The Norton Anthology of African American Literature*. Ed. by Henry Louis Gates Jr. and Nellie Y. McKay. New York: Norton Company, 1870–1877.

Genovese, Eugene D. 1976. *Roll, Jordan, Roll: The World the Slaves Made*. New York: Vintage Books.

Gilchrist, Jan Spivey. 2002. Jan Spivey Gilchrist. In *Something about the Author*. Vol. 130. Ed. by Anne Commire. Detroit: Gale Research, 61–65.

Graham, Lorenz. 1973. "An Author Speaks." *Elementary English* 50 (2): 185–188.

———. 1983. "A Writer Speaks: An Interview with Lorenz Bell Graham (June 2, 1983)." By Charles Irby. *Explorations in Ethnic Studies* 6 (July): 1–7.

———. 1988. Lorenz Graham. In *Something about the Author Autobiography Series*. Vol. 5. Ed. by Adelle Sarkissian. Detroit: Gale Research Co., 111–145.

Greenfield, Eloise. 1975. "Something to Shout About." *The Horn Book Magazine* 41 (December): 624–626.

———. 1990. Eloise Greenfield. In *Something about the Author*. Vol. 61. Ed. by Anne Commire. Detroit: Gale Research, 89–102.

"Gregarious Art Statements: The Art of R. Gregory Christie." http://www.gas-art.com/books.html.

Grimes, Nikki. 2000. "The Power of Poetry." *Booklinks* 9 (March): 32–36.

Hamilton, Virginia. 1971. "Portrait of the Author as a Working Writer." *Elementary English* 48 (4): 237–240.

———. 1981. "Changing Woman, Working." In *Celebrating Children's Books*. Ed. by Betsy Hearne and Marilyn Kaye. New York: Lothrop, Lee and Shepard, 54–61.

———. 1989. "Anthony Burns." *The Horn Book Magazine* 65 (March/April): 183–185.

———. 1993. "Everything of Value: Moral Realism in the Literature for Children." May Hill Arbuthnot Honor Lecture, Richmond, Virginia, May 4, 1993. *Journal of Youth Serviced in Libraries* 6 (Summer): 363–377.

———. 1995. "Laura Ingalls Wilder Medal Acceptance." *The Horn Book Magazine* 71 (July/August): 436–441.

Hansen, Joyce. 1999. "Memories of Reading, Memories in Writing." *The ALAN Review* 26 (3): 61–64.

Harris, Violet J. 1986. *The Brownies' Book:* Challenge to the Selective Tradition in Children's Literature. Ph.D. diss. University of Georgia.

———. 1990. "African American Children's Literature: The First One Hundred Years." *Journal of Negro Education* 59 (4): 540–555.

Heard, Josephine Henderson. 1890. *Morning Glories*. Digital Schomburg African American Women Writers of the 19th Century, http://digilib.nypl.org:80/dynaweb/digs-t/ww9710/@Generic__BookView.

Hopkins, Lee Bennett. 1969. *Books Are by People*. New York: Citation Press.

———. 1974. *More Books by More People: Interviews with Sixty-five Authors of Books for Children*. New York: Citation Books.

Hopkins, Pauline. 1900. Preface to *Contending Forces: A Romance Illustrative of Negro Life North and South*. Boston: Colored Co-operative Publishing Co.

Howard, Elizabeth Fitzgerald. 1991. Authentic Multicultural Literature for Children: An Author's Perspective. In *The Multicolored Mirror: Cultural Substance in Literature for Children and Young Adults*. Ed. by Merri Lindgren. Atkinson, WI: Highsmith Press, 91–95.

Huck, Charlotte, Susan Hepler, Janet Hickman, and Barbara Kiefer. 2001. *Children's Literature in the Elementary School*. 7th ed. Boston: McGraw Hill.

Hughes, Langston. 1926/1984. "The Negro Artist and the Racial Mountain." Repr. in *The Black Americans: A History in Their Own Words; 1619–1983*. Ed. by Milton Meltzer. New York: Thomas Y. Crowell.

———. 1932a. "Books and the Negro Child." In *Children's Library Yearbook*. No. 4. Chicago: American Library Association, 108–110. 1932b. *The Dream Keeper*. New York: Knopf.

———. 1940. *The Big Sea*. New York: Hill and Wang.

———. 1965. "Greetings." *Freedomways* 5 (1): 11.

Hunter, Kristen. 1968. "The Soul Brothers: Background of a Juvenile." *Publishers Weekly* May 27, 1968, 30–31.

Hurston, Zora Neale. 1945/1978. *Mules and Men*. Bloomington, IN: Indian University Press.

———. 1958. "Sometimes in the Mind." In *The Book of Negro Folklore*. Ed. by Langston Hughes and Arna Bontemps. New York: Dodd, Mead, 93–121.

Hutton, Frankie. 1993. *The Early Black Press in America; 1927–1860*. Westport, CT: Greenwood Press.

Ingalls, Zöe. 1996. "Images of Slavery." *Chronicles of Higher Education*. B6.

Interracial Books for Children. 1967. Vol. 1, nos. 2 and 3 (Winter).

"I Am a Painter, Not Yet an Artist." 1969. *Life*. August 29, 1969, 58–59.

Jackson, Blyden. 1989. *A History of African American Literature. Vol. 1, The Long Beginning, 1746–1895*. Baton Rouge: Louisiana State University Press.

Janeczko, Paul B., ed. 1991. *Poetspeak: In Their Work, about Their Work*. New York: Collier.

Johnson, A. E. 1890/1988. *Clarence and Corinne; or, God's Way*. New York: Oxford University Press.

Johnson, Angela. 2003. Telephone interview by Rudine Sims Bishop. September 29.

Johnson, Dianne. 1990. *Telling Tales: The Pedagogy and Promise of African American Literature for Youth*. New York: Greenwood Press.

Jones, Kirkland C. 1992. *Renaissance Man from Louisiana: A Biography of Arna Wendell Bontemps*. Westport, CT: Greenwood Press.

Jordan, June. 1969. *Who Look at Me*. New York: Thomas Y. Crowell.

Lanier, Ruby. 1977. "Profile: Call Me Jesse Jackson." *Language Arts* 54 (March): 331–339.

Larrick, Nancy. 1965. "The All-White World of Children's Books." *Saturday Review* 48 (September 11): 63–65, 84–85.

Lester, Julius. n.d. *African American Voices and Visions: Biographies of Some of Our Most Prestigious Authors and Illustrators*. New York: Penguin USA Children's Books.

———. 1996. Afterword. *Sam and the Tigers*. (n.p.) New York: Dial.

Lewis, David Leavering. 2000. *W.E.B. Du Bois: The Fight for Equality and the American Century, 1919–1963*. New York: John Macrae/Henry Holt.

Linder, Douglas. 2000. The Trial of Sheriff Joseph Shipp et al. 1907, www.law.umkc.edu/faculty/projects/ftrials/shipp/lynchingyear.html.

Locke, Alain, ed. 1925/1970. *The New Negro: An Interpretation*. Repr. New York: Atheneum.

Logan, Shirley Wilson. 1999. *We Are Coming: The Persuasive Discourse of Nineteenth Century Black Women*. Carbondale: Southern Illinois University Press.

Lofting, Hugh. 1930. Afterword to *Frawg*, by Annie Vaughan Weaver. New York: Frederick A. Stokes.

Maddox, Rosa. 2002. Interview in *Unchained Memories: Readings from the Slave Narratives*. Boston: Bullfinch Press/AOL Time Warner Book Group.

Martin, Michelle. 2004. "'Hey, Who's the Kid with the Green Umbrella?': A Reevaluation of Little Black Sambo and the Black-a-moor." In *Brown Gold: Milestones of African-American Children's Picture Books, 1845–2002*. New York: Routledge, 3–18.

Masters, Edgar Lee. 1916. *Spoon River Anthology*. New York: Macmillan.

Matthews, Victoria Earle. 1893/1998. *Aunt Lindy: A Story Founded on Real Life*. Repr. in *Afro-American Women Writers, 1746–1933: An Anthology and Critical Guide*. Ed. by Ann Allen Schockley. Boston: G. K. Hall.

Means, Florence Crannell. 1940. "Mosaic." *The Horn Book Magazine* 16 (January): 35–41.

Meltzer, Milton, ed. 1984. *The Black Americans: A History in Their Own Words; 1619–1983*. New York: Thomas Y. Crowell.

Mikkelsen, Nina. 1994. *Virginia Hamilton*. New York: Twayne.

Mitchell, Lucy Sprague. 1921. *The Here and Now Story Book*. New York: E. P. Dutton/Parents' Institute.

Montalto, Nicholas V. 1982. *A History of the Intercultural Education Movement; 1924–1941*. New York: Garland Publishing.

Moore, Joanna P. 1902. "In Christ's Stead": Autobiographical Sketches. Chicago: Women's Baptist Home Missionary Society. http://docsouth.unc.edu/church/moore/moore.html#moore217.

Mossell, F. N. 1894/1971. *The Work of the Afro-American Woman*. Repr. Freeport, NY: Books for Libraries Press.

Myers, Christopher. 1997. Telephone interview by Rudine Sims Bishop. November 26.

Myers, Water Dean. 1979. "The Black Experience in Children's books: One Step Forward, Two Steps Back." *Interracial Books for Children Bulletin* 10 (6): 14–15.

———. 1986. "I Actually Thought We Would Revolutionize the Industry." *New York Times Book Review* November 9, 50.

———. 1995. "1994 Margaret Edwards Acceptance Speech." *Journal of Youth Services in Libraries* 8 (Winter 1995): 129–133.

———. 2003. "Walter Dean Myers on *Patrol*. Acceptance Speech for the Jane Addams Peace Award for *Patrol*," www.harpercollins.com/author/authorExtra.aspx?authorID=12522&isbn13=9780060283636&displayType=bookessay.

Neal, Larry. 1994. "The Black Arts Movement." In *Within the Circle: An Anthology of African American Literary Criticism from the Harlem Renaissance to the Present*. Ed. by Angelyn Mitchell. Durham, NC: Duke University Press, 184–198.

"Negro Dialect in Children's Books." 1941. *Publishers Weekly*. 140 (October 18): 1555–1558.

Nichols, Charles, ed. 1980. *Arna Bontemps-Langston Hughes Letters 1925–1967*. New York: Dodd, Mead.

Nordstrom, Ursula. 1970. Letter to Virginia Haviland. September 30. In *Dear Genius: The Letters of Ursula Nordstrom*. Ed. by Leonard Marcus. New York: HarperCollins.

Olneck, Michael R. 1990. "The Recurring Dream: Symbolism and Ideology in Intercultural and Multicultural Education." *American Journal of Education* 98 (2): 147–174.

Ovington, Mary White. 1913/1972. *Hazel*. Repr. Freeport, NY: Books for Libraries Press.

Payne, Daniel Alexander. 1888/1968. *Recollections of Seventy Years*. Repr. New York: Arno Press and the *New York Times*.

———. 1891/1969. *History of the African Methodist Episcopal Church*. Repr. New York: Arno Press and the New York Times.

Penn, I. Garland. 1891/1969. *The Afro-American Press and Its Editors*. Repr. New York: Arno Press and the *New York Times*.

Petry, Ann. 1988. Ann Petry. In *Contemporary Authors Autobiography Series*. Vol. 6. Ed. by Adelle Sarkissian. Detroit: Gale Research, 253–269.

Pinkney, Brian. 1997. The Rhythm of My Art. In *Art and Story: The Role of Illustration in Multicultural Literature for Youth*. Ed. by Anthony L Manna and Carolyn Brodie. Fort Atkinson, WI: Highsmith Press, 51–57.

Pinkney, Brian and Andrea Pinkney. 1995. Telephone interview by Rudine Sims Bishop. September 28.

Pinkney, Jerry. 1996. "John Henry." *The Horn Book Magazine* 72 (January/February 1996): 32–33.

———. 1997. Interview by Darwin L. Henderson and Anthony L. Manna. The Wrinkle of Skin, the Fold of Cloth: Conversations with Jerry Pinkney. In *Art and Story: The Role of Illustration in Multicultural Literature for Youth*. Ed. by Anthony Manna and Carolyn S. Brodie. Fort Atkinson, WI: Highsmith Press, 19–31.

———. 1998. Interview by Edmund P. Gaither. In *Historical Tales and Legends: The Art of Jerry Pinkney*. Ed. by Edmund P. Gaither. California African American Museum. Exhibition Catalogue, December 19, 1998–April 11, 1999.

Poole, Georgia Cowen, et al. 1942. "A Further Statement on Negro Dialect in Children's Books." *Publishers Weekly* 41 (January 10): 104–105.

Pritchard, Mryon T. and Mary White Ovington, eds. 1920. *The Upward Path: A Reader for Colored Children*. New York: Harcourt Brace and Howe.

Rahn, Suzanne. 1987. "Early Images of American Minorities: Rediscovering Florence Crannell Means." *The Lion and the Unicorn* 11 (April): 98–115.

Rampersad, Arnold. 1986. *The Life of Langston Hughes. Vol. 1: 1902–1941; I, Too, Sing America*. New York: Oxford University Press.

Ransome, James. 1997. "Aunts, Uncles, Quilts, a Spotted Dog and Flowers." In *Art and Story: The Role of Illustration in Multicultural Literature for Youth*. Ed. by Anthony Manna and Carolyn S. Brodie. Fort Atkinson, WI: Highsmith Press, 95–103.

Raymond, Anthea. 1997. Oral history interview. Carole Byard, http://web.gc.cuny.edu/womencenter/AWV/Byard.html.

Redding, J. Saunders. 1939/1988. *To Make a Poet Black*. Repr. Ithaca, NY: Cornell University Press.

Rees, David. 1984. *Painted Desert, Green Shade: Essays on Contemporary Writers of Fiction for Children and Young Adults*. Boston: The Horn Book.

Rider, Ione. 1939. "Arna Bontemps." *The Horn Book Magazine* 15 (January–February 1939): 13–19.

Ringgold, Faith. 1995. *We Flew Over the Bridge: The Memoirs of Faith Ringgold*. New York: Bullfinch Press/Little, Brown.

Ringgold, Faith, Linda Freeman, and Nancy Rocher. 1996. *Talking to Faith Ringgold*. New York: Crown.

Rollins, Charlemae Hill, ed. 1941/1948/1967. *We Build Together: A Reader's Guide to Negro Life and Literature for Elementary and High School Use*. Repr. Urbana, IL: National Council of Teachers of English.

Schockley, Ann Allen. 1988. *Afro-American Women Writers, 1746–1933: An Anthology and Critical Guide*. Boston: G. K. Hall.

Sidney, Thomas. 1828/1967. "On Freedom." Repr. in *The Negro American: A Documentary History*. Ed. by Leslie H. Fishel Jr. and Benjamin Quarles. New York: William Morrow, 156.

Sims, Rudine. 1982. "Profile: Lucille Clifton." *Language Arts* 59 (2): 160–167.

———. 1982b. *Shadow and Substance: Afro-American Experience in Contemporary Children's Fiction*. Urbana, IL: National Council of Teachers of English.

Sinnette, Eleanor Des Verney. 1999. Interview by Rudine Sims Bishop. Taped telephone conversation. July 12.

Smith, Henrietta, ed. 1994. *The Coretta Scott King Awards: From Vision to Reality*. Chicago: American Library Association.

———. 1999. *The Coretta Scott King Awards Book 1970–1999*. Chicago: American Library Association.

Smith, Katherine Capshaw. 1999. "From Bank Street to Harlem: A Conversation with Ellen Tarry." *The Lion and the Unicorn* 23 (2): 271–285.

Smith, Nila Banton. 1965. *American Reading Instruction*. Newark, DE: International Reading Association.

Steele, Vincent. 1998. "Tom Feelings: A Black Arts Movement." *African American Review* 32 (1): 119–124.

Steptoe, John. 1987. "An Interview with John Steptoe." By Roni Natov and Geraldine DeLuca. *The Lion and the Unicorn* 11 (1): 122–129.

Stowe, Harriet Beecher. 1852/1982. *Uncle Tom's Cabin; or Life among the Lowly*. Repr. New York: Bantam.

Suhl, Isabelle. 1985. "The 'Real' Dr. Dolittle." In *The Black American in Books for Children*. Ed. by Donnarae MacCann and Gloria Woodard. Metuchen, NJ. Scarecrow Press, 151–161.

Tarry, Ellen. 1955/1992. *The Third Door: The Autobiography of an American Negro Woman*. Tuscaloosa: University of Alabama Press.

Taylor, Mildred D. 1977. Newbery Award Acceptance. *The Horn Book Magazine* 53 (August 1997): 401–409.

Theobold, Ruth. 1932. "Library Service for Negro Children." In *Children's Library Yearbook*. No. 4. Chicago: American Library Association, 111–121.

Trager, Helen. 1945. "Intercultural Books for Children." *Childhood Education* 22 (November): 138–145.

U.S. Census Bureau. 1860. Introduction. In *Population of the United States in 1860*. Compiled from the Original Returns, http://www2census.gov/prod2/decennial/documents/1860a-02.pdf.

Vandergrift, Kay. 1993. "A Feminist Perspective on Multicultural Children's Literature in the Middle Years of the Twentieth Century." *Library Trends* 41 (3): 354–377.

Viguers, Ruth Hill. 1966. Editorial. *The Horn Book Magazine*. February, 18–19.

Walker, Alice. 1984. *In Search of Our Mothers' Gardens*. New York: Harvest/Harcourt Brace Jovanovich.

Walter, Mildred Pitts. 1992. "The Many Faces in Children's Books." *School Library Journal*: 28–33.

Washington, Booker T. 1901/1965. *Up from Slavery: An Autobiography*. Repr. New York: Dell.

WBGU-TV. 2004. *Looking for a Face Like Mine.* Video. Bowling Green University, Bowling Green, OH.

Webber, Thomas L. 1978. *Deep Like the Rivers: Education in the Slave Quarter Community, 1831–1865.* New York: Norton.

Webster, Noah. 1880. *Elementary Spelling Book: Being an Improvement on the American Spelling Book.* Rev. ed. New York: Appleton and Co.

Wesley, Valerie Wilson. 2000. "Portfolio: African American Illustrators." *American Visions* (August/September): 20–27.

Woods, George and Julius Lester. 1972. "Black and White; An Exchange." In *The Black American in Books for Children. Readings in Racism.* Ed. by Donnarae McCann and Gloria Woodard. Metuchen, NJ: Scarecrow Press, 66–72.

Woodson, Carter G. 1933/1972. *The Miseducation of the Negro.* Repr. Washington, D.C.: Associated Publishers.

———. 1919/1968. *The Education of the Negro Prior to 1861.* New York: Arno Press and *The New York Times.*

Woodson, Jacqueline. 2001. "Fictions." *Obsidian* 3 (1): 48–50.

Yuill, Phyllis J. 1976. *Little Black Sambo: A Closer Look.* New York: Racism and Sexism Resource Center for Educators.

Index

Abolitionist schools for Blacks, 6–7
Abolitionist Society, 7
Across the Cotton Patch (Credle), 74
Adoff, Arnold, 95–96, 111
Adoff, Jaime, 111
Adventures of Sparrow Boy, The (Pinkney), 147
Aesthetic, Black, 88
Affirmation, 120; art of, 177–79. *See also* Clifton, Lucille, authenticating the world of Black children
Africa, 161–63
Africa Dream (Greenfield), 162
African American children. *See* Children
African American children's literature: catalysts for contemporary, 84–87; historical perspective on, xi–xiv, xii, 221 (*see also* Newspapers); purposes, xii; quantity, xii, 221; terminology, xiv–xv
African American writers, books unrelated to African Americans written by, 52
African Methodist Episcopal (A.M.E.) Church, 10, 11, 13
AFRO-BETS, 91
Ajeemah and His Son (Berry), 257–58
"All Alone, My Baby Boy" (poem), 12
All Jahdu Storybook (Hamilton), 200
All Us Come Cross the Water (Clifton), 120–23
"All-White World of Children's Books, The" (Larrick), 84–85
American Baptist Publication Society, 17
American Book Award, 197
American Library Association Best Book for Young Adults, 213

American Library Association Newbery Honor Books. *See* Newbery Honor Books
American Library Association Notable Books, 156, 171
American Spelling Book, The, 6
Amifika (Clifton), 122
Amistad, 274
Amistad Rising (Chambers), 253
Angel Baby (Cummings), 137
Angelou, Maya, 100
Angels (Greenfield), 178
Angel to Angel (Myers), 102
Animal tales, 2, 55–56, 58–59, 146, 167
Anthony Burns (Hamilton), 198
Araminta (Evans), 75, 80
Arilla Sun Down (Hamilton), 202–3, 243
Art, 159, 168, 170, 183, 184, 189; beauty and, 24–25; cover, 32; fusing the visual and the verbal, 99–101. *See also* Black Arts Movement; Illustrators
Ashanti to Zulu (Musgrove), 171
Associated Publishers, 42, 54–55
"As the Crow Flies" (news column), 26–28
Aunt in Our House, The (Johnson), 135
Aunt Lindy (Matthews), 18
Autobiographies, 256

Baby Grand, the Moon in July, and Me, The (Barnes), 231–32, 234
Baby Says (Steptoe), 157
Back Home (Pinkey), 143
Bader, Barbara, 58, 59, 74
Baker, Augusta, 58
Banfield, Beryl, 85
Banks, Jacqueline Turner, 232, 233

Bannerman, Helen, 82
Barnes, Joyce Annette, 231–32, 234
Barnett, Moneta, 153–55
Bearden, Romare, 187
Beautiful Blackbird (Bryan), 165
Beauty, 102; art and, 24–25. *See also*
    "Black is beautiful"
Because We Are (Walter), 227
Beim, Jerrold and Lorraine, 80
Bells of Christmas, The (Hamilton), 202
Belton, Sandra, 231–33
Berry, Erick, 53
Berry, James, 257–58
Best Illustrated Book Awards. *See*
    New York Times Best Illustrated Book
    Awards
Between Madison and Palmetto (Woodson),
    237, 238
Beyond Mayfield (Nelson), 230
Bible stories, 62, 164
Bibliographies and lists of recommended
    books, 73–74, 77. *See also We Build*
    Together
Big Jade (Nolen), 147
Bigmama's (Crews), 172
Biographical writings, 41, 52, 63, 74, 167,
    179–80, 188, 199, 249–50, 273
Biracial children, 232. *See also* Interracial
    relationships; Mixed-race families
Birthday (Steptoe), 119
Black Arts Movement, 56, 87–89, 91,
    95–97, 99, 101. *See also* Poetry,
    as social action
Black BC's, The (Clifton), 120–21
Black Child (Thomas), 100
Black Cowboy, Wild Horses (Lester), 255
Black expression, 89
"Black imagery," 168
"Black is beautiful," 139, 165, 202
Black Pilgrimage (Feelings), 99–100, 159,
    161
Black Snowman, The (Mendez), 129, 162
Blessing in Disguise, A (Tate), 226
Blue-back Speller, 6
Blues, 39, 105–6, 146
Blues Journey (Myers), 185, 186
Blues of the Flats Brown, The (Myers),
    146
Blue Tights (Williams-Garcia), 239
Bluish (Hamilton), 203
Body characteristics and body image,
    138–39
Bontemps, Arna, 45; awards and honors,
    49, 89, 249; work of, 45–52, 60

"Books About Negro Life for Negro
    Children" (Theobold), 74
Boston Globe-Horn Book Award, 120,
    156, 158, 165, 170, 197, 198, 257
Boston Globe-Horn Book Award for
    Illustration, 124, 180
Boston Globe-Horn Book Honor citations,
    185
Boy and the Ghost, The (San Souci), 179
Boyd, Candy Dawson: middle grades,
    middle school, and middle class in the
    novels of, 223–24
Boy Who Didn't Believe in Spring, The
    (Clifton), 123
Bratton, Alpha Angela, 31
Breadsticks and Blessing Places (Boyd),
    223–24
Brer Rabbit, 2
Bright April (de Angeli), 78–79
Bright Eyes, Brown Skin (Hudson and
    Ford), 139
Broadside Press, 87–88, 96
Broderick, Dorothy, 68–69
Bronzeville Boys and Girls (Brooks), 56, 98,
    111
Brooks, Gwendolyn, 45, 56, 88
Brother to the Wind (Walter), 129
Brown, Sterling, 68, 69
Brown Angels (Myers), 102
Brown Honey in Broomwheat Tea (Thomas),
    182
Brownie's Book, The (magazine), 21–22,
    52, 59, 92; contents of, 25–34;
    discontinuation of, 35; goals and values of,
    23, 231; legacies of, 35–36; as literature,
    29–34; necessity for, 23–25; photographs
    of, 33, 34; significance of, 34–35
Bruh Rabbit and the Tar Baby Girl
    (Hamilton), 182, 200
Bryan, Ashley, 53–54, 109–10; connecting
    children to their roots, 163–65
Bryant, Sara Cone, 70
Bubbles (Greenfield), 124
Bud, Not Buddy (Curtis), 269, 270
Burns, Anthony, 198
Burton, Frank, 12
Butler, James Alpheus, 29, 30
Byard, Carole, 126, 129, 142, 155, 188; as
    cultural activist, 161–63

Caines, Jeanette, 126–27
Caldecott Honor Book citations, 120, 142,
    155, 156, 158, 161, 162, 165, 168, 172,
    180, 184, 185, 187, 188

Caldecott Medal, 48, 116, 156, 165, 170, 171
Call Me Charley (Jackson), 60–61, 230
Campbell, E. Simms, 47
Captive, The (Hansen), 256–57
Caribbean: immigrant families from, 234; slavery in, 257–58
Carty, Leo, 154
Carver, George Washington, 110
Cepeda, Joe, 139, 140
Chambers, Brad, 85
Chambers, Veronica, 234–35
Characters, Black, 23–24, 67, 68; absence of, 23; relationships with White characters, 57
Chariot in the Sky (Bontemps), 50–51
Charles, Ray, 215
Charlie Pippin (Boyd), 224
Chevrolet Saturdays (Boyd), 224
Child, Lydia Maria, 9
"Childhood remembrance" stories, 143
Children, African American: affirming the lives of, 123–25; authenticating the world of, 120–23, 138, 213, 233, 244 (*see also* Self-love); celebrating, 102–9; celebrating academic and creative achievements of, 28–29; childhood before being forced into hard labor, 3; encouraged to follow their dreams, 143–45; giving them "back their own souls," 67; popular images of, 14; recognizing them as readers, 72–75. *See also specific topics*
Children of the Fire (Robinet), 262, 263
"Children of the Sun," 22
Children's Book Press, 274
Children's columns in periodicals, 15. *See also Brownie's Book*
"Children's Corner" in *Sower and Reaper*, 15
Children's Library Yearbook, 73
Children's literature, 221; defined, xiv–xv
Childress, Alice, 214–15
Chita's Christmas Tree (Howard), 141
Chocolate, Debbi, 232, 233
Christian Recorder, 11–13
Christie, R. Gregory, 188
Christopher Cat, 55–56
Churches, Black, 10
"Cinderella" story, African, 157
Circle of Gold (Boyd), 223
City life, focus on, 212–16
Civil War, novels set during, 260

Clarence and Corinne; or God's Way (Johnson), 16–18
Class differences. *See* Social class
Clean Your Room, Harvey Moon (Cummings), 137
Clifton, Lucille, 95, 125, 134, 138, 213, 217, 273; authenticating the world of Black children, 103, 104, 120–23, 244; Everett Anderson books, 102–4; picture storybooks, 120–23
C.L.O.U.D.S. (Cummings), 127–28
Cole, Nat King, 146
Coleman, Evelyn, 184
Collage, 186–87
Collier, Bryan, 187–88
Color complex in Black community, 240–41
Colored American, The (newspaper), 14
Comic Negro (stereotype), 68
Coming on Home Soon (Woodson), 187
Communality, 2, 244–45
Concord of sensibilities, xii
Connecticut Poet Laureate, 110
Conroy, Jack, 52
Cook, Mary V., 15–16
Cooper, Floyd, 124, 182–83, 188
Coretta Scott King (CSK) Author Awards, 89–90, 197, 200, 205, 215, 235, 237, 240, 269
Coretta Scott King (CSK) Author Honor Books, 108, 155, 223, 227, 237, 241, 269
Coretta Scott King (CSK) Genesis Award for African American authors, 240
Coretta Scott King (CSK) Illustrator Award, 126, 144, 154, 155, 162, 165, 169, 170, 178, 180, 181, 185, 187–88
Coretta Scott King (CSK) Illustrator Honor Books, 161, 169, 188
Coretta Scott King (CSK) Illustrator Honor Citations, 178, 180–83, 185, 187, 188
Coretta Scott King (CSK) New Author Award, 111
Cornish, Samuel, 8–9, 13
Cornrows (Yarbrough), 125–26, 161, 162, 229
Council on Interracial Books for Children (CIBC), 85–87, 205, 211; Minority Writers Contest, 215, 265, 266
Crawford, J. M., 12
Creation, The (Johnson), 181
Credle, Ellis, 74–75

Crews, Donald, 143, 156, 185; as graphic artist, 172–73
Crews, Nina, 185–87
Crichlow, Ernest, 80
Crisis, The (NAACP magazine), 21, 22
Crow columns, 26–28
Crowning Glory (Thomas), 109
Cuffe, Paul, 32, 257
Cullen, Countee, 40, 45, 55–56
Cultural heritage and identity, 243
Cultural themes, Webber's, 2
Cummings, Pat, 126, 127, 137; human kids who just happen to be Black, 168–70
Curtis, Christopher Paul, 251; recent history laced with humor in the novels of, 269–71

Davis, Ossie, 263
Day of Tears (Lester), 256
de Angeli, Marguerite, 78–79
Dear America historical series, 259–60
Dear One, The (Woodson), 238
Degrass, Isaiah, 7
Desegregation/integration, 87; stories of, 229–31
Dialect, 149, 244; Black urban, 118, 244 (*see also* "Negro dialect"; Vernacular English); Gullah, 78
Dialect poems, 53
Different Beat, A (Boyd), 224
Dillon, Leo and Diane, 155, 200; focusing on shared humanity, 170–72
Discourse styles, 244. *See also* Dialect; "Negro dialect"; Vernacular English
Discrimination. *See* Racism
Don't You Turn Back (Hughes), 96
Douglass, Frederick, 3, 5, 10, 58
"Dragon's Tooth, The" (Richardson), 30
Dragon Takes a Wife, The (Myers), 128
Draper, Sharon, 240
Dream Keeper, The (Hughes), 38–39, 41, 47, 74
Dreams, encouraging children to follow their, 143–45
Drum and Spear Press, 88, 124
Du Bois, W.E.B., 34, 35, 54, 59, 63, 90, 231; biographies of, 141, 199. *See also Brownies' Book*
Dunbar, Paul Laurence, 49, 53–54
Dustland (Hamilton), 201
Dynamic cubism, 117

Economics. *See* Social class
Edith Jackson (Guy), 214
Education, 11, 22, 87, 239; postwar, 9–10; through literature, 41–42. *See also* Intercultural education movement; Morality and moral education; Multicultural education movement; Schools for Blacks
Education Issues of *The Brownies' Book*, 28
Ego-tripping and other poems for young people (Giovanni), 97–98, 154
Elders, 123, 125, 126, 136, 148, 149, 189; wisdom from, 25–26
Elementary and Secondary Education Act (ESEA), 84
Elijah's Angel (Rosen), 183–84
Ellington Was Not a Street (Shange), 188
Ellison, Ralph, xii
Emotion, conveying, 189, 190
Enchanted Hair Tale, An (DeVeaux), 129
Epaminondas and His Auntie (Bryant), 70
Equiano, Alaudah, 256–57
Ernestine and Amanda (Belton), 232
Ethnocentric perspective, 86–87
Ets, Marie Hall, 57–58
Evans, Eva Knox, 75, 80
Everett Anderson books, 102–4, 122

"Fairies" (Hughes), 38
Fairy tales, 168, 185, 186. *See also* Picture books, folklore and fantasy in
Faithful Friend, The (San Souci), 180
Fallen Angels (Myers), 205, 210
Fall Secrets (Boyd), 224
Families, 242–43; from the diaspora, 234–35; preteens and their, 233–34; strength of Black, 124. *See also* Intergenerational relationships
Family, 2, 11, 33, 236; emphasis on, 216–18; extended, 122–23
Family love, 122, 123, 134
Family stories: passing down, 135; and sagas, 59, 264–69
Family values, 2
Fantasy, 167. *See also* Fairy tales; Picture books
Fast Sam, Cool Clyde, and Stuff (Myers), 206, 207
Fast Sooner Hound (Bontemps and Conroy), 52
Fast Talk on a Slow Track (Williams-Garcia), 239
Fathers, 185, 209
Fauset, Jessie, 25–26, 32

Feelings, Muriel, 158, 159
Feelings, Tom, 101, 105, 155, 187; on art
    and the arts, 99–100, 189; awards and
    honors, 158; on Black aesthetic, 88–89;
    Black Pilgrimage, 99–100, 159, 161;
    emotional content in the work of, 190;
    "improvising within a restricted form,"
    158–61, 190, 252; *The Middle Passage*,
    158–60, 249; R. Gregory Christie and,
    188; references to movement and music,
    189; themes in the work of, 159, 189
Female bonding, 189
Females: empowered, 130, 201. *See also*
    Women
Feminist. *See* Womanist
Ferguson, Amos, 106
"Fireside Schools," 19n.2
First Part Last, The (Johnson), 235–37
Flake, Sharon: gritty urban novels,
    240–41
Flop-Eared Hound (Credle), 75
Flossie and the Fox (McKissack), 129, 145
Flournoy, Valerie, 126, 166
Flying motif, 51, 144, 148, 149–50
Folktales and folklore, 31, 52, 133, 150,
    163, 166, 167, 199; in picture books,
    128–30, 145–48; reviving interest in
    African American, 200–201. *See also*
    Mythology; Tate, Eleanora
Ford, George, 89, 153–55
Forever Friends (Boyd), 224
Forged by Fire (Draper), 240
Forty Acres and Maybe a Mule (Robinet),
    260
Foster, Pocohantas, 30
Frawg (Weaver), 70–71, 74
Frazier, C. Lesley, 31
Freddie Found a Frog (Napjius), 154–55
Freedmen's Book, The, 9
Freedmen's Bureau, 9
Freedmen's Journal, 10
"Free within ourselves," 40
Freight Train (Crews), 172
Friends, The (Guy), 213–14
Friends and friendship, 108, 123, 216–18,
    232–33. *See also under* Myers, Walter
    Dean
Friendship, The (Taylor), 268
Frog Who Wanted to Be a Singer, The
    (Goss), 146
From the Notebooks of Melanin Sun
    (Woodson), 237, 238
Front Porch Stories at the One-Room School
    (Tate), 225

Gag, Wanda, 57
Games, in *The Brownie's Book*, 32
Gathering, The (Hamilton), 201
Gayle, Addison, 88
Gift Giver, The (Hansen), 222
Gilchrist, Jan Spivey, 101, 103, 124,
    177–79, 190
Gingerbread Days (Thomas), 109
Giovanni, Nikki, 88, 154, 188; as poet of
    the people, 97–99
Girl on the Outside, The (Walter),
    227
Girls: empowered Black, 130. *See also*
    Females
Gladiola Garden (Newsome), 37, 42,
    54–56
Glorious Angels (Myers), 102
Glory Field, The (Myers), 264–65
Going Someplace Special (McKissack),
    143
Gold Cadillac, The (Taylor), 268
Golden Slippers (Bontemps), 48–49
Gone from Home (Johnson), 236
Good, Says Jerome (Clifton), 122
Goss, Linda, 146
Govan, Christine Nobel, 71, 75, 76
Graham, Lorenz, 61–63
Grandmama's Joy (Greenfield), 125, 161,
    162
Grandparents, 189. *See also* Elders;
    Intergenerational relationships
Grandpa's Face (Greenfield), 125,
    182
Greenfield, Eloise, 88, 91–92, 95,
    100–102, 127, 217, 242; accentuating
    the positive, 104–7; affirming African
    American children's lives, 123–25; desire
    to "give children a love for the arts,"
    229; Jan Spivey Gilchrist and, 177–79,
    190; manifesto, 91–92, 178, 226, 242,
    259; objectives, 263; photographs,
    33, 34
Greer, Glyndon, 90
Griffith, Gershom, 252
Grimes, Nikki, 95, 99–102, 187; reflections
    of her world, 107–9
Growin' (Grimes), 217
"Grown-ups' Corner" (magazine column/
    forum for adults), 29
Grubbs, A. J., 146
Guy, Rosa, 213–14, 234

Hair, 129, 138–40, 189
Haiti, 46, 234

Hamilton, Virginia, 52, 111, 221, 241–43, 266; awards, 197; *Bruh Rabbit and the Tar Baby Girl*, 182, 200; chronicling the life of the people, 196–205; great-grandmother's escape from slavery, 254; on growing up Black in America, 195; on her work, 197; invented terms and concepts, 198–99; inventing African American science fiction for children and young adults, 201; Justice trilogy, 201; modern myth making, 199–200; *The People Could Fly*, 51, 171, 199, 200, 250; *The Planet of Junior Brown*, 203, 213; portrait of, 171; realistic fiction about home, history, and heritage, 201–5; reviving interest in African American folklore, 200–201; *Zeely*, 196–97, 201–2

Hans Christian Andersen Illustrator Award, 165

Hans Christian Andersen Medal, 197

Hansen, Joyce, 234, 242, 250, 259–61; fictional slave narrative, 256–57; reflecting the life of city school kids, 222–23

Happy to Be Nappy (hooks), 140

Harlem, 58, 110, 206–7

Harlem (Myers), 185, 186

Harlem Renaissance, 35, 38–40, 46, 49, 62

Harlem Summer (Vroman), 211

HarperCollins, 274

Harriet and the Promised Land (Lawrence), 117

Harrington, Oliver, 57

Harris, Violet J., 32, 46

Harry Potter's Balloon Farm (Nolen), 147

Haskins, Francine, 136, 188

Hawkins, Louretta, 211

Hazel (Ovington), 72–73

Hazelwood High Trilogy, 240

Heard, Josephine Henderson, 18

Heart Calls Home, The (Hansen), 260

Heaven (Johnson), 236

Henry, John, 199

Hero Ain't Nothin' But a Sandwich (Childress), 214–15

Heroes, 167; "sheroes" and, 117, 180

Herron, Carolivia, 139

Her Stories (Hamilton), 199

Hezekiah Horton (Tarry), 57

High John the Conquer, 147, 199

High school graduates, 28

High school students, facing issues of today, 240

His Own Where (Jordan), 213

Historical fiction, 50–51, 195–96, 249–51; for middle grades/middle school, 261–62. *See also specific topics*

History, African American, 49–50, 120, 121, 198–99, 269–71. *See also* Slavery

Hogan, Inez, 70

Hold Fast to Dreams (Pinkney), 230, 243

Home Boy (Hansen), 222

Homosexuality, 214, 238

Honey I Love and Other Love Poems (Greenfield), 105, 106, 171

hooks, bell, 140

Hoops (Myers), 205, 208

Hope, 208–9, 235–37

Hopkins, Lee Bennett, 96

Horn Book, The (Greenfield), 46, 91–92

House of Dies Drear, The (Hamilton), 202

House You Can Pass on the Way, The (Woodson), 238

Howard, Elizabeth Fitzgerald, 133, 140–42

How Mr. Monkey Saw the Whole World (Myers), 146

Hudson, Cheryl and Wade, 91

Hughes, Langston, xi, 21, 67, 173, 190; Arna Bontemps and, 46, 47, 49, 50; books recommended by, 74; in *The Brownie's Book*, 28, 29, 37–41; *The Dream Keeper*, 38–39, 41, 47, 74; *Love to Langston* (Medina), 111; manifesto, 39–41; Mexican games "arranged" by, 32; poetry, 31, 37–41, 96, 100; *Popo and Fifina*, 46–47; "The Negro Speaks of Rivers," 49; Tom Feelings's work and, 161; Walter Dean Myers and, 205; writings, 41

Humming Whispers (Johnson), 236

Humor, 206–8; recent history laced with, 269–71

Hundred Penny Box, The (Mathis), 171, 215–17

Hunter, Kristen, 211–13

Hurston, Zora Neale, 146–47

Hutton, Frankie, 13–14

Hyperion, 274

Hyppolite, Joanne, 230–32, 234

I, Momolu (Graham), 62

"I, Too" (Hughes), 39

I Am the Darker Brother (Adoff), 96

I Can Draw a Weeposaur and Other Dinosaurs (Greenfield), 107, 179

If You Please, President Lincoln (Robinet), 260

I Greet the Dawn (Bryan), 53–54

I Hadn't Meant to Tell You This (Woodson), 237–39

I Have Heard of a Land (Thomas), 182

Illustrators, African American, 40–41, 153, 177, 185–88; established women artists entering the field, 183–85; new artists beginning their careers in 1980s, 177–83; pacesetting, 155–73; a perspective on, 188–90; themes in the work and commentary of, 189; unsung beginnings, 153–55

Image of the Black in Children's Fiction (Broderick), 68–69

Imaginative literature for Black children, 16; first recorded public call for, 16

Immigrant families from Caribbean, 234

Immigrants, Black West Indian, 214

Improvisational nature of art forms, 189, 190

"Improvising within a restricted form," 160

Incest, as topic in young adult literature, 238–39

In Daddy's Arms I Am Tall (Steptoe), 185, 186

Indigo and Moonlight Gold (Gilchrist), 179

I Need a Lunch Box (Caines), 127

Integrationist stance, 41. *See also* Desegregation/integration

Intercultural education movement, 67, 81; and books about Black people, 76–80. *See also* Multicultural education movement

Intergenerational relationships, 125–26, 134–37, 148. *See also* Family

Interracial Books for Children, 85–86

Interracial relationships, 238, 240. *See also* Biracial children; Mixed-race families

In the Land of Words (Greenfield), 107

In the Time of the Drums (Siegelson), 180

Invisible Princess, The (Ringgold), 145

Irene Jennie and the Christmas Masquerade (Smalls), 252

"Is Juvenile Literature Demanded on the Part of Colored Children?" (Cook), 16

It Ain't All for Nothin' (Myers), 208

It's a New Day (Sanchez), 96

Jackson, Jesse, 60–61

Jalani and the Lock (Pace), 253

Jambo Means Hello (Feelings), 158

Jane Addams Award, 52, 210

Janie Belle (Tarry), 57

Jazz rhythms in poetry, 105

Jesus Christ, depicted as Black, 164

Jimmy Lee Did It (Cummings), 127

John Henry (Lester), 165

John Newbery Medal. *See* Newbery Medal

Johnson, Amelia Etta Hall, 15–18

Johnson, Angela, 110, 133–36, 147; novels of longing, loss, and hope, 235–37

Johnson, Dolores, 137, 252–53

Johnson, James Weldon, 164, 181

JoJo's Flying Side Kick (Pinkney), 137

Jones, Lois Mailou, 28, 54, 55

Jones, Mandy, 5–6

Jones, Thomas, 5

Jordan, June, 101, 213

Journey to Freedom (Wright), 253

Joy, The, 16

"Judge, The" (editorial column), 25–26

Julius (Johnson), 147

Jump at the Sun, 274

Jumping the Broom (Wright), 252

"Jury, The" (letters-to-the-editor column), 29

Just an Overnight Guest (Tate), 225

"Just-As-I've-a-Mind-To" (fictional creature), 12

Justice and Her Brothers (Hamilton), 201

Justin and the Best Biscuits in the World (Walter), 227, 243

Just Us Books (JUB), 91, 154, 155, 233, 274

Just Us Women (Caines), 127

Keats, Ezra Jack, xiii, 116

"Kind Little Children" (Crawford), 12–13

King, Martin Luther, Jr., 90, 144, 226

"Kitchen Clock, The" (poem), 13

Koko, 71–72

Land, The (Taylor), 266, 267

Language, 149. *See also* Dialect; Vernacular English

Larrick, Nancy, 84–85

Last Summer with Maizon (Woodson), 237

Laura Ingalls Wilder Award, 197

Lawrence, Jacob, 117

Lee, Mary Effie. *See* Newsome, Mary Effie Lee

Lee and Low, 274

Lena (Woodson), 238–39

Leonardo da Vinci, 36

Lesbianism, as topic in young adult literature, 214, 238
Lester, Julius, 89, 146, 160, 167, 249, 251; putting a human face on slavery, 255–56
Letters-to-the-editor column, 29
Lewis, E. B., 187
Lewis, Norman, 157
Liberation literature, 198–99, 250
Librarians, Black: taking a stand, 75–76
Library for the People of Color, 8–9
"Library Service for Negro Children" (Theobald), 73
Life of Alaudah Equiano, or Gustavus Vassa, the African, 256
Lift Every Voice and Sing (Johnson), 178
Like Sisters on the Homefront (Williams-Garcia), 239–40
Lillie of Watts Takes a Giant Step (Walter), 226
Lillie of Watts (Walter), 226
Listen for the Fig Tree (Mathis), 216, 243
Literacy, 2, 18; opposition to, 5, 6, 8; pursuit of, 4–10, 258–59
Little Black Sambo. See Story of Little Black Sambo
Little Brown Baby (Dunbar), 53, 74
Little Jeemes Henry (Credle), 74–75
Little Man, Little Man (Baldwin), 213
"Little Page, The" (Newsome), 36–37
"Little People of the Month, The" (magazine column), 28
Local Color Negro (stereotype), 68
Lofting, Hugh, 71
Logan family saga, 265–69
Lonesome Boy (Bontemps), 51–52
"Lonesome boy" theme, 51
Long Journey Home (Lester), 255
Lost Zoo, The (Cullen), 55–56
Love, 105, 108
Love to Langston (Medina), 111
Lucky Stone, The (Clifton), 217–18
Ludell (Wilkinson), 218

MacArthur Fellowship, 135, 183, 197
Macmillan, 23
Maddox, Rosa, 3
Ma Dear's Aprons (McKissack), 142, 143
Madelia (Gilchrist), 179
Madison, Dolley, 261, 262
Madison, James, 261
Magazines, 16; women's, 15. *See also specific magazines*

Magical Adventures of Pretty Pearl, The (Hamilton), 199
Mainstream American English (MAE), 149
Maizon at Blue Hill (Woodson), 237–38
Malcolm X, 108
Mammy (stereotype), 24
Many Thousand Gone (Hamilton), 199
Margaret Edwards Award, 205
Marguerite de Angeli Prize for New Children's Fiction, 232
Marisol and Magdalena (Chambers), 234
Marked by Fire (Thomas), 228
Martin's Big Words (Rappaport), 188
Masse, May, 57, 58
Mathis, Sharon Bell, 215–17, 243
Matthews, Victoria Earle, 18
Mayfield Crossing (Nelson), 230, 231
M.C. Higgins, the Great (Hamilton), 197, 203–4, 243
McCard, Chita, 141
McKay, Claude, 57
McKissack, Frederick, 90
McKissack, Mabel, 90
McKissack, Patricia, 129, 142, 143, 145, 167, 249, 259
Me and Nessie (Greenfield), 124, 125
Means, Florence Crannell: reflecting the American mosaic, 77–78
Medina, Tony, 111
Meet Danitra Brown (Grimes), 182
Meltzer, Milton, 101
Mental illness, as topic in children's or young adult books, 236
Michael Printz Award, 205, 235
Middle class, Black, 14, 223–24
Middle-class African American life, 136–38, 223–24
Middle grades/middle school, historical fiction for, 261–62
Middle Passage, The (Feelings), 158–60, 249
Mikkelsen, Nina, 202, 203
Miller, Don, 121
Million Fish, More or Less, A (McKissack), 145
Minority Writers Contest, 215, 265, 266
Minors' Moralist Society, 8
Miracle's Boys (Woodson), 237, 239
Mirandy and Brother Wind (McKissack), 130, 167
Missing in Haymarket Square (Robinet), 262, 263
Missionary organizations, 6
Mississippi Bridge (Taylor), 268

Mississippi Challenge (Walter), 227
Mississippi Chariot (Robinet), 262, 263
Mitchell, Lucy Sprague, 57
Mixed-race families, 232
Moja Means One (Feelings), 158
Money Hungry (Flake), 241
Monster (Myers), 205, 209–10
Moore, Joanna P., 19n.2
Moore, Yvette, 263
Morality and moral education, 11–14, 26,
    30. *See also* Religious schools for Blacks
Morning Glories (Heard), 18
Motown and Didi (Myers), 205
"Mount Ice Cream" (Lee), 35
Mouse Rap, The (Myers), 207
Mr. Monkey and the Gotcha Bird (Myers),
    128–29
Mufaro's Beautiful Daughters (Steptoe),
    120, 157
Mules and Men (Hurston), 146–47
Multicultural education movement, xiv, 76,
    95, 133. *See also* Intercultural education
    movement
Multiculturalism, 86, 170, 232; embracing,
    182–83
Multicultural literature, 171, 274
"Museum art," 181–82
Music, Black, 105–6, 111, 146, 189
My Brother Fine with Me (Clifton), 121,
    122
My Dog Rinty (Tarry and Ets), 58–59
Myers, Christopher, 148, 186, 187, 189
Myers, Walter Dean, 102, 128, 146, 212,
    221, 241; *Fly, Jimmy, Fly*, 150; focus
    on hope, 208–9; focus on humor and
    friendship, 206–8; *The Glory Field*,
    264–65; *Now Is Your Time*, 249; poetry,
    110; raising moral questions, 209–11;
    weaving the recognizable fabric of Black
    life, 205–12; *Wings*, 148, 186
My Happy Days (Shackelford), 59
My Mama Needs Me (Walter), 169
My Man Blue (Grimes), 108
Mystery of Drear House, The (Hamilton),
    202
Mythology, 148, 199, 200

Nappy Hair (Herron), 139, 140
Narcissus an' de Chillun (Govan), 71
"Nathaniel's Rap" (Greenfield), 106
Nathaniel Talking (Greenfield), 106–7,
    178
National Association for the Advancement
    of Colored People (NAACP), 22, 72

National Book Award, 213, 228, 255
National Council of Teachers of English
    (NCTE), 81, 169; Excellence in Poetry
    Award, 105, 107
Nature, as subject of poetry, 54
Neal, Larry, 87
NEATE books, 233
NEATE to the Rescue (Chocolate), 233
Neeny Coming, Neeny Going (English), 183
"Negro Artist and the Racial Mountain,
    The" (Hughes), 40
"Negro Character as Seen by White
    Authors, The" (Brown), 68
Negro characters. *See* Characters, Black
"Negro dialect," 74–75, 80. *See also*
    Dialect, Black urban; Vernacular English
"Negro Dialect in Children's Books,"
    75–76
Nelson, Kadir, 188
Nelson, Marilyn, 110
Nelson, Vaunda Micheaux, 230
Nettie Jo's Friends (McKissack), 130
Newbery Honor Books, 46, 49, 52, 89,
    110, 158, 171, 197, 209, 249, 251, 269
Newbery Honor citations, 205, 215
Newbery Medal, 50, 197, 203, 251, 265,
    269
News, world (in *The Brownie's Book*),
    26–28
Newsome, Mary Effie Lee, 35–37, 49,
    54–56
Newspapers, 10–14
New York Times Best Illustrated Book
    Awards, 117, 170, 200
New York Times Book Review Outstanding
    Book of the Year, 213, 217
Nicodemus, 70
Nicodemus and His Little Sister (Hogan),
    70
Night on Neighborhood Street (Greenfield),
    105, 178
Noah's Ark (Pinkney), 168
Nolen, Jerdine, 147, 188
Nordstrom, Ursula, 157
Now Is Your Time (Myers), 249
Now Let Me Fly (Johnson), 252–53
Now Sheba Sings the Song (Angelou), 100
Nursery rhymes, 102

Ola Shakes It Up (Hyppolite), 230–31
Old African, The (Lester), 255–56
"Old Commodore Quiver" (Newsome),
    37
Only Passing Through (Rockwell), 188

Oral culture: entertainment, knowledge, and survival, 1–4
Oral tradition, 225
Orbis Pictus Honor Books, 169
Other Side: Shorter Poems, The (Johnson), 110
Other Side, The (Woodson), 237
Our Women and Children Magazine, 15, 16
Out from This Place (Hansen), 260
Outside Shot, The (Myers), 208
Ovington, Mary White, 72–74

Palm of My Heart, The (Adedjouma), 188
Papa Tells Chita a Story (Howard), 141
Parallel culture, 198
Parks, Rosa, 144, 188
Patchwork Quilt, The (Flournoy), 126, 136, 166, 181
Patrol (Myers), 210
Payne, Daniel Alexander, 8, 11, 13
Peer relationships, 232–33. *See also* Friends and friendship
Penn, I. Garland, 15–17
People Could Fly, The (Hamilton), 51, 171, 199, 200, 250
Periodicals, 10–11, 15, 16
Peter Moroni's Camp Runamok Diary (Cummings), 137
Petry, Ann, 254–55
Physical differences between Blacks and Whites, used as excuse for racism, 138–39
Pickaninnies, 69–72, 74–76, 79
Picture book collections, 111
Picture books, 115–16, 125–28, 133, 148–50; beginnings, 57–59; defined, 115; emergence of modern African American, 116–25; encouraging Black children to love themselves, 138–40; family in, 133–36; folklore and fantasy in, 128–30, 145–48; keeping the past alive, 140–43; reality, relevance, and "Blackness," 119–20; on slavery, 252–54; slice-of-life, 136–38; tall tales as, 52; themes, 148
Picture-Poetry Book (McBrown), 55
Pictures of African American children, 102
Picture storybooks, Lucille Clifton's, 120–23
Pierce, Elijah, 183–84
Pinkney, Andrea Davis, 179–80, 230, 258, 274

Pinkney, Brian, 41, 137, 147, 189; new generation, new direction, 179–81
Pinkney, Gloria Jean, 143
Pinkney, Jerry, 181, 189, 255, 256; family, 168; portraying African Americans with dignity, 165–68
Pinkney, Sandra, 231
Planet of Junior Brown, The (Hamilton), 203, 213
Plantations, literacy on, 4–6
Poetry, 31, 95–96, 235; of African American children in 1940s and 1950s, 53–56; anthologies/volumes of, 45, 48–49, 104 (*see also specific anthologies*); of Ashley Bryan, 164; continuing and extending the tradition, 109–11; for elementary schools, 54–55; "nonracial," 40, 55; as social action, 96–102. *See also* Newsome, Mary Effie Lee
Poets, African American children's, 102–9; male, 109–10; "Negro poets," 40, 55; "new" voices, 109–11
"Poor children," 122. *See also* Social class
Popo and Fifina (Bontemps and Hughes), 46–47
Posses (peer groups), 233
Precious and the Boo Hag (McKissack and Moss), 145
Pregnancy, teenage, 239–40
Pretty Pearl (Hamilton), 200, 202
"Prize Winner, A" (Foster), 30
Promise Me the Moon (Barnes), 234
Publishing, 274; 19th century Black, 10–19
Publishing companies, Black, 87–88, 90–91

Quakers, 6–7
Quilt Counting (Ransome), 182
Quilts and quilt making, 144, 184–85, 252
Quincea Flera Means Sweet 15 (Chambers), 234

Racial heritage and identity, 243
Racism, 86, 231; and race relations, 59–63. *See also specific topics*
Raising Dragons (Nolen), 147
Randolph Caldecott Medal, 155
Ransome, James, 201, 254; "museum art" in African American children's books, 181–82
Ransome, Lesa Cline, 182
Rap a Tap Tap, Here's Bojangles–Think of That! (Dillon and Dillon), 171

Rap music, 105–6

Ray Charles (Mathis), 154

Realism: "new," 196, 197, 213, 215, 242. *See also Soul Brothers and Sister Lou*

Realistic fiction, contemporary, 195–96, 221–22; about home, history, and heritage, 201–5; burgeoning of, 229–35; highlighting the preteen years, 222–29; "new generation" of stars and rising stars, 235–41; a perspective on, 241–45; in 1970s, 212–16

Reconstruction, 260–63

Rees, David, 204

Religious literature, 17, 18, 39, 62

Religious schools for Blacks, 6–7

Renaissance. *See* Harlem Renaissance

Repository of Religion and Literature and Science and Art, 13

Rhymes, 3

Rhyming poems, 103

Rhythm: in illustrations, 188; in poetry, 105

Rich, Anna, 188

Richardson, Willis, 30

Riddles, 3

Rights of All (newspaper), 13

Ringgold, Faith, 133, 184–85, 189; the unique books of, 143–45

Robeson, Paul, 199

"Robin and the Squirrel, The" (short story), 14

Robinet, Harriet Gillem, 250, 261–63

Robinson, Aminah Brenda Lynn, 183–84, 189

Robinson, Bill "Bojangles," 171

Rodgers, Bertha, 52

Rollins, Charlemae Hill, 81–82

Roll of Thunder, Hear My Cry (Taylor), 265–67

Romiette and Julio (Draper), 240

Rosa (Giovanni), 188

Ruby (Guy), 214

Sad-Faced Boy (Bontemps), 47–48, 52

Saint James, Synthia, 183

Salem witch trials, 254

Sam and the Tigers (Lester), 167

Sambo. See Story of Little Black Sambo

Sam Patch, the High Wide and Handsome Jumper (Bontemps and Conroy), 52

Sanchez, Sonia, 96

Sargent, John Singer, 181

School activities, programs, and exhibitions: messages reporting on, 14

Schools for Blacks: religious and abolitionist, 6–7; self-help, 7–9. *See also* Education

Science fiction, inventing African American, 201

Scorpions (Myers), 205, 209

Scratchboard, 180

Secret of Gumbo Grove, The (Tate), 225

Self-empowerment, moving toward, 89–91

Self-esteem, 226, 229–30. *See also* Self-love

Self-help, institutions of, 7–9

Self-love: encouraging Black children to love themselves, 138–40; learning to love oneself, 231–32

Seminole Diary (Johnson), 253

Service, commitment to, 32

Service Bureau for Intercultural Education, 76

Seth and Samona (Hyppolite), 232, 234

Sewell, Helen, 40

Sexual abuse, as topic in young adult literature, 238–39, 258

Shades of Black (Pinkney), 139

Shange, Ntozake, 188

She Come Bringing Me that Little Baby Girl (Greenfield), 124

Shimmershine Queens, The (Yarbrough), 229

Shortcut (Crews), 172–73

Shuttered Windows (Means), 77–78

Sidewalk Story (Mathis), 215

Sidney, Thomas, 7

Signifying, 207, 244

Simpson, George Max, 29

Singers, Fisk Jubilee, 50–51

Sing to the Sun (Bryan), 109–10

Sinnette, Elinor DesVerney, 85

Sister (Greenfield), 217

Skin I'm In, The (Flake), 240–41

Slam! (Myers), 208

Slappy Hooper, the Wonderful Sign Painter (Bontemps and Conroy), 52

Slave narrative, Joyce Hansen's fictional, 256–57

Slave quarter communities, 2–3

Slavery, 50–51, 198, 250; books for older readers on, 254–62; the continuing struggle after, 262–64; and its aftermath, 251–62; literacy and fitness for, 4–7; picture books on, 252–54; themes in writings about, 251–52. *See also* Abolitionist schools for Blacks

Slaves and plantation owners, intimate relationships between, 258–59

"Slice-of-life" books, 136–38
"Slumber Song" (Bratton), 31
Smalls, Irene, 252
Smith, Hope Anita, 111
Smith, Lucy Wilmot, 15
Smith, Marcus Cornelius, 30
Snowy Day, The (Keats), xiii–xiv, 116, 117
Social action, poetry as, 96–102
Social class, 30–31, 51, 102, 104, 122
"Social conscience" books, 61
Social issues: confronting, 237–39; social
    justice and, 27, 87
Society for the Propagation of the Gospel
    in Foreign Parts (SPG), 6
"Some Little Friends of Ours"
    (photographs), 29
Something on My Mind (Feelings), 99–100
Somewhere in the Darkness (Myers), 209
Song of the Boat (Graham), 62
Song of the Trees (Taylor), 265, 266
Songs, in oral tradition, 2–3
Song Shoots Out of My Mouth, The (Adoff),
    111
Songs of Faith (Johnson), 236
"Sorrow songs," 63
Soul Brothers and Sister Lou, The (Hunter),
    196, 211–12, 243
Soul Looks Back in Wonder (Feelings), 100,
    161
South Carolina, 8, 225–26
South Town (Graham), 61–62
Sower and Reaper, "Children's Corner" in,
    15
Spin a Soft Black Song (Giovanni), 98
Spirituals, 2–3, 63, 163–64
Spirit world, 2
St. Nicholas Magazine, 24
Steptoe, John, 153–55, 186, 189; collages,
    186–87; as groundbreaking African
    American author-artist, 156–58; honors
    and awards, 156; picture books, 117–21,
    124, 125
Stereotypes, 24, 40, 68–72
Stevie (Steptoe), 117–18, 153, 156
Stories, 2; within stories, 149
Stories of Little Brown Koko (Hunt), 71–72
Story of Little Black Sambo, The
    (Bannerman), 70, 74, 82, 167
Story of the Negro, The (Bontemps), 49–50
Street Called Home, A (Robinson), 184
Sukey and the Mermaid (San Souci), 180
Sunday (Saint James), 183
Sunday school, 17
Sunday Week (Johnson), 137

Surrealism, 51–52
Sweet Whispers, Brother Rush (Hamilton),
    202, 203, 243

Tales of Momolu (Graham), 62
Talk about a Family (Greenfield), 217
Talkin' about Bessie (Grimes), 187
Talking with Artists (Cummings), 169
Tall tales as picture books, 52
Tar Beach (Ringgold), 143–44, 184, 185
Tarpley, Natasha Anastasia, 140
Tarry, Ellen, 57–59
Tate, Eleanora, 231; small town girls in the
    novels of, 225–26
Taylor, Mildred D., 251, 264; Logan family
    saga, 265–69
Teacup Full of Roses (Mathis), 216
Tears of a Tiger (Draper), 240
Teenagers, 202, 240
Thank You, Dr. Martin Luther King, Jr.
    (Tate), 226
Theobold, Ruth, 73–74
Third World Press, 87–88
This Strange New Feeling (Lester), 255,
    256
Thomas, Joyce Carol, 106, 109, 125, 221;
    African Americans in the Southwest,
    227–28
Thompson, Carolyn, 88
Thunder Rose (Nolen), 188
Time Pieces: The Book of Times (Hamilton),
    204
Times They Used to Be, The (Clifton), 217
Timothy's Flower (Van Leeuwen), 154
Tituba of Salem Village (Petry), 254
To Be a Drum (Coleman), 137
To Be a Slave (Lester), 158, 160, 249–51,
    255
Tobe (Sharpe), 75
To Everything There Is a Season (Dillon and
    Dillon), 170
*Tommy Traveler in the World of Negro
    History* (Feelings), 159
Toning the Sweep (Johnson), 235–36
Topsy as prototype, 69
Trouble's Child (Walter), 227
Truck (Crews), 172
"True Brownies, The" (Du Bois), 22
Truth, Sojourner, 188
Tubman, Harriet, 106, 117, 144, 167,
    253, 254
*Twins, the Pirates, and the Battle of New
    Orleans, The* (Robinet), 260
Two Is a Team (Beim and Beim), 80

Ugly Duckling, The (Andersen), 168
Uncle Jed's Barbershop (Mitchell), 142, 181
Uncle Tom's Cabin (Stowe), 69
Underground Railroad, 253
Uptown (Steptoe), 119, 187–88
Upward Path, The (Ovington and Pritchard), 73
"Urban literature," 196
Urban novels, 47–48

Values, 123–24. *See also* Morality and moral education
Vassa, Gustavus, 256–57
Vernacular English, Black, 47, 48, 52, 96, 118, 119, 121, 147, 149, 157, 207–8, 214, 244
Vietnam War, 210, 224
Viguers, Ruth Hill, 84
Virgie Goes to School with Us Boys (Howard), 141
Vroman, Mary Elizabeth, 211

Walker, Alice, 19n.1
Walk On! (Ford and Williamson), 155
Walter, Mildred Pitts, 129, 263; dynamics of choice, courage, and change, 226–27
War, opposition to as topic, 210
Washington, Booker T., 9, 21–22, 258
Washington City Is Burning (Robinet), 260
Watsons Go to Birmingham–1963, The (Curtis), 269
Watsons Go to Florida, The (Curtis), 269
Webber, Thomas L., 2
We Build Together: A Reader's Guide to Negro Life and Literature for Elementary and High School Use (WBT) (Rollins), 81–83
Wedding, The (Johnson), 134
Well, The (Taylor), 268
We Read: A to Z (Crews), 172
West Indian immigrants, Black, 214
When Jo Louis Won the Title (Rochelle), 136

Where Does the Day Go? (Myers), 205, 206
Which Way Freedom? (Hansen), 260
Whirlwind Is a Ghost Dancing (Dillon and Dillon), 171
Who Look at Me (Jordan), 101
Why Mosquitos Buzz in People's Ears (Aardema), 171
"Wild Honeysuckle, The" (fairy tale), 12
Wilkinson, Brenda, 218, 263
Williams-Garcia, Rita, 140; and young adults transitioning to adulthood, 239–40
Williamson, Mel, 155
Willie Bea and the Time the Martians Landed (Hamilton), 203
Wilson, Johniece Marshall, 233–34
Wings (Myers), 148, 186
"Winter Sweetness" (Hughes), 38
Witch trials, 254
Womanist, 15, 16, 19n.1, 129
Women artists, 183–85
Women's magazines, 15
Women's World (magazine), 15
Women writers, African American, 13, 190; first children's novel by, 16–18; late 19th century, 14–19
Won't Know Till I Get There (Myers), 207
Woodson, Carter G., 21, 54, 90; education through literature, 41–42
Woodson, Jacqueline, 187; confronting social issues, 237–39
Working Cotton (Williams), 142–43, 161, 162
World of Daughter McGuire, The (Wyeth), 232
Wright, Courtni, 252
Wyeth, Sharon Dennis, 138, 232

Yarbrough, Camille, 125–26, 229, 249
Yellow Bird and Me (Hansen), 222
Young adult literature, xv

Zeely (Hamilton), 196–97, 201–2

About the Author

RUDINE SIMS BISHOP is Professor Emerita of Education at Ohio State University, where she has taught courses on children's literature. Her previous books include *Shadow and Substance: Afro-American Experience in Contemporary Children's Fiction* (1982), *Presenting Walter Dean Myers* (1990), *Kaleidoscope: A Multicultural Booklist for Grades K–8* (1994), and *Wonders: The Best Children's Poems of Effie Lee Newsome* (1999). She has won several awards and has been on the selection committees for both the Caldecott and Newbery Medals.